Global Intersectionality and Contemporary Human Rights

Global Intersectionality and Contemporary Human Rights

JOHANNA BOND

Sydney and Frances Lewis Professor of Law, Washington & Lee University School of Law

OXFORD
UNIVERSITY PRESS

OXFORD
UNIVERSITY PRESS

Great Clarendon Street, Oxford, OX2 6DP,
United Kingdom

Oxford University Press is a department of the University of Oxford.
It furthers the University's objective of excellence in research, scholarship,
and education by publishing worldwide. Oxford is a registered trade mark of
Oxford University Press in the UK and in certain other countries

First Edition published in 2021

Impression: 1

Published in the United States of America by Oxford University Press
198 Madison Avenue, New York, NY 10016, United States of America

British Library Cataloguing in Publication Data
Data available

Library of Congress Control Number: 2021933318

ISBN 978–0–19–886883–5

DOI: 10.1093/oso/9780198868835.001.0001

Printed and bound in the UK by
TJ Books Limited

For Eli, Emmet, and Josie

And for J.D.

"Whatever we do together is pure invention

the maps they gave us were out of date

by years"

Adrienne Rich, Twenty-One Love Poems XIII

Acknowledgments

The origin story of this book begins decades ago when I was a law student. I had the great privilege to work with and learn from Professor John A. Powell, who was then the Founder and Director of the University of Minnesota's Institute on Race and Poverty (now called the Institute on Metropolitan Opportunity). John became a mentor and friend, who introduced me to critical race theory, encouraged me to imagine a more just and equitable world, and impressed upon me the transformative potential of social change. Now a Law Professor myself, I hope to inspire my students in much the same ways that John inspired me.

I encountered many others who helped to shape my view of women's rights and intersectionality in the context of international human rights. I am grateful to have had the opportunity to work with the International Women's Rights Action Watch (IWRAW) at the University of Minnesota during the time that I was a student there. Marsha Freeman, then Director of IWRAW, gave me my first job working on women's human rights, which allowed me to work my way through law school and also introduced me to tireless and inspiring women's rights activists around the world. IWRAW introduced me to Unity Dow, the first female High Court Justice in Botswana, and many other activists like her who were fighting for gender justice at the grassroots, national, regional, and international levels. After law school, I was fortunate to work with Advocates for Human Rights, a Minneapolis-based human rights organization doing work to promote human rights all over the world. I owe a debt of gratitude to Robin Phillips, then Director of the Women's Human Rights Program at Advocates for Human Rights, from whom I learned a great deal about cross-cultural collaboration.

I benefitted immeasurably from my participation in the Women's Law and Public Policy Fellowship Program (WLPPFP), which introduced me to teaching at Georgetown Law. I cannot even begin to capture the depth of appreciation I feel for the nourishing mentorship of Mary Hartnett. As Director of the WLPPFP Program, Mary offered professional guidance at a time when it was greatly needed. More importantly, she became a lifelong friend. Wendy Williams, Professor of Law at Georgetown, also became an indispensable mentor and friend. Deborah Epstein, Susan Deller Ross, Wally Mlyniec, and many others at Georgetown Law helped to launch my academic career with humor and compassion. There are many others—too many to mention—who helped along the way, offering encouragement and guidance.

The book would not have been possible without the support of my institution, W&L Law, particularly through the Frances Lewis Law Center. Support for the publication of this book was also provided by the Class of 1956 Provost's Faculty Development Endowment at Washington and Lee University. A number of extraordinary research assistants helped to gather the research for the book, including Sarah Ashworth, Paige Elizabeth Avery, Kelly Cunningham, Emily Dalessio, Chandler Gray, Imani Hutty, Laura Iheanachor, Carrie Macon, Andrea Marshall, Kat Phillips, Lauren Robertson,

Emily Tichenor, and Claire Williams. Professors Devon Carbado, Brandon Hasbrouck, and Jennifer Nash generously read parts of the manuscript and provided invaluable insight. Special thank you to Gay McDougall, former member of the United Nations Committee on the Elimination of Racial Discrimination, who generously sat down with me to share her perspectives. Sara Versluis helped to shape the book in ways both large and small, and I am indebted to her. Any errors are attributable only to me.

This book would never have seen the light of day were it not for the Herculean efforts of my spouse and partner, J.D. King, who meticulously read every chapter and offered laughter and distraction along the way. I will always be grateful to my parents for instilling in me a love of books and the confidence and determination to write my own and to my sister, Jen, for being my partner in crime growing up.

Thank you to the many friends who restored balance to my life by rescuing me for a glass of wine or a walk in the woods. I am eternally grateful to my children, Eli, Emmet, and Josie, who I love fiercely and who fill me with wonder, awe, and humility on a daily basis. My love for you knows no bounds.

Contents

Introduction: Centering Intersectionality

The year 2020 ushered in the worst global pandemic in a century. Around the world, over three million people lost their lives to COVID-19, a brutal, fast-spreading virus that quickly overtaxed healthcare systems around the world. As is often the case in times of disease, conflict, or social turmoil, marginalized communities suffered the most. In the case of this pandemic, "social distancing" offered one of the most effective strategies to control the spread of the virus by maintaining physical distance between individuals and limiting physical contact. Many communities, however, were unable to practice social distancing effectively, thanks to structural inequality that rendered such distancing impossible. People detained in immigration facilities and prisons, for example, were particularly affected. Impoverished communities in urban areas and homeless shelters experienced high rates of transmission, as did elderly communities in nursing homes. Those deemed "essential workers," often working in lower-income jobs, continued to report to job sites, while higher-earning workers worked from home. Women shouldered a higher burden of uncompensated caregiving and experienced increased rates of intimate partner violence during the pandemic. In short, the global crisis underscored many of the structural inequalities that have propelled discrimination and violence for hundreds of years.

Not surprisingly, the immediate response to the pandemic focused on medical interventions. Over time, however, there has been a growing realization that the social and economic costs of the crisis have been borne unequally. In São Paulo, Brazil, for example, people of color are 62 percent more likely to die from COVID-19 than their white counterparts.[1] In the United States, COVID-19 has had a particularly devastating effect on Black Americans, revealing harmful structural discrimination in healthcare manifested in "lower health insurance access, overrepresentation in essential work, greater health risk factors, poor health service coverage in certain geographic areas, and even unconscious bias among health providers."[2] Across the globe, Syrian refugees are battling COVID-19 in a refugee camp in Jordan, where they live in cramped conditions in communities with insufficient healthcare access and little access to clean water.[3] The pandemic requires a response that carefully considers how

[1] *Disproportionate Impact of COVID-19 on Racial and Ethnic Minorities Needs to Be Urgently Addressed*, U.N. High Comm'r for Hum. Rts. [hereinafter OHCHR] (June 2, 2020), https://www.ohchr.org/EN/NewsEvents/Pages/DisplayNews.aspx?NewsID=25916.

[2] Michelle Lokot & Yeva Avakyan, *Intersectionality as a Lens to the COVID-19 Pandemic: Implications for Sexual and Reproductive Health in Development and Humanitarian Contexts*, 28 Sexual & Repro. Health Matters 40, 41 (2020).

[3] *See* Reva Dhingra, *Refugees at Risk in Jordan's Response to COVID-19*, ReliefWeb (Apr. 9, 2020), https://reliefweb.int/report/jordan/refugees-risk-jordan-s-response-covid-19; *Jordan: Authorities Must Allow Urgent Medical Care for Displaced Syrians in Rukban During COVID-19*, Amnesty Int'l (May 7, 2020), https://www.amnesty.org/en/latest/news/2020/05/jordan-authorities-must-allow-urgent-medical-care-for-displaced-syrians-in-rukban-during-covid19/.

Global Intersectionality and Contemporary Human Rights. Johanna Bond, Oxford University Press. © Johanna Bond 2021.
DOI: 10.1093/oso/9780198868835.003.0001

the crisis affects different groups of people differently. Effective responses must consider how gender, race, ethnicity, religion, socioeconomic status, age, disability, and sexual orientation and gender identity intersect in people's lives to either privilege or disadvantage them vis-à-vis the likelihood of contracting the virus, dying from it, or otherwise suffering the deleterious effects of efforts to contain it. To understand the devastating consequences of COVID-19 fully one must examine its disparate impact on different communities.[4] As I will explore in this book, intersectional analysis offers one of the best theoretical and methodological tools to unpack and examine the structural conditions that lead to such disparate health effects.

Intersectionality theory posits that aspects of identity, such as race and gender, are mutually constitutive and intersect to create unique experiences of discrimination and subordination. Intersectionality offers "a lens, a prism, for seeing the way in which various forms of inequality often operate together and exacerbate each other."[5] Perpetrators of sexual violence in armed conflict, for example, often target women on the basis of both gender and ethnicity. When human rights actors intervene on behalf of those harmed by sexual violence in armed conflict, they must understand the intersectional complexity of those violations. Remedies that fail to capture the intersectional nature of human rights violations do not offer comprehensive redress to victims.

Global Intersectionality and Contemporary Human Rights examines the influence of intersectionality theory on human rights law in the modern era and its evolution as a theoretical framework in the United States and around the world. As a scholar of women's human rights, I have studied the ways in which women have organized to promote gender equality as a human right around the world. In 1995, as a law student, I attended the United Nations Fourth World Conference on Women in Beijing. The Beijing conference was a watershed moment in the evolution of women's human rights because it generated critical momentum and attention in the global fight for women's rights. Even then, I was struck by the almost singular focus on gender as an organizing principle to draw women together in common cause. At the same time, intersectionality was emerging as an influential critical theory, and I sought to apply its insights to women's human rights organizing.[6] I saw intersectionality then—and continue to see it today—as an essential tool to understand in full and remedy the complexity of rights violations that occur at the intersection of multiple subordinated identities.

In this volume, I draw on feminist theory, critical race theory, and human rights jurisprudence to argue that scholars and activists have underutilized intersectionality theory in the global discourse of human rights. In particular, this book examines the application of intersectional theory and frameworks within the structures and systems that enforce these rights, most specifically the United Nations (UN), the central intergovernmental organization charged with the protection of human rights. In so doing, I highlight both the UN's progress in incorporating intersectional analysis into

[4] Lisa Bowleg, *We're Not All in This Together: On COVID-19, Intersectionality, and Structural Inequality*, 110 Am. J. Pub. Health 917 (2020).

[5] Katy Steinmetz, *She Coined the Term 'Intersectionality' Over 30 Years Ago. Here's What It Means to Her Today*, Time (Feb. 20, 2020), https://time.com/5786710/kimberle-crenshaw-intersectionality/.

[6] Johanna Bond, *International Intersectionality: A Theoretical and Pragmatic Exploration of Women's International Human Rights Violations*, 52 Emory L. J. 71 (2003).

its work and its failure to do so in key instances. From this evidence I argue that the United Nations and other human rights organizations must do more to actively embrace intersectionality as an analytical framework. Intersectional analysis offers critical insight into the lived experience of human rights violations. Most importantly, it provides a more complete account of human rights violations and offers a broader scope of remedies to address them than does the unidimensional approach still prevalent in much of the UN's work.

The opening chapters of this book trace the evolution of contemporary intersectionality theory and its use and resonance in the global human rights context. Intersectionality theory stems from the work of critical race feminists in the United States from the 1970s through the early 2000s, although its roots can be traced to the activism of Sojourner Truth in the mid-nineteenth century. In the late 1980s and early 1990s, Kimberlé Crenshaw and others found fertile ground for an important critique of feminist legal scholarship. Critical race feminists, Crenshaw among them, explained that the prevailing feminist theories promoting "formal equality," "cultural or relational" feminism, and "dominance" feminism failed to capture the experiences of women of color. In 1993, Crenshaw highlighted the problem with universalizing feminist theories in her article *Mapping the Margins: Intersectionality, Identity Politics, and Violence against Women of Color.*[7] In her article, Crenshaw demonstrated that a woman's experiences with violence are deeply interwoven with race and class. Importantly, Crenshaw argues that the intersection of race and gender in one's life leads to experiences that are qualitatively different from the aggregation of race and gender subordination.

Although Crenshaw is credited with articulating and naming the theory, its antecedents can be found in the work of a number of critical race feminists in both the Global North and South. Throughout the evolution of the theory, it has focused primarily on the intersection of race and gender, although its tenets are applicable in ways that stretch far beyond these parameters. Because of its origins in critical race feminism, many of the scholars applying intersectionality theory do so in the context of race- and gender-based subordination. The theory must be applied more broadly so that scholars and activists working at the intersection of, for example, race and disability or sexual orientation and age may seek to fully vindicate the rights of all the people in the communities with which they work. Nevertheless, many of the examples and case studies in this volume focus on the intersection of gender and another vector of subordination, such as race or ethnicity. This is, in part, due to the relative dearth of data focusing on other critical intersections within human rights discourse. Where possible, I have tried to include examples of intersectionality in human rights that go beyond gender. The fact remains, however, that women around the globe experience continued marginalization, and women who experience intersectional discrimination are often acutely affected.

Numerous examples in this book demonstrate how human rights entities have failed to appreciate the scope and context of subordination and, in so doing, have neglected those already harmed by human rights abuses. This book examines a range of

[7] Kimberlé Crenshaw, *Mapping the Margins: Intersectionality, Identity Politics, and Violence Against Women of Color*, 43 STAN. L. REV. 1241 (1993).

human rights issues that implicate intersectionality—disability rights, the right to education, reproductive rights, rights related to sexual orientation and gender identity, citizenship and political representation, abuses in the context of armed conflict, as well as post-conflict processes. As the COVID-19 pandemic has demonstrated, emerging and unanticipated intersectional challenges will increasingly dominate the agendas of future generations, including climate change, global health care, and privacy.

In the last two decades, the United Nations, working primarily through human rights treaty-monitoring bodies, has demonstrated an increasing willingness to embrace intersectionality as a tool for human rights analysis, although as noted, progress has been slow and sporadic. In 2000, the Committee on the Elimination of Racial Discrimination (CERD) issued a general recommendation entitled Gender-Related Aspects of Racial Discrimination. CERD's General Recommendation No. 25 was one of the first significant efforts of the UN treaty bodies to explore and promote the concept of intersectionality. Because the committee that oversees implementation of the Convention on the Elimination of All Forms of Discrimination Against Women (CEDAW) offers examples of both robust intersectional analysis and missed opportunities for such analysis and because my background is in women's human rights work, I pay particular attention to its work throughout the book. Chapter 5, for example, explores the CEDAW Committee's decisions on individual complaints to assess the extent to which it is willing to consider the intersectional dimensions of the human rights complaints that it reviews. Chapter 6 examines the extent to which intersectionality factors into the Committee's responses to countries that have ratified the treaty and submitted reports detailing the government's efforts to implement it. These chapters lay bare what is lost in the failure to adopt a robust intersectional framework for human rights analysis. The focus on CEDAW merely offers a case study that facilitates a deeper dive and more detailed analysis. An intersectional lens is equally important in the work of the committees that oversee other rights treaties, such as the aforementioned Committee on the Elimination of Racial Discrimination, Human Rights Committee (HRC), Committee on Economic, Social, and Cultural Rights (CESCR), Committee on the Rights of the Child (CRC), and the Committee on the Rights of Persons with Disabilities (CRPD).

The UN treaty bodies operate in conversation with a host of other entities, including regional human rights systems, non-governmental organizations (NGOs), and national human rights institutions. In Chapter 4, I look at human rights jurisprudence in three regional systems—the European Union, the Inter-American human rights system, and the African human rights system—and highlight efforts by these regional bodies to include intersectional analysis in their work. Meanwhile, much of the most important human rights work in the world happens at the grassroots level. Chapter 7 turns to the civil society organizations that work with the treaty bodies and examines the extent to which non-governmental organizations and other entities have incorporated intersectional frameworks. These entities operate symbiotically with the UN treaty bodies, and they often guide and inform each other. As with the treaty bodies and regional human rights systems, non-governmental organizations (NGOs) need to adapt to intersectionality to keep pace with the changing landscape of contemporary human rights discourse and to improve human rights protections for the target populations they serve.

The book offers many examples in which an intersectional lens is necessary for a fuller, more nuanced understanding of how multiple and complex identities shape experiences of oppression and resistance. To date, however, the UN's approach to human rights violations has been overly compartmentalized, making it difficult for UN representatives to approach violations in an intersectional way. Structural and systemic challenges, including barriers between treaty bodies, hamper its work. In the final chapter, I review past reforms and propose changes in the UN's working methods that will facilitate intersectional analysis and remedies. Absent such changes within the United Nations itself, the UN's recent effort to encourage states to take an intersectional approach to human rights will accomplish very little.

In all, this survey of international, regional, and local human rights entities presents the case that international actors must incorporate intersectionality theory into human rights work more aggressively in order to maintain relevance in twenty-first-century human rights discourse and to provide more meaningful redress for human rights violations. The trends are encouraging and reforms are possible. An expansion of intersectional analysis will greatly benefit those harmed by human rights violations, many of whom experience violations at the intersection of critical aspects of their identities. Victims will not be forced to pursue remedies based solely on one form of subordination that does not fully capture their multifaceted experiences of subordination. An intersectional approach to human rights remedies is the only way for the system to provide comprehensive redress for violations of human rights.

1
Foundations of Intersectionality Theory

Intersectionality theory has profoundly changed how we think about equality. The notion that forms of subordination and privilege intersect in people's lives in complex and mutually reinforcing ways has replaced outdated, simplistic conceptualizations of discrimination. In rejecting the idea that individuals experience neatly compartmentalized forms of discrimination based alternately on, for example, race and gender, intersectionality recognizes the complex interplay between systems of oppression and power structures. This insight and the many others that flow from it form the basis of intersectionality theory, a theory that has transformed many of the disciplines in which it has been applied, including feminist scholarship. One commentator describes intersectionality as "the most important theoretical contribution that women's studies . . . has made so far."[1]

The notion that multiple systems of oppression intersect in people's lives and affect different individuals and groups of people differently opens up space for discussion about inter-group differences (e.g., differences between women and men) but also discussion about intragroup differences (e.g., differences in the experiences of discrimination among white women and women of color). Although its antecedents in Black feminist thought appeared much earlier, intersectionality theory surfaced in the late 1980s partly as a response to conceptual and pragmatic deficiencies in feminist legal theory and critical race theory. In 1989, Kimberlé Crenshaw published a germinal essay defining intersectionality theory. In *Demarginalizing the Intersection of Race and Sex: A Black Feminist Critique of Anti-Discrimination Doctrine, Feminist Theory and Antiracist Politics*,[2] Crenshaw demonstrated how neither feminist nor anti-racist advocacy fully captured the marginalization of women of color.[3] As Crenshaw explains in a later article, "[b]ecause of their intersectional identity as both women *and* of color within discourses that are shaped to respond to one *or* the other, women of color are marginalized within both."[4] The narrative exclusion of women of color contributes to their invisibility within both equality movements.[5]

Intersectionality is primarily a theory about marginalization and its felt experience. The theory is capacious enough to accommodate questions of privilege and

[1] Leslie McCall, *The Complexity of Intersectionality*, *in* Intersectionality and Beyond: Law, Power, and the Politics of Location 49 (Emily Grabham et al. eds., 2008).

[2] Kimberlé Crenshaw, *Demarginalizing the Intersection of Race and Sex: A Black Feminist Critique of Antidiscrimination Doctrine, Feminist Theory and Antiracist Politics*, 1989 U. Chi. Legal F. 139 (1989) [hereinafter Crenshaw, *Demarginalizing the Intersection*].

[3] *Id.* at 166.

[4] Kimberlé Crenshaw, *Mapping the Margins: Intersectionality, Identity Politics, and Violence Against Women of Color*, 43 Stanford L. Rev. 1241, 1252 (1991) [hereinafter Crenshaw, *Mapping the Margins*].

[5] Maria Lugones observes, "[i]t is only when we perceive gender and race as intermeshed or fused that we actually see women of color." Maria Lugones, *Heterosexism and the Modern/Colonial Gender System*, 22 Hypatia 186, 192–93 (2007).

Global Intersectionality and Contemporary Human Rights. Johanna Bond, Oxford University Press.
DOI: 10.1093/oso/9780198868835.003.0002

the structures that sustain dominance and privilege. Subordination and its converse, privilege, operate along multiple axes. Because multiple systems of oppression operate simultaneously, one may enjoy privilege because of, for example, one's race but suffer subordination because of gender, class, sexual orientation, or disability. In an 1888 speech recalling his own remarks forty years earlier at Seneca Falls at the first ever convention on women's rights, abolitionist and human rights activist Frederick Douglass poignantly acknowledged that he occupied this intersectional space as both subjugated and subjugator. Douglass, oppressed on the basis of race, acknowledged his gender privilege when speaking on the topic of women's suffrage. "Men," he said, "have very little business here as speakers, anyhow; and if they come here at all they should take back benches and wrap themselves in silence."[6] As Douglass understood, one may be both oppressed and oppressor.

As Crenshaw highlighted in her 1989 article, legal regimes that force victims of discrimination to frame a legal claim as based on *either* race *or* gender fail to capture the intersectional experience of discrimination.[7] Those harmed by intersectional discrimination may be forced to choose a single ground of discrimination on which to base their claims. As a result, remedies may address only part of the discrimination that victims have experienced, leading to results that are likely to be unsatisfying and potentially unsuccessful.[8] Although litigants have, at times, attempted to push courts to recognize intersectional claims, legal systems are limited by the specific laws establishing a basis for cognizable claims.[9] Systemic reform is needed to facilitate intersectional claims in many of the legal systems around the world.

In addition to changing the way we think about individual legal claims in the context of multifaceted discrimination, intersectionality also offers insight into interlocking systems of structural discrimination. Crenshaw highlights the importance of examining how systemic power operates and who benefits from it. She distinguishes between structural intersectionality, which concerns "the intersection of unequal social groups," and political intersectionality, which concerns "the intersection of political agendas and projects."[10] Political intersectionality addresses the intersection of antiracist and feminist organizing and advocacy. Structural intersectionality focuses on forms of oppression that systematically privilege certain groups over others and interrogates the structural dimensions of power and privilege.

Like Crenshaw, Patricia Hill Collins made significant early contributions to the development of intersectionality theory with the 1990 publication of her groundbreaking book, *Black Feminist Thought*.[11] Indeed, in describing Collins's influence

[6] Frederick Douglass, Speech before the International Council of Women, in Washington, D.C. (April 14, 1888), https://www.blackpast.org/african-american-history/1888-frederick-douglass-woman-suffrage/.

[7] Crenshaw, *Demarginalizing the Intersection*, *supra* note 2, at 149–50 ("Black women's experiences are much broader than the general categories that discrimination discourse provides.").

[8] *See id.* ("[T]he continued insistence that Black women's demands and needs be filtered through categorical analyses that completely obscure their experiences [by focusing on either race or gender] guarantees that their needs will seldom be addressed.").

[9] *See id.* at 141–50 (describing a series of legal challenges in which the legal system failed to sufficiently address the intersectional experiences of women of color facing discrimination).

[10] Sylvia Walby et al., *Intersectionality: Multiple Inequalities in Social Theory*, 46 SOCIOLOGY 224, 226 (2012) (discussing Crenshaw, *Mapping the Margins*, *supra* note 4).

[11] PATRICIA HILL COLLINS, BLACK FEMINIST THOUGHT (1990).

on intersectionality theory, Christine Bose observes that "few contemporary scholars have been so adept or successful at instigating a paradigmatic change in how we understand our world."[12] In particular, Collins promoted the idea of a "matrix of domination," in which interlocking systems of domination and subordination intersect and affect different groups in different ways.[13]

While this chapter traces the development and theoretical underpinnings of intersectionality theory, it does not provide an extensive history of the evolution of the theory. Such a historical framing is outside the bounds of this volume. Rather, this chapter offers a foundation for thinking about intersectionality theory and how it might positively influence human rights discourse. To that end, I trace the theory's development within the landscape of critical race feminism in the United States in the latter half of the twentieth century. I touch on but do not fully explore analogous critiques in subaltern studies that have emerged in the Global South. And while I will review some of the primary critiques of intersectionality, I do not provide an in-depth treatment. Such analysis deserves—and has elsewhere received—book-length treatment. My intent here is more modest: to offer an introduction to thinking critically about intersectionality. This foundation will allow us to adopt an intersectional lens in subsequent chapters, which discuss and analyze international human rights law and legal institutions.

Precursors and parallels

Although intersectionality is most closely associated with the emergent voices of critical race feminists in the United States in the late 1980s and early 1990s, parallel critiques emerged from the Global South around the same time.[14] In addition, women of color in the United States articulated the principles that undergird intersectionality theory long before the late twentieth century. Important antecedents to intersectionality theory can be traced back to the work of Sojourner Truth, Anna Julia Cooper, and others. Vivian May, for example, has highlighted Cooper's crucial work in the late 1800s, crediting her with an early articulation of intersectionality theory. May notes,

> While Cooper articulates how race, gender, class and region (and later, nation) interdepend and cannot be examined as isolatable, many of her contemporaries and later scholars examining her work could not seem to fully grasp her arguments—in large part because Cooper's words and ideas were examined via single-axis frameworks,

[12] Christine E. Bose, *Intersectionality and Global Gender Inequality*, 26 Gender & Soc'y 67, 67 (2012).

[13] collins, *supra* note 11, at 23.

[14] Sinah Theres Kloß notes that the concept of the Global South connotes more than mere geography. The Global South "when not simplistically referred to in terms of geography, has great potential to consolidate and empower the various social actors that consider themselves to be in subaltern(ized) positionalities of global networks of power." Sinah Theres Kloß, *The Global South as Subversive Practice: Challenges and Potentials of a Heuristic Concept*, 11 Global South 1, 1 (2017).

either/or models of thought, or measures of rationality that could not account for multiplicity.[15]

May also points to antecedents in the efforts of Sojourner Truth, whose clarion advocacy included the assertion "Now colored men have a right to vote; and what I want is to have colored women have the right to vote."[16] As May observes, Crenshaw herself recognized the critical contributions of these and other Black feminist trailblazers.[17]

Some scholars and activists and many others in the Global South were early adopters of an intersectionality-like framework, although they of course did not use the term until after Crenshaw's articulation of it. These parallel critiques, challenging the emerging international women's rights movement, fall roughly into three overlapping types: reactions against universalism and notions of addition and severability; reactions against "savior" narratives; and reactions against colonialism and ongoing North/South power differentials.

Universalism and addition/severability

In the 1970s and early 1980s, some advocates for women's rights attempted to galvanize support for women's rights around the world by focusing on women's shared experiences of oppression. Robin Morgan's 1984 anthology, *Sisterhood Is Global*, typified this approach and attempted to use the global sisterhood concept to unite women behind the cause of gender justice.[18] In so doing, however, Morgan relied on a false universalism. Many scholars in the Global South rejected the concept of a global sisterhood and believed that it had the effect of universalizing the experience of gender in ways that did not capture their own experiences. These scholars and activists resisted the totalizing rhetoric of the global sisterhood, mounting a critique that was similar in many ways to that of Crenshaw, Angela Harris, Patricia Hill Collins, and other critical race feminists in the United States.

Writing in 1992, Chandra Talpade Mohanty specifically countered Morgan's notion of the global sisterhood, arguing that Morgan depicted women as a "cross-culturally singular, homogenous group with the same interests, perspectives and goals and similar experiences."[19] Mohanty rejected the universalizing group of women *qua* women, noting that "the discursively consensual homogeneity of 'women' as a group is

[15] Vivian May, *Intersectionality*, *in* RETHINKING WOMEN'S AND GENDER STUDIES 155, 157 (Catherine M. Orr & Ann Braithwaite eds., 2012).

[16] Vivian May, *"Speaking Into the Void"? Intersectionality Critiques and Epistemic Backlash*, 29 HYPATIA 94, 98 (2014) (quoting Sojourner Truth, Address Before the First Anniversary of the American Equal Rights Association (May 9, 1867)).

[17] *Id.* at 97. ("In a gesture refusing historical erasure of black feminist theorizing, by referencing Sojourner Truth and Anna Julia Cooper as foremothers to her own analysis, Crenshaw underscores that many intersectional principles had been developed by black feminist thinkers for over a century.").

[18] SISTERHOOD IS GLOBAL: THE INTERNATIONAL WOMEN'S MOVEMENT ANTHOLOGY (Robin Morgan ed., 1984).

[19] Chandra Talpade Mohanty, *Feminist Encounters: Locating the Politics of Experience*, *in* DESTABILIZING THEORY: CONTEMPORARY FEMINIST DEBATES 74, 78 (Michèle Barrett & Anne Phillips eds., 1992).

mistaken for the historically specific material reality of groups of women."[20] Mohanty challenged the uncritical generalization of a group of "women" without regard to differences of race, ethnicity, gender, or sexuality. Mohanty's work represents a significant contribution to early intersectionality feminist theory and, in particular, to deconstructing notions of the global sisterhood.[21]

In a similar vein, other critical voices asserted the connections between subordination based on race and gender. Like Mohanty, a number of Chicana feminists rejected a universalized understanding of gender subordination.[22] Gloria Anzaldúa, for example, poignantly and beautifully described her experiences as a Chicana lesbian in intersectional-like terms in *Borderlands: La Frontera*, published in 1987.[23] Chicana feminists in the 1970s and 1980s recognized and protested the simultaneous operation of both racism and sexism, laying the foundation for intersectionality's insight concerning the interconnected and mutually constitutive nature of systems of oppression.

In the 1960s and 1970s, a few scholars gestured toward an understanding of intersectionality in ways that centered Black women as an analytical category. In 1963, for example, Black feminist activist Pauli Murray objected to the omission of women from the 1963 March on Washington, famously noting that "Negro women, historically, have carried the dual burden of Jim Crow and Jane Crow."[24] Elaborating on this duality, Murray goes on to say, "The Negro woman can no longer postpone or subordinate the fight against discrimination because of sex to the civil rights struggle but must carry on both fights simultaneously."[25] Writing in 1970, Frances Beal published *Double Jeopardy: To Be Black and Female*,[26] in which she recognized that Black women experience both racial and gender subordination. Beal was also concerned about class-based subordination. Although Beal acknowledges both forms of subordination in the lives of Black women, she does not explore how systems of oppression may interact, integrate, and mutually reinforce one another. In an analytical sense, one simply adds "race" or "gender" to the analysis, but the concepts remain theoretically separable.

Subsequent theorists, including Deborah King, added class as a category of analysis and called it "triple jeopardy" or "multiple discrimination."[27] Writing about Black women in the United States, King described the "interactive oppressions that circumscribe our lives."[28] King's analysis hinted at intersectionality, but it did not examine in

[20] Chandra Talpade Mohanty, *Under Western Eyes: Feminist Scholarship and Colonial Discourses*, 2 BOUNDARY 333, 338 (1984).

[21] *Id.* at 358.

[22] Anna Nieto-Gómez's 1974 *La Feminista* states, "These feministas are speaking out against the sexual racist oppression that they as Chicana women must contend with.... It is ... perpetuated by nationalists who demand that women must always be traditional and maintain the culture, in spite of their socio-economically oppressive conditions." Anna Nieto-Gómez, *La Feminista*, *in* CHICANA FEMINIST THOUGHT: THE BASIC HISTORICAL WRITINGS 86, 86–87 (Alma M. García ed., 1997).

[23] Gloria Anzaldúa, BORDERLANDS: LA FRONTERA (1987).

[24] Pauli Murray, Speech to the National Council of Negro Women Convention: The Negro Woman in the Quest for Equality (Nov. 14, 1963), https://cpb-us-e1.wpmucdn.com/blogs.uoregon.edu/dist/7/11428/files/2017/03/Murray-The-Negro-Woman-2clsq0g.pdf.

[25] *Id.*

[26] Frances Beal, *Third World Women's Alliance, Double Jeopardy: To Be Black and Female*, *in* BLACK WOMEN'S MANIFESTO 19–34 (1970).

[27] Deborah K. King, *Multiple Jeopardy, Multiple Consciousness: The Context of a Black Feminist Ideology*, 14 SIGNS 42, 46, 49 (1988).

[28] *Id.* at 42

depth how systems of race, gender, and class subordination are inseparable and mutually constitutive. As Anna Carastathis describes, "[t]he jeopardy model seems not to dispute the categorical distinctions among systems; rather, their fixity is assumed in the conjoining of categories of race, class, and gender."[29] Double and triple jeopardy represent attempts to grapple with the existence of multiple systems of oppression, but they do not explore how the systems of subordination relate, reinforce, and define each other. They treat race, class, and gender as aspects of identity that can be "added" together to describe the experience of, for example, Black women living in poverty or Black women engaged in low-wage labor.

Many early articulations of "intersectionality-like" thinking reflect this more limited, additive view of multiple systems of oppression.[30] Although the concepts recognize the simultaneous operation of, for example, racism and disability, they perpetuate the misunderstanding that these experiences of discrimination are additive and severable.[31] Race and disability intersect so that race changes the experience of disability and, similarly, disability changes the experience of race.[32] In this way, race and disability are mutually constitutive rather than merely the experiential sum of race and disability. The notion that experiences of discrimination because of one's race and disability, among others, can be added, separated, or both leads to a misunderstanding of the subordination at play and a destructive hierarchy of oppressions.[33]

Additive approaches fail to capture the understanding that the discrimination experienced by Black women, for example, is qualitatively different from the discrimination experienced by white women and Black men. Historian Barbara Ransby noted that race, class, gender, and sexuality are "codependent variables that cannot readily be separated and ranked in scholarship, in political practice, or in lived experience."[34] The additive concept attempts to capture race, gender, and other forms of discrimination. It does not, however, recognize that the discrimination at the intersection of gender and race is qualitatively different from the conceptual sum of race and gender discrimination. These attempts to grapple with the simultaneous operation of racism and sexism in Black women's lives laid the foundation for intersectionality's more searching inquiry into the ways in which systems of oppression intersect and mutually define and sustain other forms of oppression. Theorists such as Crenshaw rejected the understanding of complex identities as addition problems and established the inseparability of systems of oppression.

29 Anna Carastathis, Intersectionality: Origins, Contestations, Horizons 35 (2016).

30 Ange-Marie Hancock, Intersectionality: An Intellectual History 100 (2016) ("Part of why additive organizations of power are incompletely intersectionality-like thinking is because they retain an idea of the severability of race from gender and other categories of difference. Later theorists explicitly reject this additive, severable notion of identity and insist on 'ontological equality among the axes of difference.'" (citation omitted)).

31 Carastathis, *supra* note 29, at 35.

32 Ashlee Christoffersen, Equality Challenge Unit, Intersectional Approaches to Equality Research and Data 9 (2017), http://www.ecu.ac.uk/wp-content/uploads/2017/04/Research_and_data_briefing_2_Intersectional_approaches_to_equality_research_and_data.pdf.

33 Hancock, *supra* note 30, at 97.

34 Barbara Ransby, *Black Feminism at Twenty-One: Reflections on the Evolution of a National Community*, 25 Signs 1214, 1218 (2000).

A distinct antecedent to the rejection of additive approaches is found in a 1977 publication by the Combahee River Collective. The Collective grew out of the National Black Feminist Organization in the mid-1970s, with Barbara Smith, Beverly Smith, and Demita Frazier producing its groundbreaking indictment of race and gender oppression entitled "A Black Feminist Statement." The statement notes, "We are actively committed to struggling against racial, sexual, heterosexual and class oppression and see as our particular task the development of integrated analysis and practice based upon the fact that the major systems of oppression are interlocking."[35] The statement specifically recognizes "interlocking" systems of oppression and lays the foundation for the core notions of intersectionality that would surface years later in the writing of Crenshaw, Patricia Hill Collins, and others. Anna Carastathis suggests that the statement represents a clear departure from earlier, additive expressions of double and triple jeopardy.[36] The statement was an important intellectual precursor to intersectionality, significant in its recognition of interlocking systems of oppression and in its expression of a Black lesbian/feminist identity.[37]

Feminist scholar Uma Narayan, writing in the late 1980s, embraced a version of "standpoint feminism," which argued that one views the world from a particular standpoint based on unique experiences that derive from particular identity markers like gender, race, class, and geopolitical privilege. Narayan noted, "Feminist epistemology suggests that integrating women's contribution into the domain of science and knowledge ... will not merely widen the canvas but result in a shift of perspective enabling us to see a very different picture."[38] Although an important contribution in the evolution of critical race feminism, standpoint theory stops short of an intersectional framework. It does not reflect the understanding of systems of oppression as mutually constitutive. One may offer insight from a standpoint that reflects a particular racial and gendered identity, but standpoint theory does not explore how the social construction of race and gendered identities inform one another. Narayan's insights, however, helped shape the evolving notion that one might understand the world differently depending on where one stands with respect to gender, race, class, and other aspects of identity.

Saviorism

A second important critique that helped establish intersectionality's salience focused on the notion that feminists from the Global North were attempting to save the Global South from itself.[39] A number of activists in the Global South rejected what they recognized as an international effort to "civilize" or "save" them. The Third World

[35] HANCOCK, *supra* note 30, at 97 (citing Combahee River Collective, *A Black Feminist Statement*, *in* ALL THE WOMEN ARE WHITE, ALL THE BLACKS ARE MEN, BUT SOME OF US ARE BRAVE: BLACK WOMEN'S STUDIES 13–22 (Gloria Hull et al. eds., 1993).

[36] CARASTATHIS, *supra* note 29, at 36–38.

[37] *Id.* at 38.

[38] Uma Narayan, *The Project of Feminist Epistemology: Perspectives from a Nonwestern Feminist*, *in* GENDER/BODY/KNOWLEDGE: FEMINIST RECONSTRUCTIONS OF BEING AND KNOWING 256, 256 (Alison M. Jaggar & Susan R. Brodo eds., 1989).

[39] Malia Lee Womack, *Troubling Universalized Human Rights: The Complexities of Identity and Intersectionality*, 1 J. POLS. & DEMOCRATIZATION 56, 58 (2016) (noting "[s]ince human rights are designed

Approaches to International Law movement, known as TWAIL, began as a response to colonialism and rejected the portrayal of international law as an objective and neutral imposition of universal values.[40] TWAIL originated as part of the decolonization movement after World War II. In an article entitled *What Is TWAIL?*, Makua Mutua outlines three basic objectives of TWAIL: (1) "to understand, deconstruct, and unpack the uses of international law as a medium for the creation and perpetuation of a racialized hierarchy of international norms"; (2) "to construct and present an alternative normative legal edifice for international governance"; and (3) "to eradicate the conditions of underdevelopment in the Third World."[41] TWAIL scholarship specifically rejects the notion of the Global North as a savior of the Global South.

In a subsequent article, Mutua invokes the metaphor of the savage/victim/savior to critique the Eurocentric model of human rights. The metaphor depicts the non-Western state, and the culture it supports, as the savage; the victim as the helpless innocent; and Western human rights institutions and actors as the saviors. Mutua is explicit about the role of race in the metaphor, noting that the human rights narrative typically portrays victims and savages as "non-white and non-Western" and saviors—or human rights actors—as white.[42] Mutua's critique resonates with critical race theory in general, and shares intersectionality's insight about the role of race and geopolitical privilege in human rights discourse.

Colonialism and power dynamics

The third thread of critique that helped lay the groundwork for the global application of intersectionality is closely related to TWAIL's critique of Western colonization but adds a specific focus on gender. This critique builds on the focus on colonialism and the entrenched racial and geopolitical power disparities that it fostered. Mohanty argued that feminist scholarship's embrace of universalism had a colonizing effect. Feminist imperialism operated, in part, by constructing "third world women" as perpetually victimized and lacking in agency.[43] This critique also eschews ahistorical generalizations in favor of analysis of particular contexts, locations, and historical moments. Postcolonial feminist analysis requires a focus on the ongoing and lasting effects of colonialism on the construction of race, ethnicity, gender, sexuality, and nation. In this sense, postcolonial feminism and intersectionality share a commitment to challenging mutually reinforcing systems of oppression.

by elite actors and concentrate on universal needs, they abstract the concrete experiences of the most subjugated 'others' whose identities are least recognized in the human rights hierarchy").

[40] *See* Makau Mutua, *What is TWAIL?*, *in* The American Society of International Law: Proceedings of the 94th Annual Meeting 31, 37 (2000) ("TWAIL calls for the full democratization of the structures of both national and international governance so that all voices can be heard."); *see also* Anna Spain Bradley, *Human Rights Racism*, 32 Harv. Hum. Rts. J. 1, 52–54 (2019) (noting that that TWAIL theorists "rightly call for recognizing that the law is not racially neutral").

[41] Mutua, *supra* note 40, at 31.

[42] Makau Mutua, *Savages, Victims, and Saviors: The Metaphor of Human Rights*, 42 Harv. Int'l L.J. 201, 207 (2001).

[43] Mohanty, *supra* note 20, at 353.

Too often, elites in the Global North have enjoyed geopolitical advantages, making them more visible in defining a totalizing "woman's experience" that forms the basis for organizing for women's rights around the world.[44] In so doing, they have not adequately taken account of women's multiple identities. By virtue of this socioeconomic, geopolitical, and often racial privilege, dominant feminist voices neglected issues of colonialism, imperialism, and nationalism. Largely white leaders from the Global North have, until the late 1990s, ignored the notion that women experience gender and other aspects of their multiple identities in specific and important geographic, economic, and political contexts. Since the 1990s, however, scholars and activists have increasingly applied intersectionality theory in transnational contexts. Legal scholar Adrien Katherine Wing played a prominent role in promoting global critical race feminism, including early application of intersectionality theory in global feminist discourse.[45] The theory has traveled widely. This cross-border travel and wide-ranging engagement have made intersectionality theory not weary and played out but rather "more insurrectionary and capacious."[46] This book applies intersectionality theory to the international human rights context, with specific attention to the United Nations, in the spirit of just such an insurrectionary and capacious engagement.

Situating intersectionality within feminist and critical race theory within the United States

This chapter situates intersectionality theory first and foremost as a product of Black feminist voices in the United States. This positioning is intentional. As intersectionality theory is expanded and applied in a variety of fields and circumstances, there is a significant risk that the theory will become disconnected from its roots in Black feminist thought. Sirma Bilge cautions against "depoliticizing intersectionality" by disconnecting the theory from its activist, anti-racist, social justice-oriented roots.[47] Bilge notes, "While hegemonic positions are never entirely stable, hegemonic 'White' ways of knowing and 'White' entitlements are fully implicated in the feminist struggles for meaning over intersectionality and the forced take-over of intersectionality from feminists of color."[48] In her intellectual history of intersectionality theory, Ange-Marie Hancock warns of the potential "whitening" of intersectionality theory.[49] One of the risks of this appropriation is the elision of intersectionality's origin story—it is

[44] Lisa Crooms, *"To Establish My Legitimate Name Inside the Consciousness of Strangers:" Critical Race Praxis, Progressive Women-of-Color Theorizing and Human Rights*, 46 How. L.J. 229, 253 (2003) (describing the deliberations at the World Conference Against Racism: "[W]e failed to actively counter the overwhelming presence of voices from the Global North, in general, and from the U.S., in particular. As feminists of color, many of us failed to be reflexive, opting, instead, to recreate hierarchy by not relinquishing our privilege vis-à-vis our sisters from the global South.").

[45] *See generally* Global Critical Race Feminism: An International Reader (Adrien Katherine Wing ed., 2000).

[46] Devon W. Carbado, *Colorblind Intersectionality*, 38 Signs 811, 812 (2013) (citing Edward Said, *Traveling Theory Reconsidered*, *in* "Reflections on Exile" And Other Essays 436–52 (2000)).

[47] Sirma Bilge, *Intersectionality Undone: Saving Intersectionality from Feminist Intersectionality Studies*, 10 Du Bois Rev. 405, 405 (2013).

[48] *Id.* at 413.

[49] Hancock, *supra* note 30, at 10.

"the longstanding project of theorising by women of colour about identity from which [intersectionality] is born."[50]

There is a danger in describing intersectionality as resulting from some deficiency in the universalizing women's rights discourses prevalent from the 1970s to the 1990s. Intersectionality is often described as a theory borne of Black women's frustration with both racism in feminist campaigns and sexism in anti-racist campaigns.[51] This characterization, however, risks reducing the theoretical contributions of women of color to "a unified genre of thought defined solely in terms of its critique of feminism's racism."[52] The characterization of intersectionality as a theoretical corrective to white feminism falsely implies white feminism's a priori existence.[53] On the other hand, Brittney Cooper urges scholars not to ignore "the historical fact that intersectionality was developed by black women activists and intellectuals *against* white-dominated feminism, as much as against the male-dominated black liberation movement, against capitalism and heterosexism."[54] In either case, scholars must take great care not to disconnect intersectionality from its roots in Black feminist theory and advocacy.

In this volume, I attempt to preserve and honor intersectionality's origins in Black feminist thought while also recognizing new applications for the theory, such as its application in international human rights contexts. Although this is relatively new substantive terrain, Crenshaw and others have invited application of the theory in novel and expanding contexts.[55] The threat to the theory comes not from expansion but from the hegemonic erasure of Black feminism as a primary focus of inquiry.

In the 1960s and 1970s, feminist legal scholars and activists in the United States focused primarily on laws that explicitly treated women differently from men. This strategy of challenging formal inequality allowed women's rights activists to overturn laws that prohibited women from working at night[56] or in particular job categories.[57] During this era, women's rights lawyers also challenged laws that designated men as

[50] Nikol Alexander-Floyd, *Disappearing Acts: Reclaiming Intersectionality in the Social Sciences in a Post-Black Feminist Era*, 24 FEMINIST FORMATIONS 1, 4 (2012).

[51] *Id. See also* Jasbir K. Puar, *I Would Rather Be a Cyborg than a Goddess: Becoming-Intersectional in Assemblage Theory*, 2 PHILOSOPHIA 49, 51 (2012) ("While Crenshaw specifically targeted the elisions of both critical race paradigms and gender normative paradigms, intersectionality emerged from the struggles of second wave feminism as a crucial black feminist intervention challenging the hegemonic rubrics of race, class, and gender within predominantly white feminist frames.").

[52] Shireen Roshanravan, *Motivating Coalition: Women of Color and Epistemic Disobedience*, 29 HYPATIA 41, 41 (2014).

[53] CARASTATHIS, *supra* note 29, at 25 (noting that "[w]hite feminism has mistakenly been seen to originate first, with women-of-color feminisms emerging later 'to add the factor of race/ethnicity to the feminist project'") (quoting BENITA ROTH, SEPARATE ROADS TO FEMINISM: BLACK CHICANA, AND WHITE FEMINIST MOVEMENTS IN AMERICA'S SECOND WAVE 8 (2004)).

[54] JENNIFER NASH, BLACK FEMINISM REIMAGINED: AFTER INTERSECTIONALITY 40 (2019) (quoting BRITTNEY COOPER, BEYOND RESPECTABILITY: THE INTELLECTUAL THOUGHT OF RACE WOMEN (2017)).

[55] Carbado, *supra* note 46, at 841 ("[I]t is erroneous to conceptualize intersectionality as a theory whose exclusive focus is the intersection of race (read: nonwhite) and gender (read: nonmale).... [M]any scholars frame intersectionality more narrowly than is theoretically necessary."); *see also* Crenshaw, *Mapping the Margins*, *supra* note 4, at 1296 ("[I]ntersectionality might be more broadly useful as a way of mediating the tension between assertions of multiple identity and the ongoing necessity of group politics.").

[56] SUPREME COURT DECISIONS AND WOMEN'S RIGHTS 143 (Clare Cushman & Talbot D'Alemberte eds., 2001) (citing Corning Glass Works v. Brennan, 417 U.S. 188 (1974)).

[57] *See generally* Goesaert v. Cleary, 335 U.S. 464 (1948) (evaluating a Michigan law that restricted most women from working as bartenders); Craig v. Boren, 429 U.S. 190 (1976).

breadwinners and heads of households.[58] Pregnancy discrimination also became a target of women's rights lawyers in the 1970s.[59] Feminist legal scholars and activists were able to target the proverbial low-hanging fruit.

In the 1980s, activists shifted focus to more subtle forms of discrimination. In many cases, the challenged laws did not facially discriminate against women. The application of the laws, however, disproportionately affected women in negative ways. The effort in the 1970s to remove formal barriers to women's opportunities had proven insufficient to fully empower women. Activists recognized that they would need to challenge, for example, stereotypes about the inferiority of women and the double burden of domestic work and employment outside the home. The 1980s also brought challenges to sexual harassment, which had previously been accepted as a norm within the workplace.

Feminist scholars have characterized the 1980s as an era of "difference" or "cultural" or "relational" feminism. Carol Gilligan greatly influenced 1980s feminist discourse by arguing that girls and boys are socialized differently and, as a result, have different notions of morality.[60] Gilligan argued that the guiding moral principles for girls amount to an "ethic of care," whereas the guiding moral principles for boys reflect an "ethic of justice." Ultimately, Gilligan argued that girls' value systems and boys' value systems should be equally respected. Some legal scholars have applied Gilligan's theory of difference, arguing that the law should promote motherhood, alternative dispute resolution, and other legal concepts associated with "feminine" or relational values. This approach represents a departure from the liberal feminism dominant in the 1970s, in which feminists argued that the law should treat women and men the same.

Also in the 1980s, another school of feminist thought—"dominance feminism"—took hold. Feminist proponents of dominance feminism, such as legal scholar Catharine MacKinnon, maintained that the "difference" between women and men was that men occupied a place of domination, while women occupied a place of subordination. This insight proved invaluable in explaining the prevalence of social phenomena like sexual harassment in the workplace and intimate partner violence in the home.

In the late 1980s and early 1990s, Kimberlé Crenshaw and others found fertile ground for an important critique of much of the feminist legal scholarship prevalent in the 1970s and 1980s. Critical race feminists, Crenshaw among them, explained that the prevailing feminist theories promoting "formal equality," "cultural or relational" feminism, and "dominance" feminism failed to capture the experiences of women of color. In 1991, Crenshaw built on her earlier work by highlighting the problem with universalizing feminist theories in her article *Mapping the Margins: Intersectionality, Identity Politics, and Violence Against Women of Color*.[61] In *Mapping the Margins*, Crenshaw demonstrated that a woman's experiences of violence may depend on and be tightly interwoven with race and class. As Crenshaw explains, "the intersection of

[58] *See* Califano v. Westcott, 443 U.S. 76, 78 (1979) (challenging a law that provided aid to families where the father was unemployed or underemployed but not where the mother was unemployed or underemployed).

[59] Wendy Williams, *Equality's Riddle: Pregnancy and the Equal Treatment/Special Treatment Debate*, 13 N.Y.U. Rev. L. & Soc. Change 325, 325 (1984).

[60] Carol Gilligan, In a Different Voice (1982).

[61] *See* Crenshaw, *Mapping the Margins*, *supra* note 4.

racism and sexism ... cannot be captured wholly by looking at the race or gender dimensions of those experiences separately."[62] Importantly, Crenshaw argues that the intersection of race and gender in one's life leads to experiences that are qualitatively different from the simple aggregation of race and gender subordination.

In the case of intimate partner violence, for example, women of color may be reluctant to involve law enforcement even when physical safety is at stake. "Women of color are often reluctant to call the police," Crenshaw notes, "a hesitancy likely due to a general unwillingness among people of color to subject their private lives to the scrutiny and control of a police force that is frequently hostile."[63] The intersections of race, gender, sexuality, and class are highly relevant in interactions with police. This intersectional approach should inform the breadth of policy responses to intimate partner violence, encouraging holistic community responses that go beyond law enforcement.

Crenshaw also highlights the ways in which immigrant women's experiences of intimate partner violence are qualitatively different from those of socioeconomically privileged white women. Crenshaw describes the structural dimensions of intersectionality and the impact of structural intersectionality on intimate partner violence. Drawing on her observations from battered women's shelters located in minority communities in Los Angeles, Crenshaw notes that many of the women seeking shelter were unemployed or underemployed, and many of them were from low socioeconomic status groups. Poverty frequently thwarts a woman's ability to extricate herself from a violent relationship. Crenshaw observes:

> These burdens [poverty, childcare responsibilities, and lack of job skills], largely the consequence of gender and class oppression, are then compounded by the racially discriminatory employment and housing practices women of color often face, as well as by the disproportionately high unemployment among people of color that makes battered women of color less able to depend on the support of friends and relatives for temporary shelter.[64]

The structural dimensions of intersectionality reflect institutionalized racism and create conditions of poverty that limit options for many women of color. The context and structural interplays are significantly different from that of other groups, as are the understanding and responses needed to remedy them.

Intersectionality and anti-essentialism

One important critique of the prevailing feminist legal theory from the 1970s and 1980s was that it treated all women as similarly situated. With respect to the formal equality focus of the 1970s, the question for majority-white privileged legal scholars was: were women *as a category* treated differently from men *as a category*? There was little recognition among majority-white feminist legal scholars that the experiences

[62] *Id.* at 1244.
[63] *Id.* at 1257.
[64] *Id.* at 1245–46.

of discrimination might be qualitatively different for different groups of women. Similarly, in the 1980s some of the most vocal proponents of dominance feminism failed to appreciate the ways that other markers of identity, such as race, class, sexual orientation, religion, and disability, might affect a particular woman's experiences of subordination.

The notion that there can be no universal experience of gender or race is foundational to intersectionality theory. This is not a particularly novel claim; since the days of the suffrage movement, women of color have objected to universalizing claims of "women's experiences" that were largely based on the experiences of white leaders of the movement.[65] Elizabeth Spelman observes, "[T]he real problem has been how feminist theory has confused the condition of one group of women with the condition of all."[66]

In 1990, Angela Harris defined "gender essentialism" as "[t]he notion that there is a monolithic 'women's experience' that can be described independent of other facets of experience like race, class, and sexual orientation."[67] Gender essentialism privileges gender as an identity category to the exclusion of other critical aspects of identity. Harris's work on anti-essentialism is illuminating in many ways. In her 1990 article, *Race and Essentialism in Feminist Legal Theory*, she refutes the notion that "a unitary, 'essential' women's experience can be isolated and described independently of race, class, sexual orientation, and other realities of experience."[68] Harris also links additive notions of subordination with essentialism, noting that "[t]he result of essentialism is to reduce the lives of people who experience multiple forms of oppression to addition problems: 'racism + sexism = straight black women's experience,' or 'racism + sexism + homophobia = black lesbian experience.' "[69]

Harris explains the tendency to universalize through categories such as "women" by contrasting two different literary speakers.[70] At one end of the spectrum, she describes a Jorge Luis Borges character named Funes the Memorious.[71] After suffering a fall, Funes experiences perfect memory. Because he remembers images with perfect clarity of detail, he sees each image or memory as distinct. He loses the ability to group like things alike; he loses the ability to categorize. The extreme particularity of Funes's world leaves him unable to meaningfully relate to others. This level of particularity would prevent any collective organizing or social movement around a common cause. In contrast to Funes, Harris describes the voice implicit in the reference to "We the

[65] *See* Angela P. Harris, *Race and Essentialism in Feminist Legal Theory*, 42 Stan. L. Rev. 581, 586–87 (1990) ("In the first wave of the feminist movement, black women's realization that the white leaders of the suffrage movement intended to take neither issues of racial oppression nor black women themselves seriously was instrumental in destroying or preventing political alliances between black and white women within the movement.").

[66] Elizabeth V. Spelman, Inessential Woman: Problems of Exclusion in Feminist Thought 4 (1988).

[67] Harris, *supra* note 65, at 588.

[68] *Id.* at 585.

[69] *Id.* at 588.

[70] *Id.* at 582–88.

[71] I cite Harris's use of Funes the Memorious and "We the People" in a previous article. I revisit it here because it brilliantly captures the perils of universal categories and, at the opposite extreme, the inability to categorize. *See* Johanna Bond, *International Intersectionality: A Theoretical and Pragmatic Exploration of Women's International Human Rights Violations*, 52 Emory L.J. 71, 107 (2003).

People" in the preamble to the US Constitution. The voice of "We the People" purports to speak for all but fails to include people of color in profoundly harmful ways. Both voices, Harris observes, are inadequate. "Both voices are monologues; both depend on the silencing of others."[72] Harris uses this framing to propose an anti-essentialist approach that rejects these universalizing tendencies. She specifically challenges Catharine MacKinnon's dominance theory for failing to account for race in its generalized description of the experience of rape.[73]

Feminist legal scholars and others sometimes equate intersectionality and anti-essentialism.[74] Although these approaches share certain attributes, including an effort to de-center the experiences of white women, Devon Carbado and Cheryl Harris observe that intersectionality and anti-essentialism offer different theoretical contributions. Notably, Carbado and Harris reject the view that critical theorists must always avoid essentialism.[75] They suggest that essentialism can be used carefully and productively by critical theorists, and they caution that anti-essentialism can itself be used in furtherance of a conservative political agenda. "Our view is that judging a particular analysis to be essentialist does not settle normative questions," they write; "rather, the important consideration is whether the deployment of essentialism is justified empirically and normatively in a particular context."[76] This opens the door for consideration of how some degree of essentialism may be helpful or necessary for political action and normative change.

The choice to craft an essentialist narrative is often a strategic one. The focus on common experiences of oppression often functions as a call to arms. Gayatri Chakravorty Spivak describes what she calls "strategic essentialism,"[77] which attempts to strike a useful balance between the isolation and particularity of Funes and the totalizing universalization of "We the People." Spivak recognizes that there must be some degree of generalization about experiences for people to be able to organize for social change. In other words, without strategic essentialism, there can be no collective political action. Carbado and Harris observe, "[T]he deployment of the category 'African American' might be necessary to describe, organize against, or disrupt the group-based hierarchies on which racism has historically rested."[78] Patricia Williams

[72] Harris, *supra* note 65, at 583 ("In a sense, the "I" of Funes, who knows only particulars, and the "we" of "We the People," who know only generalities, are the same. Both voices are monologues; both depend on the silence of others. The difference is only that the first voice knows of no others, while the second has silenced them.").

[73] Devon W. Carbado & Cheryl I. Harris, *Intersectionality at 30: Mapping the Margins of Anti-Essentialism, Intersectionality, and Dominance Theory*, 132 HARV. L. REV. 2193, 2200–201 (2019) (quoting Angela P. Harris, *Race and Essentialism in Feminist Legal Theory*, 42 STAN. L. REV. 581, 598 (1990)). Harris criticizes MacKinnon for providing "an analysis of what rape means to white women [that] masquerade[es] as a general account; it has nothing to do with the experience of black women." *Id.*

[74] *Id.* at 2196.

[75] *Id.* at 2196 ("[The authors] contest the view that feminism and critical theory must always avoid essentialism to achieve normative commitments to social transformation."). Carbado and Harris make two other important claims about intersectionality: (1) intersectionality and dominance theory share a critique of the sameness/difference framework; and (2) intersectionality and dominance theory differ in their framing of race and gender. *Id.*

[76] *Id.* at 2204.

[77] Gayatri Chakravorty Spivak, *Subaltern Studies: Deconstructing Historiography*, *in* SELECTED SUBALTERN STUDIES 3, 13 (Ranajit Guha & Gayatri Chakravorty Spivak eds., 1988).

[78] Carbado & Harris, *supra* note 73, at 2204.

also recognizes the necessity and legitimacy of some limited generalization. In particular, Williams believes that the experience of race "so profoundly affects the way one is treated, so radically shapes what one is allowed to think and feel about this society, that the decision to generalize from such a division is valid."[79] Anti-essentialism offers a powerful critique of universalized voices that silence disempowered constituencies and generalized categories that place white experience at the center of analysis. At the same time, careful and targeted essentializing may be necessary for effective advocacy in some situations. This nuanced invocation of essentialism does not map perfectly onto the contours of intersectionality, making the distinctions between the two theories important to grasp.[80]

Crenshaw's and Collins's early articulations of intersectionality theory were invaluable in de-centering the experiences of women who were privileged along the axes of race and class. Since then, intersectionality has gained significant traction as a theoretical framework. Scholars and theorists have expanded the theory beyond race and class to include multiple axes of privilege.[81] The theory has been applied across multiple disciplines in a variety of contexts. Activists have incorporated the theory into the missions of their organizations. Perhaps most importantly, the theory is dynamic, the lessons it teaches ever-changing. In a text that traces the intellectual history of intersectionality theory, Carbado notes that "[a] work-in-progress understanding of intersectionality invites us to do just that—that is, to see the theory in places in which it is already doing work and to imagine other kinds of work that agents might employ intersectionality to perform."[82]

This volume attempts to "do just that." It applies intersectionality theory to the human rights context, recognizing the important work that intersectionality is already doing in the field of human rights and encouraging a more robust embrace of intersectionality within nongovernmental organizations and inter-governmental institutions like the United Nations.

Critiquing and refining intersectionality theory

As intersectionality has gained traction around the world, it has understandably generated scholarly criticism. The discourse around critique of intersectionality is itself controversial. Jennifer Nash describes what she calls the "intersectionality wars," in which she cautions that "black feminists are enlisted in becoming precisely what the field imagines them to be—relentless, demanding, policing disciplinarians—as they expose and condemn the critics who are imagined to fail to adequately and fairly account for intersectionality, for black feminist theory, for black women's intellectual

[79] Patricia Williams, The Alchemy of Race and Rights 256 (1991).

[80] Carbado & Harris, *supra* note 73, at 2211.

[81] Indeed, Crenshaw herself explains that the theory is not limited to race and class. She notes, "[w]hile the primary intersections that I explore here are between race and gender, the concept can and should be expanded by factoring in issues such as class, sexual orientation, age, and color." Crenshaw, *Mapping the Margins*, *supra* note 4, at 1244 n.9.

[82] Devon Carbado et al., *Intersectionality: Mapping the Movements of a Theory*, 10 Du Bois Rev. 303, 304–05 (2013).

production."[83] Nash characterizes the response of many critical race theorists to critics of intersectionality as one of defensiveness and urges Black feminist proponents of intersectionality to engage less protectively with critiques of intersectionality. She acknowledges that intersectionality risks appropriation by white feminists but attempts to shift the discussion to what she considers to be more productive and generous engagements with intersectionality. It is appropriate and enlightening to debate the theory, and we should invite ethical debates about intersectionality, including both critiques and defenses of the theory.

Although, as noted, this text does not provide an in-depth treatment of scholarly critiques of intersectionality, it is helpful to sketch out their broad parameters to provide a foundation for thinking critically about the theory. As outlined below, the primary critiques fall into three categories: critiques problematizing a focus on race; critiques of the contexts in which intersectionality has (or has not) been applied; and critiques of the theory's reliance on identity categories. Ultimately, the salience of the critiques is belied by intersectionality's continued relevance and staying power. But the critiques are invaluable in that they push proponents of the theory, of which I am one, to continue to refine it and explore new applications for it.

Some critics charge that the theory overemphasizes race and that it fails to adequately interrogate other sites of privilege and subordination such as sexuality, class, disability, and so on. Devon Carbado, Kimberlé Crenshaw, Vickie Mays, and Barbara Tomlinson note, "Despite an enormous range of intersectional research addressing concerns of many racial and ethnic groups, genders, sexual orientations, nationalities, disabilities, and so forth, some scholars have criticized intersectionality for focusing 'too much' on Black women."[84] One such critique argues that Crenshaw's articulation of intersectionality reifies race and gender as the only relevant identity markers for Black women. Nash expresses this concern, among others, in her article *Re-Thinking Intersectionality*.[85] She suggests, "Crenshaw focuses on black women because they are 'multiply burdened', yet her analysis precludes an examination of forms of 'multiple burdens' (or the intersections of privileges and burdens) beyond race and gender."[86] Similarly, Nash asserts that Crenshaw is inattentive to historical and other contexts that shape the particular experiences of race and gender for individual Black women. In other words, Nash believes that Crenshaw treats all Black women as similarly situated.[87]

[83] Jennifer Nash, Black Feminism Reimagined After Intersectionality 34 (2019).

[84] Carbado et al., *supra* note 82, at 309.

[85] Jennifer Nash, *Re-Thinking Intersectionality*, 89 Feminist Rev. 1, 7 (2008).

[86] *Id.*

[87] *Id.* at 3. Nash describes her four primarily critiques of intersectionality as: "the lack of a clearly defined intersectional methodology, the use of black women as prototypical intersectional subjects, the ambiguity inherent to the definition of intersectionality, and the coherence between intersectionality and lived experiences of multiple identities." *Id.* 3–4. The critique implicitly asserts that Black women cannot be representative of intersectionality in action. Devon Carbado rejects the notion that Black women cannot be representative of intersectional methodology, noting "[t]he critique that intersectionality is necessarily and only about Black women reflects a similar representational problem: Black women cannot specifically name themselves in a theory (they are too similar to be different), nor can they function as the backdrop for the genesis and articulation of a generalizable framework about power and marginalization (they are too different to be the same)." Carbado, *supra* note 46, at 813.

Crenshaw's work establishes a template for intersectional analysis. It does not purport to interrogate all forms of intragroup privilege exhaustively. Crenshaw, in fact, disavows this notion, noting that her articulation of intersectionality is necessarily incomplete.[88] It is unrealistic to expect Crenshaw to illustrate all possible manifestations of privilege across all possible axes. As Sumi Cho observes, "race and gender intersectionality merely provided a jumping off point to illustrate the larger point of how identity categories constitute and require political coalitions."[89] Crenshaw offers an invaluable heuristic process, one that has been expansively and vigorously taken up by other theorists to explore a multitude of other intersectional identities.

Proponents of "multidimensionality" offer a similar critique of intersectionality's purported exclusive focus on race and gender. Darren Hutchinson's insightful work on multidimensionality, for example, represents an important contribution to the social construction of race and sexuality. Hutchison's work builds on intersectionality, expanding it to sufficiently account for sexuality. He argues, "The most important substantive addition that multidimensionality and other race-sexuality models bring to intersectionality scholarship is the examination of heterosexist subordination (alongside race, gender, and class), a topic that is omitted from much of the intersectionality literature."[90] Peter Kwan explicitly criticizes intersectionality for creating a "categorical hegemony" that privileges race and gender over other markers of identity.[91] In discussing some of the alternatives to intersectionality that have arisen, including multidimensionality,[92] cosynthesis,[93] inter-connectivity,[94] and assemblages,[95] Devon Carbado notes that these alternative frameworks "artificially circumscribe the theoretical reach of intersectionality as a predicate to staging their own intervention."[96] Similarly, Sumi Cho observes, "[T]he post-intersectionality move cannot be explained as analytically or conceptually distinct from intersectionality, a point conceded by even [Athena] Mutua (2013) who admits that Darren Hutchinson's employment of multidimensionality theory to address partially privileged individuals can be traced back to intersectionality."[97] As this chapter has demonstrated, some of the early adopters of intersectionality-like thinking were Black lesbian feminists who included race, gender, and sexuality in their analyses of multifaceted subordination. Indeed,

[88] Crenshaw notes, "While the primary intersections that I explore here are between race and gender, the concept can and should be expanded by factoring in issues such as class, sexual orientation, age, and color." Crenshaw, *Mapping the Margins*, *supra* note 4, at 1244–45 nn.8–9.

[89] Sumi Cho, *Post-Intersectionality: The Curious Reception of Intersectionality in Legal Scholarship*, 10 Du Bois Rev. 385, 390 (2013).

[90] Darren Lenard Hutchinson, *Identity Crisis: "Intersectionality," "Multidimensionality," and the Development of an Adequate Theory of Subordination*, 6 Mich. J. Race & L. 285, 311 (2001).

[91] Peter Kwan, *Jeffrey Dahmer and the Cosynthesis of Categories*, 48 Hastings L.J. 1257, 1276 (1997).

[92] *See generally* Darren Hutchinson, *Ignoring the Sexualization of Race: Heteronormativity, Critical Race Theory and Anti-Racist Politics*, 47 Buff. L. Rev. 1 (1999).

[93] Kwan, *supra* note 91, at 1276.

[94] *See generally* Francisco Valdes, *Sex and Race in Queer Legal Culture: Ruminations on Identities and Inter-Connectivities*, 5 S. Cal. Rev. L. & Women's Stud. 25 (1995).

[95] *See generally* Jasbir K. Puar, Terrorist Assemblages: Homonationalism in Queer Times (2007).

[96] Carbado, *supra* note 46, at 816.

[97] *See* Cho, *supra* note 89, at 387 (referring to the work of Hutchison and Athena Mutua, *Multidimensionality is to Masculinities What Intersectionality is to Feminism*, 13 Nev. L.J. 341 (2013)).

in naming and describing "intersectionality," Crenshaw did not intend for the framework to be applied in the limited case of only race and gender.[98]

Another category of critiques focuses on how intersectionality has, or has not, been applied in particular contexts. Here, I would include the critique that intersectionality has not been used to elucidate sites of privilege as well as sites of subordination and discrimination.[99] Scholars have infrequently invoked intersectionality to shed light on the privileged identity of white, heterosexual men, for example.[100] There is some validity to these critiques. Hae Yeon Cho and Myra Marx Ferree observe, "While the theory calls for critical consideration of the normative cases as well as the excluded or marginalized, a methodological emphasis on inclusion sometimes fetishizes study of 'difference' without necessarily giving sufficient attention to its relation to unmarked categories, especially to how the more powerful are defined as normative standards."[101] Jasbir Puar, who is often described as a critic of intersectionality,[102] also observes that "intersectionality always produces an Other, and that Other is always a Woman of Color . . . who must invariably be shown to be resistant, subversive, or articulating a grievance."[103] Puar, too, suggests that, at best, intersectionality could shed light on privilege even though it has not typically been used in this way. At worst, Puar suggests that intersectional analysis has reinscribed the dominance of white women by defining women of color only in terms of "difference."[104]

Intersectionality theory can and should be used to examine the ways in which those in power construct social norms in order to maintain that power.[105] In fact, intersectionality encourages us to consider how individuals may be both privileged along some axes and subordinated along other axes of identity. Nothing in it suggests otherwise. That the theory has been used less frequently to elucidate sites of privilege suggests not that it is flawed but that it has been used first and foremost to expose and combat marginalization. Although it is appropriate that the theory has primarily been used to interrogate and combat marginalization, intersectionality theory also accommodates the critical examination of privilege.

Although her perspective is not quite a critique of intersectionality, Vrushali Patil encourages the expanded use of intersectionality to explore transnational processes such as colonialism and European imperialism.[106] After a cross-disciplinary review

[98] *See* Crenshaw, *Mapping the Margins*, *supra* note 4, at 1244–45 nn.8–9.

[99] *See, e.g.*, Nash, *supra* note 85, at 10 ("Generally, intersectional literature has excluded an examination of identities that are imagined as either wholly or even partially privileged, although those identities, like all identities, are always constituted by the intersections of multiple vectors of power.").

[100] Carbado, *supra* note 46, at 817. Carbado coins the phrase "colorblind intersectionality" to refer to "instances in which whiteness helps to produce and is part of a cognizable social category but is invisible or unarticulated as an intersectional subject position." *Id.*

[101] Hae Yeon Choo & Myra Marx Ferree, *Practicing Intersectionality in Sociological Research: A Critical Analysis of Inclusions, Interactions, and Institutions in the Study of Inequality*, 28 Socio. Theory 129, 133 (2010).

[102] *But see* Jennifer Nash, Black Feminism Imagined After Intersectionality 53 (2019) (contesting the characterization of Puar as *the* critic of intersectionality).

[103] Puar, *supra* note 51, at 52.

[104] Puar calls this the "ironic othering of WOC through an approach that meant to alleviate such othering." *Id.*

[105] Carbado, *supra* note 46, at 814 ("[I]t is a mistake to conceptualize intersectionality as a 'race to the bottom.' . . . The theory seeks to map the top of social hierarchies as well." (internal citations omitted)).

[106] Vrushali Patil, *From Patriarchy to Intersectionality: A Transnational Feminist Assessment of How Far We've Really Come*, 38 Signs 847, 848 (2013).

of applications of intersectionality, Patil notes three primary problems. First, most of the analysis focuses on the Global North. Second, the vast majority of applications of intersectionality focus on domestic issues, reifying nation-state borders. Third, there is considerably more focus on the local and intra-national rather than the international, regional, or global levels. Patil suggests that "complications in how intersectionality shapes international, regional, and global forces, processes, institutions, and organizations, as well as connections between these scales and more local scales, remain largely unexamined."[107] Patil's intervention encourages more robust use of intersectionality frameworks to explore global processes, including colonization.[108]

Finally, a third category of critique relates to intersectionality's reliance on enumerated—and sometimes unenumerated—categories of identity markers. Some argue that intersectionality invites a discussion of limitless identity categories and, as a corollary, which groups are the most marginalized.[109] Richard Delgado, for example, cautions against an unconstrained list of identity categories and the essentialism that necessarily stems from them.[110] Relatedly, Joanne Conaghan and others charge that intersectionality's focus on identity categories moves the theory toward a focus on individual rather than structural inequality.[111] Conaghan urges us to "*ground* the grounds—in their historical and social contexts and in the processes and (inter)relations which constitute and maintain them."[112]

Crenshaw's original articulation, however, focuses explicitly on structural aspects of power and their effects on Black women, in particular. Proponents of intersectionality explicitly value its emphasis on systems of oppression and structural inequality, which are necessarily historically contingent and contextually specific. In short, intersectionality, when appropriately applied, is already doing the important work that Conaghan suggests must be done. This critique undervalues the contextual and historical analysis that forms the basis of an intersectional approach. Intersectionality recognizes that identities are not rigid and fixed but contested and contingent, and the methodological approach requires an historical and contextual inquiry.[113] As such, it is not possible or desirable to rank identities in a fixed, hierarchical way or even to

[107] *Id.* at 853; *see* Richard Delgado, *Rodrigo's Reconsideration: Intersectionality and the Future of Critical Race Theory*, 96 Iowa L. Rev. 1247, 1268–69 (2011).

[108] *Id.* at 855 ("Thus, the patriarchal model in its absolutist form enabled interrelated discourses of the irrationalization, feminization, and infantilization of conquered peoples and constitutes a key moment in the construction of transterritorial racial and cultural hierarchy.").

[109] Nira Yuval-Davis, *Intersectionality and Feminist Politics*, 13 Eur. J. Women's Stud. 193, 202 (2006) (noting that "Judith Butler (1990) mocks the 'etc.' that often appears at the end of lists of social divisions mentioned by feminists ... and sees it as an embarrassed admission of a sign of exhaustion as well as of the illimitable process of signification itself." (internal quotation omitted)).

[110] Richard Delgado, *Rodrigo's Reconsideration: Intersectionality and Future of Critical Race Theory*, 96 Iowa L. Rev. 1247, 1264 (2011).

[111] Intersectionality and Beyond: Law, Power, and the Politics of Location 5 (Emily Grabham et al. eds., 2008).

[112] Joanne Conaghan, *Intersectionality and UK Equality Initiatives*, 23 S. Afr. J. on Hum. Rts. 317, 332 (2007).

[113] Ben Smith, *Intersectional Discrimination and Substantive Equality: A Comparative and Theoretical Perspective*, 16 Equal Rts. Rev. 73, 84 (2016) ("Conaghan criticises intersectionality for failing to grapple with the underlying inequalities that create patterns of discrimination. However, this criticism seems mistaken. A legal recognition of intersectionality in discrimination law arguably requires that in assessing discrimination courts *must* examine the structural disadvantages operating in the background.").

determine which identities are most relevant without engaging in historically, spatially, contextually specific analysis designed to elucidate and dismantle structural inequality.

Conaghan provocatively asks whether intersectionality has "reached the limits of its potential."[114] She values intersectionality's contributions to critical race feminism and law but worries that the theory is limited by its very grounding in law and identity categories. Because of its reliance on legal categories, Conaghan is skeptical that intersectionality can capture the varied, complex lived experiences of discrimination.[115] She also expresses concern that the metaphor of an intersection is itself limiting in its focus on the two-dimensional points of intersection. The strands of discrimination or inequality reflected in a particular intersection are, she argues, inseparable and multidimensional.[116] These assertions, however, do not contradict but rather reinforce intersectionality's major theoretical contributions.[117] Conaghan is correct that there are limitations to the law and to legal remedies. The legal system will never fully capture the lived experience of discrimination and inequality, and it will consistently fail to offer full recompense for discriminatory harm. That is not a reason to abandon legal theory, however. Intersectionality comes closer than other theories to helping us conceive of the mutually reinforcing and mutually constitutive systems of oppression that affect lived experiences of inequality.

Jasbir Puar critiques intersectionality as overly focused on identity and suggests that the emphasis on intersectionality within women's studies has worked against women of color (WOC).[118] Puar argues, "[T]he heuristic of intersectionality has produced a tremendous amount of work on WOC while concomitantly excusing white feminists from this work, re-centering gender and sexual difference as foundational and primary—indeed, this amplification of knowledge has in some senses been at the cost of WOC."[119] Puar's critique focuses less on the theoretical dimensions of intersectionality itself and more on the dominant role it plays in contemporary women's studies. Nash also points out that Puar is perceived as questioning intersectionality's centrality within feminist theory. She observes, "[W]hat Puar performs is less critique than a critical inquiry surrounding intersectionality's circulation and institutionalization."[120] Nash contends that Puar's critique has not been well received, in part, "because of her imagined status as an outsider to black feminism."[121] Nash contrasts her own scholarship, which is largely considered an insider's critique.

[114] Joanne Conaghan, *Intersectionality and the Feminist Project in Law*, *in* INTERSECTIONALITY AND BEYOND: LAW, POWER, AND THE POLITICS OF LOCATION 21 (Emily Grabham et al. eds., 2008); *see also* Pok Yin S. Chow, *Has Intersectionality Reached its Limits? Intersectionality in the UN Human Rights Treaty Body Practice and the Issue of Ambivalence*, 16 HUM. RTS. L. REV. 452 (2016).

[115] Joanne Conaghan, *supra* 112, at 325 (noting that intersectionality is "demonstrative of the broader limits of law in the context of lived complexity").

[116] *Id.* at 329.

[117] HANCOCK, *supra* note 30, at 100–02 (arguing that a central tenet of intersectionality is that multiple categories of difference are not severable).

[118] Puar, *supra* note 51, at 63 ("Therefore, to dismiss assemblages in favor of retaining intersectional identitarian frameworks is to dismiss how societies of control tweak and modulate bodies as matter, not predominantly through signification or identity interpellation but rather through affective capacities and tendencies.").

[119] *Id.*

[120] NASH, *supra* note 83 at 52.

[121] NASH, *supra* note 83, at 53.

As part of intersectionality discourse, critiques of intersectionality that engage ethically with the theory help proponents to refine and sharpen it. Despite this process of refinement, or perhaps because of it, intersectionality continues to figure prominently in the discourses of critical race feminism and other theories of subordination. As with this project, scholars and activists have identified new terrain in which to apply intersectionality theory. Each new instantiation of the theory contributes to the larger mapping of intersectionality, expanding its reach and reshaping its contours.

2
Global Application of Intersectionality Theory

Intersectionality theory has transformed the notion of equality in both theoretical and pragmatic ways. Since the early 1990s, scholars and activists across the globe have adopted the theory to guide their scholarly and programmatic efforts. An intersectional lens facilitates a deeper understanding of how systems of oppression and resistance intersect in women's lives across the globe. As I discussed in the previous chapter, feminists from the Global North have, at times, been the most visible in defining the "woman's experience" that forms the basis for organizing women's rights around the world. By virtue of socioeconomic and geopolitical privilege, elites in the Global North have too often dominated in setting the prevailing agenda for international women's rights advocacy. In so doing, they have neglected issues of colonialism, imperialism, and nationalism. The largely white leaders from the Global North have often overlooked the notion that women experience gender and other aspects of their multiple identities in a specific and important geographic, economic, and political context. The almost singular focus on gender to the exclusion of other aspects of identity in some instances led to a myopic approach to international women's rights advocacy and scholarship. In 1997, Lisa Crooms asked the question, 'What do women's rights have to do with the Race Convention,' in an early invocation of intersectionality theory in the context of human rights.[1] As Crooms recognized, an intersectional lens is necessary for a fuller, more nuanced understanding of the ways in which multiple and complex identities shape experiences of oppression and resistance.

This chapter delves into examples of global intersectionality to illustrate the need for a thorough and consistent intersectional approach to human rights violations around the world. Intersectionality, and the more nuanced understanding of human rights that stems therefrom, applies to a range of issues beyond gender and feminist advocacy. As I noted in the Introduction, intersectionality's origins in critical race feminism explains, in part, why intersectional analysis is increasingly applied in discussions of women's human rights. Intersectionality is equally relevant to discussions of complex human rights violations involving, for example, intersecting forms of subordination based on race and gender identity or age and disability. Yet in human rights discourse, the United Nations (UN) human rights treaty bodies most frequently invoke intersectional analysis in the context of rights violations based on gender and another facet of identity. Thus many of the examples I offer here draw upon the nexus of gender subordination and other forms of subordination. The theory itself is not limited in its application, and I strive to offer expansive and varied examples.

[1] Lisa A. Crooms, *Indivisible Rights and Intersectional Identities or, 'What Do Women's Human Rights Have to Do with the Race Convention?'* 40 HOWARD L.J. 619 (1997).

Global Intersectionality and Contemporary Human Rights. Johanna Bond, Oxford University Press. © Johanna Bond 2021.
DOI: 10.1093/oso/9780198868835.003.0003

There are countless iterations of intersectional human rights. Although it is impossible to provide exhaustive analysis of the many and varied types of intersectional human rights violations, the case studies in this chapter offer multiple examples of intersectional human rights violations, including (1) gender-based violence, including both non-state actors who commit intimate partner violence and sexual violence in armed conflict; (2) maternal mortality and inadequate prenatal care in Brazil; (3) coerced sterilization among the Roma in Europe; (4) disproportionate discipline and punishment of Black girls in the United States; and (5) inconsistent lesbian, gay, bisexual, transgender, queer and/or questioning, and intersex (LGBTQI) rights. Although these examples implicate different human rights, ranging from the right to be free from violence to the right to education to the right to the highest attainable standard of health, each example demonstrates how a more nuanced, intersectional lens is necessary to capture the rights at stake and to fully contemplate appropriate remedies.

Gender-based violence

The United Nations has defined gender-based violence to include "any act ... that results in, or is likely to result in, physical, sexual or psychological harm or suffering to women, including threats of such acts, coercion or arbitrary deprivation of liberty, whether occurring in public or in private life."[2] The committees that oversee implementation of the major human rights treaties periodically adopt guidance documents that assist countries in the implementation of those treaties. These guidance documents, referred to as either General Recommendations or General Comments, offer helpful interpretations of the treaty provisions. In its General Recommendation No. 19, for example, the committee that oversees the Convention on the Elimination of All Forms of Discrimination Against Women (CEDAW Committee) provides specific examples of gender-based violence, including family violence and abuse, forced marriage, dowry deaths, acid attacks, female circumcision, pornography, trafficking, rape, and other forms of sexual assault and sexual harassment.[3]

Intersectionality theory provides critical perspectives on gender-based violence. Indeed, Kimberlé Crenshaw's early writing on intersectionality focused on the ways in which intimate partner violence affected women of color in qualitatively different ways than white women in the United States.[4] Crenshaw's engagement with questions of state power and how that power is deployed against women of color provides an important foundation for exploring the discourse of human rights violations involving gender-based violence.

Rashida Manjoo, the UN Special Rapporteur on Violence Against Women, remarked in 2010 that "multiple and intersecting forms of discrimination have

[2] G.A. Res. 48/104, at 3, Declaration on the Elimination of Violence Against Women (Feb. 23, 1994).

[3] Comm. on the Elimination of Discrimination Against Women [CEDAW], General Recommendation No. 19: Violence Against Women, ¶¶ 11, 15 (1992), https://www.refworld.org/docid/52d920c54.html.

[4] *See, e.g.*, Kimberlé Crenshaw, *Mapping the Margins: Intersectionality, Identity Politics, and Violence Against Women of Color*, 43 STAN. L. REV. 1241, 1242 (1991) (exploring how the intersection of race and gender discrimination influences violence against women of color).

contributed to and exacerbated violence against women .... [yet] information on the intersections between gender-based discrimination and other forms of discrimination is too often overlooked."[5] Women who face economic, social, and geographic barriers to accessing services experience additional complications in combatting gender-based violence. This section explores several key aspects of gender-based violence: accountability for private actors, intimate partner violence, and gender-based violence in the context of armed conflict. By no means do these case studies reflect the full scope of gender-based violence, but I discuss them here to illustrate how intersectional theory may be applied in the context of a range of issues related to gender-based violence.

Non-state actors and intimate partner violence

Before the late 1980s, the prevailing view limited human rights violations to the actions of government officials or private citizens whose actions were ordered or explicitly supported by the state. The traditional rule covered human rights violations perpetrated by government officials acting with the authority of the state, such as a prison guard in a state-run prison. Women, however, suffered many violations of their rights in their homes at the hands of family members or other non-state actors. Traditionally, women were unable to claim a rights violation in circumstances such as these.

In the 1990s, a series of events at the international and regional levels signaled an important evolution in the understanding of accountability for human rights violations. This seismic shift had dramatic positive repercussions for victims of human rights violations, particularly women. The traditional view limiting human rights violations to those perpetrated by a state representative gave way to an expanded view of state responsibility that encompassed the state's failure to act with due diligence to prevent, investigate, punish, and redress violations of rights. This expanded interpretation of state responsibility applies even when the perpetrator is a non-state actor acting without the authority of the state government. This shift in understanding happened relatively quickly and opened the door for a range of complaints from women suffering human rights violations at the hands of family members and other non-state actors.

Several factors contributed to this rapid shift in thinking. For one, a landmark decision in 1988 gave activists a way to hold states accountable when they failed to act with due diligence to protect women from abuses long considered "private" and outside the realm of state concern. The Inter-American Court of Human Rights, a judicial and autonomous organ of the Organization of American States (OAS), decided the case of *Velásquez Rodríguez v. Honduras*[6] on the basis of the Inter-American Convention, which obligates states to "ensure" the full exercise of the rights contained

[5] *International: Violence Against Women—Missing Millennium Development Goal*, PEACE WOMEN (Dec. 7, 2010), https://www.peacewomen.org/content/international-violence-against-women-missing-millennium-development-goal.

[6] Velásquez Rodríguez v. Honduras, Judgment, Inter-Am. Ct. H.R. (ser. C) No. 4 (July 29, 1988).

in the convention. *Velásquez Rodríguez* involved a disappearance in Honduras that was one of several attributed to a quasi-governmental group. The Court decided that Honduras, in failing to prevent, investigate, and punish the disappearance, had violated Angel Manfredo Velásquez Rodríguez's right to life as provided by the convention. The Court stated that even if it could not be proven that those responsible had "acted under cover of public authority," the state's failure to act was "a failure on the part of Honduras to fulfill" its duties.[7] The precedent set by this decision required states to act with "due diligence" to prevent, investigate, and punish human rights violations even when those violations occur at the hands of private citizens. The CEDAW Committee built on the *Velásquez Rodríguez* precedent, incorporating its insights about the due diligence standard into the Committee's subsequent work.

Furthermore, before the early 1990s, "[t]he UN had failed to effectively promote women's rights"[8] framed in the language of equality and non-discrimination. The 1990s brought increased attention to rape in armed conflict, particularly in the former Yugoslavia and in Rwanda. In the words of one scholar:

> [Violence against women] as a claim to rights worked because it embodied a horror that could not be ignored; and it also worked, as Ratna Kapur notes, because stories of the victim subject could enter the mainstream of representation and reaffirm the image of women (especially Southern women) as without power and in need of protection.[9]

As a result, violence against women surfaced as a primary focal point for women's human rights advocacy during that time.

Although the Convention itself does not mention violence against women, the CEDAW Committee adopted a general recommendation in 1992 that directly addresses gender-based violence. General Recommendation No. 19 specifically applies the *Velásquez Rodríguez* notion about due diligence as a metric to determine whether states had fulfilled their obligations to combat violence against women. In 1993, the General Assembly of the United Nations adopted the Declaration on the Elimination of Violence Against Women (DEVAW). This Declaration further established the due diligence standard as the measurement by which to determine if states had met their burden in eliminating violence against women.[10] As a UN declaration, DEVAW is not binding, but it represents the consensus of member states that all states have an obligation to eradicate violence against women, whether that violence is perpetrated by public or private actors.

In the mid-1990s, the global human rights community increasingly addressed issues of gender-based violence. The 1993 UN Human Rights Conference in Vienna highlighted the global impact of gender-based violence.[11] In 1995, gender-based

[7] *Id.* ¶ 182.

[8] Alice M. Miller, *Sexuality, Violence Against Women, and Human Rights: Women Make Demands and Ladies Get Protection*, 7 Health & Hum. Rts. 16, 20 (2004).

[9] *Id.* at 21.

[10] G.A. Res. 48/104, Art. 3(c), Declaration on the Elimination of Violence Against Women (Feb. 23, 1994).

[11] *See* Miller, *supra* note 8, at 24 ("The 1993 World Conference on Human Rights was a political watershed in this process of transformation and the moment when VAW took the lead in bringing attention to the human rights of women.").

violence was a significant focus of the UN Fourth World Conference on Women in Beijing. Other regional and international efforts paralleled these significant developments at the United Nations. In 1994, for example, the General Assembly of the OAS adopted the Inter-American Convention on the Prevention, Punishment and Eradication of Violence Against Women (Convention of Belém Do Pará).

These important developments broadened the scope of cognizable women's human rights claims. Changes in the collective understanding of state action under international human rights law dramatically expanded common approaches to women's human rights. These changes broke down the barrier between so-called public and private rights. Whereas previously only violations of rights in the public realm were considered worthy of state attention and redress, expanding notions of state responsibility forced states to address abuses against women in the private sphere.

As intersectionality theory has gained traction around the world, more scholars and activists have begun to appreciate the ways in which intersecting forms of discrimination and subordination make women's experiences of gender-based violence qualitatively different. Intersectionality, for example, underscores the ways in which a focus on criminalization and mass incarceration disserves women of color who may experience both gender-based violence in their homes and the racist violence of the carceral state in their daily lives. The International Network of Women with Disabilities notes that women with disabilities face a high risk of violence that results from both gender- and disability-based discrimination.[12] Women living in poverty may lack access to healthcare and medical treatment in the aftermath of intimate partner violence. Migrant women may be unable to reliably access services for victims of intimate partner violence for fear of immigration reprisals. Intersectional analysis in the context of intimate partner violence allows for a more thorough and nuanced analysis of the challenges different groups of women face because of intersecting and mutually reinforcing forms of discrimination and subordination.

As noted, Kimberlé Crenshaw's early work on intersectionality is particularly relevant and useful in the context of intimate partner violence. *Mapping the Margins: Intersectionality, Identity Politics, and Violence Against Women of Color* demonstrates the critical need for an intersectional lens in combatting intimate partner violence. In it, Crenshaw discusses how the intersection of race, gender, and class shapes violence against women of color, and how non-intersectional approaches fail to "disrupt the patterns" that led to the violence.[13] Although Crenshaw's early work focuses on the United States, the lessons it offers are applicable to the broader, global discourse around intimate partner violence. An intersectional approach recognizes that women's experiences are not shaped exclusively by any one aspect of identity but rather by their intersections, and therefore allows for a more complete analysis of rights violations.

[12] Int'l Network of Women with Disabilities (INWWD), *Document on Violence Against Women with Disabilities*, at 7 (Oct. 4, 2010), https://inwwd.wordpress.com/publications-of-the-inwwd/.

[13] Crenshaw, *supra* note 4, at 1260.

Armed conflict and sexual violence

Sexual violence has been a tragic part of armed conflict across the globe. It is a reality in contemporary conflicts in the Central African Republic, Colombia, Democratic Republic of the Congo (DRC), Mali, South Sudan, and Syria.[14] In the early to mid-1990s, it was armed conflicts in the former Yugoslavia and in Rwanda that brought intersectional human rights analysis to the foreground. In both conflicts, women were targeted for rape and sexual violence based on gender and ethnic identity.

Sexual violence in conflict may take many forms, including "systematic mass rape, forced maternity, rape as a means of murder, and sexual torture, gang rape, coerced rape between family members, sexual mutilation, forced prostitution, sexual slavery, rape in rape camps, women forced to 'marry' *génocidaires*, and so forth."[15] Intersectionality fosters a deeper understanding of the human rights violations and the appropriate remedies by considering the ways in which gender and ethnic identity intersect to shape experiences of conflict.

War in the former Yugoslavia resulted in the deaths of over 100,000 people, the displacement of two million others, and the rape of approximately 20,000 to 50,000 women.[16] In 1993, the UN Security Council created the International Criminal Tribunal for the former Yugoslavia (ICTY) to hold leaders accountable for the violence. The sexual violence, which affected all communities but was disproportionately perpetrated by Bosnian Serb forces, amounted to ethnic cleansing and included the abduction of women and girls into "rape camps." In these camps, women and girls "were raped repeatedly until they became pregnant, and held to ensure they delivered a child born of rape; or held in domestic and sexual slavery for extended periods."[17]

The Rwandan genocide in 1994 provides a difficult but illuminating case study through which to more fullyexplore the intersection of ethnicity and gender in the context of armed conflict. As many as one million people were killed[18] and some 150,000 to 200,000 women were raped during the conflict. The victims of the genocide were predominantly members of the Tutsi ethnic group and the perpetrators largely members of the Hutu ethnic group. The large-scale targeting of Tutsi women for rape and sexual violence reflects a deeply intersectional human rights violation based simultaneously on gender and ethnicity. Following the counsel of Joanne Conaghan,

[14] *See ICRC President Calls for Action on Sexual Violence in Conflict*, INT'L COMM. OF THE RED CROSS (June 12, 2014), https://www.icrc.org/en/doc/resources/documents/statement/2014/06-12-sexual-violence-statement-maurer.htm (discussing the troubling reality of sexual violence worldwide).

[15] Elisa von Joeden-Forgey, *Gender and the Future of Genocide Studies and Prevention*, 7 GENOCIDE STUD. & PREVENTION 89, 92 (2012).

[16] KEN BOOTH, THE KOSOVO TRAGEDY: THE HUMAN RIGHTS DIMENSIONS 73 (2001).

[17] *See* Aisha Nicole Davis, Note, *Intersectionality and International Law: Recognizing Complex Identities on the Global Stage*, 28 HARV. HUM. RTS. J. 205, 224 (2015) (citing MEGAN BASTICK ET AL., SEXUAL VIOLENCE IN ARMED CONFLICT: GLOBAL OVERVIEW AND IMPLICATIONS FOR THE SECURITY SECTOR 113 (2007)).

[18] *See* Alan Cowell, *Rwanda Marks 25 Years Since the Genocide. The Country is Still Grappling with Its Legacy*, N.Y. TIMES (Apr. 6, 2019), https://www.nytimes.com/2019/04/06/world/africa/rwanda-genocide-25-years.html (describing the breadth of harm from the Rwandan genocide).

who instructs intersectionality practitioners to "*ground* the grounds,"[19] it is important to consider the deep historical and social context.

Ethnic conflict in Rwanda existed in the pre-colonial era, with the Tutsi ethnic group generally possessing higher social status than members of the Hutu ethnic group.[20] After the 1884–85 Berlin Conference "assigned" Rwanda to Germany,[21] German colonization further entrenched ethnic hierarchies by empowering Tutsi chiefs to "maintain order" over Hutu populations.[22] After the First World War, Belgium gained control of Rwanda.[23] Ethnic tensions increased in the 1950s during the era of decolonization on the continent, as Hutus organized to assert political power over minority Tutsis. In 1959, the "Hutu Peasant Revolution" flared and continued to exacerbate ethnic tensions until Rwanda gained independence in 1962. Prior to independence, large numbers of Tutsis had fled to Tanzania and what was then called Zaire (now known as the DRC) and continued to stage attacks on the Hutu government in Rwanda.[24] The exodus of Tutsis continued through the 1980s with many Tutsis seeking refuge in Burundi, Uganda, Zaire, and Tanzania, bringing the total of Rwandan refugees to approximately 480,000 by the end of the decade.[25]

Exiled Tutsis and a smaller number of Hutus in Uganda formed the Rwandan Patriotic Front (RPF), which planned and executed an attack on Rwanda on October 1, 1990. After the attack, the Tutsis within Rwanda were targeted as RPF members, and large-scale radio campaigns exacerbated ethnic tensions. In August 1993, the Organisation of African Unity (OAU) and other regional governments brokered a peace deal, known as the Arusha Accords, between the largely Hutu government and the RPF. That peace, however, was short-lived.

On April 6, 1994, the plane carrying the presidents of Burundi and Rwanda was shot down in a rocket attack.[26] The deaths inflamed ethnic violence in the region within an hour after the plane crash. In the weeks and months that followed, the Hutu majority systematically identified and murdered some 800,000 Tutsis and committed mass rapes of Tutsi women. Although both sides of the conflict committed atrocities against the other, the slaughter of hundreds of thousands of Tutsis amounted to genocide under international law.[27]

[19] Joanne Conaghan, *Intersectionality and UK Equality Initiatives*, 23 S. Afr. J. on Hum. Rts. 317, 332 (2007).

[20] *See Outreach Programme on the 1994 Genocide Against the Tutsi in Rwanda and the United Nations* [hereinafter *Outreach Programme*], United Nations, https://www.un.org/en/preventgenocide/rwanda/historical-background.shtml (last visited Apr. 29, 2021) (describing the socioeconomic structure of pre-colonial Rwanda).

[21] *See* Usta Kaitesi, Genocidal Gender and Sexual Violence: The Legacy of the ICTR, Rwanda's Ordinary Courts and Gacaca Courts 33 (2014) (outlining the changes of power over Rwanda).

[22] *See Outreach Programme*, *supra* note 20 (laying out the timeline of the political and social development of Rwanda); *id.* at 33 (stating that the Europeans treated the Tutsi as superior to the Hutus during their occupation of Rwanda).

[23] *See* Kaitesi, *supra* note 21, at 33.

[24] *Outreach Programme*, *supra* note 20.

[25] *Id.*

[26] Cowell, *supra* note 18 .

[27] *See* Kaitesi, *supra* note 21, at 13 ("The central characteristics of the crime of genocide are first the specific intent to destroy a group and, second, the existence of a distinct or specific group that is national, ethnic, racial or religious.").

The United Nations Security Council established the International Criminal Tribunal for Rwanda (ICTR) in November 1994.[28] The ICTR indicted ninety-three people, including government officials, members of the military, politicians, business people, religious leaders, and other community leaders deemed to be responsible for violations of international humanitarian law. In 1998, the ICTR issued a judgment in *Prosecutor v. Jean-Paul Akayesu*, a historic decision defining rape as an act of genocide. In 2001, the Rwandan government instituted a participatory justice system called Gacaca to address the large backlog of cases in its own genocide trials.

The scale and violence of the 1994 genocide shocked the international community. In addition to the mass killings, the Hutu majority systematically targeted some 150,000 to 200,000 Tutsi women for rape and other forms of sexual violence. Female victims of rape, targeted on the basis of ethnicity and structural gender subordination, experienced severe human rights violations at the intersection of ethnic and gender oppression.[29] An intersectional lens allows us to see how ethnicity and gender are mutually constitutive and, together, contributed to the victimization of Tutsi women. Collectively, Tutsi women's experiences of gender and ethnic violence differed from the experiences of Tutsi men and Hutu women. At the individual level, of course, Tutsi men were also victims of sexual violence in the conflict, as were Hutu women. Intersectionality, however, offers insight into the widespread victimization of Tutsi women in particular.

Intersectionality contemplates identity categories that are not fixed or static. As such, intersectionality encourages the consideration of social processes that assign meaning to identity categories.[30] Within Rwandan society before colonialism, Hutu and Tutsi "denoted social and economic status as opposed to ethnic differences."[31] In the colonial and post-colonial period, ethnic identity emerged as a social construction and hierarchy among groups.[32] Tutsi women were seen as overly sexualized, and a Tutsi mistress or wife could increase the social standing of a Hutu man.[33] Carey Hogg notes,

> Evidence of the gendered nature of the genocide can be found in much of the Hutu extremist ideology used to promote the ethnic cleansing; portraying Tutsi women as seductresses who would use their sexuality to trick and entrap Hutu men, identifying even Hutus who married or associated with Tutsi women as traitors to their "kind."[34]

These economic and class-based hierarchies informed the social construction of ethnic identities throughout the conflict. Intersectionality sheds light on the structural inequalities that predate conflict and often give rise to it.

[28] *Id.* at 49.

[29] *See* Llezlie L. Green, Note, *Gender Hate Propaganda and Sexual Violence in the Rwandan Genocide: An Argument for Intersectionality in International Law*, 33 COLUM. HUM. RTS. L. REV. 733, 761 (2002).

[30] *See* ANGE-MARIE HANCOCK, INTERSECTIONALITY: AN INTELLECTUAL HISTORY 169–71 (2015).

[31] KAITESI, *supra* note 21, at 29.

[32] *See id.* at 33.

[33] *See id.* at 7 n.22 (describing the "inferiority complex" of the abusers who "employed gender and sexual violence as a means of conquest and a sense of achieving an impossible objective.").

[34] Carey Leigh Hogg, *Women's Political Representation in Post-Conflict Rwanda: A Politics of Inclusion or Exclusion?*, 11 J. INT'L WOMEN'S STUD. 34, 38 (2009).

Legal scholar Doris Buss has argued that intersectionality theory offers important but limited insight into the ways in which identity is constructed *through* conflict.[35] She is concerned with the potential for essentializing ethnicity and reinforcing the very constructions of ethnicity that fostered conflict in the first place. Intersectionality, however, provides precisely the tools to dispel notions of ethnicity as static and permanent. In the case of Rwanda, the Hutu/Tutsi distinction traditionally functioned as a class-based distinction.[36] Noting that ethnic identity has evolved over time, the ICTR judges remarked, "the emergence of Hutu, Tutsi, and Twa ethnic group identity over the course of Rwandan history, and the concomitant ethnic prejudice that resulted from the differential distribution of social and political privilege along ethnic lines, [was] fostered by and during colonial rule."[37] Intersectionality theory interrogates the social construction of ethnic identity as well as its interaction and intersection with other aspects of identity, such as gender. In this way, it avoids precisely the static and ahistorical understanding of identity with which Buss is concerned.

Sexual violence during armed conflict must be considered against the backdrop of women's status during times of peace. Sexual violence during war is not "exceptional." Rather, it is an unfortunate reality for many women during times of peace as well as war. Noting this link, human rights activist LaShawn Jefferson observes that "[s]exual violence has continued to be systematic and unrelenting in part because of state failure to take seriously, prevent, and prosecute routine and widespread discrimination and violence against women during times of 'peace.'"[38] Contextual analysis of women's status during peacetime demonstrates that women's lower status in legal and socio-economic contexts often provides the foundation for sexual violence in times of both peace and armed conflict.

In many countries, women's sexuality is closely related to notions of honor and reputational concerns of the family and community.[39] Families and communities guard and police the sexual activity of women and girls. In these contexts, sexual violence in armed conflict becomes a way to inflict severe harm on an individual and to inflict collective, symbolic harm on the community and, at times, the targeted ethnic group.[40] Hoesch and Saniei-Pour write, "[S]exual violence is used as an instrument to build up group solidarity by rewarding participation and fragmenting opponent communities."[41] When the motivation for sexual violence stems, in part, from this

[35] *See* Doris Buss, *Performing Legal Order: Some Feminist Thoughts on International Criminal Law*, 11 Int'l Crim. L. Rev. 409, 414–15 (2011) ("[O]fficial recognition of gendered experiences of conflict, has influenced related developments in mainstreaming gender in post-conflict peace building. . . .").

[36] Kaitesi, *supra* note 21, at 31.

[37] Prosecutor v. Nahimana, Case No. ICTR-99-52-T, Judgment and Sentence, ¶ 108 (Dec. 3, 2003).

[38] LaShawn R. Jefferson, *In War as in Peace: Sexual Violence and Women's Status*, *in* Hum. Rts. Watch, World Report 2004: Human Rights and Armed Conflict 325, 326–27 (2004), https://www.hrw.org/legacy/wr2k4/download/wr2k4.pdf.

[39] *See* Tzili Mor, *Feminist Rule of Law Reform and Health Impact of Legal Systems Premised on Women as Communal Gauges of Honor*, 44 U. Balt. L. Rev. 237, 250 (2015) ("Any damage to the girls' reputation damages that of the family; consequently, any actual or suspected transgression by girls—but not by boys—can lead to swift reactions, such as the killing of the girl by her relatives to 'restore' the honor of the family.").

[40] *See* Jefferson, *supra* note 38, at 328.

[41] Sarah Hoesch & Alireza Saniei-Pour, *Marginalised Minorities in Conflict: Women and Millennium Development Goals*, *in* Did the Millennium Development Goals Work?: Meeting Future Challenges with Past Lessons 217, 228 (Hany Besada et al. eds., 2017).

desire to inflict communal harm, intersectionality provides a vehicle for recognizing and examining individual and collective harms.

As Eilish Rooney notes, "[i]n intersectional analysis, conflict-related identities are treated as socially produced critical sites of power and oppression that govern women's access to resources and their visibility in conflict discourse."[42] In the context of the conflicts in the former Yugoslavia and Rwanda, intersectional analysis considers how the social construction of gender and ethnicity impacts experiences of violence. It also allows us to unpack how the conflict underscores or redefines gender and ethnic identity. Intersectionality recognizes that a Hutu woman, for example, may have been both oppressed and oppressor during the 1994 genocide. She may have, for example, encouraged the rape of a Tutsi neighbor and simultaneously been a long-standing victim of intimate partner violence. This social positioning makes her simultaneously a victim of gender oppression and a beneficiary of ethnic hierarchy.

Because it reflects a core notion of the social construction of identity across categories such as gender, ethnicity, race, disability, religion, and sexual orientation and gender identity, intersectionality also resists oversimplified understandings of masculinity and femininity in the context of armed conflict. Too often, conflict narratives oversimplify the experiences of women as consisting solely of victimization and the experiences of men as perpetrators of sexual violence. Rooney observes, "The already noted categorization of innocence as essentially female enters war discourse as an exploitable rhetoric of vulnerability requiring masculine protection."[43] Kimberly Theidon describes how intersectionality can help us to fully appreciate the role of women as perpetrators of human rights violations in armed conflict as well as the role of men as victims.[44] In her study of conflicts in Peru and Colombia, Theidon describes how "rape of men by other men was a form of establishing relations of power and domination at the nexus of gender, ethnicity, and social class."[45] Intersectionality allows us to unpack the social construction of gender that leads to the oversimplified characterization of women as victims and men as perpetrators. It also offers a way to explore the inextricably linked constructions of gender and ethnicity in the context of conflict.

As these many examples demonstrate, gender and ethnicity are mutually constitutive. When considering the social construction of gender, one must also consider the role that ethnicity plays in its construction, and vice versa. The mutually constitutive roles of gender and ethnicity make these identity categories inextricably linked and

[42] Eilish Rooney, *Intersectionality: Working in Conflict*, *in* The Oxford Handbook Of Gender And Conflict 328 (Fionnuala Ní Aoláin et al. eds., 2018).

[43] *Id.* at 336.

[44] Theidon explains, "Included in the verbal harassment were ethnic insults. The recruits were darker-skinned men from the sierra serving under lighter skinned officers from the coast. Class standing and military rank magnified ethnic difference, which was further enforced by the use of sexual violence, especially rape.... Who could "*tirar*" (rape) another was a determining factor is [*sic*] deciding who was the "más macho," and the first one to anally rape another man came out, literally, on top.... Rape was a means of establishing hierarchies, between armed groups and the population, and within the armed forces themselves."Kimberly Theidon, *Conclusion: Reflections on the Women, Peace, and Security Agenda*, *in* Gender Violence in Peace and War: States of Complicity 184, 193–94 (Victoria Sanford et al. eds., 2016).

[45] *Id.* at 186.

highly relevant to an analysis of the human rights issues at stake. An intersectional framework is, therefore, necessary to understand the parameters of the human rights violations, the full impact on victims, and the remedies required to provide redress for victims for the harms they have suffered, which I address more fully in the last section of this chapter.

Maternal mortality and healthcare in Brazil

In Brazil, structural inequality impedes access to high-quality healthcare. In particular, the combination of racism, sexism, and discrimination based on socioeconomic status affects access to healthcare for Black women in Brazil. Black women, for example, are "disproportionately affected by . . . fibroid tumors, maternal mortality, and clandestine abortions."[46] In addition, "Black women health activists [in Brazil] have also argued that race plays a major role in worsening the health status of black women when compared to white women."[47]

In recent years, Black feminist health activists have begun to use an intersectional framework to explore how structural racism and sexism are mutually constituted and combine to affect healthcare access and outcomes for Black women negatively. The intersection of race and gender subordination has influenced Black women's experience of healthcare. As such, "employing an intersectional approach to health policy analysis is particularly important for black women, because their treatment in the health-care system and health outcomes lie at the crossroads of gendered and racialized forms of social experience and social inequality."[48]

Up until the end of the twentieth century, Brazilian national identity was grounded in the idea that the country functioned as a "racial democracy" and that it largely avoided racial stratification.[49] The myth of racial harmony was perpetuated in large part by sociologist Gilberto Freyre, who attributed it to Portugal's unique brand of colonialism, one that promoted "cordial" and "harmonious" race relations.[50] As Kia Lilly Caldwell notes, "in Freyre's representation of Brazilian colonial history, the sexual violence and exploitation experienced by enslaved African women and indigenous women was discursively erased and reimagined as the foundation of Brazil's egalitarian and raceless *mestiço* (mixed race) society."[51] Despite challenges from Black activists beginning in the early twentieth century, this romanticized image of a racial democracy persisted well into the mid-1980s.[52]

In recent decades, scholars and activists have chipped away at this mythology and exposed both the racism and sexism in Brazilian society. Starting in the early 1980s, activists organized in support of healthcare for all. The 1988 Brazilian Constitution

46 Kia Lilly Caldwell, Health Equity In Brazil: Intersections of Gender, Race, and Policy 11 (2017).
47 *Id.* at 49.
48 *Id.* at 13.
49 *Id.* at 4.
50 *Id.* at 5.
51 *Id.*
52 *Id.*

recognizes health as a "right of all and the duty of the National Government and shall be guaranteed by social and economic policies aimed at reducing the risk of illness and other maladies and by universal and equal access to all activities and services for its promotion, protection and recovery."[53] This constitutional commitment to health as a human right both reflected the efforts of and energized an activist movement designed to improve the quality of and access to healthcare in the country. In 1990, Brazil adopted a unified health system in an effort to democratize and improve the healthcare system. But at the time, drafters did not consider race to be a salient factor in the delivery or experience of healthcare in the country.[54]

Later studies on health outcomes for Black Brazilians revealed racial and ethnic disparities in life expectancy and other indicators of health.[55] Black Brazilian women experience disparities in health outcomes across a range of metrics. Caldwell writes, "[A]ctivists in the black women's movement have long suspected that Afro-Brazilian women have been subjected to sterilization, including forced sterilizations, at higher rates than white women."[56] It is common for women to be forced to travel to multiple hospitals for treatment in childbirth, an endeavor sometimes called "pilgrimage."[57] Women of color experience higher rates of pilgrimage while in labor.[58] In one study in Rio de Janeiro, for example, 31.8 percent of Black women, 28.8 percent of Brown women, and 18.5 percent of white women were forced to travel to multiple maternity hospitals in search of care in childbirth.[59] (The Brazilian census separates the country's population into Brown, Black, and white racial categories.[60]) Researchers also found disparities in access to anesthesia during childbirth.[61]

In addition, unsafe abortion differently impacts women of color in Brazil.[62] Abortion is widespread but illegal in Brazil, causing women to seek unsafe, illegal abortions.[63] In one study, abortion-related deaths between 2000 and 2004 were nearly two times greater for Brown women and three times greater for Black women than for white women.[64] Black Brazilians are overrepresented among those living in poverty,[65] making it clear that race, gender, and poverty intersect and affect a woman's health and experience in the context of abortion.

53 CONSTITUIÇÃO FEDERAL [CONSTITUTION] art. 196 (Braz.).
54 CALDWELL, *supra* note 46, at 8.
55 *See id.* at 10 (presenting data on the differing life expectancy of white and Afro-descendant Brazilians).
56 *Id.* at 11.
57 *Id.* at 117.
58 *Id.*
59 *Id.*
60 *Id.* at 9.
61 *Id.*
62 *Id.* at 9. Census data in Brazil controversially breaks down the Afro-descendant population in Brazil into *preto* (Black) and *pardo* (Brown) populations. This chapter makes the distinction only because the available data are disaggregated in this way.
63 *Id.* at 41 (internal citations omitted). The 2010 National Abortion Survey indicates that in urban areas, 15 percent of women had undergone an illegal abortion. "[T]he survey found that one out of five Brazilian women terminated a pregnancy before age forty. Moreover, in 2013, 205,000 Brazilian women were hospitalized in the public health system for attempting to terminate a pregnancy. A study conducted by the State University of Rio de Janeiro (UERJ) also found that there were 865,000 illegal abortions in the country the same year." *Id.*
64 *Id.* at 39.
65 *Id.*

In the 1980s, Black feminist activists in Brazil grew concerned about population control initiatives that targeted women of color. An internal government document, written by economist Benedito Pio da Silva, "outlined concerns about the growth of the *parda* [Brown] and *negra* [Black] populations based on data from the 1980 census."[66] As an effort to control the reproduction of Black Brazilian women, the document reflects the intersection of racial subordination and gender subordination. It targeted women of color in ways that were qualitatively different from the subordination faced by Black men and by white women. The contents of the document became public when a state deputy made a 1982 speech referencing da Silva's proposal that "population control in the *parda* and *negra* populations through sterilizations that could be carried out by the organization Pró-Família."[67]

The backlash was swift and fueled health-related activism of Black women in Brazil. By 1990, Black women activists had organized the National Campaign against the Sterilization of Black Women.[68] In 2000, Black Brazilian women played a prominent role in the country's organizing for the 2001 World Conference Against Racism, as described more fully in chapter 3 of this volume. As awareness of racism within Brazilian society grew in the 1990s, the Brazilian government made important attempts to address both health equity and racism, in general. Many are concerned, however, about whether the policy advances are sufficiently intersectional and provide adequate protection to Black women in their experiences with the healthcare system. Indeed, writes Caldwell, "how prominently gender and the health needs of black women will be incorporated into these policies remains an open question, particularly because this would require an intersectional perspective that addresses the ways in which gender, race, class, and other forms of identity shape experiences and expressions of health and wellness."[69]

The Zika crisis further demonstrates the limitations of a health policy response that does not adequately consider the intersection of gender, race, and poverty.[70] In 2016, the Zika virus swept across much of Latin America, causing an unusually high number of babies in the region to be born with microcephaly. The condition, in which a baby's head is smaller than expected, is associated with seizures, developmental delay, intellectual disabilities, and problems with balance and movement.[71] The virus can be transmitted if a pregnant woman is bitten by an infected mosquito, or it can be transmitted through sexual intercourse.[72]

In late 2015, Brazilian health officials warned women to delay pregnancy until the virus was contained. Shortly thereafter, health officials in Colombia, Ecuador, and El Salvador issued similar guidance to people considering pregnancy. The public health

[66] *Id.* at 49.

[67] *Id.*

[68] *Id.* at 52.

[69] *Id.* at 90.

[70] *See* Johanna Bond, *Zika, Feminism, and the Failures of Health Policy*, 73 Wash. & Lee L. Rev. Online 841, 851 (2017) (discussing the failures of countries and organizations to recognize the ways that "multiple systems of oppression" intersect and harm women in the context of a health care crisis).

[71] *Id.* at 843.

[72] *See Zika Virus: Prevention and Transmissions*, Ctrs. for Disease Control & Prevention, https://www.cdc.gov/zika/prevention/index.html (May 20, 2019) (describing the possible methods of transmission including mosquito bites, mother-to-child, sexual intercourse, and blood transfusion).

response also included travel warnings for women of childbearing age living outside the region. Pregnant women were cautioned against travel to Zika-infected areas. In short, while travel warnings discouraged tourists from visiting affected areas, women living in those areas were simply discouraged from getting pregnant.

The official public health response was inadequate for two primary reasons. First, the advice simply to avoid pregnancy failed to account for the fact that women often become pregnant from non-consensual sexual intercourse or may consent to intercourse but have limited options for preventing pregnancy. Second, the response in Brazil focused on avoiding travel to infected areas, which was impossible for women residing in those areas. The public health response neglected the ways in which the virus might impact women living in poverty, many of whom live in houses that lack screens on windows and doors, do not have air conditioning, and are in areas with abundant standing water, which serves as a breeding ground for mosquitos. Although the coronavirus and Zika virus have different transmission vectors and cause vastly different diseases, there are echoes of the latter's inadequate public health response in the contradictory and insufficient response to the COVID-19 pandemic.

The response failed to consider issues of structural inequality. Because there is considerable overlap in Brazil between women living in poverty and Black women,[73] socioeconomic status, gender, and race intersect in ways that impede healthcare access, including Zika prevention and treatment, for Black Brazilian women. As with other elements of disproportionate care and health outcomes for women in Brazil, intersectional analysis illustrates the mutually reinforcing ways that gender, race, and class affect women's abilities to abide by the government's guidelines for Zika and COVID-19 prevention and treatment.

Coerced sterilization and reproductive rights among Romani women

Regulation of reproductive rights has long been a way for states to exert control over women's bodies. Throughout history, these regulations have affected different groups of women differently. Often, gender-based subordination intersects with other vectors of discrimination such as those based on race, ethnicity, religion, disability, socioeconomic status, and sexual orientation or gender identity. Intersectional analysis illuminates how state regulation of reproductive rights reinforces intersecting systems of subordination and affects different groups of women differently.

Throughout Europe, Romani women experience intersectional discrimination based on gender, ethnicity, and class.[74] Among other concerns, racist and sexist

[73] *See Summary of Social Indicators*, AGENCIA IBGE, https://agenciadenoticias.ibge.gov.br/en/agencia-press-room/2185-news-agency/releases-en/29439-sintese-de-indicadores-sociais-em-2019-proporcao-de-pobres-cai-para-24-7-e-extrema-pobreza-se-mantem-em-6-5-da-populacao-2 (Nov. 30, 2020, 5:53 PM) (reporting that in 2019, 42 percent of Brazilian Black women lived in poverty or extreme poverty, compared with 18.5 percent of white women).

[74] *See* Siobhan Curran, Intersectionality and Human Rights Law: An Examination of the Coercive Sterilisations of Romani Women, at 12 (2014) (LLM thesis, University of Ulster) (noting that the axes of ethnicity, gender, and class need to be examined when analyzing the discrimination faced by Romani women);

narratives that have been used to justify the coercive sterilization of Romani women. The Czech Republic's Ombudsman "estimates that as many as 90,000 Romani women from the former Czechoslovakia became infertile due to coercive sterilisation between 1970 and 1990."[75] The Czech Republic's Public Defender of Rights asserted that Roma sterilizations were justified because they applied to "citizens showing an extensively negative attitude to work and learning, a high crime rate, an inclination to alcoholism, female promiscuity, and … lagging behind the cultural and social development of other population groups."[76] Romani women, in particular, face stereotypes that they are "lazy," "dirty," "unable to look after their own health," or "not capable of looking after their own children."[77]

In 2003, the Center for Reproductive Rights issued a report documenting 110 cases of coercive sterilization of Romani women in Slovakia. The report also documents race-based segregation in maternity wards in the country. The former Slovakian Minister of Health remarked in 1995, "The government will do everything to ensure that more white children than Romani children are born."[78] The high number of coerced sterilizations among Romani women in the region combined with the explicit racism of government officials and healthcare providers establishes that Romani women were subjected to intersectional discrimination based on gender, ethnicity, and class.

Viewing the coercive sterilization of Romani women as solely a product of gender discrimination, ethnic discrimination, *or* class-based discrimination would paint a woefully incomplete picture of the systems of oppression at work.[79] Although Roma feminists have begun to embrace intersectionality as a framework in which to examine and combat coerced sterilization, proposed policy solutions have largely failed to incorporate intersectional insights.[80] For Romani women to achieve justice through legal reform or compensation in the court system, they will need to be recognized as complex, intersectional subjects deserving of comprehensive, intersectional remedies. Later chapters in this volume return to particular cases and human rights violations of Roma individuals.

Johanna Bond, *Intersecting Identities and Human Rights: The Example of Romani Women's Reproductive Rights*, 5 GEO. J. GENDER & L. 897, 908–09 (2004) (discussing the different factors that contribute to a woman's identity and how each factor plays into intersectional oppression).

[75] Sioban Curran, *Intersectionality and Human Rights Law: An Examination of the Coercive Sterilisations of Romani Women*, 16 EQUAL RTS. REV. 132, 139 (2016).

[76] *See id.* at 141 (citing CZECH PUBLIC DEFENDER OF RIGHTS, FINAL STATEMENT OF THE PUBLIC DEFENDER OF RIGHTS IN THE MATTER OF STERILISATIONS PREFORMED IN CONTRAVENTION OF THE LAW AND PROPOSED REMEDIAL MEASURES 78 (2005)).

[77] *See* Curran, *supra* note 74, at 20 (internal quotations omitted).

[78] Curran, *supra* note 75, at 141.

[79] *See* Curran, *supra* note 74, at 19 ("Experiences of discrimination and subordination across different and mutually reinforcing axes have shaped the social location of Romani women and made them vulnerable to a range of serious human rights abuses.").

[80] *See* Angéla Kóczé, *Missing Intersectionality: Race/Ethnicity, Gender, and Class in Current Research and Policies on Romani Women in Europe* 55–56 (Central Eur. Univ., Working Paper, 2009) (discussing the disadvantages of Romani women that the United Nations has failed to take into account).

Education: discipline and punishment in the United States

Research in the United States shows that Black girls are perceived to be more adultlike and less innocent than white girls of the same age.[81] This stereotypical perception profoundly affects Black girls in the United States in numerous ways. Black girls who encounter the juvenile justice system, for example, are more likely to be perceived as adult or adultlike offenders. As such, they may experience "more punitive exercise of discretion by those in positions of authority, greater use of force, and harsher penalties."[82] In school settings, teachers and administrators perceive Black girls to be older than white girls in the same age group. This misperception impacts the frequency with which Black girls are disciplined and how they are disciplined. Out-of-school suspensions reflect a significant racial disparity,[83] unfairly and disproportionately affecting Black girls and interfering with their enjoyment of the right to education in the United States.

One 2017 study revealed that survey participants perceived Black girls as needing less nurturing, protection, support, and comfort than white girls.[84] The participants also viewed Black girls as being more independent, more knowledgeable about adult topics, and more knowledgeable about sex. Authors of the study suggest that "the perception of Black girls as less innocent may contribute to harsher punishment by educators and school resource officers."[85] Relatedly, the perception of Black girls as needing less support and nurturing may lead to fewer leadership and mentorship opportunities in schools.[86]

Recognizing that children are still developing socially and psychologically, the United States legal system has traditionally treated children with more leniency than adults. Childhood, however, is a social construct that simultaneously shapes perceptions of race and is shaped by perceptions of race in the United States. As such, the leniency typically afforded children disproportionately favors white children and disfavors Black children.[87]

In a 2014 study, a group of psychologists found that beginning at the age of ten, Black boys are perceived to be older and less innocent than their white peers.[88] In that

[81] *See* Rebecca Epstein et al., Girlhood Interrupted: The Erasure of Black Girls' Childhood 4 (2017) [hereinafter girlhood interrupted] (presenting data on the adultification of Black girls).

[82] *Id.* at 1.

[83] *See* off. for civ. rts., u.s. dep't of educ., 2015–16 civil rights data collection: school climate and safety 13 (2018), https://www2.ed.gov/about/offices/list/ocr/docs/school-climate-and-safety.pdf (showing that although female black students accounted for only 8 percent of school enrollment they accounted for 14 percent of out-of-school suspensions).

[84] girlhood interrupted, *supra* note 81, at 1.

[85] *Id.*

[86] *Id.*

[87] *See* Priscilla A. Ocen, *(E)racing Childhood: Examining the Racialized Construction of Childhood and Innocence in the Treatment of Sexually Exploited Minors*, 62 UCLA L. Rev. 1586, 1606 (2015) ("[A]s the notion of the innocent, developmental child emerged, white children began to enjoy greater [legal] protections while Black children's position remained relatively unchanged.").

[88] Phillip Atiba Goff et al., *The Essence of Innocence: Consequences of Dehumanizing Black Children*, 106 J. Personality & Soc. Pysch. 526, 529 (2014).

study, veteran police officers and others overestimated the age of Black boys by approximately four-and-a-half years. Police officer misperceptions about advanced age were also used to justify police violence.[89] Although less research has been conducted on the adultification of Black girls (a trend that aligns with the very patterns Crenshaw named in her early work), preliminary studies suggest that gender, race, and age intersect in ways that leave Black girls in the United States subject to less leniency, greater punishment, and oversexualization in public and private school systems across the country.[90]

Stereotypes of Black girls have their roots in the racist constructions of femininity that date back to slavery in the United States. Three dominant stereotypes can be traced to the slavery era, which the authors of *Girlhood Interrupted* identify as "Sapphire (e.g., emasculating, loud, aggressive, angry, stubborn, and unfeminine); Jezebel (e.g., hypersexualized, seductive, and exploiter of men's weaknesses); and Mammy (e.g., self-sacrificing, nurturing, loving, asexual)."[91] These stereotypes continue to inform the social construction of race and gender for Black girls and women in the United States. The racial and gendered construction of Black femininity also intersects with age, resulting in the adultification of Black girls, which as noted above, negatively affects their educational experiences and their experiences in other state systems such as the juvenile justice and child welfare systems.[92]

School discipline often depends on the subjective assessment of a teacher or school administrator. Black girls experience significantly higher rates of school discipline and some studies indicate that they are disciplined more harshly than their peers for the same behavior.[93] Discipline for school dress code violations, for example, involves precisely the kind of subjective decision-making that disproportionately harms Black girls. In one study in Washington, DC, for example, researchers found that dress code violations disproportionately affected Black girls in significant ways.[94] In its report, the National Women's Law Center concluded:

> [S]ome schools ban styles associated with Black girls and women, like hair wraps. Black girls also face adults' stereotyped perceptions that they are more sexually provocative because of their race, and thus more deserving of punishment for a low-cut shirt or short skirt.... Dress codes also communicate to students that girls are to be blamed for "distracting" boys, instead of teaching boys to respect girls, correct their

[89] *See* GIRLHOOD INTERRUPTED, *supra* note 81, at 4 (noting that the adultification of Black boys has increased the amount of police violence used against them).

[90] *See* Ocen, *supra* note 87, at 1610 (arguing that from the era of slavery in America and moving forward in history, Black girls in particular have been "marginaliz[ed] not only within the category of child, but also within the category of female").

[91] GIRLHOOD INTERRUPTED, *supra* note 81, at 5.

[92] *See id.* (citing Jamilia J. Blake et al., *Challenging Middle-Class Notions of Femininity: The Cause of Black Females' Disproportionate Suspension Rates*, *in* CLOSING THE SCHOOL DISCIPLINE GAP: EQUITABLE REMEDIES FOR EXCESSIVE EXCLUSION 75, 76 (Daniel J. Losen et al. eds., 2015)) (explaining the intersectional issues that arise from the adultification of Black girls).

[93] *See id.* at 9 (discussing the higher rate and severity of punishment for Black female students).

[94] NAT'L WOMEN'S L. CTR., DRESS CODED: BLACK GIRLS, BODIES AND BIAS IN D.C. SCHOOLS (2018), https://nwlc-ciw49tixgw5lbab.stackpathdns.com/wp-content/uploads/2018/04/5.1web_Final_nwlc_DressCodeReport.pdf.

> behavior and be more responsible. This dangerous attitude promotes sexual harassment in schools.[95]

Black girls were often disciplined for these low-level and highly subjective infractions, resulting in significant amounts of missed class time because of in- and out-of-school suspensions. Black girls in Washington, D.C. are 20.8 times more likely to be suspended than their white counterparts.[96] The report concludes that dress codes in Washington, DC "promote race and sex discrimination and pull students out of the classroom for no good reason .... Black girls fall behind in school, which threatens their long-term earning potential while also exacerbating longstanding and widespread racial and gender inequalities."[97] Dress code expectations are also damaging to transgender students and students who are gender fluid or non-binary.

Research strongly suggests that adultification based on racial and gender stereotypes impinges on Black girls' right to education by unjustly and disproportionately removing them from the classroom.[98] An intersectional view of childhood, gender, and race reveals that Black girls experience the right to education in the United States differently than white girls and Black boys in the same age group.

Black girls' right to education is also negatively affected by the juvenile justice system. The juvenile justice system historically relies on judges and other decision-makers to exercise discretion in meting out punishment to children. In fact, notes law professor Jyoti Nanda,

> a complex set of legal rules gives each system actor the discretion either to treat [a girl of color] as a child with background social problems for which she is not responsible or to commit her to the juvenile justice system as a delinquent who should be held accountable for her conduct.[99]

Nanda continues, "[R]ace, gender, and class intersect to create a distorted image of girls of color."[100] Decision-makers in the juvenile justice system often view Black girls and other girls of color as the source of problems rather than as the victims of intersecting structural systems of subordination. Some studies have found that "Black girls received harsher punishment than White girls despite controlling for the seriousness of the offense, prior record, and age."[101] It is precisely the exercise of this discretion that invites reliance on racialized and gendered stereotypes and implicit bias

[95] *Id.* at 1.
[96] *Id.* at 16.
[97] *Id.* at 1. *See also id.* at 26 ("Black girls are missing out on class time because of dress and grooming codes. Some are suspended, while others are pulled out of the classroom informally. Both formal and informal classroom removals cause these girls to lose out on the opportunity to learn.").
[98] *See, e.g.*, Kimberlé Williams Crenshaw, Black Girls Matter: Pushed Out, Overpoliced and Underprotected 16–21 (2015), https://44bbdc6e-01a4-4a9a-88bc-731c6524888e.filesusr.com/ugd/b77e03_e92d6e80f7034f30bf843ea7068f52d6.pdf (illustrating the clear disparity in the instances of out of school suspension and expulsion between Black girls and white girls of the same age range).
[99] Jyoti Nanda, *Blind Discretion: Girls of Color & Delinquency in the Juvenile Justice System*, 59 UCLA L. Rev. 1502, 1505 (2012).
[100] *Id.* at 1507.
[101] *Id.* at 1530.

to unfairly determine outcomes for Black girls. In these discretionary juridical moments, racial and gender stereotypes intersect to influence decision-makers in ways that punish Black girls more frequently and more severely than their white counterparts. Race and gender stereotypes intersect and influence the exercise of discretion to the social, emotional, and economic detriment of Black girls.

Intersectional analysis is necessary to fully comprehend and address the structural racism and gender bias that, together, negatively affect individual girls in school and in the justice system, as well as have long-term impacts on employment, earning potential, mental health, and other lingering effects of trauma. Although several studies have examined how juveniles enter the delinquency system, few of them explore the intersection of race and gender and how their intersection creates qualitatively different issues for Black girls and other girls of color. As Nanda notes, "With more proper documentation of these intersectional issues, decision makers .... will then be better informed on factors essential to the exercise of their discretion to the betterment of girls of color, and possibly also begin to create and implement effective solutions."[102]

Sexual orientation, gender identity, and LGBTQI rights

International human rights law has slowly and inconsistently embraced human rights norms related to sexuality. Trend lines certainly suggest that rights related to sexual orientation and gender identity are largely accepted within international legal institutions. At the grassroots level, however, activists continue to fight for basic rights in many countries around the world.

Within some domestic legal systems, courts have determined that prohibitions on "sex" or "gender" discrimination encompass a prohibition against discrimination based on sexual orientation and gender identity. Similarly, international human rights treaty bodies within the United Nations have expanded the definition of sex discrimination to include discrimination based on sexual orientation and gender identity. This section traces the evolution of this trend within international human rights law and explores how an intersectional framework has facilitated this normative expansion.

The UN Human Rights Council has unequivocally asserted that States have an obligation to "safeguard the human rights of LGBT people."[103] Importantly, in 2007, a group of almost thirty international experts gathered to draft a set of guiding principles on the application of international human rights law to issues related to sexual orientation and gender identity. The "Yogyakarta Principles" describe a range of human rights related to sexual orientation and gender identity, including non-discrimination; security of person; economic, social, and cultural rights; expressive and associational

[102] *Id.* at 1539. *See also* JAMILIA J. BLAKE & REBECCA EPSTEIN, LISTENING TO BLACK WOMEN AND GIRLS: LIVED EXPERIENCES OF ADULTIFICATION BIAS 16 (2019) (finding that "[i]mproved cultural competency and gender-responsiveness can help educators and other authorities better understand black girls and address bias or lack of cross-cultural experience").

[103] *Combatting Discrimination Based on Sexual Orientation and Gender Identity*, UNITED NATIONS OFF. OF THE HIGH COMM'R FOR HUM. RTS., http://www.ohchr.org/EN/Issues/Discrimination/Pages/LGBT.aspx (last visited May 1, 2021).

rights; movement and asylum; cultural and family life; human rights defenders; and redress for violations.[104] Noting that the international response up to that point had been "fragmented and inconsistent," the drafters hoped to provide guidance and promote consistency in the response to LGBTQI[105] rights violations from both activists and UN treaty bodies alike.[106]

In 2008, the UN General Assembly adopted a declaration promoting the rights of LGBTQI individuals.[107] In 2011, the Human Rights Council adopted a resolution on sexual orientation and gender identity, a highly significant development in the evolution of the UN's embrace of LGBTQI rights.[108] The Human Rights Council reinforced this commitment to rights related to sexual orientation and gender identity in a 2014 follow-up resolution.[109]

Several of the UN treaty bodies have articulated a commitment to protect and promote LGBTQI rights. For example, the Human Rights Committee, the Committee on Economic, Social and Cultural Rights, the CEDAW Committee, the Committee on the Rights of the Child, and the Committee Against Torture all prohibit discrimination against LGBTQI individuals to some degree.[110] Some human rights treaties benefited from open-ended language in their non-discrimination provisions, making it easier to expand prohibitions on discrimination to include LGBTQI discrimination and violence.[111] The treaty bodies have articulated support for LGBTQI rights in a variety of ways, including in decisions in individual cases brought under the various optional protocols[112] (described in greater detail in chapter 5), in concluding observations as

[104] Int'l Panel of Experts in Int'l Hum. Rts. L. & on Sexual Orientation & Gender Identity, *The Yogyakarta Principles: Principles on the Application of International Human Rights Law in Relation to Sexual Orientation and Gender Identity* (Mar. 2007), https://www.refworld.org/pdfid/48244e602.pdf.

[105] This volume uses the expansive descriptor "LGBTQI" whenever possible to designate lesbian, gay, bisexual, transgender, queer, and intersex. At times, the text reflects a narrower category such as "LBT" such as when CEDAW is specifically referring to lesbian, bisexual, or transgender women. At other times, usage may reflect the choices of cited reference material.

[106] THE YOGYAKARTA PRINCIPLES, *The Yogyakarta Principles - An Overview*, http://yogyakartaprinciples.org/wp-content/uploads/2016/08/backgrounder_en.pdf (last visited May 1, 2021).

[107] *See UN: General Assembly Statement Affirms Rights for All*, HUM. RTS. WATCH (Dec. 18, 2008, 7:28 PM), http://www.hrw.org/news/2008/12/18/un-general-assembly-statement-affirms-rights-all (explaining that the UN General Assembly confirmed "international human rights protections include sexual orientation and gender identity").

[108] *See* Paula Gerber, *Living a Life of Crime: The Ongoing Criminalization of Homosexuality Within the Commonwealth*, 39 ALT. L.J. 78, 81 (2014) (describing the SOGI Resolution as a "landmark" development).

[109] *See* Human Rights Council Res. 27/32, U.N. Doc. A/HRC/RES/27/32, at 1–2 (Oct. 2, 2014) (underscoring the importance of LGBTQI rights around the world).

[110] For a more complete discussion of UN treaty body action on this issue, *see* Johanna Bond, *Gender and Non-Normative Sex in Sub-Saharan Africa*, 23 MICH. J. GENDER & L. 65, 79 (2016) (discussing the receptivity of different UN treaty bodies to addressing LGBTQI issues).

[111] *See id.* at 74 ("Some treaties open the door for an expansive interpretation of discrimination, because they prohibit discrimination based on a number of enumerated categories and 'any other status,' which has been interpreted to include sexual orientation and gender identity.").

[112] *See, e.g.*, Toonen v. Australia, Communication No. 488/1992, U.N. Human Rights Committee [H.R.C.], U.N. Doc. CCPR/C/50/D/448/1992, ¶ 8.7 (Mar. 31, 1994) ("The Committee confines itself to noting, however, that in its view the reference to 'sex' . . . is to be taken as including sexual orientation."). The Human Rights Committee issued this decision in 1994 clarifying that the prohibition on sex discrimination in the International Covenant on Civil and Political Rights includes discrimination on the basis of sexual orientation and gender identity. *Id.*

part of the state reporting process[113] (described in greater detail in chapter 6), and in general recommendations or general comments[114] (described in greater detail in chapter 3).

Despite its focus on gender discrimination, the CEDAW Committee has been relatively slow to embrace LGBTQI rights.[115] The International Gay and Lesbian Human Rights Commission observes, "[O]ther treaty bodies have looked at the issue [of LGBTQI rights] in a more comprehensive way than the CEDAW Committee and have given serious consideration to sexual rights abuses in their review of states."[116] The CEDAW Committee has made progress, albeit slowly, in the last decade in embracing rights related to sexual orientation and gender identity. One example is CEDAW's General Recommendation No. 28, which provides that "[t]he discrimination of women based on sex and gender is inextricably linked with other factors that affect women, such as race, ethnicity, religion or belief, health, status, age, class, caste and *sexual orientation and gender identity*."[117]

An intersectional lens is crucial in exploring discrimination and violence perpetrated against LGBTQI individuals. All over the world, for example, women have experienced targeted homophobic violence, sometimes called "curative rape." This type of violence has been documented in numerous countries where women describe being targeted for sexual violence because they did not conform to traditional gender-based roles. Conceived of in this way, the links between being targeted because of real or perceived sexual orientation or gender identity and because of gender are readily apparent. The structural inequality faced by women intersects with the forms of

[113] *See, e.g.*, Comm. on the Elimination of All Forms of Discrimination Against Women [CEDAW], Rep. of the Comm. on the Elimination of All Forms of Discrimination Against Women on its Twentieth Session, ¶ 128, U.N. Doc. A/54/38/Rev.1 (1999) ("The Committee recommends that lesbianism be conceptualized as a sexual orientation and that penalties for its practice be abolished.").

[114] *See, e.g.*, Comm. on Econ., Soc. and Cultural Rts., Gen. Comment No. 20: Non-Discrimination in Economic, Social and Cultural Rights, ¶ 32, U.N. Doc. E/C.12/GC/20 (2009) (providing that "a person's sexual orientation is not a barrier to realizing Covenant rights"); Comm. on Econ., Soc. and Cultural Rts., Gen. Comment No. 19: The Right to Social Security, ¶ 29, U.N. Doc. E/C.12/GC/19 (2008) (noting that social security may not be denied based on a person's sexual orientation); Comm. on Econ., Soc. and Cultural Rts., Gen. Comment No. 18: The Right to Work, ¶ 12(b), U.N. Doc. E/C.12/GC/18 (2006) (stating that "[t]he labour market must be open to everyone" and prohibiting discrimination based on sexual orientation); Comm. on Econ., Soc. and Cultural Rts., Gen. Comment No. 15: The Right to Water, ¶ 13, U.N. Doc. E/C.12/2002/11 (2003) (explaining that the Covenant prevents discrimination based on sexual orientation); Comm. on Econ., Soc. and Cultural Rts., Gen. Comment No. 14: The Right to the Highest Attainable Standard of Physical and Mental Health, ¶ 18, U.N. Doc. E/C.12/2000/4 (2000) (prohibiting discrimination based on sexual orientation for access to healthcare).

[115] As of 2012, when the UN Office of the High Commissioner for Human Rights (UNHCHR) issued an important report on LGBTQI discrimination, the CEDAW Committee had not referenced LGBTQI rights as frequently as many of the other committees. A tally of the treaty bodies' references to LGBTQI rights in concluding observations reveals that "[t]he report cites thirty-eight concluding observations from the Human Rights Committee about LGBTQI discrimination and violence, eleven concluding observations from the Committee on Economic, Social, and Cultural Rights about LGBTQI rights, and eight references to LGBTQI rights in the concluding observations of each of the following committees: the Committee Against Torture, the Children's Rights Committee, and the CEDAW Committee." Bond, *supra* note 110, at 79.

[116] Int'l Gay & Lesbian Hum. Rts. Comm'n, Equal and Indivisible: Crafting Inclusive Shadow Reports for CEDAW 7 (2009), http://www.iglhrc.org/sites/default/files/287-1.pdf.

[117] Comm. on the Elimination of Discrimination Against Women [CEDAW], Gen. Recommendation No. 28 on the Core Obligations of States Parties Under Art. 2 of the Convention on the Elimination of All Forms of Discrimination Against Women, ¶ 18, CEDAW/C/GC/28 (Dec. 16, 2010) (emphasis added).

structural inequality that LGBTQI individuals face because they do not conform to gender role expectations around sexuality.

Zanelle Muholi, a South African artist and activist, notes, "In South African black culture, being a black lesbian is seen as negative, as destroying the nuclear family, and as un-African. There are expectations that African women must have children and procreate with a male partner who is to be head of the family."[118] Perpetrators target Black South African lesbians in part for their failure to conform to these gender role expectations.[119] Black lesbians in South Africa are exposed to violence fueled by the intersection of subordination based on race, gender, and sexuality.

In addition to exploring the mutually constitutive nature of discrimination based on race, gender, and sexual orientation, an intersectional framework also facilitates exploration of the many ways in which colonialism continues to construct identity based on race and gender. Anne McClintock traces the overlapping and mutually generative aspects of race, gender, and nation-building in the context of colonial occupation.[120] McClintock notes, "[T]he colonies—in particular Africa—became a theater for exhibiting, amongst other things, the cult of domesticity and the reinvention of patriarchy."[121] Fully understanding the harmful legacies of colonialism and its lasting effects on contemporary race and gender identity requires an intersectional lens.[122] It facilitates a complex, context-specific analysis of human rights violations based simultaneously on the juncture of race, gender, and sexual orientation.

Focusing on intersectional remedies

The case studies in this chapter do not illustrate the full range of intersectional human rights issues. That would be impossible in a single volume. However, they illuminate the role of intersectional analysis in understanding the complexity and lived experience of human rights violations. This enhanced—and complicating—perspective also informs our understanding of appropriate and intersectional remedies.

Consider, for example, citizenship rights and rights related to political representation. Among countries of the world, national gender quotas have become a common strategy to increase the representation of women in national politics. By 2008, over one hundred countries had adopted some type of gender quota and twenty countries had implemented quotas for minority groups.[123] There are little data, however,

[118] *see* Bond, *supra* note 110, at 85 (quoting Zanele Muholi, Mapping Our Histories: A Visual History of Black Lesbians in Post-Apartheid South Africa 19 (2013)).

[119] *Id.*

[120] Anne McClintock, Imperial Leather: Race, Gender, and Sexuality in the Colonial Contest 16–17 (1995).

[121] *Id.*

[122] *See id.* at 353. *See also* Lisa Yarwood, *Women, Transitional Justice and Indigenous Conflict: The Role of Women in Addressing New Zealand's Colonial Past*, *in* Women and Transitional Justice: the Experience of Women as Participants 9, 12 (Lisa Yarwood ed., 2013) ("The actions of the colonial settlers in the nineteenth century were spurious and motivated by the acquisition of land, but as time progressed the consequences of these actions and the marginalisation of Maori simply became normalized in society.").

[123] Melanie M. Hughes, *Intersectionality, Quotas, and Minority Women's Political Representation Worldwide*, 105 Am. Pol. Sci. Rev. 604, 605 (2011).

analyzing the effect of those quotas on minority women. An intersectional analysis is necessary to determine if the remedial efforts of the majority of states are improving the representation of minority women, in particular. In one study, Melanie Hughes found that the effect of quota systems on women from underrepresented groups is mixed, depending on the precise parameters of the quota system.[124]

Even if we had data showing their effectiveness, quotas are an insufficient intervention to ensure public engagement. Beyond quotas at the national level, intersectional structural discrimination prevents some women from fully engaging in public life. Time use studies that explore disparities in the demands on men's and women's time in sub-Saharan Africa, for example, demonstrate that women experience more significant, multiple, and varied demands on their time than do men, frustrating women's participation in public life.[125] For rural women living in poverty, labor devoted to subsistence takes a significant amount of time and energy, leaving little time for public engagement.[126] An intersectional lens reveals the particular challenges faced by women living in impoverished rural areas who wish to participate in local governance. Efforts to include more women in decision-making at the national and sub-national level must address the intersectional structural impediments to women's participation.

In the realm of employment, domestic workers around the world often suffer from intersectional human rights abuses stemming from discrimination based on gender in combination with race, ethnicity, nationality, or migrant status. Of the fifty million people who work as domestic workers across the globe, many are female migrant workers.[127] Domestic workers are among the most exploited and least protected workers in the world.[128] Women who are hired to provide domestic labor often travel abroad in the hope of sending money back to their families. They may face unsafe working conditions, severe limitations on their freedom of movement, isolation, low or no compensation, long hours, and physical and sexual abuse.

The abuses are distinctly intersectional in nature and any human rights remedies must be broad enough to encompass the intersectional nature of the violations. Structural discrimination based on gender, socioeconomic status, race, ethnicity, nationality, and/or religion intersect to create conditions that that are ripe for employers to abuse migrant workers. In addition to the intersectional economic forces that drive migrant labor, a 2014 Al Jazeera news article describes how racial and ethnic stereotypes are used in the recruitment of domestic laborers in Singapore:

[124] *Id.* at 604.

[125] *See* Johanna Bond, *The Challenges of Parity: Increasing Women's Participation in Informal Justice Systems within Sub-Saharan Africa*, *in* GENDER PARITY & MULTICULTURAL FEMINISM 175, 176 (Ruth Rubio-Marín & Will Kymlicka eds., 2018).

[126] *See id.* ("Thus, even when gender role expectations have sufficient flexibility to allow women a meaningful role in community decision-making, pragmatic demands on their time may frustrate women's efforts to inhabit the public sphere.").

[127] *See* OFF. OF THE HIGH COMM'R FOR HUM. RTS., UNITED NATIONS, BEHIND CLOSED DOORS: PROTECTING AND PROMOTING THE HUMAN RIGHTS OF MIGRANT DOMESTIC WORKERS IN AN IRREGULAR SITUATION 2 (2015) [hereinafter OHCHR] (discussing the statistics on migrant domestic workers).

[128] *See* ELIZABETH FRANTZ, OPEN SOC'Y FOUNDS., BREAKING THE ISOLATION: ACCESS TO INFORMATION AND MEDIA AMONG MIGRANT DOMESTIC WORKERS IN JORDAN AND LEBANON 6 (2014) (outlining the disproportionate burden placed on domestic workers).

> Go to ... a 1970s [era] mall in central Singapore, and you will find five levels of brightly lit rooms and galleries called "Homekeeper" and "Budget Maid." Inside these rooms, dozens of women sit in a listless, artificial silence. They nod respectfully as you enter, and some watch closely as you speak to staff. You might take one home with you—for two years, or longer. The women, domestic workers, come from Indonesia, the Philippines, and Myanmar. They sit beneath garish signs and posters, testifying to their friendliness and industriousness.... [The] executive director of the Humanitarian Organisation of Migration Economics (HOME), a migrant workers advocacy group based in Singapore, said that some agencies market their domestic workers like "commodities." He adds that racial stereotypes are sometimes used in transactions with patrons. 'Some of the stereotypes include Filipinos as "smarter," Indonesians as "less bright," and Burmese as "sweet-natured and compliant."[129]

The United Nations defines migrants who are in "an irregular situation" as people who "are not authorized to enter, to stay and to engage in a remunerated activity in a transit or destination country."[130] Migrants working in an irregular situation often lack legal status and are reluctant to seek redress for intersectional rights violations that may include unfair labor practices, forcible confinement, lack of privacy, and gender-based violence.[131] To protect migrant workers from these and other intersectional abuses, some countries that send migrant workers abroad have signed protective bilateral treaties with countries in which their nationals often find exploitative work. In 2014, for example, Saudi Arabia signed a memorandum of understanding with Indonesia designed to provide minimal protections for Indonesian migrants in an irregular situation (those whose entry or exit into the country occurs outside of the law or regulations), many of whom are women, in Saudi Arabia.[132] In some cases, domestic laws address the needs of migrants working in irregular situations, at least on paper. Argentina's Migration Law No. 25.971 gives all migrants access to healthcare and social assistance. Bolivia's Migration Law No. 370 recognizes the rights of migrants to enjoy health and reproductive rights.[133] Other countries have taken steps to ensure that migrants in irregular situations have access to information about courts and complaint procedures and about their rights throughout the recruitment and placement process. The Committee on the Rights of Migrant Workers noted in its General Comment No. 2 that "regularization," which grants legal status and protection to migrants, "is the most effective measure to address the extreme vulnerability of migrant

[129] Michael Malay, *Buy a Discount Maid at Singapore's Malls*, Al Jazeera (June 27, 2014), https://www.aljazeera.com/indepth/features/2014/06/buy-discount-maid-at-singapore-malls-201462495012940207.html.

[130] OHCHR, *supra* note 127, at 1 n.2.

[131] *See id.* at 13. "Migrants in an irregular situation are more likely to face discrimination, exclusion, exploitation and abuse at all stages of the migration process. They often face prolonged detention or ill-treatment, and in some cases enslavement, rape or even murder. They are more likely to be targeted by xenophobes and racists, victimized by unscrupulous employers and sexual predators, and can easily fall prey to criminal traffickers and smugglers. Rendered vulnerable by their irregular status, these men, women and children are often afraid or unable to seek protection and relief from the authorities of countries of origin, transit or destination." *Id.*

[132] *See id.* at 13 (citing *Saudi Arabia Moves to Protect Rights of Indonesian Maids*, BBC News (Feb. 19, 2014), http://www.bbc.com/news/world-middle-east-26259326).

[133] *Id.* at 21.

workers and members of their families in an irregular situation."[134] For the greatest impact, countries should take a multifaceted approach to rights protection that addresses the underlying structural and deeply intersectional nature of these abuses.

In parts of South-East Asia, discrimination based on caste, a form of descent-based discrimination, harms large numbers of people. In India, for example, Dalits experience descent-based discrimination and are often excluded from socioeconomic and cultural benefits. In 2008, a group of caste members in Uttar Pradesh accused several Dalits of encroaching on their land. In retribution for this perceived encroachment, the caste members attacked and sexually assaulted a number of Dalit women.[135] An intersectional approach to the human rights violations at issue reveals that both descent-based subordination and gender-based subordination intersected in ways that caused a specific harm to the Dalit women. Intersectional analysis goes beyond the limited appreciation that these women were particularly vulnerable or experienced discrimination based on gender plus discrimination based on descent. Intersectionality requires that one examine how gender and caste are mutually constitutive or, in other words, how the experience of caste shapes gender, and vice versa. Intersectionality requires an examination of how structural power relationships construct identity along both the social axes of caste and gender. In this case, intersectionality reveals that socioeconomics and politics define gender and caste in particular ways for Dalit women, rendering them "dispensable" and therefore "rapable."

Importantly, intersectional theory offers a more comprehensive understanding of appropriate remedies for this group of Dalit women. Remedies must include prevention measures, compensation for victims, and accountability for perpetrators. Remedies must ensure that all women, including Dalit women, have access to appropriate healthcare and social services in the aftermath of sexual assault. Remedies must also include non-discrimination training for government authorities and community members across the caste system that specifically addresses the targeting of Dalit women. Programs aimed at sexual assault victims in general may not reach Dalit communities. Similarly, programming that is generally designed to ensure access to health and social services within Dalit communities may not specifically address sexual assault in Dalit communities. An intersectional approach encourages the dismantling of mutually reinforcing stereotypes and social hierarchies of descent and gender that shape the experiences of Dalit women in harmful ways.

Around the world, women with disabilities routinely face physical and emotional abuse at the hands of family members and caregivers. An intersectional framework considers how gender norms and expectations construct women's experiences of disability and how living with a disability informs the social construction of gender. One example of the confluence of gender and disability in women's lives is the frequency with which women with disabilities experience sexual violence.[136]

[134] *Id.* at 33.

[135] *See* Hum. Rts. Council [H.R.C.], Rep. of the Special Rapporteur on Contemporary Forms of Racism, Racial Discrimination, Xenophobia and Related Intolerance, Doudou Diène, ¶¶ 56, 60, UN Doc. A/HRC/7/19/Add.1 (2008) (describing attacks on Dalit women and their homes).

[136] *See* Beth Ribet, *Surfacing Disability Through a Critical Race Theoretical Paradigm*, 2 Geo. J. L. & Mod. Critical Race Persps. 209, 214 (2010) ("Disability, like race, has been framed as a supposedly solely medical, immutable and indisputably real physical or psychiatric disease or defect. This presumption

One study in Bangladesh, for example, found that Bangladeshi women who were suffering from chronic maternal disabilities, such as uterine prolapse or obstetric fistula, suffered high rates of violence.[137] Researchers indicated that the intimate partner violence experienced by women in the study was triggered, in part, by the women's inability to perform domestic work and satisfy a husband's sexual demands. The study revealed that "most of the women living with a chronic maternal disability—stress incontinence, uterine prolapse, or fistula—were subjected to emotional violence, and almost half of them were sexually abused."[138]

A woman's disability may affect her willingness or ability to fulfill gender role expectations, including, if she is married, meeting the sexual or domestic demands of her spouse. The study concludes that there is a

> need to develop programmatic approaches to: prevent chronic maternal disabilities; educate the family and the community about causes and prevention of these conditions; and enhance opportunities for women outside marriage through education and employment leading to enhancement of their status and rights in the household, community and broader society, making them less vulnerable to violence and more knowledgeable of their rights as human beings.[139]

Intersectional analysis is necessary to fully address the interconnected gendered and disability-related needs of women with disabilities who face such violence.

As a final example, intersectionality also sheds light on potential remedies in the context of armed conflict. In the context of post-conflict peace building, UN Security Council Resolution 1325 "calls for women's equal participation with men and for their full involvement in all efforts for the maintenance and promotion of peace and security."[140] Christine Bell and Catherine O'Rourke found that UNSC Resolution 1325 had a limited effect on peace processes between 1990 and 2010.[141] Of the relatively small number of agreements that specifically refer to women, Bell and O'Rourke note that "[t]here is evidence of quotas for women proving difficult to reconcile with ethnic or clan quotas.... both Bangladeshi and Somali examples illustrate the difficulty in dealing with the intersectionality of gender identity and other forms of identity within peace agreement texts."[142] In these cases, the authors of the peace agreements fail to consider the impact of separate gender and ethnic quotas on women from marginalized ethnic communities. Similarly, women with disabilities are also often absent in

has historically been a valid legal and social basis for the deprivation of a wide range of human rights.... includ[ing]... freedom from physical and sexual violence....").

[137] *See* et al., *Violence Against Women with Chronic Maternal Disabilities in Rural Bangladesh*, 30 J. Health, Population & Nutrition 181, 181 (2012) (reporting the results from a study on the abuse suffered by women with chronic maternal disabilities).

[138] *Id.* at 189.

[139] *Id.* at 191.

[140] Christine Bell & Catherine O'Rourke, *Peace Agreements or Pieces of Paper? The Impact of UNSC Resolution 1325 on Peace Processes and Their Agreements*, 59 Int'l & Compar. L.Q. 941, 942 (2010).

[141] *See id.* ("In summary, we find that only 16 per cent of peace agreements contain specific references to women.").

[142] *Id.* at 960–61.

peace building and little attention is given to the intersectional human rights violations they face in armed conflict.[143] Considerations of intersectionality must be front and center in the negotiations over the participation of women from marginalized groups in conflict resolution and peace building.

An intersectional lens deepens our understanding of human rights violations. It opens up space for inquiry about complex, intersecting, and mutually constitutive sources of discrimination and subordination. Rather than a unidimensional analysis of gender discrimination, for example, intersectionality fosters a richer understanding of the many mutually reinforcing ways gender subordination intersects with discrimination based on race, ethnicity, religion, socioeconomic status, disability, sexual orientation, and gender identity. From a human rights perspective, this deeper, more nuanced approach allows for broader human rights remedies that more fully redress the human rights violations in question.

[143] *See* Stephanie Ortoleva, *Women with Disabilities: The Forgotten Peace Builders*, 33 Loy. L.A. Int'l & Compar.. L. Rev. 83, 88 (2010) (noting the insufficient attention given to the needs of women with disabilities and their lack of representation in UN programs).

3
Evolution of Intersectionality in the UN Treaty Bodies

As the world's pre-eminent intergovernmental organization dedicated to peace, security, humanitarian aid, sustainable development, and human rights, the United Nations plays a significant role in promoting global recognition of international human rights. Although scholars and activists have explored and advocated for intersectionality theory in the international human rights context for almost twenty years, the UN has been slow to incorporate and make use of intersectionality's insights. Since approximately 2000, UN treaty bodies—committees of experts who oversee implementation of the human rights treaties—have cautiously begun to explore intersectionality as a theoretical framework for examining rights violations. The results of this trend are encouraging. When the treaty bodies embrace intersectionality, they are better able to reflect and remedy the complexity of human rights violations.[1] Remedies focused only on one axis of discrimination, in contrast, provide only limited relief for victims and stymie a full and nuanced understanding of the violations at issue.

The UN treaty bodies have articulated a limited but evolving understanding of intersectionality's potential. The analysis often approaches intersectionality but falls short of a robust intersectional framework. In these instances, the treaty bodies may recognize that women experience "multiple" discrimination or that women from certain groups are "particularly vulnerable." As discussed in chapter 1, the idea of multiple discrimination, however, reflects an additive understanding of intersectionality that fails to capitalize on the theory's transformative potential. Multiple discrimination views identity categories, and the concomitant subordination or privilege attached to those categories, as fixed and layered. Multiple discrimination is a nod in the direction of intersectionality because it reflects the understanding that, for example, a woman may experience discrimination based on gender and ethnicity. Intersectionality, by contrast, views intersecting identities as dynamic and mutually constitutive, combining to form new and unique experiences of subordination, privilege, or both. Often, the UN's articulations of intersectionality reflect this more limited, additive understanding of "double" or multiple forms of discrimination.

[1] Meghan Campbell, *CEDAW and Women's Intersecting Identities: A Pioneering Approach to Intersectional Discrimination*, 11 DIREITO GV L. REV. 479, 499–500 (2015). *See generally* Johanna Bond, *International Intersectionality: A Theoretical and Pragmatic Exploration of Women's International Human Rights Violations*, 52 EMORY L.J. 71 (2003).

Global Intersectionality and Contemporary Human Rights. Johanna Bond, Oxford University Press. © Johanna Bond 2021.
DOI: 10.1093/oso/9780198868835.003.0004

Treaty body structure and functions

The UN has nine core multilateral treaties obligating states to uphold and promote human rights.[2] Each primary treaty has an enforcement body, or committee, that oversees implementation of the treaty in the countries that have ratified it. The treaty bodies are composed of independent human rights experts who are nominated and elected by States parties for fixed, renewable terms of four years. The treaty bodies monitor states' compliance with the treaty in several ways, as defined by the individual treaties themselves. In general, treaty bodies oversee compliance with the treaties through a system of state reporting and, in some cases, consideration of individual complaints or an inquiry procedure in the case of serious human rights violations. Later chapters of this volume focus on those treaty body mechanisms.

Human rights law requires that States parties (those states that have agreed to be bound by the terms of a treaty) have a duty to respect, protect, fulfill, and promote the human rights standards contained in those treaties.[3] States parties must act in good faith and with due diligence to implement the human rights treaties to which they have agreed to be bound.[4] Significantly, with respect to states' obligations, states generally may not invoke domestic law as a defense for failing to implement binding international law.[5] The treaties allow states that ratify or accede to them to make reservations to specific treaty provisions, indicating that they agree to be bound by the treaty *except* for the reserved provisions. Reservations, however, may not be incompatible with the object and purpose of the treaty.[6]

All of the core human rights treaties require a state that has ratified or acceded to[7] the treaty to report periodically to the relevant treaty body on the state's progress in

[2] *Human Rights Treaty Bodies*, Off. of the High Comm'r for Hum. Rts., https://www.ohchr.org/EN/HRBodies/Pages/TreatyBodies.aspx (last visited Oct. 8, 2020). Those treaties include the International Covenant on Civil and Political Rights (ICCPR), the International Covenant on Social, Economic and Cultural Rights (ICESCR), the Convention on the Elimination of Racial Discrimination (CERD), the Convention on the Elimination of All Forms of Discrimination Against Women (CEDAW), the Convention Against Torture (CAT), the Convention on the Rights of the Child (CRC), the Convention on the Rights of Migrant Workers (CMW), the Convention for the Protection of All Persons from Enforced Disappearances (CPED), and the Convention on the Rights of Persons with Disabilities (CRPD).

[3] Rikki Holtmaat & Jonneke Naber, Women's Human Rights and Culture: From Deadlock to Dialogue 17 (2011).

[4] *Id.*

[5] *Id.*

[6] Jane Connors, *Article 28*, *in* The UN Convention on the Elimination of All Forms of Discrimination Against Women: A Commentary 565, 575 (Marsha A. Freeman et al. eds., 2012) Article 20 of the [Vienna Law of Treaties] provides that States parties to a treaty may object to reservations made by other States parties within twelve months from the date of the depository notification of the reservation or that on which the reserving State expressed its consent to be bound by the treaty, whichever is later. Several commentators have noted States parties' general unwillingness to object to incompatible reservations, owing to diplomatic sensibilities, as well as the practical difficulties and resource constraints they face in monitoring and formulating their positions on doubtful reservations, particularly taking into account the short time frame for objection.

[7] A country may be bound by the terms of the treaty when it either ratifies the treaty or accedes to the treaty. *See Glossary*, united nations treaty collection, https://treaties.un.org/Pages/Overview.aspx?path=overview/glossary/page1_en.xml#:~:text=%22Accession%22%20is%20the%20act%20whereby,treaty%20has%20entered%20into%20force (last visited Oct. 15, 2020) ("Ratification defines the international act whereby a state indicates its consent to be bound to a treaty if the parties intended to show

treaty implementation. States parties must submit periodic reports highlighting the successes and challenges in ongoing efforts to implement the treaty.[8] Often, non-governmental organizations (NGOs) also submit their own reports, called "shadow reports," detailing relevant human rights issues in the country.[9] The committee then engages in a "constructive dialogue" with a representative of the state.[10] The committee concludes the process by issuing "concluding observations" or "concluding comments" which summarize the committee's assessment of the state's progress in fulfilling its obligations under the treaty.[11]

Many of the treaties also have an Optional Protocol that establishes the authority of the committee to hear complaints from individuals in ratifying states.[12] Individuals must exhaust domestic remedies before bringing a complaint under an Optional Protocol. Once the treaty body hears the complaint, it will issue a decision, but the process can be long and burdensome for complainants.[13] Although the decisions of the treaty body are not legally binding, they often carry significant weight in national policy discussions.[14] Individual complainants sometimes explicitly invoke intersectionality in their complaints. At other times, the treaty bodies themselves use intersectional analysis in their consideration of individual complaints. Chapter 5 analyzes intersectionality in the context of individual complaints of human rights violations brought before the Committee on the Elimination of All Forms of Discrimination Against Women (CEDAW). I argue that intersectional complaints are likely to continue to increase, and the treaty bodies must improve their capacity to address intersectional violations in their jurisprudence.

Each committee adopts General Comments or General Recommendations (the term varies by treaty body) to guide states in their interpretations of the treaty provisions.[15] These are not legally binding but they offer guidance to States parties concerning the substantive human rights obligations in the treaty. General Comments and General Recommendations are critical vehicles for the treaty bodies to communicate

their consent by such an act."); *id.* ("'Accession' is the act whereby a state accepts the offer or the opportunity to become a party to a treaty already negotiated and signed by other states. It has the same legal effect as ratification. Accession usually occurs after the treaty has entered into force.").

[8] Walter Kälin, *Examination of State Reports*, *in* UN HUMAN RIGHTS TREATY BODIES 16, 20–21 (Helen Keller & Geir Ulfstein eds., 2012).

[9] *Id.* at 23.

[10] *Id.* at 24–25.

[11] Helen Keller & Geir Ulfstein, *Introduction*, *in* UN HUMAN RIGHTS TREATY BODIES 1, 4–5 (Helen Keller & Geir Ulfstein eds., 2012).

[12] Geir Ulfstein, *Individual Complaints*, *in* UN HUMAN RIGHTS TREATY BODIES 73, 73 (Helen Keller & Geir Ulfstein eds., 2012).

[13] *Id.* at 103, 115.

[14] Helen Keller & Geir Ulfstein, *Introduction*, *in* UN HUMAN RIGHTS TREATY BODIES 1, 4 (Keller and Ulfstein eds., 2012).

[15] Some treaty bodies call these documents General Comments and other call them General Recommendations. They perform the same function and differ only in nomenclature. Phillip Alston describes General Comments as "a means by which a UN human rights expert committee distills its considered views on an issue which arises out of the provisions of the treaty whose implementation it supervises and presents those views in the context of a formal statement of its understanding to which it attaches major importance." Philip Alston, *The Historical Origins of "General Comments" in Human Rights Law*, *in* THE INTERNATIONAL LEGAL SYSTEM IN QUEST OF EQUITY AND UNIVERSALITY 763, 764 (Laurence Boisson de Chazournes & Vera Gowlland-Debbas eds., 1st ed. 2001).

with States parties and others about the meaning and scope of particular treaty provisions. In recent years, many of the treaty bodies have used General Comments or General Recommendations to address intersectionality.

The treaty bodies vary in the extent to which they have embraced an intersectional analytical framework in their work, including in their General Comments and General Recommendations. As I discussed in the Introduction, this volume skews toward a focus on the CEDAW Committee, although my arguments about the need for a more robust focus on intersectionality apply to all the human rights treaty bodies. All the treaty bodies offer valuable examples of both intersectional approaches and missed opportunities to use intersectionality as a guiding principle in the important work of interpreting and enforcing human rights. This chapter traces the evolution of intersectionality theory within the work of the treaty bodies, focusing in turn on early conceptions of human rights within the UN, gender mainstreaming within the UN, the role of UN human rights conferences in fostering intersectional analysis, intersectionality as reflected in the text of the treaties, and General Comments and General Recommendations as vehicles through which the treaty bodies have increasingly articulated a commitment to intersectionality.

Human rights and the history of the UN

In the aftermath of World War II, nations around the globe expressed a commitment to the protection of fundamental human rights. The effort to create universal standards for human rights led to the creation of the United Nations. The UN Charter was signed in 1945,[16] obligating members to promote human rights "without distinction as to race, sex, language, or religion."[17] In 1948, the UN General Assembly adopted the Universal Declaration of Human Rights, which established core human rights principles and was to be a "common standard of achievement for all peoples and all nations."[18]

Almost twenty years later, the UN General Assembly adopted two international human rights treaties: the International Covenant on Civil and Political Rights (ICCPR) and the International Covenant on Economic, Social and Cultural Rights (ICESCR). The two covenants differ in the types of rights protected and their protection mechanisms. Some have described civil and political rights as "negative" rights that require the state to cease doing something, such as torturing political prisoners.[19] In contrast, economic, social, and cultural rights are often characterized as "positive"

[16] *Charter of the United Nations*, UNITED NATIONS, https://www.un.org/en/charter-united-nations/index.html (last visited Oct. 15, 2020).

[17] *Chapter IX*, UNITED NATIONS, https://www.un.org/en/about-us/un-charter/chapter-9 (last visited Oct. 15, 2020).

[18] *Universal Declaration of Human Rights*, UNITED NATIONS, https://www.un.org/en/universal-declaration-human-rights/index.html (last visited Oct. 15, 2020).

[19] Ran Hirschl, *"Negative" Rights vs. "Positive" Entitlements: A Comparative Study of Judicial Interpretations of a Rights in an Emerging Neo-Liberal Economic Order*, 22 HUM. RTS. Q. 1060, 1071 (2000).

rights in which the state has some obligation to affirmatively provide something, like access to healthcare or education.[20]

Because ensuring the enjoyment of economic, social, and cultural rights would theoretically require a state to devote substantial financial resources to the effort, the ICESCR generally does not require immediate implementation. Instead, it requires those states that have ratified the convention to "take steps ... to the maximum of [their] available resources, with a view to achieving progressively the full realization of the rights recognized in the present Covenant."[21] However, states that have ratified the ICESCR are still expected to implement certain rights, such as the right to non-discrimination, immediately. The implementation expectations of the ICCPR are considered more stringent, with the expectation that ratifying countries fulfill their obligations under the treaty without delay.[22]

Historically, civil and political rights have occupied a privileged place compared to economic, social, and cultural rights.[23] For decades, the rights in the two treaties were largely treated as separate and disconnected. As Hilary Charlesworth observes, "The primacy traditionally given to civil and political rights by western international lawyers and philosophers is directed toward protection for men within public life, their relationship with government."[24] In contrast to this focus on men in public life, women have more frequently faced violence and other human rights violations at the hands of family members or other private actors. The focus on human rights violations perpetrated by the state against men, often for political or public acts, meant that many of the human rights violations commonly perpetrated against women went unrecognized.[25]

In the 1990s, however, activists and scholars began to articulate a view of human rights as not only universal and inalienable but also indivisible, interdependent, and interrelated.[26] The concepts of indivisibility, interdependence, and interrelatedness grew out of a recognition that the infringement or violation of one right impacts the enjoyment of other rights. This represents a more holistic and realistic view of human rights than the more compartmentalized view commonly held before the 1990s. The UN's Vienna Conference on Human Rights in 1993 helped solidify international recognition of the interconnectedness of human rights.[27] This recognition that rights are dependent on each other began to dismantle the hierarchy of rights that traditionally privileged civil and political rights. The notion of rights as interdependent and interconnected also paved the way for a more nuanced and intersectional understanding of rights.

[20] *Id.*

[21] International Covenant on Economic, Social and Cultural Rights, Art. 2, *opened for signature* Dec. 16, 1966.

[22] *See* Johanna Bond, *International Intersectionality: A Theoretical and Pragmatic Exploration of Women's Human Rights*, 52 EMORY L.J. 71, 86 n.54 (2003) (comparing the obligatory language of the ICESCR to that of the ICCPR).

[23] *Id.* at 87.

[24] Hilary Charlesworth, *What Are "Women's International Human Rights"?*, *in* HUMAN RIGHTS OF WOMEN: NATIONAL AND INTERNATIONAL PERSPECTIVES 58, 71 (Rebecca J. Cook ed., 1994).

[25] Bond, *supra* note 22, at 88–89.

[26] *Id.* at 90 n.71.

[27] *Id.* at 91 nn.72–73.

Gender mainstreaming as a precursor to intersectionality within the United Nations

Gender mainstreaming gained currency in the 1980s and 1990s as a strategy to promote women's rights. International, regional, and national organizations began to insist that all parts of their organization analyze whether a particular law, policy, or other initiative would have a positive or negative effect on women. The UN Economic and Social Council describes gender mainstreaming as "a strategy for making women's as well as men's concerns and experiences an integral dimension of the design, implementation, monitoring and evaluation of policies and programmes ... so that women and men benefit equally and inequality is not perpetuated."[28] Some referred to this as "asking the 'woman' question."[29] The strategy remains a successful way to integrate a gender perspective into the work and, sometimes, the structure of an organization. Some gender mainstreaming initiatives include "gender budgeting" efforts designed to highlight potential financial impact on women or to ensure the inclusion of gender programs within institutional budgets.[30]

The United Nations has widely embraced gender mainstreaming as a strategy to integrate a gender perspective into all of its work more fully.[31] Gender mainstreaming initially surfaced within UN discussions at the Third World Conference on Women in Nairobi in 1985.[32] A decade later, at the 1995 UN Fourth World Conference on Women in Beijing, the concept of gender mainstreaming had firmly taken hold and figured prominently in the conversations and official documents emanating from the conference.[33]

I do not diminish the important contributions of gender mainstreaming as a strategy to bring attention to women's rights within many male-dominated institutions or programs. Gender mainstreaming has undoubtedly improved policy and program outcomes for women throughout the institutions that have embraced the strategy. Although not without drawbacks, the gender mainstreaming campaign has brought attention to the ways in which seemingly gender-neutral policies have a beneficial or adverse effect on women. The approach has opened countless opportunities for women to "take a seat at the table." UN Women, a UN entity dedicated

[28] U.N. Econ. & Soc. Council, Rep. of the Econ. & Soc. Council for the Year 1997, at 24, U.N. Doc. A/52/3/Rev.1 (1999).

[29] *See, e.g.*, Katharine T. Bartlett, *Feminist Legal Methods*, 103 HARV. L. REV. 829, 831 (1990) (defining "asking the 'woman question'" as a feminist legal method that entails "identifying and challenging those elements of existing legal doctrine that leave out or disadvantage women and members of other excluded groups").

[30] *Mainstreaming Gender Perspectives in National Budgets*, UN OFF. OF THE SPECIAL ADVISER ON GENDER ISSUES & ADVANCEMENT OF WOMEN (Jan. 2001), https://www.un.org/womenwatch//osagi/gmtoolsnatlbudgets.htm.

[31] *See generally* UN WOMEN, GENDER MAINSTREAMING: A GLOBAL STRATEGY FOR ACHIEVING GENDER EQUALITY AND THE EMPOWERMENT OF WOMEN AND GIRLS (2020), https://www.unwomen.org/-/media/headquarters/attachments/sections/library/publications/2020/gender-mainstreaming-strategy-for-achieving-gender-equality-and-empowerment-of-women-girls-en.pdf.

[32] Hilary Charlesworth, *Not Waving but Drowning: Gender Mainstreaming and Human Rights in the United Nations*, 18 HARV. HUM. RTS. J. 1, 3 (2005).

[33] *Id.*

to gender equality, suggests that gender mainstreaming is transformative, promoting "changes in norms, cultural values, power structures, and the roots of inequalities and discrimination."[34]

I believe the approach offers considerable value in the promotion of women's rights. Gender mainstreaming, however, must be pursued in combination with other significant strategies for challenging intersectional subordination. For one, a gender mainstreaming approach is attractive in its concreteness and measurability,[35] making it an appealing way to "check a box" in the name of gender justice. In other words, it may offer an easy and concrete way for institutions to fulfill a gender equality mandate while avoiding the difficult work of creating cultural change.

Second, although the move toward gender mainstreaming is, on balance, a positive one, an exclusive focus on gender as an analytical category necessarily limits the intersectional work that it can do. Gender mainstreaming is, in many ways, "intersectionality lite." It is a strategy that encourages limited analysis that gestures at intersectionality but falls short because it runs in only one direction. Mainstreaming encourages institutions to consider the impact on women of a particular policy or initiative. But no corollary encourages gendered institutions such as the CEDAW Committee or UN Women to consider the impact of its initiatives on racial minorities in general or minority women in particular. Gender mainstreaming elevates gender subordination above and possibly to the exclusion of other types of intersecting systems of subordination. Gender mainstreaming efforts might, for example, lead a division focused on disability rights to consider the impact of its disability advocacy on women with disabilities. In fact, gender mainstreaming does quite well in this regard, but it fails to encourage intersectionality that runs in multiple directions. It does little work to encourage gender-based entities or organizations to adopt an intersectional lens in their work on women's rights. It leaves unexamined the many vectors through which other systems of subordination intersect with gender in ways that are critically important for women in communities that vary by, for example, race, ethnicity, religion, disability, sexual orientation, and gender identity.

Exploring intersectionality in the work of the UN treaty bodies, Pok Yin S. Chow cites the example of the Tenth Meeting of the Chairpersons of the Human Rights Treaty Bodies on Integrating a Gender Perspective into the Work of the UN Human Rights Treaty Bodies in 1998 as an important development. Chow quotes the report of the meeting of Chairpersons:

> In order to strengthen the knowledge base about the impact of gender on the conceptualization and implementation of human rights, treaty bodies could call on their secretariats to commission, and on NGOs and the academic community to undertake, studies that would contribute to the clarification of the gender dimensions of

[34] UN WOMEN, *supra* note 31.

[35] *See* Charlesworth, *supra* note 32, at 15 (noting that gender mainstreaming's elision of sex and gender "does not capture the ways in which gender is constructed in a particular society so as to make some actions seem natural and others controversial").

rights. Such studies might, for example, explore the intersection of race and gender in the context of the [CEDAW].[36] (*bracketed text in original*)

Notably, Chow's citation mistakenly inserts "CEDAW" for "CERD," the Committee on the Elimination of Racial Discrimination, in the bracketed text.[37] Although certainly understandable, particularly in light of the UN's penchant for acronyms, the inadvertent substitution is revealing. The original quote from the chairpersons' report encourages CERD to engage in intersectional analysis. The widespread embrace of gender mainstreaming makes it more likely that the chairpersons would encourage non-gender-related entities like CERD to explore the impact of gender, or the intersection of race and gender, in their work. It would be unusual for the treaty body chairpersons to encourage intersectional race and gender analysis in the context of CEDAW, although I argue that they certainly should encourage CEDAW's use of an intersectional framework. The firmly entrenched concept of gender mainstreaming, however, leads the treaty bodies to focus more often on integrating a gender lens into, for example, the work of the CERD Committee, which is precisely what the chairpersons were doing in this example. The success of gender mainstreaming makes it more likely for the treaty bodies to "see" intersectionality in the context of pushing bodies and institutions that are not focused on gender to incorporate a gender perspective. Because intersectionality offers insight into subordination that transcends gender, it goes considerably further than gender mainstreaming in capturing the complexity of multiple intersecting systems of subordination.

The role of UN conferences in fostering intersectional analysis

The 1995 World Conference on Women in Beijing laid the groundwork for wider recognition of intersectionality. The Beijing Declaration and Platform for Action, the outcome document adopted at the Conference, represents an early effort to explore intersectionality.[38] The Declaration recognized that race, ethnicity, age, disability, and socioeconomic position could create additional vulnerability for certain groups of women.[39]

This insight suggests significant movement away from the representation of all "women" as similarly situated in their experiences of discrimination. The universalized

[36] Pok Yin S. Chow, *Has Intersectionality Reached its Limits? Intersectionality in the UN Human Rights Treaty Body Practice and the Issue of Ambivalence*, 16 Hum. Rts. L. Rev. 453, 465 (2016).

[37] *Id.*

[38] *See* Sylvanna M. Falcón, Power Interrupted: Antiracist and Feminist Activism Inside the United Nations 98 (2016) ("The success of world conferences, for NGOs and governments alike, is determined in large part by the content of the accords that are known as the Declaration and the Programme of Action. One way to assess the impact of activism is through these official documents.").

[39] Fourth World Conference on Women, *Beijing Declaration*, U.N. Doc. A/CONF/177/20 (Sept. 15, 1995). The Declaration calls on states to "to ensure equal enjoyment of all human rights and fundamental freedoms for all women and girls who face multiple barriers to their empowerment and advancement because of factors as their race, age, language, ethnicity, culture, religion or disability or because they are indigenous people." *Id.* ¶ 32.

experience of female identity had begun to give way to a more complex and multifaceted understanding of the human condition. The Platform for Action approach, however, was still a long way from fully embracing intersectionality. An "added vulnerability" approach is similar to the additive understanding of multiple identities. It stops short of intersectionality in the sense that it fails to acknowledge that the experience of discrimination at the intersection of sexual orientation and race, for example, is qualitatively different from the experience of discrimination based on sexual orientation or race alone and different from the mere aggregation of sexual orientation discrimination and race discrimination. As discussed in chapter 1, intersectional discrimination is more than the sum of its parts; sexual orientation-based discrimination changes the nature of race discrimination and vice versa. They are mutually constitutive, making it impossible to simply add or subtract one from the other. Nevertheless, the Platform for Action opened the door for intersectionality to play a more prominent role in the UN's preparations for the 2001 Third World Conference against Racism, Racial Discrimination, Xenophobia and Related Intolerance (the WCAR) in Durban.

The WCAR followed two prior UN world conferences addressing racism. The first World Conference to Combat Racism and Racial Discrimination was held in 1978. On the same day that the UN General Assembly approved the first world conference on race, it passed a resolution demanding "the release of all individuals detained or imprisoned as a result of their struggle against apartheid, racism, racial discrimination, colonialism, aggression, and foreign occupation, and for self-determination and independence as well as social progress for their people."[40] The 1978 conference generated considerable controversy stemming from the Israeli–Palestinian conflict, prompting a walkout by some government representatives.[41] The 1978 Declaration and the Programme of Action laid the foundation for intersectionality by calling for "special efforts . . . to eliminate the effect of racial discrimination on the status of women."[42]

The Second World Conference to Combat Racism and Racial Discrimination occurred five years later.[43] During the 1983 conference, organizers celebrated an International Day of Solidarity with the Struggle of Women in South Africa and Namibia.[44] Conference President Héctor Charry-Samper, of Colombia, remarked, "It is an occasion to recall the plight of women who suffer particular indignities under *apartheid* and to promote appropriate assistance to them."[45] Like its 1978 counterpart, the 1983 Declaration and Programme of Action recognized that the racism experienced by women was different in important ways from the racism experienced by men.[46] Sylvanna Falcón notes the brief mention in each declaration that "women are often doubly discriminated against."[47] Although only a small part of the

[40] G.A. Res. 32/122, ¶ 3 (Dec. 16, 1977).

[41] FALCÓN, *supra* note 38, at 100.

[42] Rep. of the World Conference to Combat Racism and Racial Discrimination, Declaration and Programme of Action, 22, U.N. Doc. A/CONF.92/40 (Aug. 25, 1978), https://digitallibrary.un.org/record/2019/files/A_CONF-92_40-EN.pdf.

[43] FALCÓN, *supra* note 38, at 102.

[44] *Id.* at 104.

[45] *Id.*

[46] *Id.* at 107.

[47] *Id.* ("Paragraph 22 of the 1978 Declaration and paragraph 23 of the 1983 Declaration state that 'women are often doubly discriminated against.'").

Declarations and Programmes of Action for both conferences, the recognition of gender-based differences in the experiences of racism opened the door for discussions of intersectionality at the 2001 WCAR.

In the months preceding the 2001 WCAR, the UN hosted four regional preparatory meetings and three additional "PrepCom" meetings in Geneva.[48] The UN also organized an Expert Group Meeting on "Gender and Racial Discrimination." In November 2000, experts gathered in Zagreb, Croatia, to explore the intersection of race and gender in human rights discourse.[49] Kimberlé Crenshaw participated in this expert group meeting, and her influence is palpable in the report of the consultation.[50] This Zagreb meeting placed intersectionality theory firmly on the agenda of the WCAR and emphasized the potential contributions of intersectionality theory within the UN's human rights work.

Also in the lead-up to the WCAR, the UN Special Rapporteur on Violence Against Women, Radhika Coomaraswamy, issued a report about race, gender, and gender-based violence.[51] The report framed its discussion in explicitly intersectional terms and provided background on the theoretical basis of intersectionality. It applied intersectionality theory in the context of the criminal justice system, trafficking, armed conflict, and health. The report, coming from a well-known and well-respected international expert on gender-based violence, offered a detailed road map for applying intersectionality in the human rights context.[52]

Other events organized in preparation for the 2001 WCAR also emphasized intersectionality as an important analytical framework. In 2000, for example, a Bangkok gathering of experts on migration and trafficking embraced an intersectional approach, concluding that "women of certain racial or ethnic groups were subjected to abuses in larger measure than other women, while particular forms of violations, such as trafficking in women and girls frequently involved racist attitudes and perceptions, and were often directed at certain racial and ethnic groups."[53] The preparatory events leading up to the 2001 WCAR generated considerable interest in intersectionality and helped raise awareness of the approach before the conference even began.

The WCAR outcome document included an explicit reference to "multiple forms of discrimination," a concept that would later pave the way for a greater focus on intersectionality in the UN's work.[54] That document, which represents a consensus of the UN General Assembly, reaffirmed that

[48] *Id.* at 109.

[49] World Conference Against Racism, Racial Discrimination, Xenophobia and Related Intolerance, Rep. of the Expert Group Meeting on Gender and Racial Discrimination, 3, U.N. Doc. A/CONF.189/PC.2/20 (May 11, 2001).

[50] *See id.* at annex 1 (listing Kimberlé Crenshaw as a consultant).

[51] Radhika Coomaraswamy (Special Rapporteur of the Commission on Human Rights on Violence Against Women), *Review of Reports, Studies and Other Documentation for the Preparatory Committee and the World Conference*, U.N. Doc. A/CONF.189/PC.3/5 (July 27, 2001).

[52] *See id.* ¶ 8 ("This report attempts to consider the various ways that the lives of some women, particularly migrant, indigenous, immigrant, minority and marginalized women, around the world are shaped, constrained and sometimes lost by the nexus between gender, race, colour or ethnicity and other axes of subordination.").

[53] World Conference Against Racism, Racial Discrimination, Xenophobia and Related Intolerance, *supra* note 49, at 8.

[54] World Conference Against Racism, Racial Discrimination, Xenophobia and Related Intolerance, Declaration and Programme of Action, 7, U.N. Doc. A/CONF.189/12 (Sept. 8, 2001), https://www.oas.org/

> [s]tates have the duty to protect and promote the human rights and fundamental freedoms of all victims, and that they should apply a gender perspective, recognizing the multiple forms of discrimination which women can face, and that the enjoyment of their civil, political, economic, social, and cultural rights is essential for the development of societies throughout the world.[55]

As Falcón observes, the 2001 WCAR Declaration and Programme of Action urged a "broadened approach to racism that introduces new topics such as gender inequality in access to education, violence against women, freedom of religious expression, modern-day human trafficking, and women migrants."[56] The declaration also stated, "[T]he intersection of discrimination on grounds of race and gender makes women and girls particularly vulnerable to ... violence, which is often related to racism, racial discrimination, xenophobia and related intolerance."[57] Patricia Hill Collins and Sirma Bilge note that "[t]he importance of [WCAR] for intersectionality's global reach cannot be overstated."[58] Because WCAR brought together government representatives from 170 states and human rights activists from all over the world, the nascent discussions around intersectionality offered the opportunity to explore the concept in the context of far-reaching and geographically diverse conversations.

Intersectional conversations at the WCAR, however, were not always successful in achieving widespread acceptance of the notion of intersectionality. Toward the end of the conference, as negotiations over the final language of the Declaration and Programme of Action drew to a close, the delegation from Morocco proposed placing brackets around all references to "gender" in the outcome documents. Human rights activists and others speculated that this was a reaction against efforts to conceptualize gender as fluid and encompassing of sexual diversity.[59] As a compromise, the Declaration and Programme of Action did not bracket "gender," but it defined it narrowly, referring to "the two sexes, male and female."[60] Indeed, the outcome documents did not address sexuality, despite the efforts of lesbian, gay, bisexual, transgender, queer and/or questioning, and intersex (LGBTQI) individuals and organizations.[61]

dil/afrodescendants_Durban_Declaration.pdf [hereinafter 2001 WCAR Declaration and Programme of Action].

[55] *Id.* The WCAR NGO Forum Declaration specifically defines intersectionality. The Declaration states An intersectional approach to discrimination acknowledges that every person be it man or woman exists in a framework of multiple identities, with factors such as race, class, ethnicity, religion, sexual orientation, gender identity, age, disability, citizenship, national identity, geo-political context, health, including HIV/AIDS status and any other status are all determinants in one's experiences of racism, racial discrimination, xenophobia and related intolerances. An intersectional approach highlights the way in which there is a simultaneous interaction of discrimination as a result of multiple identities. *WCAR NGO Forum Declaration*, ¶ 119 (Sept. 3, 2001), https://www.hurights.or.jp/wcar/E/ngofinaldc.htm.

[56] Sylvanna M. Falcón, Power Interrupted: Antiracist and Feminist Activism Inside the United Nations 117 (2016).

[57] 2001 WCAR Declaration and Programme of Action, *supra* note 54, at Art. 54(a).

[58] Patricia Hill Collins & Sirma Bilge, Intersectionality 90 (2016).

[59] Jennifer Chan-Tiberghien, *Gender-Skepticism or Gender Boom? Poststructural Feminists, Transnational Feminisms and the World Conference Against Racism*, 6 Int'l Feminist J. of Pol. 454, 462–64 (2004).

[60] 2001 WCAR Declaration and Programme of Action, *supra* note 54, at 8 n.1. *See also* Falcón, *supra* note 56, at 118.

[61] Falcón, *supra* note 56, at 118–19.

In 2001, the same year as the third WCAR, the Commission on the Status of Women (CSW) held its forty-fifth session.[62] Significantly, at this session, the CSW articulated a meaningful commitment to exploring the intersection of gender and other forms of discrimination. At the session, the CSW produced its "draft agreed conclusions on gender and all forms of discrimination, in particular racism, racial discrimination, xenophobia and related intolerance."[63] The document underscored the need to analyze the multiple ways in which different forms of discrimination might affect women and girls.

In 2009, the UN held a follow-up conference to the 2001 WCAR called the Durban Review Conference, with the goal of assessing the progress made in the years since 2001.[64] The 2009 conference "proved extremely disappointing to activists who sought to pick up where the 2001 WCAR had left off."[65] Antiracist feminist activists had hoped to build on the successes of the WCAR in integrating intersectionality into human rights frameworks. But the 2009 follow-up conference largely failed to live up to these expectations. It quickly became bogged down in political battles and strategic posturing by governmental representatives, derailing hopes of advancing the intersectionality conversations that had gained traction in 2001.[66]

More recently, two other UN world conferences reflect modest gains in the use and understanding of intersectionality within the UN's human rights framework. The outcome document of the 2014 World Conference on Indigenous Peoples includes several intersectional commitments, although it does not use the language of intersectionality. The outcome document, for example, notes, "We also commit ourselves to ensuring that national legislative, policy and institutional structures relating to indigenous peoples are inclusive of indigenous persons with disabilities and contribute to the advancement of their rights."[67] The document also urges states to disaggregate data to achieve a better understanding of how Indigeneity intersects with age, gender, and disability.[68] The 2016 UN Summit for Refugees and Migrants also produced a declaration emphasizing that migrant and refugee women are "particularly vulnerable" to rights violations. The declaration uses the language of intersectionality in some places, recognizing the need to "tackle the multiple and intersecting forms of discrimination against refugee and migrant women and girls."[69]

[62] Econ. & Soc. Council, Comm. on the Status of Women, Rep. on the Forty-Fifth Session, U.N. Doc. E/CN.6/2001/14 (2001), https://www.un.org/womenwatch/daw/csw/45sess.htm.

[63] *See* Econ. & Soc. Council Res. 2001/5 (July 24, 2001) (endorsing the agreed conclusions adopted by the CSW at its forty-fifth session).

[64] FALCÓN, *supra* note 56, at 99.

[65] *Id.*

[66] *Id.* at 120.

[67] G.A. Res. 69/2, ¶ 9, Outcome Document of the High-Level Plenary Meeting of the General Assembly Known as the World Conference on Indigenous Peoples (Sept. 25, 2014).

[68] The outcome document commits states to "working with indigenous peoples to disaggregate data … and to utilizing holistic indicators of indigenous peoples' well-being to address the situation and needs of indigenous peoples and individuals, in particular older persons, women, youth, children and persons with disabilities." *Id.* at ¶ 10. The outcome document also makes a commitment to work with indigenous peoples to "prevent and eliminate all forms of violence and discrimination against indigenous peoples and individuals, in particular women, children, youth, older persons and persons with disabilities, by strengthening legal, policy and institutional frameworks." *Id.* at ¶ 18.

[69] G.A. Res. 71/1, ¶ 31, New York Declaration for Refugees and Migrants (Oct. 3, 2016).

UN world conferences such as the 1995 Beijing Conference on Women and the 2001 WCAR in Durban have helped significantly to advance conversations about intersectionality in the human rights context. In the case of both the Beijing and Durban conferences, some of the most important developments stemmed from NGO organizing conferences that preceded the official UN conferences. In the case of the third WCAR, the NGO version of the Declaration and Programme of Action included numerous references to intersectionality, many of which grew out of conversations that occurred during the NGO conference. Although this capacious conception of intersectionality is somewhat pared down in the official WCAR Declaration and Programme of Action, the WCAR outcome documents are highly significant in their broad embrace of intersectionality as a framework for thinking about rights related to race and gender.[70]

Evidence of intersectionality in CEDAW and other UN treaties

As intersectionality theory has gained purchase within human rights discourse since the early 2000s, intersectional frameworks increasingly surface in the text of new international legal instruments. Generally speaking, the more recent the adoption of a human rights treaty, the more likely it is that the treaty will reflect intersectional insights. The 2006 Convention on the Rights of Persons with Disabilities (CRPD) is an example of a treaty that was drafted after intersectionality had begun to influence human rights discourse. As this section demonstrates, the CRPD includes more intersectional language than do earlier treaties such as CEDAW.

The non-binding preamble to CEDAW refers to poverty, racial discrimination, neo-colonialism, and colonialism.[71] The text of the treaty itself mentions neither these issues nor the concept of intersectionality. When the treaty was adopted in 1979, intersectionality had not yet been identified as a formal theoretical approach. Instead, CEDAW defines discrimination in the formal equality terms that were prevalent in discrimination discourse when the treaty was drafted. Article 1 of CEDAW states,

> '[D]iscrimination against women' shall mean any distinction, exclusion or restriction made on the basis of sex which has the effect or purpose of impairing or nullifying the recognition, enjoyment or exercise by women, irrespective of their marital status, on a basis of equality of men and women, of human rights and fundamental freedoms in the political, economic, social, cultural, civil or any other field.[72]

CEDAW's definition of discrimination is both broad and narrow. CEDAW includes a broad definition of prohibited discrimination, encompassing not only the concept

[70] Falcón notes that the NGO and government representatives have different objectives and roles in navigating the sometimes fraught politics of a world conference. SYLVANNA M. FALCÓN, POWER INTERRUPTED: ANTIRACIST AND FEMINIST ACTIVISM INSIDE THE UNITED NATIONS 116–17 (2016).

[71] Convention on the Elimination of All Forms of Discrimination Against Women, *opened for signature* Mar. 1, 1980, 1249 U.N.T.S. 13 [hereinafter CEDAW].

[72] *Id.* at Art. 1.

of formal equality but also the notion of substantive equality. The Convention, for example, requires States parties to take temporary special measures to promote women in certain circumstances, going beyond what would be required by a simple formal equality requirement. The Convention also requires substantive equality in terms of equality of opportunity, meaning that States parties not only must provide equal opportunities for women and girls, but must also work to dismantle the structural barriers that might prevent women and girls from accessing opportunities.[73]

The language of the Convention also prohibits treatment which "has the effect or purpose" of discriminating against women.[74] The Convention's prohibition on discrimination thus does not require intent to discriminate. Differential treatment that merely has the effect of impairing women's enjoyment of their rights, as compared to men, runs afoul of the treaty's non-discrimination provision. The Convention prohibits both de jure and de facto discrimination, making the Convention's prohibition of discrimination quite broad.

At the same time, the drafters chose language that limits the reach of the Convention. The Convention, for example, limits complainants to women rather than to anyone who has suffered discrimination on the basis of sex. Among drafters, "the overwhelming view was that such a symmetrical approach would fail to recognize the pervasive discrimination against women on the basis of their sex."[75] Yet by focusing on women, the Convention's text "enshrines the male/female binary in the core of international law when CEDAW's goals would be better served by seeking the elimination of the categories themselves."[76] Gender stereotyping can certainly have a negative impact on men and can perpetuate rigid gender roles for both men and women. The Convention's reach is constrained, however, by allowing only complaints from women.

Although CEDAW's text prohibits "sex" discrimination rather than "gender" discrimination, subsequent communications from the Committee have established that the prohibition on discrimination extends well beyond biological sex. The concept of gender was not yet part of the common vocabulary in international human rights law at the time of CEDAW's drafting. The treaty, however, is a "dynamic instrument that accommodates the development of international law."[77] It is now, in fact, commonly understood to encompass gender discrimination as well as discrimination based on biological sex. The drafters' inclusion of Article 5, which focuses on gender stereotypes, confirms that they were concerned with the social construction of gender and hoped to combat rigid role definition for women and men.[78]

I argue that it is precisely this elasticity in the concept of gender that brings issues related to sexuality and gender identity within the purview of the Convention. Several developments in international human rights law support this expansive reading of

[73] Andrew Byrnes, *Article 1*, *in* The UN Convention on the Elimination of All Forms of Discrimination Against Women: A Commentary 51, 53 (Marsha A. Freeman et al. eds., 2012).

[74] CEDAW, *supra* note 71, at Art. 1.

[75] Byrnes, *supra* note 73, at 52.

[76] Darren Rosenblum, *Unsex CEDAW, or What's Wrong with Women's Rights*, 20 Colum. J. Gender & L. 98, 101 (2011).

[77] Christine Chinkin & Marsha A. Freeman, *Introduction*, *in* The UN Convention on the Elimination of All Forms of Discrimination Against Women: A Commentary 1, 13 (Marsha A. Freeman et al. eds., 2012).

[78] Byrnes, *supra* note 73, at 64.

gender discrimination. Indeed, "[t]here is, in principle, no reason why the Convention should not be applied to provide protection for women who are discriminated against because of their sexuality."[79] The CEDAW Committee, however, has been cautious in evaluating rights violations based on sexual orientation and gender identity.[80] As I have argued elsewhere, an expansive understanding of gender discrimination would allow the CEDAW Committee to meaningfully combat the criminalization of same-sex sexual activity and to extend protection from gender-based violence to victims who are targeted based on non-conforming gender or sexuality.[81] This understanding of the relationship between gender and sexuality is consistent with an intersectional approach that explores the intersecting systems of subordination based on gender, sexual orientation, gender identity, and other aspects of identity.

Other human rights entities both within and beyond the UN have gone further than the CEDAW Committee in denouncing and specifically prohibiting discrimination and violence against LGBTQI individuals.[82] In 2007, a group of internationally recognized experts released the "Yogyakarta Principles," a set of guiding principles that apply international human rights law to sexual orientation and gender identity.[83] Since then, the notion that general prohibitions on gender discrimination include non-discrimination protection for LGBTQI individuals has gained currency within the human rights treaty bodies.[84] Rather than leading the charge, however, the CEDAW Committee has been reluctant to embrace LGBTQI rights in a robust and consistent way. As I argue more fully in chapter 5, this reluctance represents a missed opportunity for the CEDAW Committee to use an intersectional framework to recognize, promote, and protect LGBTQI rights.

Although it does not delve deeply into intersectionality, CEDAW's text opens the door for consideration of the different ways that certain subgroups of women might experience discrimination. CEDAW includes several articles addressing specific forms of discrimination that affect certain women, including discrimination because of living in rural areas,[85] nationality,[86] age,[87] and marital status.[88] This more particular understanding of discrimination represents a departure from the rest of the treaty

[79] *Id.*

[80] *Id. See also* Rosenblum, *supra* note 76, at 175 ("The focus on 'women' in CEDAW leaves transgender individuals in the difficult position of questionable international law subjectivity.").

[81] Johanna Bond, *Gender and Non-Normative Sex in Sub-Saharan Africa*, 23 MICH. J. GENDER & L. 65, 71 (2016).

[82] *See, e.g.*, U.N. High Comm'r for Human Rights, *Discriminatory Laws and Practices and Acts of Violence Against Individuals Based on Their Sexual Orientation and Gender Identity: Report of the United Nations High Commissioner for Human Rights*, U.N. Doc. A/HRC/19/41 (Nov. 17, 2011) (arguing that the Human Rights Council's mandate requires it to combat violence and discrimination based on sexual orientation and gender identity); *see also* Ignacio Saiz, *Bracketing Sexuality: Human Rights and Sexual Orientation: A Decade of Development and Denial at the UN*, 7 HEALTH & HUM. RTS. 48, 51–52 (2004) (providing examples of how "treaty-monitoring bodies of the UN have helped consolidate the principle that sexual-orientation discrimination is proscribed in international human rights law").

[83] Bond, *supra* note 81, at 73–74.

[84] *Id.* at 75–81 (detailing the progress in recognizing LGBTQI rights within the human rights treaty bodies).

[85] CEDAW, Art. 14, *opened for signature* Mar. 1, 1980, 1249 U.N.T.S. 13.

[86] *Id.* at Art. 9.

[87] *Id.* at Art. 10.

[88] *Id.* at Art. 1, Art. 16.

text, which skews toward universalizing women's experiences of discrimination. The universalizing tendency of most of the convention is a product of both history and strategy. As noted earlier, the insights of intersectionality simply were not widely understood at the time of CEDAW's drafting. Moreover, the strategy of aligning women in and organizing women around the common experience of gender discrimination was a crucial strategy in the late 1970s, when the world had not yet been convinced that gender discrimination was a large-scale, global problem worthy of international, regional, and local attention.

Like CEDAW, the Migrant Workers Convention, which was adopted by the UN General Assembly in 1990, does not reflect the insights of intersectionality theory in the text of the treaty.[89] In contrast, later UN treaties, such as the Convention on the Rights of Persons with Disabilities, evidence a more developed understanding of intersectionality.[90] The UN General Assembly adopted the CRPD in 2006, making it one of the newest multilateral human rights treaties, and one drafted after intersectionality theory had surfaced intermittently in human rights discourse. The Convention's text and supporting documents reflect the evolving understanding and embrace of intersectionality by international actors within the UN system. The preamble to the Convention recognizes the difficult conditions faced by persons with disabilities, "who are subject to multiple or aggravated forms of discrimination on the basis of race, colour, sex, language, religion, political or other opinion, national, ethnic, indigenous or social origin, property, birth, age or other status."[91] Articles 6 and 7 of the Convention, addressing women with disabilities and children with disabilities, respectively, with the latter specifically recognizing multiple discrimination.[92] This treaty language acknowledging "multiple discrimination" represents an embrace of intersectionality that was largely nonexistent in the human rights context even fifteen years before the drafting of the convention.

Like the CRPD, the International Convention for the Protection of All Persons from Enforced Disappearances (CPED), which the UN General Assembly also adopted in 2006, reflects gradual movement toward intersectional analysis. Although the treaty does not use explicitly intersectional terminology, it does differentiate the

[89] Convention on the Protection of the Rights of All Migrant Workers and Members of Their Families, *adopted* Dec. 18, 1990, 2220 U.N.T.S. 3 (entered into force July 1, 2003). Margaret Satterthwaite has persuasively argued, however, that an intersectional approach to migrant workers' rights is essential and can be situated within the existing rights guarantees of other human rights treaties. *See generally* Margaret L. Satterthwaite, *Crossing Borders, Claiming Rights: Using Human Rights Law to Empower Women Migrant Workers*, 8 YALE HUM. RTS. & DEV. L.J. (2005).

[90] Convention on the Rights of Persons with Disabilities and its Optional Protocol, U.N. Doc. A/RES/61/106, *opened for signature* Mar. 30, 2007 [hereinafter CRPD]. The International Convention on the Protection of the Rights of All Migrant Workers and Members of Their Families, adopted in 1990, includes provisions that reflect implicit concern for the intersection of socioeconomic status and membership in minority ethnic and linguistic minority communities. *See, e.g.*, International Convention on the Protection of the Rights of All Migrant Workers and Members of their Families, Art. 25(1), U.N. Doc. A/RES/45/158, *adopted on* Dec. 18, 1990, 2220 U.N.T.S. 3 ("Migrant workers shall enjoy treatment not less favourable than that which applies to nationals of the State of employment in respect of remuneration.").

[91] CRPD, *supra* note 90, Preamble.

[92] *Id.* at Arts. 6, 7. *See also* U.N. Comm. on the Rts. of Persons with Disabilities, General Comment No. 3 on Article 6: Women and Girls with Disabilities, U.N. Doc. CRPD/C/GC/3 (2016) (explaining ways in which women and girls with disabilities are subject to multiple discrimination and positive measures States parties should take to ensure full implementation of the provisions of CRPD Article 6).

circumstances of "pregnant women, minors, persons with disabilities or other particularly vulnerable persons."[93] The language in both the CRPD and the CPED represents a shift toward intersectionality-like analysis. In both cases, the conventions stop short of robust intersectional language, opting instead for a more limited recognition of circumstances that might make a human rights victim "particularly vulnerable."

Evolving intersectional understanding in general comments and recommendations

General Recommendations and General Comments offer guidance to states in interpreting treaty provisions. Although they are not legally binding, these documents offer vital information about the meaning and breadth of particular treaty provisions. In recent years, many of the treaty bodies have used these as vehicles to address intersectionality.

One of the earliest articulations of a treaty body's commitment to intersectional analysis came from the Committee on the Elimination of Race Discrimination. In March 2000, CERD adopted General Recommendation No. 25 entitled "Gender Related Dimensions of Racial Discrimination."[94] It observes:

> Certain forms of racial discrimination may be directed towards women specifically because of their gender, such as sexual violence committed against women members of particular racial or ethnic groups in detention or during armed conflict; the coerced sterilization of indigenous women; abuse of women workers in the informal sector or domestic workers employed abroad by their employers.[95]

General Recommendation No. 25 expressed a commitment to intersectionality in the committee's work and laid the foundation for other treaty bodies to incorporate an intersectional approach. Also in 2000, the Human Rights Committee adopted a General Comment noting that "[d]iscrimination against women is often intertwined with discrimination on other grounds."[96] Although General Comment No. 28 does not refer to intersectionality, the notion of "intertwined" rights opened the door for an emerging understanding of intersectional human rights.

[93] Convention for the Protection of All Persons from Enforced Disappearances, Art. 7, U.N. Doc. A/61/448, *adopted on* Dec. 20, 2006. 2716 U.N.T.S. 3. Additionally, the CPED states, "Nothing in this Convention shall be interpreted as imposing an obligation to extradite if . . . the request has been made for the purpose of prosecuting or punishing a person on account of that person's sex, race, religion, nationality, ethnic origin, political opinions or membership of a particular social group, or that compliance with the request would cause harm to that person for any one of these reasons." *Id.* at Art. 13.

[94] Comm. on the Elimination of Race Discrimination, Rep. of the Comm. on the Elimination of Race Discrimination on Its Fifty-Sixth and Fifty-Seventh Sessions, General Recommendation No. 25: Gender Related Dimensions of Racial Discrimination, U.N. Doc. A/55/18 (2000).

[95] *Id.* ¶ 2.

[96] Off. of the High Comm'r for Hum. Rts., General Comment 28: Article 3 (The Equality of Rights Between Men and Women), ¶ 30, U.N. Doc. CCPR/C/21/Rev.1/Add.10 (Mar. 29, 2000).

The CERD Committee reiterated its commitment to an intersectional approach when it adopted a General Recommendation concerning the scope of obligations under CERD. General Recommendation No. 32, adopted in 2009, states:

> The 'grounds' of discrimination are extended in practice by the notion of 'intersectionality' whereby the Committee addresses situations of double or multiple discrimination—such as discrimination on grounds of gender or religion—when discrimination on such a ground appears to exist in combination with a ground or grounds listed in article 1 of the Convention.[97]

Another CERD General Recommendation, No. 30, focuses on the rights of non-citizens and mentions the need to "pay greater attention to the issue of multiple discrimination faced by non-citizens."[98]

By 2009, the Committee on the Rights of the Child (CRC) was also beginning to explore notions of intersectionality in its work on children's human rights.[99] The CRC recognized that multiple forms of discrimination might intersect in a child's life. In 2009, the CRC adopted General Comment No. 11, which noted the particular challenges faced by indigenous girl children and indigenous children with disabilities.[100] An earlier General Recommendation on HIV/AIDS recognized how discrimination because of age and HIV status could simultaneously shape a child's experiences of discrimination.[101] By recognizing the particular challenges faced by, for example, indigenous girl children, the CRC began to explore the intersecting effects of structural racism and gender subordination in its General Comments.

Other treaty bodies also began to use General Comments or General Recommendations as a vehicle for exploring intersecting forms of subordination and the resulting human rights violations. In a 2009 General Comment, for example, the Committee on Economic, Social and Cultural Rights (CESCR) noted that "[s]ome individuals or groups of individuals face discrimination on more than one of the prohibited grounds, for example women belonging to an ethnic or religious minority. Such cumulative discrimination has a unique and specific impact on individuals and merits particular consideration and remedying."[102] The Committee gave the example

[97] Off. of the High Comm'r for Hum. Rts., Comm. on the Elimination of Race Discrimination General Recommendation No. 32: The Meaning and Scope of Special Measures in the International Convention on the Elimination of All Forms of Racial Discrimination, ¶ 7, U.N. Doc. CERD/C/GC/32 (Sept. 24, 2009).

[98] Off. of the High Comm'r for Hum. Rts., Comm. on the Elimination of Race Discrimination General Recommendation No. 30 on Discrimination Against Non-Citizens, ¶ 8, U.N. Doc. CERD/C/64/Misc.11/rev.3 (Oct. 1, 2002).

[99] *See, e.g.*, Comm. on the Rts. of the Child, General Comment No. 15 (2013) on the Right of the Child to the Enjoyment of the Highest Attainable Standard of Health (Art. 24), ¶ 8, U.N. Doc. CRC/C/GC/15 (Apr. 17, 2013) ("Attention should also be given to any other forms of discrimination that might undermine children's health, and the implications of multiple forms of discrimination should also be addressed.").

[100] Comm. on the Rts. of the Child, General Comment No. 11 on Indigenous Children and Their Rights Under the Convention, ¶ 29, U.N. Doc. CRC/C/GC/11 (2009).

[101] *See* Comm. on the Rts. of the Child, General Comment No. 3 on HIV/AIDS and the Rights of the Child, ¶ 1 U.N. Doc. CRC/GC/2003/3 (Mar. 17, 2003) ("The [HIV/AIDS] epidemic . . . increases the victimization and marginalization of children, especially those living in particularly difficult circumstances.").

[102] Comm. on Econ., Soc., & Cultural Rights, General Comment No. 20 on Non-Discrimination in Economic, Social, and Cultural rights, ¶ 17, UN Doc. E/C.12/GC/20 (July 2, 2009).

of a woman denied social services on the basis of gender and disability discrimination.[103] The Committee's recognition of the cumulative effects of gender and disability discrimination demonstrated its willingness to move beyond the overly simplistic analysis of single-axis discrimination. Like those of many of the other treaty bodies, these early forays into intersectional-like analysis took the form of recognition that one might experience two forms of discrimination simultaneously. It fell short of a full-throated endorsement of intersectionality, but pronouncements like this opened the door for the development of intersectionality in more fulsome and nuanced forms in later years.

The CEDAW Committee has made similar progress in recognizing the complexity of gender discrimination and the many ways that gender discrimination intersects with other forms of discrimination. The CEDAW Committee first recognized the intersection of sex discrimination and discrimination based on disability in 1991 in General Recommendation No. 18.[104] The Committee continued to develop its intersectional analysis in General Recommendations over the years. By 2004, the CEDAW Committee recognized that

> [c]ertain groups of women, in addition to suffering from discrimination directed against them as women, may also suffer from multiple forms of discrimination based on additional grounds such as race, ethnic or religious identity, disability, age, class, caste or other factors.... States parties may need to take specific temporary special measures to eliminate such multiple forms of discrimination against women and its compounded negative impact on them.[105]

The Committee further explored intersectional discrimination in 2008 when it adopted a General Recommendation on migrant women and expressly recognized that women migrant workers may experience intersectional rights violations.[106] In 2008, the CEDAW Committee adopted Reporting Guidelines that required states to disaggregate data when reporting to the Committee.[107] Specifically, the Guidelines required states to include information related to "different groups of women, in particular those subject to multiple forms of discrimination."[108] The Committee's desire for disaggregated statistics, as articulated in the 2008 Reporting Guidelines, offers further evidence that it wanted to track the effects of intersectional discrimination.

[103] *Id.* ¶ 27.

[104] Comm. on the Elimination of Discrimination Against Women, 10th Sess., General Recommendation No. 18 on Disabled Women, U.N. Doc. A/46/38 (1991).

[105] Comm. on the Elimination of Discrimination Against Women, 30th Sess., General Recommendation No. 25 on Article 4, Paragraph 1 of the Convention on the Elimination of All Forms of Discrimination Against Women, on Temporary Special Measures), ¶ 12, U.N. Doc. A/59/38 (2004).

[106] Comm. on the Elimination of Discrimination Against Women, 42d Sess., General Recommendation No. 26 on Women Migrant Workers, U.N. Doc. CEDAW/C/2009/WP.1/R (Dec. 5, 2008). *See id.* ¶ 14 ("Women migrant workers often experience intersecting forms of discrimination, suffering not only sex—and gender-based discrimination but also xenophobia and racism.").

[107] Comm. on the Elimination of Discrimination Against Women, Decision 40/I: Convention-Specific Reporting Guidelines of the Committee on the Elimination of All Forms of Discrimination Against Women, Annex 1 ¶ 12, U.N. Doc A63/38 (Aug. 6, 2008).

[108] *Id.* Annex 1 ¶ E.5.

In late 2010, the CEDAW Committee adopted General Recommendation No. 28 on "the core obligations of States parties under Article 2 of the Convention on the Elimination of All Forms of Discrimination Against Women."[109] The General Recommendation underscored the importance of intersectionality, stating that "[i]ntersectionality is a basic concept for understanding the scope of the general obligations of States parties contained in Article 2."[110] Also in 2010, the Committee adopted a General Recommendation concerning older women.[111] In it, the Committee recognized that "the discrimination experienced by older women is often multidimensional, with the age factor compounding other forms of discrimination based on gender, ethnic origin, disability, poverty levels, sexual orientation and gender identity, migrant status, marital and family status, literacy and other grounds."[112] The Committee has continued to apply intersectionality—to varying degrees—in several of its subsequent General Recommendations, including those dealing with women and armed conflict,[113] rural women,[114] and women's access to justice.[115]

CEDAW has, on occasion, missed important opportunities to use an intersectional framework to promote human rights. In the 2013 General Recommendation No. 29 on the Economic Consequences of Marriage, Family Relations, and Their Dissolution (Article 16),[116] the Committee notes that families come in many forms but stops well short of fully recognizing the intersectional rights of LGBTQI women. The General Recommendation notes that same-sex relationships "are not legally, socially or culturally accepted in a considerable number of States parties."[117] Instead of using an intersectional approach to demonstrate that CEDAW requires States parties to prohibit discrimination against LGBTQI women, the Committee merely notes that where states recognize same-sex relationships, they should protect women's economic rights.[118]

In 2014, the CEDAW Committee and the CRC adopted a Joint General Recommendation No. 31/General Comment No. 18 on harmful practices.[119]

[109] Comm. on the Elimination of Discrimination Against Women, General Recommendation No. 28 on the Core Obligations of States Parties Under Article 2 of the Convention on the Elimination of All Forms of Discrimination Against Women, UN Doc. CEDAW/C/GC/28 (Dec. 16, 2010).

[110] *Id.* ¶ 18.

[111] *See* Comm. on the Elimination of Discrimination Against Women, General Recommendation No. 27 on Older Women and Protection of Their Human Rights, UN Doc. CEDAW/C/GC/27 (Dec. 16, 2010) (affirming a commitment to the protection of all women, regardless of their age).

[112] *Id.* ¶ 13.

[113] Comm. on the Elimination of Discrimination Against Women, General Recommendation No. 30 on Women in Conflict Prevention, Conflict and Post-Conflict Situations, ¶¶ 6–7, U.N. Doc. CEDAW/C/GC/30 (Nov. 1, 2013).

[114] Comm. on the Elimination of Discrimination Against Women, General Recommendation No. 34 on the Rights of Rural Women, ¶¶ 14–15, U.N. Doc. CEDAW/C/GC/34 (Mar. 4, 2016).

[115] Comm. on the Elimination of Discrimination Against Women, General Recommendation No. 33 on Women's Access to Justice, ¶ 8, UN Doc. CEDAW/C/GC/33 (Aug. 3, 2015).

[116] Comm. on the Elimination of Discrimination Against Women, General Recommendation No. 29 on Article 16 of the Convention on the Elimination of All Forms of Discrimination Against Women (Economic Consequences of Marriage, Family Relations and Their Dissolution), UN Doc. CEDAW/C/GC/29 (Oct. 30, 2013).

[117] *Id.* ¶ 24.

[118] *Id.*

[119] Comm. on the Elimination of Discrimination Against Women & Comm. on the Rts. of the Child, Joint General Recommendation No. 31 of the Committee on the Elimination of Discrimination Against Women / General Comment No. 18 of the Committee on the Rights of the Child on Harmful Practices,

Significantly, it was the first time that two UN treaty bodies had collaborated on and jointly issued a General Recommendation.[120] The document states:

> The Committees draw States parties' attention to the fact that sex- and gender-based discrimination intersects with other factors that affect women and girls, in particular those who belong to, or are perceived as belonging to, disadvantaged groups, and who are therefore at a higher risk of becoming victims of harmful practices.[121]

Notably, the General Recommendation specifically uses intersectional terminology, stating, "Harmful practices are persistent practices and forms of behaviour that are grounded in discrimination on the basis of, among other things, sex, gender age, in addition to multiple and/or intersecting forms of discrimination that often involve violence and cause physical and/or psychological harm or suffering."[122] Although it makes only a passing reference to intersectionality, the jointly authored General Recommendation signals a burgeoning commitment to intersectional theory.

Perhaps even more important than the substance of Joint General Recommendation No. 31 was the committees' willingness to collaborate on a joint General Recommendation. International human rights scholars, including myself, have criticized the primary human rights treaty bodies in the past for their compartmentalized approach to human rights violations.[123] Historically, the treaty bodies have shown little inclination toward collaboration or joint work, despite considerable overlap in certain rights and treaty language.[124] The CRC and CEDAW joint General Recommendation represents a step in the right direction. As described more fully in chapter 8, more collaborative work will help to break down the institutional barriers that continue to inhibit the full embrace of an intersectional rights framework.

A subsequent General Recommendation in 2014 reaffirmed the CEDAW Committee's evolving commitment to intersectionality, naming the gender-related dimensions of refugee status, asylum, nationality, and statelessness of women.[125] In this articulation of intersectionality, the CEDAW Committee expresses an increasingly

U.N. Doc. CEDAW/C/GC/31-CRC/C/GC/18 (Nov. 14, 2014) [hereinafter Joint General Recommendation No. 31].

[120] Ivona Truscan & Joanna Bourke-Martignoni, *International Human Rights Law and Intersectional Discrimination*, 16 Equal Rts. Rev. 103, 125 (2016). *See also* Bond, *supra* note 1 (arguing for greater collaboration between human rights treaty bodies as a way to foster intersectionality, including through jointly issued General Recommendations).

[121] Joint General Recommendation No. 31, ¶ 6.

[122] *Id.* ¶ 15.

[123] *See* Bond, *supra* note 1, at 74 ("The current theoretical foundations, organizational structure, and practice of the United Nations and many nongovernmental organizations (NGOs) does not permit a nuanced human rights analysis that would account for multiple forms of human rights abuses occurring simultaneously.").

[124] *See, e.g., id.* at 164 (noting that even when chairpersons of treaty bodies have had formal opportunities to "engage in cross-treaty dialogue and share substantive and procedural information," these meetings "have not resulted in significantly greater coordination or collaboration between the Committees").

[125] Comm. on the Elimination of Discrimination Against Women, General Recommendation No. 32 on the Gender-Related Dimensions of Refugee Status, Asylum, Nationality and Statelessness of Women, U.N. Doc. CEDAW/C/GC/32 (Nov. 14, 2014).

sophisticated understanding of intersectionality as well as an ideological commitment to intersectionality as a theoretical framework. The Committee states:

> Discrimination against women based on sex and/or gender is often inextricably linked with and compounded by other factors that affect women, such as race, ethnicity, religion or belief, health, age, class, caste, being lesbian, bisexual or transgender and other status. Discrimination on the basis of sex or gender may affect women belonging to such groups to a different degree or in different ways to men. States parties must legally recognize such intersecting forms of discrimination and their compounded negative impact on the women concerned and prohibit them.[126]

This excerpt from General Recommendation No. 32 represents a significant change in the way that the CEDAW Committee approaches intersectionality. In addition to a deeper understanding of how intersectional discrimination affects the lives of many, the Committee also clearly articulates a related state obligation to do something to remediate it. By specifically cautioning that "States parties must legally recognize" intersectionality, the CEDAW Committee offers its most forceful articulation of state obligations concerning intersectionality to date. General Recommendation No. 32 demonstrates a clear and steady evolution in the Committee's willingness to consider discrimination through an intersectional lens.

Building on this strong foundation, CEDAW further elaborates its understanding of intersectionality in the context of gender-based violence in General Recommendation No. 35, which it adopted in 2017. General Recommendation No. 35 recognizes the disparate effects of gender-based violence stemming from intersecting forms of discrimination.[127] In discussing remedies for gender-based violence, General Recommendation No. 35 specifically calls on States parties to consider intersectionality in "areas of prevention, protection, prosecution and punishment, redress, data collection and monitoring and international cooperation."[128] General Recommendation No. 35 continues CEDAW's trajectory toward increased recognition of intersectionality in its General Recommendations. Because General Comments and General Recommendations often provide states with a roadmap for treaty implementation, the treaty bodies' inclusion of intersectionality in these documents can have a significant impact on the extent to which states internalize the normative content of rights guarantees, including intersectional interpretations of rights.

Further developments

There is further evidence that the UN's human rights apparatus is increasingly committed to exploring intersectionality in its work. The Conference of States Parties to

[126] *Id.* ¶ 6.

[127] Comm. on the Elimination of Discrimination Against Women, General Recommendation No. 35 on gender-based violence against women, updating General Recommendation No. 19, ¶ ¶ 12, 23, 28, 30, 31, 32, 34, U.N. Doc. CEDAW/C/GC/35 (July 26, 2017).

[128] *Id.* ¶ 28.

the CRPD held a roundtable discussion in 2017 on the theme "Addressing the impact of multiple discrimination on persons with disabilities, and promoting their participation and multi-stakeholder partnerships for achieving the Sustainable Development Goals in line with the Convention."[129] Drafters, who prepared the document to facilitate discussion at the roundtable explicitly embraced an intersectional approach to the human rights issues faced by persons with disabilities. The document states, "The realization of the human rights and fundamental freedoms of all persons with disabilities, and their full and effective participation and inclusion in society, are hindered by the impact of multiple and intersecting forms of discrimination."[130] The document frames the roundtable discussion by establishing the relevance of intersectionality and then proposing several questions for consideration. It sets the stage for an intersectional discussion, observing:

> Available data show that the employment rate for women with disabilities is more than 30 per cent lower than that for men with disabilities (19.6 per cent compared with 52.8 per cent, respectively), while girls with disabilities are more likely to be socially excluded than boys with disabilities, which has a direct bearing on their educational trajectory. Women and girls with disabilities experience violence at a rate that is up to 3 times higher than that of their peers without disabilities, and they are up to 10 times more likely to experience sexual violence. In addition, indigenous persons with disabilities often experience multiple and intersecting forms of discrimination on the basis of both their indigenous identity and as persons with disabilities.[131]

The grounding of this 2017 roundtable conversation within the Conference of States Parties to the CRPD is significant in the extent to which the drafters incorporated intersectional analysis into the discussion of disability-related human rights violations.

Meanwhile, the United Nations High Commissioner for Human Rights issued a 2017 report to the Human Rights Council at its 35th Session entitled "Impact of multiple and intersecting forms of discrimination and violence in the context of racism, racial discrimination, xenophobia and related intolerance on the full enjoyment of all human rights by women and girls."[132] The High Commissioner prepared his report pursuant to a request from the Human Rights Council that the Commissioner explore intersectional human rights violations based on race and gender "with a view to identifying challenges and good practices."[133]

The 2017 report details many of the UN's efforts to recognize the intersectional human rights violations faced by women and girls.[134] It also explores a number of

[129] Conference of States Parties to the Convention on the Rights of Persons with Disabilities, 10th Sess., Addressing the Impact of Multiple Discrimination on Persons with Disabilities, and Promoting their Participation and Multi-Stakeholder Partnerships for Achieving the Sustainable Development Goals in Line with the Convention, U.N. Doc. CRPD/CSP/2017/2 (Mar. 27, 2017).

[130] *Id.* ¶ 1.

[131] *Id.* ¶ 3 (internal citations omitted).

[132] U.N. High Comm'r for Hum. Rts., *Impact of Multiple and Intersecting Forms of Discrimination and Violence in the Context of Racism, Racial Discrimination, Xenophobia and Related Intolerance on the Full Enjoyment of All Human Rights by Women and Girls*, U.N. Doc. A/HRC/35/10 (Apr. 21, 2017).

[133] *Id.* ¶ 1.

[134] *Id.* ¶¶ 4–13.

intersectional human rights violations that affect women and girls throughout the world, including socioeconomic exclusion and poverty, education, health, violence against women and girls, limits on autonomy, participation and representation of women in public life, and equality before the law and access to justice.[135] The report is impressive in its scope and mentions several examples of intersectional human rights abuses, including labor conditions faced by female migrant workers, indigenous women's access to land, and access to medical treatment for women and girls from ethnic minority groups.[136] The High Commissioner recognized a range of intersectional issues and explicitly embraced an intersectional framework for further investigation of the human rights violations at stake.[137]

The report represents considerable progress in the UN's commitment to exploring a wide range of intersectional human rights violations. As such, it is highly significant in the evolution of the UN's commitment to intersectionality in the human rights context. Although the report focuses on intersectional violations faced by women and girls, it is surely a harbinger of an increased commitment to intersectionality in human rights that extends beyond gender-based violations.

As this chapter's survey of the history of intersectionality in the UN demonstrates, the treaty bodies have moved from a focus on singular, mutually exclusive grounds for discrimination to occasional references to "multiple" or "double" discrimination to a more explicit embrace of "intersectionality." Intersectionality has evolved in the work of the treaty bodies along four primary vectors: the promotion of gender mainstreaming; the discourse on intersectionality at major UN conferences; the text of the treaties themselves; and the content of the treaty bodies' oversight efforts, including General Comments or General Recommendations. These developments demonstrate a trend within the more recent work of the human rights treaty bodies toward greater recognition of intersectionality. This evolution in thinking about discrimination represents a shift away from the notion of discrimination resulting from a single ground to discrimination based on multiple, intersecting identity categories. As I will explore in the next chapter, parallel trends within regional human rights systems similarly show an increasing commitment to and embrace of intersectional human rights violations.

[135] *Id.* at Parts III.A–F.

[136] *Id.* at ¶¶ 13, 19, 25.

[137] *See, e.g.*, *id.* at ¶ 65 (recommending that "indicators be developed to measure inequalities on the basis of a combination of such variables as race, ethnicity, religion or gender" and that "[r]esearch and analysis on intersecting forms of discrimination against women and girls be strengthened").

4
Intersectionality and Human Rights within Regional Human Rights Systems

Regional human rights systems have become increasingly important in the protection of human rights. Although they have their own human rights treaties and enforcement mechanisms, the regional systems operate alongside and complement the UN's human rights treaty system. They provide a complaint mechanism through which individuals may seek redress for a violation of rights and monitor and promote human rights within the region. Each of the regional systems consists of an intergovernmental organization composed of member states, such as the African Union, the Organization of American States, the Council of Europe, the League of Arab States, and the Association of Southeast Asian Nations (ASEAN). This chapter limits its analysis to the three most well-established regional systems: the African system, the inter-American system, and the European system. The two other regional systems, the ASEAN Intergovernmental Commission on Human Rights and the Arab Human Rights Committee, began operations in 2009 and are too new to assess meaningfully.[1]

Regional systems are, in theory, particularly responsive to regional concerns and reflective of regional norms. They are closer to the people they are intended to serve. As such, they supplement and reinforce international human rights norms in ways that are imbued with more localized norms and methods. Imani Perry, a professor at the Center for African American Studies at Princeton University, describes the influences of contextual factors in the construction of race, observing that race "is produced by social arrangements and political decision making" and stating, "race is something that happens, rather than something that is."[2] Perry's observations about the constructed nature of race underscore the importance of local and regional context. Regional approaches to intersectionality may reflect regional differences in the construction of and emphasis on, for example, racial, ethnic, or religious identity:

[1] ASEAN is an intergovernmental organization consisting of ten Member States (Brunei Darussalam, Cambodia, Indonesia, Laos, Malaysia, Myanmar, the Philippines, Singapore, Thailand, and Vietnam). In 2012, ASEAN adopted the ASEAN Human Rights Declaration, which guides the development of human rights in the region. *See Asia*, Int'l Just. Res. Ctr., https://ijrcenter.org/regional/asia/ (last visited May 2, 2021). The Arab Human Rights Committee was established by the Arab Charter on Human Rights, which entered into force in 2008. The League of Arab States adopted a plan to establish a human rights court that would hear human rights complaints. The Statute for the Arab Court of Human Rights will enter into force one year after it has been ratified by seven states in the region. *See Middle East and North Africa*, Int'l Just. Res. Ctr., https://ijrcenter.org/regional/middle-east-and-north-africa/ (last visited May 2, 2021).

[2] Imani Perry, More Beautiful and More Terrible: The Embrace and Transcendence of Racial Inequality in the United States 23–24 (2011).

Global Intersectionality and Contemporary Human Rights. Johanna Bond, Oxford University Press. © Johanna Bond 2021.
DOI: 10.1093/oso/9780198868835.003.0005

> Since the construction of ethnicity in Europe is strongly bound to nation-states (e.g. immigrants' sending and receiving countries), we expect that the experience of African-American women in the USA differs substantially from the experience of ethnic minorities in Western Europe due to differences in migration history, length of stay, language, integration, citizenship, religion, and the way in which minorities are accommodated by society.[3]

Similarly, the intersectional issues that receive the most attention in sub-Saharan Africa, for example, may differ from the predominant intersectional issues in North America.[4] Yet there are similarities in the ways that the regional human rights systems have approached intersectionality. The three older regional systems (the African, inter-American, and European systems) share a recent commitment to intersectionality but also exhibit certain limitations, such as an additive framework of intersectional analysis. Across all three regional systems, intersectional issues tend to be described as "multiple," "double," or "triple" discrimination rather than as truly mutually constitutive and intersectional.

Before I consider these trends in greater depth, the following sections explore, in turn, the extent to which the three regional human rights systems have embraced intersectional analysis. After a review of each system's basic structure and primary human rights treaties, I will briefly examine the ways in which the treaty language itself includes, or does not include, intersectional principles. The chapter then reviews the "soft law" related to intersectionality within the regional system: the non-binding law or policy reflected in regional recommendations, guidelines, or programs.[5] Although it is impossible to cover the jurisprudence comprehensively given the scope of the chapter, each section also offers a generalized overview of the regional system's approach to intersectionality in its non-discrimination jurisprudence. Finally, each section provides an example of intersectional discrimination and a more detailed description of how the relevant judicial bodies have approached intersectionality. The chapter uses an intersectional lens to explore LGBTQI (lesbian, gay, bisexual, transgender, queer and/or questioning, and intersex) rights in the African region, the rights of poor and Indigenous women to be free from violence in the Americas, and the equality rights of Roma women in the European system.

Intersectionality and the African human rights system

Basic structure and human rights treaties

The push for independence from colonial rule and the desire for a united regional strategy to promote human rights prompted the formation of the Organisation

[3] Liza Mügge & Sara de Jong, *Intersectionalizing European Politics: Bridging Gender and Ethnicity*, 1 Pol., Grps., & Identities 380, 384 (2013).

[4] *See* Talia Meer & Alex Müller, *Considering Intersectionality in Africa*, 31 Agenda 3, 3–4 (2017).

[5] *See* Gregory C. Shaffer & Mark A. Pollack, *Hard vs. Soft Law: Alternatives, Complements, and Antagonists in International Governance*, 94 Minn. L. Rev. 706, 715 (2010) (explaining the general difference between hard and soft law).

Table 4.1 African Union: Key institutions and instruments

Founding treaties	Organization of African Unity Charter (1963) AU Constitutive Act (2000)
Primary human rights institutions	African Commission on Human and Peoples' Rights (1987)* African Court (1998)
Primary human rights instruments	African Charter on Human and Peoples' Rights (1981)** African Charter on Rights and Welfare of the Child (1990) Maputo Protocol (2003) Key articles: 22, 23, 24 Disability Protocol (2018) Key articles: 5, 27, 28, 29, 30

*1987 was the date of formal installation.
**The Charter was formally approved in 1981 and came into effect in 1986.

of African Unity (OAU) in 1963.[6] The OAU's early interest in human rights was rather limited, focusing on anti-colonialism, sovereignty, and independence. The Charter establishing the OAU, which was later replaced by the African Union (AU) Constitutive Act, obligated states to have regard for the rights embodied in the Universal Declaration of Human Rights. Although the Charter contained no express human rights obligations for states, the OAU nevertheless took steps to address human rights issues, particularly in the areas of decolonization, racial discrimination, the environment, and migration and refugee populations. The OAU faced criticism, however, for omitting from the Charter the large-scale human rights violations perpetrated by some authoritarian leaders.[7]

The primary regional human rights treaty is the African Charter on Human and Peoples' Rights (known as the African Charter, or Banjul Charter) (see Table 4.1)[8] The OAU adopted the African Charter in 1981, and all member states of the OAU (later the AU) ratified the African Charter by 1999. As legal scholar Michael Addo observes, "[w]ith the Charter came a transformative value change from a policy of limited and selective focus on human rights to a wholesale commitment to the promotion and protection of human rights."[9] As a multilateral, regional human rights treaty, the African Charter provides a legal framework for analyzing human rights in Africa. The

[6] *See* MICHAEL K. ADDO, THE LEGAL NATURE OF INTERNATIONAL HUMAN RIGHTS 343–44 (2010) ("Not unlike [the Treaty of Westphalia], African countries were keen to consolidate their recently won freedom, in furtherance of which the Charter of the OAU gave a prominent place to the defence of sovereignty, territorial integrity, and independence.").

[7] *See* CTR. FOR HUM. RTS., FAC. OF L., UNIV. OF PRETORIA, & AFR. COMM'N H.P.R., A GUIDE TO THE AFRICAN HUMAN RIGHTS SYSTEM 1 (2016), http://www.corteidh.or.cr/tablas/31712.pdf(PDF).

[8] *See generally* African Charter on Human and Peoples' Rights, *adopted* June 27, 1981, 21 I.L.M. 58 (entered into force Oct. 21, 1986) [hereinafter African Charter].

[9] ADDO, *supra* note 6, at 346.

African Charter offers protection of both civil and political rights as well as economic, social, and cultural rights.[10] It also offers human rights protection for group or collective rights.

In addition to providing a basic framework for human rights in the region, the African Charter created the African Commission on Human and Peoples' Rights. The African Commission is charged with promoting, protecting, and interpreting the human rights included in the African Charter. The Commission interprets the African Charter and hears individual complaints concerning potential violations of the Charter. Although the decisions of the African Commission are non-binding upon the states,[11] they have influenced domestic law and policy in countries within the region.

The AU adopted the Protocol to the African Charter on the Establishment of an African Court on Human and Peoples' Rights (now the African Court of Justice and Human Rights) in 1998; it entered into force in 2004. The African Court, with the ability to issue legally binding decisions, significantly expanded human rights jurisprudence in the region.[12] As of 2020, thirty states had ratified the Protocol establishing the Court, and nine of those thirty had made a declaration recognizing the competence of the Court to hear cases from individuals and non-governmental organizations.[13] The Protocol establishing the Court also gives the Commission the ability to refer a case to the Court.[14] The Court has a mandate to support and complement the work of the Commission.[15]

In 1990, the OAU also adopted the African Charter on the Rights and Welfare of the Child (ACRWC), which entered into force in 1999. The ACRWC promotes children's healthy development and bans discrimination against children. It addresses children's rights in the context of, *inter alia*, child marriage, child labor, child abuse, juvenile justice, armed conflict, and sexual exploitation and human trafficking.[16] Although the Charter does not specifically mention intersectionality, it recognizes that gender and age bias may combine to subject young girls to mutually reinforcing forms of subordination.[17] Similarly, the ACRWC includes special protection for disabled children and

[10] *See* CTR. FOR HUM. RTS., *supra* note 7, at 5.

[11] Victor Oluwasina Ayeni, *The African Human Rights Architecture: Reflections on the Instruments and Mechanisms within the African Human Rights System*, 10 BEIJING L. REV. 302, 309–10 (2019).

[12] *See* CTR. FOR HUM. RTS., *supra* note 7, at 43–46.

[13] The thirty states that have ratified the Protocol are: Algeria, Benin, Burkina Faso, Burundi, Cameroon, Chad, Côte d'Ivoire, Comoros, Congo, Gabon, The Gambia, Ghana, Kenya, Libya, Lesotho, Mali, Malawi, Mozambique, Mauritania, Mauritius, Nigeria, Niger, Rwanda, Sahrawi Arab Democratic Republic, South Africa, Senegal, Tanzania, Togo, Tunisia, and Uganda. The nine states that specifically recognize the rights of individuals and NGOs to bring complaints are: Benin, Burkina Faso, Côte d'Ivoire, Gambia, Ghana, Mali, Malawi, Tanzania, and Tunisia. *See* Afr. Union, *List of Countries Which Have Signed, Ratified/Acceded to the Protocol to the African Charter on Human and People's Rights on the Establishment of an African Court on Human and Peoples' Rights*, https://au.int/sites/default/files/treaties/36393-sl-protocol_to_the_african_charter_on_human_and_peoplesrights_on_the_estab.pdf.

[14] Yakaré-Oulé (Nani) Jansen Reventlow & Rosa Curling, *The Unique Jurisdiction of the African Court on Human and Peoples' Rights: Protection of Human Rights Beyond the African Charter*, 33 EMORY INT'L L. REV. 203, 205 (2019).

[15] *Id.*

[16] *See* CTR. FOR HUM. RTS., *supra* note 7, at 51.

[17] *See* African Charter on the Rights and Welfare of the Child, art. 21, OAU Doc. CAB/LEG/24.9/49 (1990) (entered into force Nov. 29, 1999).

protection against harmful social and cultural practices that might be discriminatory toward girls.[18]

In 2003, the AU (formerly the OAU) adopted a supplemental protocol to the African Charter dealing with women's human rights. The Protocol to the African Charter on Human and Peoples' Rights on the Rights of Women in Africa (the "Maputo Protocol") came into force in November 2005. Although the African Charter included basic guarantees of gender equality, activists and member states felt the need for a supplemental protocol that would specifically protect women from discrimination and inequality.[19] The Maputo Protocol offers broad protection against gender-based discrimination. It includes provisions related to the rights to life, integrity, and security of person; right to be free from harmful practices; and equal rights in marriage.[20] The Maputo Protocol guarantees a number of other human rights designed to comprehensively protect aspects of women's public and private lives. For many in the region, this broad articulation of women's rights to non-discrimination and gender equality has become the focus of much women's rights activism, along with continued attention to state obligations under the Convention on the Elimination of All Forms of Discrimination Against Women (CEDAW).

The Maputo Protocol lacks an explicit reference to intersectionality. Several articles, however, indicate a recognition of the existence of intersecting forms of discrimination: Articles 22, 23, and 24 detail state obligations to certain vulnerable populations of women.[21] For example, Article 22 offers protection for elderly women.[22] It requires States parties to take measures to meet older women's physical, economic, social, and employment needs. States parties also agree to protect elderly women from violence and discrimination based on age.

Article 23 offers protection for women with disabilities.[23] Similar to Article 22, Article 23 requires States parties to take measures to meet the physical, economic, social, and employment needs for women with disabilities, as well as to protect women with disabilities from violence and discrimination based on disability. It also requires that States parties take steps to ensure women with disabilities participate in decision-making.

Finally, Article 24 offers protection to "[w]omen in [d]istress"—poor women and women from marginalized populations.[24] This article requires states to provide these women, including those who are pregnant, nursing, or heads of households, suitable environments to meet their needs and protect their dignity.

These articles reflect one of the core principles of intersectionality theory: that different subgroups of women experience inequality differently depending on intersecting markers of identity. Although the Maputo Protocol does not explicitly discuss

[18] *See id.* art. 13.

[19] *See* CTR. FOR HUM. RTS., *supra* note 7, at 6.

[20] *See* Protocol to the African Charter on Human and Peoples' Rights on the Rights of Women in Africa (Maputo Protocol), *adopted* July 11, 1995, CAB/LEG/66.6 (entered into force Nov. 25, 2005).

[21] *See id.* arts. 22, 23, 24.

[22] *Id.* art. 22.

[23] *Id.* art 23.

[24] *Id.* art. 24.

intersectionality in the terms of the treaty, this recognition of intragroup privilege and subordination opens the door for consideration of intersectionality more broadly.[25]

The African Commission adopted a General Comment to guide states' interpretation of Article 14 of the Maputo Protocol, which recognizes reproductive rights. In a nod toward intersectionality, the Commission notes that States parties must ensure health and reproductive services that are "sensitive to the reality of women in all contexts, and adapted to women living with disabilities."[26] Even more pointedly, the Commission remarks in another General Comment that "this article should not be read and understood in isolation from other provisions of the Protocol dealing with the intersecting aspects of women's human rights, such as gender inequality, gender-based violence, harmful customary practices, and access to socio-economic rights."[27] The Commission's use of intersectional language in these guidance documents demonstrates that the Commission is receptive to intersectional analysis.

In January 2018, the AU adopted another supplemental protocol to the African Charter—the Protocol to the African Charter on Human and Peoples' Rights on the Rights of Persons with Disabilities in Africa (the "Disability Protocol").[28] The Disability Protocol creates broad protections against disability-based discrimination.[29] It includes provisions related to equal recognition before the law, the right to life, and the right to access to justice, among others.[30] As of 2020, no states had ratified the Disability Protocol so it has yet to enter into force.[31]

The Disability Protocol, like the Maputo Protocol, includes provisions to protect individuals facing multiple forms of discrimination.[32] For example, Article 27 addresses protections for women and girls with disabilities.[33] With twelve subsections, this article is arguably more comprehensive than the Maputo Protocol's provision on the same topic. It encompasses protections related to participation in decision-making,

[25] *See* CTR. FOR HUM. RTS., *supra* note 7, at 6 (discussing the Maputo Protocol's recognition of multiple forms of discrimination in its provisions related to widows, elderly women, and women with disabilities).

[26] African Comm'n on Human and People's Rights [Afr. Comm'n H.P.R.], Gen. Comment No. 2 on Article 14.1(a), (b), (c) and (f) and Article 14.2 (a) and (c) of the Protocol to the African Charter on Human and Peoples' Rights on the Rights of Women in Africa, ¶ 53 (2014).

[27] African Comm'n on Human and People's Rights [Afr. Comm'n H.P.R.], Gen. Comment No. 1 on Article 14(1)(d) and (e) of the Protocol to the African Charter on Human and Peoples' Rights on the Rights of Women in Africa, ¶ 7 (2012).

[28] *African States Affirm the Rights of Persons with Disabilities in a New Landmark Protocol*, OFF. OF THE HIGH COMM'R FOR HUM. RTS. (Feb. 15, 2018), https://www.ohchr.org/EN/NewsEvents/Pages/DisplayNews.aspx?NewsID=22661&LangID=E.

[29] *See* Protocol to the African Charter on Human and Peoples' Rights on the Rights of Persons with Disabilities in Africa, pmbl., Jan. 29, 2018 [hereinafter Disability Protocol] (recognizing that "the rights and dignity of persons with disabilities should be promoted, protected to enable them to enjoy fully and equally all their human rights and fundamental freedoms").

[30] *See id.* arts. 7–8, 13.

[31] *See* Afr. Union, *List of Countries Which Have Signed, Ratified/Acceded to the Protocol to the African Charter on Human and People's Rights on the Rights of Persons with Disabilities* (June 18, 2020), https://au.int/sites/default/files/treaties/36440-sl-PROTOCOL%20TO%20THE%20AFRICAN%20CHARTER%20ON%20HUMAN%20AND%20PEOPLES%E2%80%99%20RIGHTS%20ON%20THE%20RIGHTS%20OF%20PERSONS%20WITH%20DISABILITIES%20IN%20AFRICA.pdf.

[32] *See* Women ENABLED INT'L, ACCOUNTABILITY TOOLKIT: AFRICAN HUMAN RIGHTS SYSTEM FACTS SHEET 1, https://www.womenenabled.org/atk/Women%20Enabled%20International%20accountABILITY%20toolkit%20-%20African%20Human%20Rights%20System%20-%20FINAL.pdf (highlighting that the Disability Protocol "recognizes intersectional forms of discrimination").

[33] Disability Protocol, *supra* note 29, art. 27.

participation in women's organizations, access to information, protection from economic isolation, participation in sports and culture, and reproductive rights.[34]

The Disability Protocol also includes provisions related to disability discrimination's intersection with age-related discrimination. For instance, Articles 28 and 29 specifically address protections for children and youth with disabilities.[35] Examples of specific protections detailed in these provisions relate to family separation, education, abuse, and barriers in societal participation.[36] Article 30 covers older persons with disabilities.[37] This article includes specific protections such as access to social programs, support with regard to legal capacity, and protection from neglect and violence.[38]

Like the Maputo Protocol, the Disability Protocol does not explicitly reference intersectionality. However, its provisions on women, children and youth, and older persons indicate an intersectional approach to tackling regional discrimination. The Disability Protocol contains a broad definition of discrimination that includes a catch-all prohibition for discrimination based on "any status."[39] The Protocol implicitly adopts an intersectional framework, particularly in its provisions addressing the rights of women (Article 27), children (Article 28), youth (Article 29), and elderly people with disabilities (Article 30). More recent human rights treaties, such as the Maputo Protocol and the Disability Protocol, which were drafted after intersectionality theory had surfaced in global human rights discourse, reflect modest gains in the acceptance and promotion of intersectionality in the context of human rights.

"Soft law" commitments to intersectionality

In addition to these regional human rights treaties, several non-binding guidelines or "soft" law documents express an emerging commitment to intersectionality within the African regional system. For example, the African Commission published a guide on the implementation of economic, social, and cultural rights in the African Charter.[40] The guide references intersectional discrimination, noting, "States should recognise and take steps to combat intersectional discrimination based on a combination of (but not limited to) the following grounds: sex/gender, race, ethnicity, language, religion, political and other opinion, sexuality, national or social origin, property, birth, age, disability, marital, refugee, migrant and/or other status."[41] Through the use of references to intersectionality in the guide, the African Commission demonstrates an understanding of the importance of intersectionality to its work. Ensuring that this non-binding, expressive commitment to intersectionality has a real impact on the

[34] *See id.*
[35] *See id.* arts. 28–29.
[36] *See id.*
[37] *See id.* art. 30.
[38] *See id.*
[39] *See id.* art. 5.
[40] AFR. COMM'N H.P.R., PRINCIPLES AND GUIDELINES ON THE IMPLEMENTATION OF ECONOMIC, SOCIAL, AND CULTURAL RIGHTS IN THE AFRICAN CHARTER ON HUMAN AND PEOPLES' RIGHTS, https://www.achpr.org/public/Document/file/English/achpr_instr_guide_draft_esc_rights_eng.pdf.
[41] *See id.* at 16 (addressing steps to combat intersectional discrimination).

work and jurisprudence of the African Commission, however, is a more significant challenge.

In 2015, various UN and regional entities issued a joint statement that again demonstrated a theoretical commitment to intersectionality. The joint statement was issued by UN human rights experts, the Rapporteur on the Rights of Women of the Inter-American Commission on Human Rights, and the Special Rapporteurs on the Rights of Women and Human Rights Defenders of the African Commission on Human and Peoples' Rights. The statement recognizes that "[v]iolence against women, harmful gender stereotypes and multiple and intersectional forms of discrimination based on sex and gender lead to the violation of women's sexual and reproductive health rights."[42]

Similarly, the Special Rapporteur on the Rights of Women in Africa issued a statement for the "Global Day of Action for Access to Safe and Legal Abortion" on September 28, 2018. In this statement, Justice Lucy Asuagbor urged States parties to take all necessary measures to protect women's sexual and reproductive rights and ensure their access to safe and legal abortion, as set out in the Maputo Protocol. Asuagbor contrasts requirements from the Maputo Protocol that states must protect the reproductive rights of women by "authorizing medical abortion in cases of sexual assault, rape, incest, and where the continued pregnancy endangers the mental and physical health of the mother or the life of the mother or the fetus"[43] with the realities that many States parties still criminalize abortions. In ten of Africa's fifty-four countries, abortion is still not permitted for any reason. Further, many States parties continue excessively restricting women and girls' right to access safe and legal abortion services under the conditions provided by the Maputo Protocol. The statement fails to make a meaningful, overt intersectional argument about many different forms of oppression, but does note that victims of sexual violence are particularly affected by restrictions on abortions.[44]

Beginning in 2016, the AU also commissioned a periodic report, with support from the UN Office of the High Commissioner for Human Rights, assessing progress in rights implementation in the region.[45] The report identifies thematic gaps in international human rights standards within Africa. Intersectional discrimination is not the focus of the report, and the report mentions intersectionality only in a footnote. It states that "there is a need for acceleration of full implementation of the Maputo

[42] Joint Statement by UN Human Rights Experts, The Rapporteur on the Rights of Women of the Inter-American Commission on Human Rights and the Special Rapporteurs on the Rights of Women and Human Rights Defenders of the African Commission on Human and Peoples' Rights (Sept. 24, 2015), https://www.ohchr.org/EN/NewsEvents/Pages/DisplayNews.aspx?NewsID=16490.

[43] Statement by the Special Rapporteur on the Rights of Women in Africa on the Occasion of the "Global Day of Action for Access to Safe and Legal Abortion" (Sept. 28, 2018), https://www.achpr.org/pressrelease/detail?id=22.

[44] *See id.*

[45] *See* AFR. COMM'N H.P.R., OFF. OF THE HIGH COMM'R FOR HUM. RTS. & UN WOMEN, WOMEN'S RIGHTS IN AFRICA 8 (2017), https://www.ohchr.org/Documents/Issues/Women/WRGS/WomensRightsinAfrica_singlepages.pdf. "This report is the first in a series of analytical reports on the situation of women human rights on the continent that will be issued periodically and should be read in conjunction with existing African Union reports on women's human rights such as the States parties report on the Solemn Declaration on Gender Equality in Africa, State[s] parties reports on the Maputo Protocol and reports from the Special Rapporteur on the rights of women in Africa, among others." *Id.*

Protocol's norms, be it in the form of new laws to cover gaps in existing legislation or policies."[46] The gaps in policies, as suggested in footnote 9 of the article, are most often policies addressing multiple discriminations.[47] The report, however, relegates these important concerns to a footnote. In so doing, the drafters of the report missed an opportunity to raise concerns specifically and more comprehensively about albinism, colorism, and the effects of multiple discrimination on women in the region.

Although the soft law documents do not have a binding effect on policies and jurisprudence in the region, the inclusion of intersectional language in these reports indicates that key regional policy-makers understand the importance of an intersectional approach to human rights issues.

Intersectionality jurisprudence within the African regional system

Intersectionality has surfaced infrequently in the jurisprudence of the African system. In 2011, the African Commission issued its opinion in *Egyptian Initiative for Personal Rights and Interights v. Egypt*.[48] The case involved female journalists who alleged that they were physically and sexually assaulted, insulted, intimidated, and sexually harassed during a May 2005 demonstration.[49] The plaintiffs asserted that Egypt violated several provisions of the African Charter because law enforcement officers both perpetrated some of the assaults and failed to intervene in others.[50] The plaintiffs argued, in part, that this constituted a violation of Articles 2 and 18(3) of the African Charter because the victims were discriminated against on the basis of sex and because Egypt failed "to protect the Victims from discrimination against women."[51] The African Commission found that Egypt violated both Articles 2 and 18(3).[52]

In analyzing the issues in *Egyptian Initiative*, the African Commission recognized, albeit without using the term *intersectionality* or similar language, that the Complaint implicated an intersectional issue:

> The Complainants argue that, in violation of Article 2 of the African Charter, the Victims were discriminated against in the enjoyment of their rights in violation of the African Charter on the basis of their sex and political opinion. They further allege that, there was differential treatment between men and women during the riot and that the main reason why the Victims were assaulted by the authorities is basically because they are women and journalists.[53]

[46] *Id.* at 20.
[47] *See id.* at 20 n.9.
[48] Egyptian Initiative for Personal Rights and Interights v. Egypt, Communication 323/2006, African Commission on Human and Peoples' Rights [Afr. Comm'n H.P.R.] (Dec. 16, 2011), https://www.achpr.org/public/Document/file/English/achpreos10_232_06_eng.pdf.
[49] *See id.* ¶¶ 1–19.
[50] *See id.* ¶¶ 1–19, 23.
[51] *See id.* ¶¶ 75, 86–87.
[52] *See id.* ¶¶ 117–67, 275.
[53] *See id.* ¶ 124.

In essence, the African Commission acknowledged that the plaintiffs were seeking relief on the grounds that the victims were discriminated against based on sex and political views.[54] Nevertheless, the African Commission's analysis focused on the "gender-specific" nature of the acts, rather than the intersection between the victims' gender and political status.[55] Thus, while the case is regarded by some as a step towards holding states accountable for violations of the African Charter,[56] it indicates that the African Commission has failed to truly incorporate an intersectional analysis into its rulings.

The African Court issued its first judgment in a women's human rights case in 2018 in *Association pour le Progrès et la Défense des Droits des Femmes Maliennes (APDF) and the Institute for Human Rights and Development in Africa (IHRDA) v. Mali*.[57] Two non-governmental organizations (NGOs) in Mali brought the complaint against Mali alleging that the revised 2011 Family Code violated the rights of women and girls. The 2011 Family Code set the minimum age for marriage for females at sixteen and males at eighteen, in violation of international standards that establish eighteen years as the minimum age for all. The Code also did not require religious ministers to obtain consent from both parties of the marriage before performing the marriage. The complainants also alleged that the Code violated the right to equitable inheritance for women and children born out of wedlock, because the Code required the application of Islamic law in inheritance matters. Islamic law entitles women to half of what men receive in inheritance. For all of these reasons, the complaint alleged that the Family Code violated the Maputo Protocol, the African Charter on the Rights and Welfare of the Child, and CEDAW.

Although the Court did not approach this case as one involving intersectional rights, it is helpful to consider the intersectional aspects of the case. The Court recognized that Muslim women and girls, in particular, were detrimentally affected by the revised code. The Court observed, "the extant Family Code envisages the application of Islamic law (Article 751) and entitles religious ministers to celebrate marriages, but does not require them to verify the free consent of the parties."[58] Although without doing so explicitly, the Court grappled with discrimination at the intersection of gender and religion in the lives of women in Mali. The Court reasoned that Muslim women and girls were situated in a particular context in which both their gender and their religion had the potential to intersect and circumscribe their rights in marriage and inheritance.

[54] *See id.* ¶ 128.
[55] *See id.* ¶¶ 117–67.
[56] *See* Mariam Kirollos, *The Daughters of Egypt Are a Red Line*, 24 SUR—INT'L J. ON HUM. RTS. 137, 141 (2016) ("Though the case still remains ignored by the Egyptian government, the ruling was regarded as a victorious step towards accountability.").
[57] Association pour le Progrès et la Défense des Droits des Femmes Maliennes (APDF) and the Institute for Human Rights and Development in Africa (IHRDA) v. Mali, No. 046/2016, African Court on Human and Peoples' Rights [Afr. Ct. H.P.R.] (May 11, 2018), https://www.african-court.org/en/images/Cases/Judgment/046%20-%202016%20-%20Association%20Pour%20le%20Progr%C3%A8s%20et%20la%20Defense%20Des%20Droits%20Des%20Femmes%20Maliennes%20-%20APDF%20Vs.%20Mali%20-%20Judgement%20of%2011%20Mai%202018%20-%20Optimized.pdf.
[58] *See id.* ¶ 91.

After finding violations of the Maputo Protocol, the ACRWC, and CEDAW, the Court considered reparations and other appropriate remedies. The Court required that Mali amend its Family Code to bring it into conformity with international human rights law.[59] The Court also required Mali to "promote and ensure through teaching, education and publication, the respect of the rights and freedoms contained in the present Charter and to see to it that these freedoms and rights as well as the corresponding obligations and duties are understood."[60] A more robust intersectional approach to the question of remedies might have led the Court to consider the ways in which the government of Mali could promote changes in the law and public education within the most affected communities—in this case, within Muslim communities in Mali. By foregrounding context and the particular circumstances facing communities, intersectionality offers remedies that are likely to reach and provide redress for those living at the intersection of specific identity markers, such as youth, gender, and religion. In this way, the "teaching, education and publication" required by the Court would be targeted and most effective.

In addition to being its first decision on women's rights, the Court's decision was significant for other reasons. The Court invoked its broad jurisdiction to decide the case despite the absence of alleged violations of the African Charter. The African Court Protocol defines the jurisdiction of the Court to include not only the African Charter but "any other relevant human rights instrument ratified by the States concerned."[61] By contrast, the European Court of Human Rights and the Inter-American Court of Human Rights have more limited jurisdiction that is confined to the interpretation of the European Convention on Human Rights and the American Convention on Human Rights, respectively. Prior to the APDF case, however, the African Court has been reluctant to rely exclusively on this expanded jurisdiction, limiting its consideration to cases in which violations of the Charter are alleged in addition to other treaties.[62] The Court's willingness to apply "any other human rights instrument" ratified by the state in this case suggests it may be moving toward bolder, more expansive protection of human rights than in the past.

The Court's jurisdictional breadth has generated anxiety on the part of some legal commentators.[63] Some of these concerns reflect Eurocentric skepticism that the African system cannot handle the jurisprudential responsibility of interpreting other human rights instruments.[64] I reject these concerns and argue that this jurisprudential breadth presents a unique opportunity for the Court. Other concerns relate to the possibility that the Court's expansive jurisdiction will detract from its focus on developing

[59] *See id.* ¶ 130.

[60] *See id.* ¶ 131 (internal quotations omitted).

[61] Protocol to the African Charter on Human and Peoples' Rights on the Establishment of an African Court on Human and Peoples' Rights, art. 3.1, *adopted* June 10, 1998 (entered into force Jan. 25, 2004).

[62] *See* Adamantia Rachovitsa, *On New 'Judicial Animals': The Curious Case of an African Court with Material Jurisdiction of a Global Scope*, 19 Hum. Rts. L. Rev. 255, 269 (2019) ("It is the first case in which the Court decided a complaint strictly on the basis of other treaties on human rights without implicating the [ACHPR].").

[63] *See id.* at 255 ("Its jurisdiction has been received with skepticism and fear arguing that, if the Court extends its jurisdiction over treaties other than the African Charter on Human and Peoples' Rights, this will lead to jurisprudential chaos and will undermine the formation of the African *corpus juris*.").

[64] *See id.* at 279.

its own normative framework for interpreting the rights in the African Charter.[65] I believe that the Court will inevitably develop the corpus of law under the African Charter and that this concern is exaggerated.

To the contrary, I believe that the Court's expansive jurisdiction is an asset that may facilitate intersectional analysis. As commentator Adamantia Rachovitsa observes, "In light of the distinctive material jurisdiction of the ACtHPR [African Court on Human and Peoples' Rights] extending over a variety of human rights treaties, one could argue that the ACtHPR may develop a practice of 'calibrating' the dispute and finding the heart of the matter brought before it."[66] Finding the "heart of the matter" may well involve an exploration of intersectional violations. Because the Court is explicitly authorized to consider any other human rights instrument ratified by the offending State, it may be more open to intersectional analysis than treaty bodies that are more accustomed to operating within their normative silos. Time will tell whether the Court will liberally exercise its expanded jurisdiction in cases like *Association pour le Progrès et la Défense des Droits des Femmes Maliennes (APDF) and the Institute for Human Rights and Development in Africa (IHRDA) v. Mali* and whether that expansive jurisdiction will facilitate intersectional analysis in the Court's decisions.

The example of LGBTQI rights

Despite the inclusion of intersectional provisions in both the Maputo Protocol and Disability Protocol, neither document demonstrates an attempt to combat intersectional discrimination in the context of LGBTQI rights. Article 5 of the Disability Protocol states:

> Every person with a disability shall be entitled to the enjoyment of the rights and freedoms recognised and guaranteed in this Protocol without distinction of any kind on any ground including race, ethnic group, colour, sex, language, religion, political or any other opinion, national and social origin, fortune, birth or any status.[67]

Broad phrasing such as "without distinction of any kind on any ground" and "any status" arguably should include LGBTQI status. Nevertheless, explicit reference to LGBTQI status is noticeably absent from the Protocol's enumerated protections.

Moreover, the African Union's shortfall with regard to intersectionality and LGBTQI rights is apparent in the African Commission's treatment of the Coalition of African Lesbians (CAL), a group engaged in raising awareness "on sexuality and gender and its intersections."[68] In 2010, the African Commission rejected CAL's application for observer status, denying the group the opportunity to participate in the African human rights system. (Observer status generally allows accredited NGOs

[65] *See id.* at 283.
[66] *See id.* at 281–82.
[67] Disability Protocol, *supra* note 29, art. 5.
[68] *About Us: Why We Exist*, Coal. of Afr. Lesbians, http://www.cal.org.za/about-us/why-we-exist/ (last visited May 2, 2021).

to submit shadow reports to the Commission and to attend and participate in the Commission's sessions according to its rules of procedure.) The African Commission's decision was based on concerns regarding the alleged incompatibility between same-sex conduct and African values.[69]

Between 2014 and 2015, the African Commission took steps that seemingly indicated the AU would begin to recognize LGBTQI rights within its human rights framework. For example, in 2014 the African Commission adopted the Resolution on Protection against Violence and Other Human Rights Violations against Persons on the Basis of Their Real or Imputed Sexual Orientation or Gender Identity.[70] Within this resolution, the African Commission specifically condemned acts of violence perpetrated because of imputed or real sexual orientation or gender identity.[71] Additionally, in 2015, the African Commission reversed course and granted CAL observer status.[72]

Nonetheless, this progress was limited and was, at least with respect to CAL, short-lived. The AU's Executive Council sought withdrawal of CAL's observer status shortly after the African Commission granted it, again because of the alleged contradiction between CAL's work and "African values."[73] In 2018, the African Commission revoked CAL's observer status—a decision that CAL asserts occurred because of the African Commission's "bowing to the pressure of the Executive Council of the African Union, and its regressive interpretation of the African Charter on Human and Peoples' Rights."[74] The African Commission's treatment of CAL illustrates that the AU has yet to fully embrace the notionthat LGBTQI rights are human rights. In essence, the AU ignores one of the several forms of discrimination that individuals face. Until the AU fully recognizes LGBTQI rights, its emerging intersectional approach will remain deficient.

[69] *See* Monica Mbaru et al., *Cultural Discourse in Africa and the Promise of Human Rights Based on Non-Normative Sexuality and/or Gender Expression: Exploring the Intersections, Challenges and Opportunities*, *in* Envisioning Global LGBT Human Rights: (Neo)colonialism, Neoliberalism, Resistance and Hope 177, 189 (Nancy Nicol et al. eds., 2018) ("Many of the concerns raised were related to 'family and African values', and the argument that same-sex sexual conduct contradicts what the African Charter has inspired.").

[70] *See id.* at 190–91.

[71] *See* African Commission on Human and Peoples' Rights Res. 275(LV)2014 (May 12, 2014).

[72] *See* Mbaru, *supra* note 69, at 191.

[73] *See, e.g.*, *Decision on the 38th Activity Report of the African Commission on Human and Peoples' Rights—Doc.EX.CL/921(XXVII)*, Executive Council, Twenty-Seventh Ordinary Session, EX.CL/Dec.887(XXVII), ¶ 7 (June 12, 2015), https://au.int/sites/default/files/decisions/31762-ex_cl_dec_873_-_898_xxvii_e.pdf (requesting that the African Commission "take into account the fundamental African values, identity and good traditions, and to withdraw the observer status granted to NGOs who may attempt to impose values contrary to the African values"). *See also* Abadir M. Ibrahim, *LGBT Rights in Africa and the Discursive Role of International Human Rights Law*, 15 Afr. Hum. Rts. L.J. 263, 274 (2015) ("Even after the Commission decided in 2015 to grant CAL observer status, the AU's Executive Council, which is composed of Ministers from all member states, asked the Commission to withdraw the observer status of CAL, which it accused of trying to 'impose values contrary to the African values.'") (quoting *Decision on the 38th Activity Report of the African Commission on Human and Peoples' Rights–Doc.EX.CL/921(XXVII)*, Executive Council, Twenty-Seventh Ordinary Session, EX.CL/Dec.887(XXVII), ¶ 7 (June 12, 2015)).

[74] *Women and Sexual Minorities Denied a Seat at the Table by the African Commission on Human and Peoples' Rights*, Coal. of Afr. Lesbians (Aug. 17, 2018), https://www.cal.org.za/2018/08/17/women-and-sexual-minorities-denied-a-seat-at-the-table-by-the-african-commission-on-human-and-peoples-rights/.

Sub-regional examples of intersectional approaches

Within the regional human rights system, South African law offers an example of domestic law that facilitates intersectional claims and analysis. The South African Promotion of Equality and Prevention of Unfair Discrimination Act of 2000 (the "Promotion of Equality Act") facilitates intersectional analysis by focusing on substantive rather than formal equality and offering broad grounds for discrimination claims, including an open-ended ground.[75] This open-ended ground allows a complainant to define her identity-related discrimination in new and different ways, depending on the discrimination she has suffered, as long as the harm is similar in kind to discrimination described by traditional grounds. Paola Uccellari writes, "The fluid South African approach is thus able to address any ground, howsoever defined by the claimant, so long as it can be shown to constitute a 'marker of disadvantage,' or that it is an important element of a person's sense of self."[76] As Adrien Katherine Wing notes:

> In South Africa, the justices are particularly attuned to the plight of people who have faced multiple forms of discrimination, such as black women. Justice O'Regan noted that they face "particularly acute" disadvantage. Justice Goldstone warned of the complex relationship between identities and urged "neatly self-contained categories should be resisted." In *National Coalition for Gay and Lesbian Equality v. Minister of Justice*, Justice Sachs noted that grounds may intersect, and thus discriminatory impact could not be evaluated on one ground only. For example, African widows have suffered as "blacks, as Africans, as women, as African women, as widows and usually, as older people, intensified by the fact that they are frequently amongst the lowest paid workers."[77]

Unlike the finite lists of prohibited grounds found in much domestic and international anti-discrimination law, the flexibility in the definition of prohibited discrimination in South Africa's law invites intersectional claims.

In 2020, the Consitutional Court of South Africa issued a highly significant decision related to intersectional rights. In that case, the Court invalidated part of the

[75] *See* Paola Uccellari, *Multiple Discrimination: How Law Can Reflect Reality*, 1 EQUAL RTS. REV. 24, 37–38 (2008). The law prohibits discrimination based on:

(a) race, gender, sex, pregnancy, marital status, ethnic or social origin, colour, sexual orientation, age, disability, religion, conscience, belief, culture, language, and birth; or
(b) any other ground where discrimination based on that other ground—
 (i) causes or perpetuates systemic disadvantage;
 (ii) undermines human dignity;
 (iii) adversely affects the equal treatment of a person's rights and freedoms in a serious manner that is comparable to discrimination on a ground in paragraph (a)

Promotion of Equality and Prevention of Unfair Discrimination Act, Act 4 of 2000, ch.1, § 1(1)(xxii) (S. Afr.).

[76] Uccellari, *supra* note 75, at 38.

[77] Adrien Katherine Wing, *The South African Constitution as a Role Model for the United States*, 24 HARV. BLACKLETTER L.J. 73, 79 (2008) (internal citations omitted).

Compensation for Occupational Injuries and Diseases Act (COIDA) because the Act specifically excluded domestic workers. Recognizing that "domestic workers are predominantly Black women," the Court engaged in a lengthy intersectional analysis. It stated, "Adopting intersectionality as an interpretive criterion enables courts to consider the social structures that shape the experience of marginalized people."[78] The majority's extensive and enthusiastic embrace of intersectionality may influence jurisprudence within the regional human rights system in the future.

The Southern African Development Community (SADC) is a subregional organization of sixteen Southern African countries that strive to use regional integration and cooperation to achieve economic, quality of life, and human rights goals.[79] In 2008, the SADC adopted the SADC Protocol on Gender and Development, which laid out six objectives to creating and implementing gender-conscious policies and legislation.[80] In addition to encouraging countries to adopt specific quotas for women in parliamentary bodies,[81] the Gender Protocol focuses on issues such as gender-based violence.[82] Some of the reports written by SADC include intersectional language, such as when recognizing that women are vulnerable to human trafficking because of their gender as well as socioeconomic status and their existence in violent communities.[83] The Gender Protocol also spurred the creation of advocacy groups such as the Southern African Gender Protocol Alliance. The alliance produces issue briefs discussing the status of marginalized female groups within SADC and monitors the efforts of SADC members in implementing the Gender Protocol.[84]

[78] Mahlangu v. Minister of Lab. [2020] ZACC 24, ¶ 79 (S. Afr.).

[79] *See History and Treaty*, SADC, https://www.sadc.int/about-sadc/overview/history-and-treaty/ (last visited May 2, 2021).

[80] Malebakeng Forere & Lee Stone, *The SADC Protocol on Gender and Development: Duplication or Complementarity of the African Union Protocol on Women's Rights?*, 9 Afr. Hum. Rts. L.J. 434, 438 (2009). The six objectives are:

1. Eliminate discrimination and achieve gender equality;
2. Harmonise and co-ordinate the implementation of the various obligations imposed by the instruments to which SADC member states have subscribed;
3. Address emerging gender issues and concerns and fill gaps where existing treaties are inadequate or insufficient;
4. Set realistic, measurable targets, time frames, and indicators for achieving gender equality and equity;
5. Strengthen, monitor and evaluate the progress made by the member states towards reaching the targets and goals set out in the Protocol; and
6. Deepen regional integration, attain sustainable development and strengthen community building.

Id. at 438–39. *See also* Southern African Development Community, Protocol on Gender and Development, Aug. 17, 2008, https://www.sadc.int/files/8713/5292/8364/Protocol_on_Gender_and_Development_2008.pdf.

[81] *See Women in Politics & Decision-Making*, SADC, https://www.sadc.int/issues/gender/women-politics/ (last visited May 2, 2021).

[82] *See Gender Based Violence*, SADC, https://www.sadc.int/issues/gender/gender-based-violence/ (last visited May 2, 2021).

[83] *See* SADC, Trafficking in Persons in the SADC Region: A Baseline Report 59–60 (2016), https://www.sadc.int/files/3514/7505/0085/SADC_Baseline_Report_Low_Resolution.pdf ("The strategies depended on the circumstances of the victim .... Female victims, especially girls, were more likely to be subjected to commercial sexual exploitation than male victims.").

[84] *See Vision and Mission*, Gender Links for Equal. & Just., https://genderlinks.org.za/who-we-are/vision-and-mission/ (last visited May 2, 2021).

Another subregional entity charged with rights protection is the Economic Community of West African States Court of Justice (ECOWAS Court of Justice), which is the judicial organ of ECOWAS, a group of fifteen West African countries formed in 1975 to promote economic integration in the region. In 2005, a supplementary protocol granted the ECOWAS Court of Justice jurisdiction to hear human rights complaints interpreting the African Charter on Human and Peoples' Rights.[85] To date, the Court has not taken an intersectional approach in its handful of human rights cases.

Intersectionality and the inter-American system

Basic structure and human rights treaties

The Organization of American States (OAS) consists of thirty-five countries in the Americas. The inter-American regional human rights system, which is part of the OAS, monitors, promotes, and protects human rights within OAS member states.[86] The inter-American system consists primarily of two institutions: the Inter-American Commission on Human Rights (IACHR) and the Inter-American Court of Human Rights (IACtHR). The Inter-American Commission, which consists of seven independent commissioners, is a charter-based institution, meaning that it applies to all OAS member states. In contrast, the Inter-American Court is a treaty-based institution and, as such, applies only to states that have ratified the American Convention on Human Rights. The Inter-American Commission and Inter-American Court are responsible for interpreting the primary regional human rights instruments (see Table 4.2). The inter-American human rights system includes a declaration of principles entitled the American Declaration on the Rights and Duties of Man and a legally binding treaty called the American Convention on Human Rights. For the purposes of this chapter, two other regional instruments are particularly important: the Inter-American Convention on the Prevention, Punishment and Eradication of Violence Against Women (the "Belém do Pará Convention") and the Inter-American Convention on the Elimination of All Forms of Discrimination Against Persons with Disabilities.

The Commission and the Court share certain responsibilities within the regional system (see Table 4.2). For example, both may issue decisions in individual cases of alleged human rights violations. The Court hears cases submitted to it by the Commission or by a State party to the American Convention on Human Rights. The Court's decisions are legally binding on the relevant state. The Court also issues advisory opinions concerning enforcement of the Convention or other human rights instruments in the region. Both the Commission and the Court have opportunities to consider intersectionality in the context of rights claims within the region. In general,

[85] *See* Supplementary Protocol A/SP.1/01/05 Amending the Preamble and Articles 1, 2, 9 and 30 of Protocol A/P.1/7/91 Relating to the Community Court of Justice and Article 4 Paragraph 1 of the English Version of the Said Protocol, Jan. 19, 2005.

[86] *See Inter-American Human Rights System*, INT'L JUST. RES. CTR., https://ijrcenter.org/regional/inter-american-system/#:~:text=The%20Inter%2DAmerican%20System%20for,of%20American%20States%20(OAS) (last visited May 2, 2021).

Table 4.2 Organization of American States: Key institutions and instruments

Founding treaty	OAS Charter (1967)
Primary human rights institutions	Inter-American Commission on Women (IACW; 1928)
	Inter-American Commission on Human Rights (IACHR; 1959)
	Inter-American Court of Human Rights (IACtHR; 1979)
	Rapporteurship on the Rights of Indigenous Peoples (1990)
	Rapporteurship on the Rights of Women (1994)
	Rapporteurship on the Rights of Migrants (1996)
	Rapporteurship on the Rights of the Child (1998)
	Rapporteurship on the Rights of Afro-Descendants and Against Racial Discrimination (2005)
	Rapporteurship on the Rights of Lesbian, Gay, Trans, Bisexual, and Intersex Persons (2011)
Primary human rights instruments	American Declaration on the Rights and Duties of Man (1948)
	American Convention on Human Rights (ACHR; 1969)
	Inter-American Convention on the Prevention, Punishment and Eradication of Violence Against Women (Belém Convention; 1994)
	Key article: 9
	Inter-American Convention on the Elimination of All Forms of Discrimination Against Persons with Disabilities (CEDPD; 1999)
	Inter-American Convention Against All Forms of Discrimination and Intolerance (2013)
	American Declaration on the Rights of Indigenous Peoples (ADRIP; 2016)
	Key article: 7

however, the Commission has been more open than the Court to the consideration and articulation of intersectionality in its analysis of human rights.[87]

The Commission's work extends to human rights monitoring and promotion outside of the context of individual complaints. The Commission also monitors human rights situations in member states and addresses thematic issues through a system of rapporteurships. As of July 2018, eight thematic rapporteurships in the inter-American system were dedicated to collecting and disseminating information on specific, potentially intersectional issues, including the Rapporteurship on the Rights of Afro-Descendants and against Racial Discrimination; Rapporteurship on the Rights of the Child; Rapporteurship on the Rights of Indigenous Peoples; Rapporteurship

[87] *See* Lorena P.A. Sosa, *Inter-American Case Law on* Femicide: *Obscuring Intersections?*, 35 Neth. Q. Hum. Rts. 85, 102 (2017) ("The Commission has shown more inclination than the Court towards the adoption of an intersectional approach, particularly in recent reports.").

on the Rights of Lesbian, Gay, Trans, Bisexual, and Intersex Persons; Rapporteurship on the Rights of Migrants; and the Rapporteurship on the Rights of Women. By establishing thematic rapporteurships on these potentially intersectional issues, the inter-American system implicitly recognizes that each of these subgroups may experience the rights embodied in the primary regional human rights treaties differently than most rights holders.

The American Convention on Human Rights (ACHR) makes no reference to intersectionality in its provisions but does include a prohibition on discrimination based on "race, colour, sex, language, religion, political or another opinion, national or social origin, economic status, birth, or any other social condition." By including discrimination based on "any other social condition," the American Convention leaves open the possibility of crafting an intersectional claim to discrimination. In practice, however, the list of enumerated grounds tends to become the focus of any non-discrimination claim or inquiry.[88] In these cases, "where the applicant cannot categorise him/herself under only one ground, the claim of discrimination may be dropped, or the analysis of the case may be incomplete, leading to ineffective remedies and ultimately failing to provide justice."[89]

In 1994, the OAS adopted the Belém do Pará Convention, the first treaty in history to focus specifically on violence against women. The Belém Convention is the most ratified Convention of the inter-American human rights system, with only Canada, Cuba, and the United States not party to it.[90] The OAS has embraced intersectionality, to some extent, in Article 9 of the Belém do Pará Convention. While the Belém Convention does not explicitly reference intersectional discrimination, the Rapporteur on the Rights of Women (RRW) interprets Article 9 as establishing the principle of intersectionality within the Convention by acknowledging that not all women experience gender violence in similar ways.[91] Article 9 requires that member states

> take special account of the vulnerability of women to violence by reason of ... their race or ethnic background or their status as migrants, refugees or displaced persons.... [and give] [s]imilar consideration ... to women subjected to violence while pregnant or who are disabled, of minor age, elderly, socio-economically disadvantaged, affected by armed conflict or deprived of their freedom.[92]

[88] *See id.* at 90–91.

[89] *Id.* at 91.

[90] Ctr. for Just. & Int'l L., Evaluation of the Statute of the Mechanism to Follow-Up on the Implementation of the Convention of Belém do Pará 9 (2006), https://www.cejil.org/sites/default/files/legacy_files/position_paper_2.pdf.

[91] *See* Inter-American Commission on Human Rights [Inter-Am. Comm'n H.R.], *Report on Legal Standards Related to Gender Equality and Women's Rights in the Inter-American Human Rights System: Development and Application*, ¶ 28, OEA/Ser.L/V/II.143, Doc. 60 (Nov. 3, 2011) ("The principle of intersectionality has been established in Article 9 of the Convention of Belem do Para, since discrimination and violence do not always affect women in the same measure.").

[92] *See* Inter-American Convention on the Prevention, Punishment and Eradication of Violence Against Women, June 9, 1994, 33 I.L.M. 1534 (commonly referred to either as the Convention of Belém do Pará or the Inter-American Convention Against Violence).

While Article 9 acknowledges the structural elements that lead to special vulnerability for women,[93] the RRW's interpretation of Article 9 is additive and describes these factors as "expos[ing] women to discrimination *along with* their sex," rather than characterizing multiple identities as mutually constitutive.[94] The RRW has also noted, however, that the "principle of intersectionality has been established in Article 9 of the Convention of Belém do Pará."[95] In addition, the OAS General Assembly has explicitly affirmed its commitment to implementing the Belém Convention "from an approach based on intersectionality and the human rights of women throughout their entire life cycle."[96] Reflecting the distinction between additive and intersectional approaches, the General Assembly's most recent strategic plan for implementing the Belém Convention signaled its desire to promote gender equality "by addressing the multiple and intersectional forms of discrimination and violence suffered by women belonging to vulnerable groups."[97]

Specific consideration of multiply marginalized groups in the inter-American system: the example of Indigenous women

No specific legal instruments protect Indigenous women in the inter-American system. While the principles of race and sex equality are enshrined in Article 3 of the OAS Charter, the primary legal instruments of the inter-American human rights system, the American Declaration and the American Convention, do not discuss Indigenous peoples or Indigenous women. Historically, advocates seeking to enforce Indigenous women's rights have relied on broad provisions like Article 1(1)[98] and Article 21[99] of the American Convention, which insufficiently address Indigenous peoples' intersectional experiences of subordination. OAS's decades-long work to remedy this omission culminated in the American Declaration on the Rights of Indigenous Peoples (ADRIP), a comprehensive regional human rights instrument proposed in 1997 and adopted in 2016 after complex negotiations between member states and representatives of Indigenous peoples of the Americas.

[93] *See* Sosa, *supra* note 87, at 92.

[94] *See* Inter-Am. Comm'n H.R., *supra* note 91, ¶ 28 (emphasis added).

[95] *Id.*

[96] *See* Organization of American States [OAS], General Assembly Res. 2928, Promotion and Protection of Human Rights, OEA/Ser.P/AG/RES. 2928 (XLVIII-O/18), at xv(2) (June 5, 2018) (noting the adoption of the MESECVI Strategic Plan for 2018–2023).

[97] *Id.* at xv(1).

[98] *See* Organization of American States, American Convention on Human Rights, art. 1, §1, *opened for signature* Nov. 22, 1969, 1144 U.N.T.S. 123 (entered into force July 18, 1978). The Inter-American Court has observed that the American Convention's obligation of non-discrimination requires States to effectively protect Indigenous people by taking into account their "particularities, social and economic characteristics, as well as their situation of special vulnerability, customary law, values, customs and traditions." *See also* Rosendo Cantú et al. v. Mexico, Preliminary Objections, Merits, Reparations, and Costs, Judgment, Inter-Am. Ct. H.R. (ser. C) No. 216, ¶ 184 (Aug. 31, 2010) (internal quotations omitted).

[99] *See id.* art. 21. The right to property codified in Article 21 has been interpreted to encompass Indigenous peoples' physical and intangible relationship to ancestral land, regardless of ownership. *See also* Case of the Yakye Axa Indigenous Community v. Paraguay, Merits, Reparations, and Costs, Judgment, Inter-Am. Ct. H.R. (ser. C) No. 12, ¶ 137 (June 17, 2005).

ADRIP contains specific provisions enumerating Indigenous women's rights. Article 7 provides that:

> Indigenous women have the right to the recognition, protection, and enjoyment of all human rights and fundamental freedoms provided for in international law, free from discrimination of any kind. States recognize that violence against indigenous peoples and individuals, particularly women, hinders or nullifies the enjoyment of all human rights and fundamental freedoms. States shall adopt, in conjunction with indigenous peoples, the necessary measures to prevent and eradicate all forms of violence and discrimination, particularly against indigenous women and children.[100]

Similarly, Article 30(4)(c) instructs that in times of armed conflict, states must adopt measures in collaboration with Indigenous peoples to ensure "that indigenous women and children live free from all forms of violence, especially sexual violence, and shall guarantee the right of access to justice, protection, and effective reparation for harm caused to the victims."[101] While ADRIP echoes the Belém Convention's refrain for the eradication of violence against women, its focus on Indigenous women's "particular" vulnerability to violence is not explicitly intersectional and fails to meaningfully address their increased exposure to other human rights violations. It is a nod toward intersectionality, but it needs to provide states with more guidance as to the operation of intersecting systems of subordination and the ways that unequal power and structural inequality operate to the detriment of Indigenous women and girls.

In 2013, OAS adopted the Inter-American Convention Against All Forms of Discrimination and Intolerance, which calls on states to prevent, eliminate, prohibit, and punish all acts and manifestations of discrimination and intolerance.[102] The Convention explicitly includes sexual orientation and gender identity and expression as protected grounds.[103] However, only twelve states are signatory to the Convention, and Uruguay and Mexico are the only states to have ratified the Convention.[104]

OAS adopted the Inter-American Convention on the Elimination of All Forms of Discrimination Against Persons with Disabilities (CEDPD) in 1999.[105] The instrument, which entered into force in 2001, created a framework for protecting the rights of disabled individuals.[106] Unlike other conventions adopted by the inter-American system, the CEDPD does not include specific provisions on disabled women or other disabled marginalized populations.[107]

[100] Organization of American States [OAS], General Assembly Res. 2888, American Declaration on the Rights of Indigenous Peoples, art. VII, OAS Doc. AG/RES. 2888 (XLVI-O/16) (June 15, 2016).

[101] *Id.* art XXX(4)(c).

[102] *See* Organization of American States [OAS], Inter-American Convention Against All Forms of Discrimination and Intolerance, *adopted* June 5, 2013, A-69 (entered into force Feb. 20, 2020) [hereinafter Convention Against Discrimination].

[103] *See id.* at pmbl., art. 1, § 1.

[104] *See A-69 Signatories and Ratifications*, OAS, http://www.oas.org/en/sla/dil/inter_american_treaties_A-69_discrimination_intolerance_signatories.asp (last visited May 3, 2021).

[105] Diana Guarnizo-Peralta, *Disability Rights in the Inter-American System of Human Rights: An Expansive and Evolving Protection*, 36 Neth. Q. Hum. Rts. 43, 44 (2018).

[106] *See id.*

[107] *See id.* at 46.

Soft law commitments to intersectionality

In recent years, the OAS has highlighted in its standards the duty of states to take special account of the "inextricable link between the factors that expose women to discrimination along with their sex, such as their age, race, ethnicity, and economic position, among others."[108] The Inter-American Commission has articulated a commitment to intersectionality in its 2017–2021 Strategic Plan. One of the objectives of the five-year plan is to "ensure that all of [its] work is carried out in coordination and strategically considering principles of equality and non-discrimination and the *intersection* of identities and risks that can accentuate human rights violations against diverse persons."[109] The Commission is also encouraging intersectional analysis through its thematic rapporteurships. For example, the Rapporteurship on the Rights of Indigenous Peoples notes that it will "seek to implement activities that allow it to address . . . structural, generalized and intersectional discrimination faced by indigenous peoples, including indigenous women."[110]

In particular, there are other indications that the Inter-American Commission has begun to embrace intersectional analysis in its work to promote human rights in the region, including in its work on gender-based human rights violations and LGBTQI rights.

Inter-American Commission report on LGBTQI rights and other LGBTQI reports

The Inter-American Commission has noted the importance of an intersectional approach in its analysis of LGBTQI rights. In particular, the Commission issued a report in 2018 that explicitly recognizes the intersectional rights of LGBTQI individuals.[111] The Commission recognizes the rights of "lesbian, gay, trans, bisexual and intersex persons" and uses the abbreviation "LGBTI." (Note: in other instances that do not specifically refer to the work of the Commission, this chapter uses the more expansive acronym LGBTQI.) The thematic report states,

> A fundamental perspective is the indivisibility and interdependence of civil, political, economic, social and cultural rights, and the holistic nature of State interventions in this area, considering the particular risks faced by LGBTI persons in exercising all their human rights, as well as intersectionality with other criteria such as ethnicity, sex, gender, race and socio-economic status.[112]

[108] *See* Inter-Am. Comm'n H.R., *supra* note 91, ¶ 28.

[109] Inter-American Commission on Human Rights [Inter-Am. Comm'n H.R.], Strategic Plan 2017–2021, at 54, OEA/Ser.L/V/II.161, Doc. 27/17 (2017), https://www.oas.org/en/iachr/mandate/StrategicPlan2017/docs/StrategicPlan2017-2021.pdf (emphasis added).

[110] *Id.* at 31.

[111] *See* Inter-American Commission on Human Rights [Inter-Am. Comm'n H.R.], *Recognition of the Rights of LGBTI Persons: Advances and Challenges Towards the Recognition of the Rights of LGBTI Persons in the Americas*, OEA/Ser.L/V/II.170, Doc. 184 (Dec. 7, 2018) [hereinafter *Recognition of the Rights of LGBTI Persons*].

[112] *See id.* ¶ 21.

The report specifically indicates that states lack sufficient data to understand intersectional LGBTQI identities[113] and recommends that states "collect and analyze statistical data on violence and discrimination affecting LGBTI persons, as well as on the various aspects of the lives of lesbian, gay, bisexual, trans and intersex people (e.g. education, work, housing, health)."[114] The report emphasizes that the data needs to be "as disaggregated as possible so that it can be determined when violations result from the intersection of discrimination based on sexual orientation, gender identity or expression and body diversity with other grounds of discrimination such as race, ethnicity, disability, age, nationality and socioeconomic status of the victims, among other factors."[115] This call for disaggregation signals the Commission's desire to better quantify, identify, and understand potential intersectional subordination, and likely reflects what it believes to be the first step in implementing an intersectional analysis.

The report acknowledges that intersectional identities complicate the analysis that states must undergo to formulate effective protections for LGBTQI individuals. It does not, however, fully implement intersectional analysis itself. For example, the report notes that the Commission has expressed "special concern" about the vulnerability of particular groups like "young trans women," and refers to data indicating that "80% of trans persons killed were 35 years of age or younger."[116] But in discussing causes of violence against LGBTQI individuals, the Report refers to "cross-sectional"—as opposed to intersectional—"factors" that motivate violence and influence the personal safety of LGBTQI people.[117] Essentially, the report analyzes identities like youth, homelessness, female identity, and race as "factors" that "multiply" or "increase" the vulnerability of LGBTQI individuals.[118] The report describes these factors as "links" (e.g., "there is a strong link between poverty, exclusion and violence").[119] Although this represents significant movement toward an intersectional understanding of human rights, merely treating intersectional identities as a form of layered vulnerability misses an important insight of intersectionality. Specifically, intersectionality reflects an understanding that systems of subordination (such as those based on poverty, age, and gender) are mutually constitutive and result in complex forms of oppression that cannot be simply reduced to their constituent parts. As described in chapter 1, anti-essentialism, which is related to but not identical to intersectionality, cautions that we cannot " 'reduc[e] the lives of people who experience multiple forms of oppression to addition problems,'

[113] *See id.* ¶ 189 ("States generally do not have sufficient information to evaluate the effectiveness of the measures adopted [to prevent violence against LGBTI individuals]. Nor do they have information on the *intersectionality* with other groups, at the root of the problem of violence caused by prejudice, due to the lack of official data collection.") (emphasis added). *See also id.* ¶ 263 ("States do not have reliable statistics that reflect the true dimension of discrimination suffered by LGBTI persons in the Americas....").

[114] *Id.* ¶ 267(1). *See also* ¶ 6 (For more effective progress in the protection of the rights of LGBTQI persons, the Commission stresses the crucial importance for States to develop adequate data collection mechanisms with particular attention to the disaggregation of data regarding persons belonging to the acronym LGBTQI, as well as taking into account the specific types of vulnerability to which they are subject.)

[115] *Id.* ¶ 263.

[116] *Id.* ¶ 185 (quotations omitted).

[117] *See id.* (listing age, gender, "economic well-being," and race and ethnicity—particularly "Afro-descendent"—as factors).

[118] *See id.* ¶ 187.

[119] *See id.* ¶ 185.

in which racism is added to sexism in ways that obscure fundamental realities of Black women's social experience."[120]

In another example, the report adopts additive language when discussing intersectional identities. The report says, for example, that the Commission has noted "the multiple forms of discrimination and violence experienced by Afro-descendant women with diverse sexual orientations and gender identities, as well as the intersectionality of different factors, such as gender, race and extreme poverty," but concludes by saying these factors "constitut[e] a triple historical discrimination"—indicating an additive, not intersectional, approach to these factors.[121] The Commission should be commended for its embrace of intersectionality and the more nuanced understanding of the rights at issue here. The additive language of "triple discrimination," however, is reminiscent of that critiqued by Kimberlé Crenshaw and some of the other intersectionality scholars mentioned in chapter 1. To be sure, the Commission has come a long way in its embrace of intersectional analysis. Understanding that intersectionality results in *different* not simply *more* or *layered* subordination is the next step.

Between 2008 and 2017, the OAS General Assembly approved nine resolutions concerning human rights, sexual orientation, and gender identity.[122] The resolutions acknowledge and condemn discrimination and acts of violence against members of the LGBTQI community. They also call on states, the Inter-American Commission, and other bodies to take appropriate measures to address the problem. One resolution requested that the Inter-American Commission prepare a report on the "legal implications and conceptual and terminological developments as regards sexual orientation, gender identity, and gender expression."[123] In response, the Commission issued a report entitled "Sexual Orientation, Gender Identity, and Gender Expression: Key Terms and Standards." This report clarifies the IACHR's use of LGBTQI terminology (e.g., the difference between "sex" and "gender") and highlights the IACHR's commitment to non-discrimination for LGBTQI individuals, noting "[A]ny difference in treatment based on sexual orientation is a suspect category and presumed to be incompatible with the American Convention."[124] In addition, the Inter-American Commission developed an Action Plan to address the ongoing issue of discrimination and violence against LGBTQI people and proposed to "establish legal standards, rule on cases, and issue reports on the situation of members of the LGBTI communities in the American States."[125] The Commission has been working to protect and promote

[120] Devon W. Carbado & Cheryl I. Harris, *Intersectionality at 30: Mapping the Margins of Anti-Essentialism, Intersectionality, and Dominance Theory*, 132 HARV. L. REV. 2193, 2200 (2019) (quoting Angela P. Harris, *Race and Essentialism in Feminist Legal Theory*, 42 STAN. L. REV. 581, 588 (1990)).

[121] *Recognition of the Rights of LGBTI Persons*, *supra* note 110, ¶ 185.

[122] *See, e.g.*, Organization of American States [OAS], G.A. Res. 2908, Promotion and Protection of Human Rights, AG/RES. 2908 (XLVII-O/17) (June 21, 2017). *See also Links*, OAS, http://www.oas.org/en/iachr/lgtbi/links/ (listing OAS General Assembly resolutions).

[123] Organization of American States [OAS], G.A. Res. 2653, Human Rights, Sexual Orientation and Gender Identity, ¶ 6, AG/RES. 2653 (XLI-O/11) (June 7, 2011).

[124] Inter-American Commission on Human Rights [Inter-Am. Comm'n H.R.], *Sexual Orientation, Gender Identity, and Gender Expression: Key Terms and Standards*, at 6–7, 29, OEA/Ser.G CP/CAAP-INF. 166/12 (Apr. 23, 2012).

[125] Inter-American Commission on Human Rights [Inter-Am. Comm'n H.R.], Strategic Plan 2011–2015: Action Plan 4.6.i (2011–2012), at 2 (2011).

LGBTQI rights in the region, and its commendable efforts will help to dismantle the structural subordination facing LGBTQI individuals and communities.

The IACHR has made significant strides in the recognition of LGBTQI rights in the region. In the last decade, much of the Commission's work has also recognized the crucial intersections of rights related to sexuality and those related to race, ethnicity, disability, age, nationality, and socioeconomic status. Importantly, the Commission has called for data disaggregated by multiple identity categories, making intersectional analysis easier to accomplish. The next step for the IACHR will be to shift from the notion of added or layered vulnerability of victims to a more robust understanding of intersectionality as intersecting, mutually constitutive systems of subordination that result in different and complex forms of discrimination and subordination.

Inter-American Commission report on legal standards related to gender equality and women's rights

The IACHR report "Legal Standards related to Gender Equality and Women's Rights in the Inter-American Human Rights System" addresses the Commission's efforts to integrate intersectional approaches within its legal standards.[126] The report notes IACHR's emerging expectation that states "take special account of the inextricable link between the factors that expose women to discrimination along with their sex, such as their age, race, ethnicity, and economic position, among others."[127] One IACHR standard concerning the problem of violence against women includes "the duty of the states to consider, in the policies they adopt to promote gender equality, the particular risk of human rights violations that women may face due to factors combined with their sex, such as age, race, ethnicity, and economic position, among others."[128] This language represents an obligation to consider intersectional concerns. The report then outlines (a) decisions on the merits of the IACHR, (b) decisions of the inter-American Court, (c) thematic reports, and (d) country reports.

Included in section (a) is an analysis of the case of *Ana, Beatriz and Celia Gonzalez Perez*, which involves Indigenous women from Mexico who were illegally detained, raped, and tortured by a group of soldiers. Their case highlights how the principle of intersectionality, established in Article 9 of the Belém do Pará Convention, addresses the problem of how discrimination and violence do not always affect women in the same measure, particularly in the case of Indigenous females accessing the guarantees of exercising their human rights.[129] The case of Valentina Rosendu Cantú, another Indigenous woman raped by military members, highlights similar concerns of sex, race, ethnicity, and economic position.[130] The report highlights this case, among others, as "Multiple Forms of Discrimination," which essentially addresses intersectional discrimination concerns.

A recent Commission report, "Indigenous Women and Their Human Rights in the Americas," contains a detailed discussion of intersectional principles and explicitly

[126] *See* Inter-Am. Comm'n H.R., *supra* note 91, ¶ 28.
[127] *Id.*
[128] *Id.* ¶ 18.
[129] *See id.* ¶¶ 25, 28.
[130] *See id.* ¶¶ 41–43.

enumerates intersectionality as a guiding principle when evaluating and addressing the forms of discrimination faced by women in the Americas.[131] The report acknowledges that Indigenous women have a "multidimensional identity," and "a unique worldview and cultural identity, and a sense of collective membership in their peoples, which calls for an intersectional approach."[132] Similarly, the Commission's report "Missing and Murdered Indigenous Women in British Columbia, Canada," on the epidemic of disappearances and murders of such women, echoes the call by the UN Special Rapporteur on Violence Against Women for a "holistic model" for examining the "institutional and structural inequalities [which] exacerbate violence through multiple and intersecting forms of discrimination."[133]

The OAS General Assembly announced in its Plan of Action of the American Declaration of the Rights of the Rights of Indigenous Peoples (2017–2021), adopted through resolution AG/RES. 2913 (XLVII-O/17), that "particular attention will be given to marginalized and vulnerable groups within indigenous communities, who suffer multiple, aggravated and concomitant forms of discrimination." The plan instructs civil servants to promote intersectoral dissemination and awareness of ADRIP across all state institutions, "not only those responsible for indigenous issues," and explicitly uses intersectional language to describe these efforts.

Overall, OAS has emphasized intersectionality within the instruments of the inter-American system. In its more recent reports, OAS indicates an embrace of intersectional theories and an understanding of different aspects of human identity. However, several Commission reports still adhere to an additive understanding of identities rather than a truly intersectional approach to data analysis and understanding multiple identities. By adopting a true intersectional analysis, OAS could improve its already robust use of intersectional language in order to provide more comprehensive redress to victims of intersectional rights violations.

Intersectionality jurisprudence within the inter-American system

Cases brought before the Inter-American Court (IACtHR) frequently involve intersectional issues, but the Court has taken an uneven approach to employing intersectional analysis in its decisions. The Commission (IACHR) acts as a gatekeeper to the Court, as only the Commission may receive individual complaints directly from affected individuals. This section will examine some of the decisions of the Commission

[131] *See* Inter-American Commission on Human Rights [Inter-Am. Comm'n H.R.], *Indigenous Women and Their Human Rights in the Americas*, ¶¶ 38–41, OEA/Ser.L/V/II., Doc. 44/17 (Apr. 17, 2017), oas.org/en/iachr/reports/pdfs/indigenouswomen/pdf.

[132] *Id.* ¶ 32.

[133] Inter-American Commission on Human Rights [Inter-Am. Comm'n H.R.], *Missing and Murdered Indigenous Women in British Columbia, Canada*, ¶ 148, OEA/Ser.L/V/II., Doc. 30/14 (Dec. 21, 2014), oas.org/en/iachr/reports/pdfs/indigenous-women-bc-canada-en.pdf. The Report states, "[T]he creation and use of stereotypes becomes one of the causes and consequences of gender violence practiced against women. The stereotypes in an investigation are the result of the existing situation of inequality and discrimination that many women confront due to multiple factors that are interrelated with their sex, such as race, age, ethnicity, socioeconomic condition and others." *Id.* ¶ 175.

and the Court, looking specifically at their use of intersectional language in three areas: non-discrimination claims, LGBTQI issues, and gender-based violence claims.

Non-discrimination jurisprudence

Over the past three decades, the IACtHR has heard numerous cases regarding gender-based human rights violations.[134] Until 2004, however, the IACtHR had not fully articulated the impact of gender on specific human rights violations.[135] The *Case of the Plan de Sánchez Massacre v. Guatemala* concerned a horrific massacre of a predominantly Mayan village in Guatemala by military forces in 1982.[136] The military also raped and tortured the women in the village.[137] In the court's judgment of the case, the IACtHR acknowledged that women experience torture and rape in a gender-specific way because of the historical employment of rape as a means of controlling women.[138] Although the Court did not employ a thorough intersectional analysis, the affirmation that women experience situations differently than men was an important step.

In 2016, the IACtHR heard *I.V. v. Bolivia*, which involved the sterilization of I.V. without her informed consent.[139] The Court found that Bolivia violated I.V.'s right to humane treatment, right to privacy, and right of family, as well as the state's duty to prevent violence against women, among other violations.[140] This case is remarkable because the IACtHR employed an intersectional analysis when discussing the importance of informed consent to women in particular and how the sterilization specifically harmed I.V.[141] The Court examined how I.V.'s status as an immigrant and a person of modest socioeconomic means impacted her ability to receive adequate medical care.[142] The Court did employ additive language, looking for factors in addition to I.V.'s sex.[143] IACtHR also highlighted that the doctors' gender stereotypes influenced their decision to make I.V.'s medical choices for her since the male doctors believed they were in a better position to make reproductive health decisions for a female patient.[144] The language used in this case illustrates an important use of intersectional analysis by the IACtHR.

[134] *See* Patricia Palacios Zuloaga, *The Path to Gender Justice in the Inter-American Court of Human Rights*, 17 Tex. J. Women & L. 227, 231 (2008) ("The majority of victims in cases brought before the Court have been male, however when women have been victims, the allegations against the state do not necessarily disclose gender sensitive violations.").

[135] *See id.* at 232 ("The issue that most concerns the author is the fact that before 2004, the Court had not issued a ruling the recognized a gender-sensitive human rights violation ....").

[136] Case of the Plan de Sánchez Massacre v. Guatemala, Reparations, Judgment, Inter-Am. Ct. H.R. (ser. C) No.116, ¶¶ 32 (a)–(b), 38, 49(2)–49(4) (Nov. 19, 2004).

[137] *See id.*

[138] *See id.*

[139] *See* I.V. v. Bolivia, Preliminary Objections, Merits, Reparations and Costs, Judgment, Inter-Am. Ct. H.R. (ser. C) No. 329, at ¶ 19 (Nov. 30, 2016).

[140] *See* Martín Hevia & Andrés Constantin, *Gendered Power Relations and Informed Consent: The* I.V. v. Bolivia *Case*, 20 Health & Hum. Rts. J. 197, 199 (2018).

[141] *See I.V. v. Bolivia*, No. 329, ¶ 136.

[142] *See id.*

[143] *See id.* ¶ 236 ("[T]he physician acted with a stereotype rationale according to which only I.V. was responsible for the couple's contraceptive actions.").

[144] *See id.*

LGBTQI jurisprudence

In recent years, the OAS, including the Inter-American Commission and the Inter-American Court, has begun to address patterns of violence and other human rights abuses affecting LGBTQI persons in the Americas. In 2011, OAS created the Rapporteurship on the Rights of Lesbian, Gay, Bisexual, Trans and Intersex (LGBTI) Persons, whose mandate is to monitor the situation of human rights of LGBTQI persons in the region. The IACHR acknowledges that many OAS member states, including the United States, frequently adopt laws that explicitly discriminate against LGBTQI people. LGBTQI individuals experience the criminalization of their identity and activities; discrimination in access to adequate and appropriate healthcare, the justice system, and education; marginalization in labor and political participation; and the exclusion and invisibility that accompanies these human rights violations. Intersectional subordination of LGBTQI people also contributes to their experiences of poverty, high rates of violence, and related impunity for perpetrators.

The right to non-discrimination on the basis of sexual orientation and gender identity is not explicitly described in any international human rights treaty. The primary legal instruments of the inter-American human rights system, the American Declaration and the American Convention, protect individuals from discrimination based on limited categories, including physical characteristics like race, ideological characteristics like religious belief and political opinion, and social characteristics like poverty.[145] The Inter-American Commission and Court maintain that protection from discrimination based on sexual orientation and gender identity are covered under the phrase "any other social condition" in Article 1(1) of the American Convention.[146] While this interpretation recognizes that gender and sexual orientation are socially constructed, it fails to address the general physical reality of LGBTQI individuals and their particular susceptibility to bodily violence. Further, sex discrimination is often limited to the heteronormative conception of male and female, ignoring the intersectional issues raised by complex identities of nonbinary, trans, and intersex people.

Jurisprudence has focused on the legal rights, such as the right to obtain identity documents that correspond with one's gender and the recognition of same-sex or nontraditional family units. No recent jurisprudence has directly addressed concerns for LGBTQI individuals' bodily autonomy. Jurisprudence on the rights of LGBTQI individuals in the Americas is in its infancy and is ripe for the application of intersectional principles. To date, the Inter-American Court has heard only three cases concerning sexual orientation and gender identity. While these cases have expanded LGBTQI rights and recognition, their results are limited by perfunctory intersectional analysis.

In 2012, the Court decided *Atala Riffo and Daughters v. Chile*, its first case directly addressing LGBTQI rights and discrimination on the basis of sexual orientation.[147] The Court found Chile violated the rights of Karen Atala Riffo, a Chilean judge who

[145] *See* American Convention on Human Rights, *supra* note 98, art. 1, §1 ("The States Parties to this Convention undertake to respect the rights and freedoms recognized herein . . . without any discrimination for reasons of race, color, sex, language, religion, political or other opinion, national or social origin, economic status, birth, or any other social condition.").

[146] *See* Inter-Am. Comm'n H.R., *supra* note 91, ¶ 137.

[147] *See* Shushan Khorozyan, *Atala Riffo and Daughters v. Chile*, 40 Loy. L.A. Int'l & Compar. L. Rev. 1513, 1513–16 (2017) (summarizing case).

lost custody of her children after coming out as lesbian, by arbitrarily discriminating against her and interfering with a protected same-sex family unit.[148] *Atala Riffo* set important precedent that a state's different treatment of LGBTQI individuals and their non-traditional family units must be presumed incompatible with the American Convention.[149] The Court did not elaborate on the intersection of gender stereotypes and discrimination based on sexual orientation.

The Court's later jurisprudence on LGBTQI issues similarly carved out important human rights victories for LGBTQI individuals. The Court determined in the 2013 case *Flor Freire v. Ecuador* that perceived or imputed LGBTQI identity is a protected category. Homero Flor Freire was an Ecuadorian soldier who was discharged after being accused of engaging in homosexual conduct with another soldier; Flor Freire denied engaging in the act and did not identify as homosexual.[150] The Court ultimately found that Ecuador's military discipline regulation penalizing soldiers for homosexual acts violated the American Convention's principle of equality and prohibition on discrimination.[151]

The Court nods toward intersectional analysis in the case of *Alberto Duque v. Colombia*.[152] The Court found that Colombia discriminated against Ángel Alberto Duque, an HIV-positive gay man whose situation of poverty was largely attributable to HIV treatment costs, by denying him the right to receive his partner's survivor's pension solely because they were a same-sex couple.[153] Notably, although the Court recognized that "multiple vulnerability factors"—including his sexual orientation, HIV-positive status, and situation of poverty[154]—impacted Alberto Duque's right to humane treatment and also acknowledged that "persons living with HIV are in an especially vulnerable situation,"[155] it failed to find evidence that Alberto Duque's right to life was violated when he received lower-quality HIV treatment after his partner's death required him to change to a subsidized health plan.[156] While the Court acknowledged that multiple facets of Alberto Duque's identity impacted the discrimination he

[148] *See* Atala Riffo and Daughters v. Chile, Merits, Reparations and Costs, Judgment, Inter-Am. Ct. H.R. (ser. C) No. 254, ¶ 146 (Feb. 24, 2012) ("On the contrary [the Juvenile Court of Villarrica] used abstract, stereotyped, and/or discriminating arguments to justify their decisions . . . for which reason said decisions constitute discriminatory treatment against Ms. Atala."). *See also* Atala Riffo and Daughters v. Chile, Provisional Measures, Order of the President of the Court, Inter-Am. Ct. H.R. (ser. E) (Nov. 26, 2013).

[149] *See generally* Inter-American Commission on Human Rights [Inter-Am. Comm'n H.R.], *Violence against Lesbian, Gay, Bisexual, Trans and Intersex Persons in the Americas*, OAS/Ser.L/V/II.rev.1, Doc. 36 (Nov. 12, 2015).

[150] *See* The Global Community Yearbook of International Law and Jurisprudence 2017, at 692–93 (Giuliana Ziccardi Capaldo ed., 2018).

[151] *See Inter-American Court: Ecuador Discriminatorily Discharged Soldier for Sexual Orientation*, Int'l Just. Res. Ctr. (Nov. 14, 2016), https://ijrcenter.org/2016/11/14/inter-american-court-ecuador-discriminatorily-discharged-soldier-for-sexual-orientation/.

[152] Ángel Alberto Duque v. Colombia, Preliminary Objections, Merits, Reparations and Costs, Judgment, Inter-Am. Ct. H.R. (ser. C) No. 310 (Feb. 26, 2016).

[153] *See* Avani Uppalapati et al., *International Regulation of Sexual Orientation, Gender Identity, and Sexual Anatomy*, 18 Geo. J. Gender & L. 635, 705 (2017) (describing Alberto Duque's condition).

[154] *See IACHR Takes Case Involving Colombia to the Inter-American Court*, Org. of Am. States (Dec. 1, 2014), http://www.oas.org/en/iachr/media_center/PReleases/2014/144.asp.

[155] Ángel Alberto Duque v. Colombia, Case 12,841, Inter-Am. Comm'n H.R., Report No. 5/14, ¶ 100 (Apr. 2, 2014).

[156] *See id.* ¶ 102.

experienced, it found no violations of his right to personal integrity, right to life, or right to judicial protection.[157]

In 2016, the Republic of Costa Rica requested that the Inter-American Court interpret whether the American Convention protects rights relating to gender identity. In January 2018, the Court responded by issuing a landmark advisory opinion on gender identity, equality, and non-discrimination of same-sex couples[158] declaring that "the change of name and the rectification of public records and identity documents to conform to a person's gender identity are protected by the American Convention on Human Rights."[159] This advisory opinion described the confluence of identity factors as creating "cyclical" and "multiple" discrimination.[160]

Gender-based violence jurisprudence

The IACHR has also issued decisions in cases involving gender-based violence, some of which involved intersectional issues. *Castro-Castro Prison v. Peru* specifically addresses violence against women. The Court found a violation of Article 5 of the American Convention and interpreted its scope through reference to the Belém do Pará Convention. In addition, the Court held for the first time that gender-based violence is a form of discrimination according to the precedents of the Committee on the Elimination of Discrimination against Women. Furthermore, this case provides an expansive definition of sexual violence: "actions with a sexual nature committed with a person without their consent, which besides including the physical invasion of the human body, may include acts that do not imply penetration or even any physical contact whatsoever." Finally, the Court referred to the obligation to act with due diligence in cases of violence against women, set forth in Article 7(b) of the Belém Convention to determine state responsibility for violating the duty to investigate and punish contained at Articles 8(1) and 25 of the American Convention.[161]

The case of *Gonzales Lluy* et al. *v. Ecuador* involves errors committed by doctors during a blood transfusion that resulted in a young girl contracting HIV.[162] The Inter-American Court engaged in intersectional analysis by considering poverty as one of several factors that combined to give rise to the discrimination suffered by the victim. The court identified a confluence of multiple intersecting factors and risks of discrimination associated with Gonzales Lluy's status as a girl, a person living in poverty, and someone living with HIV.[163] The Inter-American Commission noted, "According to

[157] *See* Uppalapati et al., *supra* note 153, at 705.

[158] *See* State Obligations Concerning Change of Name, Gender Identity, and Rights Derived from a Relationship Between Same-Sex Couples (Interpretation and Scope of Articles 1(1), 3, 7, 11(2), 13, 17, 18 and 24, in Relation to Article 1, of the American Convention on Human Rights), Advisory Opinion OC-24/17, Inter-Am. Ct. H.R. (ser. A) No. 24 (Nov. 24, 2017).

[159] Jorge Contesse, *The Inter-American Court of Human Rights' Advisory Opinion on Gender Identity and Same-Sex Marriage*, AM. SOC'Y INT'L L. (July 26, 2018), https://www.asil.org/insights/volume/22/issue/9/inter-american-court-human-rights-advisory-opinion-gender-identity-and.

[160] *See id.*

[161] *See* Miguel Castro-Castro Prison v. Peru, Merits, Reparations and Costs, Judgement, Inter-Am. Ct. H.R. (ser. C.) No. 160, at 90, 116, 125, 131 (Nov. 25, 2006).

[162] *See* Gonzales Lluy et al. v. Ecuador, Preliminary Objections, Merits, Reparations and Costs, Judgment, Inter-Amer. Ct. H.R. (ser. C) No. 298, ¶ 85 (Sept. 1, 2015).

[163] *See* Inter-American Comm'n on Human Rights [Inter-Am. Comm'n H.R.], *Report on Poverty and Human Rights in the Americas*, ¶¶ 172–73, OEA/Ser.L/V/II.164, Doc. 147 (Sept. 7, 2017).

the concurring opinion of Judge Juan Eduardo Ferrer MacGregor, it was the first time that the Court had used the concept of "intersectionality," and it examined in depth the scope of the principle of non-discrimination, taking into account that in that case, multiple discrimination occurred based on the composite nature of the causes of discrimination."[164]

The example of the right to be free from violence for poor and Indigenous women in the Americas

Over fifty million people in the Americas self-define as Indigenous.[165] The legacy of colonialism has contributed to the historical and ongoing subjugation of Indigenous people in the Americas, who continue to endure human rights violations including forced assimilation and sterilization; natural resource exploitation of ancestral lands; and other forms of state violence. Indigenous women in the Americas are subject to discrimination from both outside and within their own communities, leading to increased exposure to enduring violations of their civil and political rights; their economic, social, and cultural rights; and their right to live free from violence. The intersection of Indigeneity with sex, gender, ethnic origin, youth or old age, ability, language, and situation of poverty hampers Indigenous women's ability to exercise their human rights in full and raises significant barriers to accessing basic health and education services, decent employment, and the justice system. The widespread epidemic of violence against Indigenous women in the Americas signals a growing need for regional policies informed by an intersectional perspective.[166]

The Inter-American Commission and Court have increasingly addressed Indigenous peoples' human rights concerns over the past two decades. The focus of the Court's jurisprudence regarding Indigenous peoples almost exclusively concerns resource extraction in ancestral lands.[167] While Indigenous women remain disproportionately affected by the effects of extractive industries, these cases neglect gendered and other intersectional perspectives, instead favoring community-level analysis. The few cases that directly address Indigenous women's rights exclusively concern violence against Indigenous women. These cases, however, take important steps toward intersectional analysis by acknowledging that violence affects Indigenous women in particular and contextually specific ways.

164 *See id.* ¶ 172 n.209.

165 Press Release, Org. of Am. States, A 17-Year Wait Pays Off for Indigenous Peoples, OAS Press Release E-075/16 (June 15, 2016).

166 *See* Dan Bilefsky, *'Why Are So Many of Our Girls Dying?' Canada Struggles With Violence Against Indigenous Women*, N.Y. Times (May 30, 2019), https://www.nytimes.com/2019/05/30/world/canada/canada-indigenous-violence.html.

167 *See, e.g.*, Kichwa Indigenous People of Sarayaku v. Ecuador, Merits, Reparations and Costs, Judgment, Inter-Am. Ct. H.R. (ser. C) No. 245, ¶ 278 (June 27, 2012) (finding Ecuador violated the American Convention by permitting private oil companies to excavate Kichwa territory without their consent, failed to provide them judicial protection, and limited their rights to freedom of movement and cultural expression); Mayagna (Sumo) Awas Tingni Community v. Nicaragua, Merits, Reparations and Costs, Judgment, Inter-Am. Ct. H.R. (ser. C) No. 79, ¶ 164 (Aug. 31, 2001) (finding Nicaragua violated the American Convention by granting resource extraction concession on Indigenous lands without the community's consent).

Two such landmark cases, *Fernández Ortega v. Mexico*[168] and *Rosendo Cantú v. Mexico*,[169] involved young members of the Me'phaa Indigenous community who were raped and tortured by Mexican military personnel in 2002. In *Fernández Ortega*, the Court acknowledged that States must pay "special attention" when responding to rape victims who "belong to vulnerable groups, such as indigenous women."[170] The Court observed that inadequate procedures adopted by Mexico to investigate human rights violations exacerbated the "difficulties encountered by indigenous people, indigenous women in particular, to obtain access to justice,"[171] including language barriers, legal fees, and potential community ostracization. The Court reflected at length on the unique challenges Indigenous women face when seeking justice:

> The alleged victim is an indigenous woman, who lives in an isolated mountainous area, who had to walk several hours to file a complaint about a rape that would, in all probability, have negative repercussions in her social and cultural medium—such as possible rejection by her community—before justice and health care authorities who did not speak her language.... [S]he pressed charges and was persistent with her claim, knowing that in the area in which she lives there is a continuing presence of soldiers, some of whom had been criminally charged with committing a serious crime.[172]

While the Court's analysis described Indigeneity and poverty as separate factors enhancing the baseline vulnerability experienced by women, *Fernández Ortega* is notable for its observation that Indigenous women's overlapping social identities and situation of poverty present obstacles to accessing the legal system.

Rosendo Cantú, decided the same year, marked the first time the Court found that rape and sexual violence constituted torture.[173] The Court reached this conclusion by implementing an intersectional analysis of the human rights violations endured by the seventeen-year-old Valentina Rosendo Cantú. The Court analyzed the intersection of different categories protected against discrimination, including gender, race, age, and poverty, and determined the violations of Cantú's rights to personal integrity, private life, and personal dignity resulted from her unique intersectional subordination. Rather than separately assessing the human rights violations against Cantú, the Court took a holistic approach and acknowledged that the Mexican military members, as State actors, committed torture by violating Cantú's sexual autonomy to intentionally

[168] *See* Fernández Ortega et al. v. Mexico, Preliminary Objections, Merits, Reparations, and Costs, Judgment, Inter-Am. Ct. H.R. (ser. C) No. 215, ¶¶ 219–20 (Aug. 30, 2010) (finding Mexico's failure to adequately investigate the rape of a twenty-seven-year-old Me'phaa woman by Mexican military personnel violated the American Convention and the Belém Convention, among others).

[169] *See* Rosendo Cantú et al. v. Mexico, Preliminary Objections, Merits, Reparations, and Costs, Judgment, Inter-Am. Ct. H.R. (ser. C) No. 216, ¶ 3 (Aug. 31, 2010) (finding Mexico's ambivalence regarding the rape of a seventeen-year-old Me'phaa girl by military personnel violated Article 5(2) of the American Convention and Article 7(a) of the Belém Convention).

[170] *Fernández Ortega*, No. 215 ¶ 259.

[171] *Id.* ¶ 2 (internal quotations omitted).

[172] *Id.* ¶ 107.

[173] *See Cantú*, No. 216 ¶ 118.

inflict physical and mental suffering. *Rosendo Cantú* is significant for its intersectional discussion of the "special needs of women, minors, and indigenous peoples."[174]

The Commission and Court have also handled several cases related to the intersection of socioeconomic status and gender. *Gonzales* et al. *v. Mexico ("Cotton Field")* involved the murder of three young women whose bodies were found in a cotton field in Ciudad Juárez. Their murder was part of a systemic pattern of violence targeting women in Ciudad Juárez. Because of its location near the US/Mexico border, Ciudad Juárez has numerous factories that are part of the maquila industry,[175] which means that the city has a high percentage of migrant workers. The socioeconomic context leads to "the convergence between social inequalities and the proximity of the international border as conducive to the development of different types of organized crime, high rate of school desertion and the presence of sexual predators and military officials."[176] These factors have contributed to an exceptionally high rate of gender-based violence in the region.

Like many victims of gender-based violence in Juárez, the victims in the *Cotton Field* case were young working-class women and girls. One victim, Esmeralda Herrera, was a fifteen-year-old domestic worker. Another, Laura Ramos, was a seventeen-year-old high school student. The final victim in the case was Claudia González, a twenty-year-old worker in the maquila industry. All the victims faced intersecting systems of subordination based on class and gender.

In considering the case, the Court alluded to these issues without engaging in a probing analysis of intersectionality. The Court remarked on the "risk factors" that should be "taken into account in prevention strategy."[177] It also noted the existence of "high risk" areas requiring additional surveillance.[178] The representatives in the case noted that

> over and above gender-based violence, the girls and women of Ciudad Juárez suffer a double discrimination, because the humble origins of Claudia, Laura and Esmeralda, and of the other girls and women who have been murdered or reported missing, and of their mothers and their next of kin, also generates discrimination against a social class.[179]

The Court, however, largely limited its analysis to aspects of gender discrimination. It missed a significant opportunity to probe deeply into the intersection of gender, class, and age. A comprehensive intersectional analysis would have allowed the Court to carefully consider how the structural dimensions of class, age, and gender combine to render young, poor women in Juárez victims of a type of subordination that is qualitatively different from gender subordination operating alone. This kind of

[174] Amy Choe, *Rosendo Cantú et al. v. Mexico*, 36 LOY. L.A. INT'L & COMPAR. L. REV. 1353, 1353 (2014).
[175] A maquiladora is a foreign-owned factory or production plant where lower-paid workers assemble goods or products for export.
[176] *See* Sosa, *supra* note 86, at 94.
[177] González *et al.* ("Cotton Field") v. Mexico, Preliminary Objection, Merits, Reparations, and Costs, Judgment, Inter-Am. Ct. H.R. (ser. C) No. 205, ¶ 258 (Nov. 16, 2009).
[178] *See id.* ¶¶ 503–04.
[179] *Id.* ¶ 391.

intersectional analysis would have led the Court to consider comprehensive remedies aimed at combatting class, age, and gender subordination. Instead, the Court focused almost exclusively on gender discrimination, missing the opportunity to enrich its analysis and provide more comprehensive remedies.

Several other cases illustrate the Commission's and the Court's view of the intersectional issues presented in cases of gender-based violence within the region. In *Escobar Ledezma* et al. *v. Mexico*, a young female maquila worker named Paloma Angélica Escobar disappeared and was later found murdered in Chihuahua. The Commission found that Mexico violated the deceased's right to equality under the law according to the American Convention. In the *Escobar Ledezma* case, representatives of the victims advocated an intersectional approach, although they did not use the term *intersectionality*. Instead, they argued that the systemic violence in Chihuahua was the result of not only structural gender subordination but also structural class inequality. They noted that the violence stemmed from "a class problem since the women most affected are young and poor women who have to travel by bus to go to work and to move about normally."[180] The Commission however, failed to explore the intersectional issues involving socioeconomic status and gender, despite the intersectional framing of the issues in the complaint. Two subsequent cases, *Veliz Franco* et al *v. Guatemala* and *Velásquez Paiz* et al *v. Guatemala*, also involved the disappearance and murder of young girls.[181] In both cases, the Court also concluded that the State had violated each woman's right to equality under the American Convention and Article 7 of the Belém Convention. In these cases, the Commission and the Court seem willing to gesture toward intersectionality when it comes to gender and age. Because these cases all involved young women under the age of eighteen, the Court analyzed the ways in which youth made the young women more likely to be murdered.

Sub-regional examples facilitating intersectional analysis

Canada offers an example of a country that has invited intersectional interpretations of the equal protection provisions into its Constitution. Article 15 of the Canadian Charter of Rights and Freedoms ("the Canadian Charter") includes a non-exhaustive list of grounds for prohibited discrimination.[182] The Supreme Court of Canada has "held that an intersection of grounds can be considered as analogous to, or a synthesis of the listed grounds."[183] Proving such intersectional discrimination may be challenging, but the possibility of a legally cognizable intersectional claim is a first step. Other institutions in Canada, such as the Ontario Human Rights Commission (OHRC), have embraced an intersectional approach to human rights work.[184] The

[180] Paloma Angélica Escobar Ledezma et al. v. Mexico, Case 12,551, Inter. Am. Comm'n H.R., Report No. 51/13, ¶ 27 (July 12, 2013).

[181] Veliz Franco et al. v. Guatemala, Preliminary Objections, Merits, Reparations and Costs, Judgment, Inter-Am. Ct. H.R. (ser. C) No. 277 (May 19, 2014); Velásquez Paiz et al. v. Guatemala, Preliminary Objections, Merits, Reparations and Costs, Judgment, Inter-Am. Ct. H.R. (ser. C) No. 307 (Nov. 19, 2015).

[182] Canadian Charter of Rights and Freedoms Apr. 17, 1985, art. 15.

[183] *See* Uccellari, *supra* note 76, at 38 (citing *Law v. Canada* [1991] 1 S.C.R. 497, ¶¶ 554–55).

[184] *See id.* at 41.

OHRC is a government agency that is empowered to make inquiries into Ontarian institutions to address any sources of conflict as well as bring a complaint directly to the Human Rights Tribunal of Ontario.[185]

The Canadian Supreme Court's declaration that it recognizes intersectional claims as legally cognizable differs from the approach in the United States. Ironically, since many of the early architects of intersectionality theory were critical race feminists in the United States, intersectionality has not enjoyed the same degree of formal juridical recognition in US courts. In the United States, in fact, studies have found that plaintiffs who bring intersectional claims for employment discrimination are less likely to win than plaintiffs who bring a claim under only one form of discrimination.[186] The US government has repeatedly failed to address systemic intersectional human rights violations such as violence against trans women held in US immigration detention.

Overall, jurisprudence in the inter-American system is increasingly incorporating intersectional analysis and recognition of intersectional issues. The United States must do more to keep pace with regional efforts to recognize intersectionality in human rights frameworks. The progress on intersectionality within the inter-American system, however, has the potential to influence national human rights discourse positively in all countries in the region, including the United States.

Intersectionality and the European system

Basic structure and human rights treaties

The European human rights system is the oldest regional system, dating back to the adoption of the European Convention on Human Rights in 1950.[187] It consists of the Council of Europe, the European Union, and the Organization for Security and Cooperation in Europe. Each of these institutions has its own mechanisms for ensuring the protection and promotion of human rights within the region. I focus here on the European Court of Human Rights (ECtHR) and on the human rights law of the European Union, as interpreted by the Court of Justice of the European Union (CJEU). Although these represent two distinct systems of law, in practice the institutions of the Council of Europe and the EU influence each other. In case law, for example, the ECtHR refers to relevant EU legislation and the jurisprudence of the CJEU.[188]

[185] *See Litigation and Inquiry Strategy*, Ontario Hum. Rts. Comm'n, http://www.ohrc.on.ca/en/about-commission/litigation-and-inquiry-strategy (last visited May 3, 2021). For example, the OHRC brought a complaint on behalf of Black lawyers who were racially profiled at a library and successfully argued for the adoption of a three-part test for discrimination. *Id.*

[186] *See* Rachel Kahn Best et al., *Multiple Disadvantages: An Empirical Test of Intersectionality Theory in EEO Litigation*, 45 L. & Soc'y Rev. 991, 1011 (2011) ("[P]laintiffs making intersectional claims have only about half the odds of attaining at least a partial victory and approximately one-third the odds of a complete victory.").

[187] Carol M. Tucker, *Regional Human Rights Models in Europe and Africa: A Comparison*, 10 Syr. J. Int'l L. & Com. 135, 140 (1983).

[188] *See* Eur. Comm'n on Hum. Rts., Handbook on European Non-Discrimination Law 17 (2018) [hereinafter ECHR Handbook].

Table 4.3 Council of Europe: Key institutions and instruments

Founding treaty	Treaty of London (1949)
Primary human rights institutions	European Commission on Human Rights (1954–98) European Court of Human Rights (1959) European Committee on Social Rights (ECSR; 1961)
Primary human rights instruments	European Convention on Human Rights (ECHR; 1950) Key articles: 14, Protocol 12 European Social Charter (1961; revised 1996) European Convention for the Prevention of Torture and Inhuman or Degrading Treatment or Punishment (1987) Framework Convention for the Protection of National Minorities (1994) Convention on Action Against Trafficking in Human Beings (2005) Convention on Preventing and Combatting Violence Against Women and Domestic Violence (Istanbul Convention; 2011)

The Council of Europe and the European Court of Human Rights

In the aftermath of World War II, the Council of Europe was created to promote reconstruction in Europe as well as human rights, the rule of law, and social development.[189] As of 2018, the Council of Europe included forty-seven Member States, with twenty-eight of those states also belonging to the European Union.[190] The Council of Europe drafted and adopted some of the foundational human rights instruments in the region, including the European Convention on Human Rights (ECHR), the European Social Charter, and the European Convention for the Prevention of Torture and Inhuman or Degrading Treatment or Punishment (see Table 4.3). All the Member States of the Council of Europe have ratified the ECHR. In 1959, the Council established the European Court of Human Rights to hear complaints of rights violations from individuals and states. Originally, the now-defunct European Commission of Human Rights determined which claims were admissible before the Court. In 1998, a protocol to the European Convention, Protocol No. 11, entered into force and established the status of the European Court of Human Rights as a permanent, full-time institution without the European Commission of Human Rights as a gatekeeper. As of 2018, the Court, which is based in Strasbourg, France, had delivered over 21,000 judgments.[191]

[189] *See* Statute of the Council of Europe, 87 U.N.T.S. 103, E.T.S. 1, pmbl. & art. 1.
[190] *Who We Are*, COUNCIL OF EUR., https://www.coe.int/en/web/about-us/who-we-are?desktop=true (last visited May 3, 2021).
[191] *See* EUR. CT. HUM. RTS., THE ECHR IN FACTS AND FIGURES 5 (2018), https://www.echr.coe.int/Documents/Facts_Figures_2018_ENG.pdf.

In addition to the European Convention on Human Rights, the Council of Europe's other primary human rights treaty is the European Social Charter, which was revised in 1996.[192] The Council created the European Committee on Social Rights (ECSR) to monitor State compliance with the European Social Charter. The European Social Charter includes a non-discrimination provision similar to Article 14 of the ECHR, discussed below. Unlike the ECHR, however, the Social Charter allows complaints from collective entities such as non-governmental organizations.[193]

The European Convention on Human Rights includes a provision guaranteeing equal treatment in the enjoyment of the rights in the Convention.[194] In other words, the non-discrimination provision, Article 14, is not a free-standing non-discrimination provision but limits the reach of its equality guarantee to the other rights in the Convention. A subsequent protocol to the ECHR, Protocol 12, which opened for signature in 2000, expands non-discrimination protection to cover any right guaranteed at the national level.[195] Protocol 12 would expand Article 14's non-discrimination protection beyond the rights in the Convention to include "any right set forth by law." As of 2020 however, only twenty states had ratified Protocol 12.[196] Protocol 12 represents a significant expansion of non-discrimination protection. Regarding Protocol 12, the European Commission on Human Rights observes:

> [W]hile the Protocol principally protects individuals against discrimination from the state, it will also apply to those relationships between private persons, which should normally be regulated by the state. These may include, "for example, arbitrary denial of access to work, access to restaurants, or to services which private persons may make available to the public such as medical care or utilities" .... Protocol 12 will prohibit discrimination outside purely personal contexts, where individuals exercise functions placing them in a position to decide on how publicly available goods and services are offered.[197]

Protocol 12 makes individuals accountable for discrimination when they offer goods and services to the public, which significantly increases the reach of the non-discrimination provision.

Most complaints alleging a violation of the non-discrimination provision of Article 14 also allege a violation of one of the substantive rights in the ECHR. A complaint may allege that the complainant experienced a violation of the substantive rights and that the interference with the enjoyment of the right was discriminatory. When the ECtHR finds a violation of the substantive right, it does not consider whether there

[192] *The European Social Charter*, COUNCIL OF EUR., https://www.coe.int/en/web/european-social-charter? (last visited May 3, 2021).

[193] *The Charter in Four Steps*, COUNCIL OF EUROPE, https://www.coe.int/en/web/european-social-charter/about-the-charter (last visited May 3, 2021).

[194] Convention for the Protection of Human Rights and Fundamental Freedoms, Nov. 4, 1950, art.14, 213 U.N.T.S. 221, 232 [hereinafter European Convention on Human Rights].

[195] *See* Niels Peterson, *The Principle of Non-discrimination in the European Convention on Human Rights and in EU Fundamental Rights Law*, in CONTEMPORARY ISSUES IN HUMAN RIGHTS LAW: EUROPE AND ASIA 129, 130 (Yumiko Nakanishi ed., 2018).

[196] *See id.*

[197] *See* ECHR HANDBOOK, *supra* note 188, at 34.

has been a violation of the specific rights listed in Article 14's non-discrimination provision.[198]

In its interpretation of Article 14, the Court recognizes both direct and indirect discrimination. In cases involving direct discrimination, the Court treats as discriminatory differential treatment of people who are similarly situated when the different treatment demonstrates bias based on a particular, identifiable characteristic. The Court also recognizes cases involving indirect discrimination in which "a difference in treatment may take the form of disproportionately prejudicial effects of a general policy or measure which, though couched in neutral terms, discriminates against a group."[199]

In cases of direct discrimination, the Court requires the complainant to establish different treatment and then requires the government to show that the differential treatment was justifiable.[200] In cases of indirect discrimination, the Court adopts a burden-shifting approach, requiring the complainant to provide prima facie evidence that a policy or practice disproportionately affects a protected group. The burden then shifts to the government to prove that the difference in treatment is justifiable.[201] The Court considers statistical evidence of differential impact when presented with such evidence.[202] Statistical data that is disaggregated by gender, race, ethnicity, religion, disability, and/or sexual orientation and gender identity may, in theory, help facilitate the Court's consideration of intersectional claims.[203] The availability of disaggregated data, however, is only the first step. The Court must also consistently demonstrate its willingness to consider intersectional discrimination that is revealed through the examination of disaggregated data.

In addition to indirect discrimination claims, two other features of the Convention and the Court's interpretation may help to facilitate consideration of intersectional claims. Article 14 establishes certain grounds for prohibited discrimination, including "sex, race, colour, language, religion, political or other opinion, national or social origin, association with a national minority, property, birth or other status."[204] The open-ended category of discrimination based on "other status" has allowed the Court to consider discrimination based on "sexual orientation, disability, age, military rank, parenthood of a child born out of wedlock, fatherhood, marital status, membership of an organization and place of residence."[205] The Court has also noted that the Convention is a "living" document that must evolve with the times.[206] The

[198] *See id.* at 29.

[199] D.H. and Others v. The Czech Republic, App. No. 57325/00, 47 Eur. H.R. Rep. 3, ¶ 184 (2008). *See also* Opuz v. Turkey, App. No. 33401/02, 48 I.L.M. 909 (2009).

[200] LORENA SOSA, INTERSECTIONALITY IN THE HUMAN RIGHTS LEGAL FRAMEWORK ON VIOLENCE AGAINST WOMEN 124 (2017).

[201] *See id.*

[202] *See, e.g.*, Hoogendijk v. The Netherlands, Decision, App. No. 58461/00 (2005).

[203] *See* SOSA, *supra* note 200, at 124.

[204] European Convention on Human Rights art.14, 213 U.N.T.S. 221, 232.

[205] *See* Jess Bullock & Annick Masselot, *Multiple Discrimination and Intersectional Disadvantages: Challenges and Opportunities in the European Union Legal Framework*, 19 COLUM. J. EUR. L. 57, 72 (2013). *See also* SOSA, *supra* note 200, at 124.

[206] Tyrer v. United Kingdom, 25 Eur. Ct. H.R. 5856/72, ¶ 31 (1978) ("The Court must also recall that the Convention is a living instrument which, as the Commission rightly stressed, must be interpreted in the light of present-day conditions.").

Table 4.4 European Union: Key institutions and instruments

Founding treaties	Maastricht Treaty (1993) Treaty of Lisbon (2007)
Primary human rights institutions	Court of Justice of the European Union (CJEU; 1952) European Commission (1958)
Primary human rights instruments	Treaty on the Functioning of the European Union (originally Treaty of Rome, 1957; renamed 2009) Amsterdam Treaty (1999) EU Charter of Fundamental Rights (2000) Key articles: 20, 21 Employment Equality Directive (2000) Racial Equality Directive (2000) Gender Equality Directive (2006)

Convention benefits from interpretive flexibility stemming from open-ended grounds of discrimination as well as the understanding of rights evolving in a dynamic, "living" document.

Several other Council of Europe treaties contain important non-discrimination provisions. The Framework Convention for the Protection of National Minorities and the Convention on Action Against Trafficking in Human Beings, for example, include provisions prohibiting discrimination. The Convention on Preventing and Combatting Violence Against Women and Domestic Violence (the "Istanbul Convention"), which the Council of Europe adopted in 2011, is particularly significant in discussions of non-discrimination. The Council of Europe also established the European Commission against Racism and Intolerance, which focuses on combatting discrimination based on, for example, race, ethnicity, religion, sexual orientation, or gender identity.

The European Union and the Court of Justice of the European Union

The original treaties of the European Communities focused on free trade and contained few references to human rights. Over time, however, the CJEU confronted several cases that involved human rights violations. As a result, the CJEU developed a number of judicially articulated laws known as the "general principles of Community Law."[207] As EU treaties have been revised over the years, human rights have become increasingly prominent and vitally important to EU law (see Table 4.4).

EU Member States are bound by multiple sources of law. Council of Europe law and decisions of the ECtHR are binding on EU states. In addition, EU states are

[207] *See* ECHR HANDBOOK, *supra* note 188, at 20 (internal quotations omitted).

bound by EU law and decisions of the CJEU. The two sources of law overlap in the non-discrimination area, and the CJEU looks to the ECHR and the European Social Charter for guidance in implementing EU human rights law.[208]

EU non-discrimination law was originally quite narrow, as it was limited to non-discrimination in employment. Until 2000, "non-discrimination law in the EU only applied to employment and social security, and only covered the grounds of sex."[209] The Treaty on the Functioning of the EU also prohibited discrimination on the basis on nationality.[210] Significantly, in 1999, the EU adopted the Amsterdam Treaty, which greatly expanded the grounds for which discrimination was prohibited.

In 2000, the EU significantly reformed its equality legislation. It passed legally binding directives that expanded non-discrimination provisions to include grounds beyond the existing prohibitions on gender discrimination. The EU adopted new equality directives, including the Employment Equality Directive (which bans discrimination on the basis of sexual orientation, religion or belief, age, and disability); the Racial Equality Directive (which bans race discrimination in the context of social security and the welfare system and in the provision of goods and services); and the Gender Equality Directive (recast 2006). In 2019, the EU was considering a proposal, called the "Horizontal Directive," that would broaden non-discrimination protection on the basis of sexual orientation, religious belief, disability, and age beyond the employment context to include access to goods and services.[211]

The EU also adopted the EU Charter of Fundamental Rights in 2000. Although the Charter began as a non-binding declaration, the 2009 Lisbon Treaty converted it into a "legally binding document with the same value as the EU treaties."[212] Article 21 of the EU Charter of Fundamental Rights contains a non-exhaustive list of seventeen grounds for prohibited discrimination.[213] Along with the expansion of the grounds for prohibited discrimination, the new EU laws established new entities to provide oversight of the implementation of the new laws—for example, the EU Agency for Fundamental Rights (FRA) and the European Institute for Gender Equality (EIGE).[214]

The EU expanded the grounds on which one may claim a violation of anti-discrimination law, implicitly encouraging Member States to enact legislation that contemplates claims of intersectional discrimination.[215] This expansion, along with

[208] *See id.* at 17.

[209] *See id.* at 21.

[210] Treaty on the Functioning of the EU arts. 18, 45, May 9, 2008, 2008 O.J. (C 115).

[211] *See* ECHR HANDBOOK, *supra* note 188, at 22.

[212] *See id.* at 23.

[213] Andrea Krizsan et al., *Institutionalizing Intersectionality: A Theoretical Framework, in* INSTITUTIONALIZING INTERSECTIONALITY: THE CHANGING NATURE OF EUROPEAN EQUALITY REGIMES 1, 13 (Andrea Krizsan et al. eds., 2012). The Charter prohibits discrimination on the basis of "any ground such as sex, race, colour, ethnic or social origin, genetic features, language, religion or belief, political or any other opinion, membership of a national minority, property, birth, disability, age or sexual orientation." *See* ECHR HANDBOOK, *supra* note 188, at 35.

[214] *See* ECHR HANDBOOK, *supra* note 188, at 23.

[215] *See* Krizsan, *supra* note 213, at 13 ("Although these requirements cover only race or ethnic origin and gender, the European Commission encourages the creation of integrated equality bodies covering all protected inequalities through its soft law recommendations."). *See also* Sarah Hannatt, *Equality at the Intersections: The Legislative and Judicial Failure to Tackle Multiple Discrimination*, 23 OXFORD J. LEGAL STUD. 65, 66 (2003).

other recent developments, "mark[s] a shift from 'gender to diversity' in EU equality policies."[216] This significant expansion of non-discrimination grounds within the EU opened the door for consideration of intersectionality in discrimination cases. Some commentators have noted, however, that the EU needs to clarify that it will recognize intersectional claims of discrimination, arguing that "[t]he legislative innovation that is needed is one which states that unlawful discrimination includes discrimination based on more than one ground."[217]

Since the early 2000s, intersectionality theory has gained traction in Europe.[218] As Andrea Krizsan, Hege Skjeie and Judith Squires explain,

> [w]here states have previously operated with equality legislation that addresses only particular forms of inequality they are now under pressure not only to address multiple forms of discrimination, but also to consider the interaction between these strands. European states are increasingly attempting to engage, at both a conceptual and policy level, with the fact that gender discrimination and inequality are shaped in fundamental ways by different inequality axes: by race, ethnicity, class, sexuality, disability, and others.[219]

At the domestic level, many states have reformed their equality legislation in an effort to incorporate intersectional insights. Some countries have expanded the grounds for prohibited discrimination.[220] Several European countries have created new institutions with more comprehensive oversight responsibilities. In Britain, for example, the Equality and Human Rights Commission oversees implementation and enforcement of legislation prohibiting discrimination on the basis of age, disability, gender, race, religion or belief, and sexual orientation or transgender status.[221] Other countries, such as Belgium, maintain separate enforcement bodies for sex discrimination and race discrimination.[222]

Different actors within the EU system have embraced intersectionality at different levels throughout the system, often referring to intersectionality as "multiple discrimination."[223] However, this new recognition of intersectionality has not altered the legal framework within the EU, so intersectionality has not had maximum impact on victims of discrimination.[224] In fact, the "EU's anti-discrimination law does not explicitly cover intersectionality or even multiple discrimination."[225] Although Member States

[216] *See* Krizsan, *supra* note 213, at 13.

[217] Johanna Kantola & Kevät Nousiainen, *The European Union: Initiator of a New European Anti-Discrimination Regime?*, *in* Institutionalizing Intersectionality: The Changing Nature of European Equality Regimes 33, 55 (Andrea Krizsan et al. eds., 2012).

[218] See Krizsan et al, *supra* note 213, at 5 ("[T]here is evidence of a shared determination to address multiple inequalities, which is creating a pluralized equalities framework—political, legal and institutional.").

[219] *Id.* at 4.

[220] *See* Hannatt, *supra* note 215, at 66.

[221] *See* Krizsan et al., *supra* note 213, at 4.

[222] *See id.*

[223] *See* Kantola & Nousiainen, *supra* note 217, at 55.

[224] *See* Gauthier de Beco, *Protecting the Invisible: An Intersectional Approach to International Human Rights Law*, 17 Hum. Rts. L. Rev. 633, 657 (2017) (stating that engagement with intra-group differences has largely been unequal).

[225] Kantola & Nousiainen, *supra* note 217, at 55.

may address intersectionality in their own non-discrimination laws, the EU has not created structural space within its own legal apparatus to accommodate intersectional claims.[226] Instead, EU law continues to focus on "the relatively limiting principle of (formal) equality."[227] The CJEU, for example, continues to "define non-discrimination through a formal lens that derives discrimination from a difference in treatment in comparable situations" rather than emphasizing the broader context in which discrimination occurs.[228] This legal definition of discrimination makes it more difficult for claimants to raise intersectional arguments before CJEU.

In sum, the European system has been uneven, at best, in its embrace of intersectionality. International human rights instruments drafted after 2010 would seem to provide an opportunity to incorporate intersectional principles, the relevance of which were commonly accepted at that point. But even human rights instruments drafted as recently as 2011 do not embody intersectional principles. The Convention on Preventing and Combatting Violence Against Women and Domestic Violence (Istanbul Convention), which entered into force in 2014, does not explicitly embrace an intersectional framework.[229] The Istanbul Convention has a broad range of grounds for prohibited discrimination, including a catch-all category for "other status," but it does not mention intersectionality.

In December 2010, the EU ratified the Convention on the Rights of Persons with Disabilities (CRPD). Historically, international human rights treaties had been open to ratification only by states. The CRPD, however, allows for ratification by regional entities such as the European Union. In its review of the EU's compliance with the terms of the CRPD, however, the CRPD Committee expressed disappointment that the European Union had not incorporated disability-related concerns into EU directives such as the Racial Equality Directive, the Gender Goods and Services Directive, and the Gender Equality Directive but instead let these directives exist in silos. By ratifying the CRPD, the European Union has an opportunity to embrace intersectionality in its commitment to persons with disabilities by incorporating disability-related concerns into its existing directives. An intersectional approach would include examining the intersection of disability discrimination with other forms of discrimination, such as that based on race, gender, or sexual orientation.

The European Union has mentioned intersectionality sparingly and has not incorporated the concept into its analysis of human rights violations in a meaningful and systematic way. The Racial Equality Directive and the Employment Equality Directive acknowledge that "women are often the victims of multiple discrimination."[230] These brief references, however, do not reflect a deep commitment to analyzing intersectional discrimination.

[226] *See* Dagmar Schieck, *Revisiting Intersectionality For EU Anti-Discrimination Law in an Economic Crisis—A Critical Legal Studies Perspective*, 2 Sociologia del Diritto 23, 30 (2016).

[227] *See* Kantola & Nousiainen, *supra* note 217, at 55.

[228] Marc De Vos, *Substantive Formal Equality in EU Non-Discrimination Law*, in The European Union as Protector and Promoter of Equality 245, 248 (Thomas Giegerich ed., 2020).

[229] For enforcement, the Istanbul Convention relies on a group of experts to evaluate state compliance rather than creating a quasi-judicial system of individual complaints. *See* sosa, *supra* note 200, at 133.

[230] Council Directive 2000/43/EC, 2000 O.J. (L 180), ¶ 14.

The CJEU has been reluctant to use Article 21 of the EU Charter of Fundamental Rights (mentioned above) to expand the scope of non-discrimination protection to include an intersectional claim. Although Article 21 has an open-ended set of grounds for discrimination claims, the EU equality directives each list a limited, closed list of prohibited grounds. The EU handbook on non-discrimination law states that CJEU

> has repeatedly emphasized that it is not within its power to extend those grounds, and it has so far not invoked Articles 20 or 21 of the EU Charter to overturn this position. This means that it would not be possible to create new grounds to reflect the specific situations of discrimination experienced by certain groups, such as black women.[231]

In other words, the CJEU has shown little inclination to consider new categories of discrimination that might include intersectional discrimination.

While the Council of Europe and the European Union have overlapping interests in human rights and while their institutions and law influence each other, there is a notable distinction in their use of (or disregard for) intersectionality. Given the CJEU's reluctance to approach intersectionality expansively, the ECtHR is more likely to embrace intersectional approaches in its analysis of complaints. Article 14 of the ECHR has a broader, open-ended scope, making it more likely for the ECtHR to interpret discrimination claims in an intersectional way. The ECtHR is less bound than the CJEU to the specific grounds listed in the treaty, and it is therefore more likely to consider a claim based on an intersectional combination of grounds.

Soft law commitments to intersectionality

Progress in recognizing intersectional discrimination claims has been more apparent in the EU's non-binding, "soft law" context (guidelines, recommendations, suggested programs, etc.) than in legally binding, "hard law."[232] Additionally, the EU has encouraged Member States to embrace intersectionality in domestic anti-discrimination laws. The European Parliament (the legislative branch of the EU) established a Committee on Women's Rights and Gender Equality (FEMM), which has been active in promoting women's rights in the region and has also promoted intersectionality in limited ways. For example, FEMM has drafted reports and initiated parliamentary dialogue concerning intersectionality in the context of Roma women in 2006 and disabled women in 2007.[233] In 2007, the European Commission (the EU's executive branch) drafted a report entitled *Tackling Multiple Discrimination: Practices, Policies and Laws*.[234] Subunits within the European Commission, however, which are often tasked with drafting such reports, continue to hew closely to their own mandates and to consult with the same civil society organizations with which they typically collaborate. This tendency

[231] *See* ECHR HANDBOOK, *supra* note 188, at 62–63.

[232] *See* NIALL CROWLEY ET AL., EMPOWERMENT OF ROMANI WOMEN WITHIN THE EUROPEAN FRAMEWORK OF NATIONAL ROMA INCLUSION STRATEGIES 15–16 (2013). *See also* Kantola & Nousiainen, *supra* note 217, at 55.

[233] *See* Kantola & Nousiainen, *supra* note 217, at 44.

[234] *Id.* at 45.

to remain focused on one type of discrimination, even in the context of research on intersectionality, functionally limits the work and the outcome documents.[235] In fact, civil society organizations are not immune from criticism that they have remained too focused on one particular ground of discrimination and insufficiently engaged with intersectionality. The European Women's Lobby, for example, which is the largest pan-European women's rights organization, has come under criticism for failing to focus on minority women and diversity within the group.[236]

FEMM's September 2019 newsletter signals steps towards intersectionality in the European Parliament.[237] In late 2019, FEMM conducted a hearing in conjunction with the Committee on Employment and Social Affairs (EMPL) on the candidacy of Helena Dalli for Equality Commissioner.[238] Dalli, a Maltese citizen, gave an introductory speech in which she spoke about creating a task force on equality that would build "an intersectional approach on gender mainstreaming in all EU policies."[239] Dalli also pledged to communicate with ministers to advance several stagnant files, including an Anti-discrimination Directive.[240] Further, Dalli fielded several questions from committee members on issues such as LGBTQI rights and disability rights.[241] The creation of an Equality Commissioner and the consideration of a candidate who openly speaks about the importance of intersectionality in the European system represents movement in the right direction.

Soft law in the Council of Europe acknowledges some forms of intersectionality without fully implementing an intersectional analysis. In 2002, the Committee of Ministers introduced a recommendation on gender-based violence.[242] The recommendation, which has widespread support among Member States of the Council of Europe, reflects a sensitivity to intersectionality. The recommendation refers to "multiple discrimination," stating, "Women are often subjected to multiple discrimination on ground of their gender as well as their origin, including as victims of traditional or customary practices inconsistent with their human rights and fundamental freedoms."[243] This reference, however, occurs in the Preamble and is not the subject of extended discussion in the recommendation. The Committee of Ministers also operates rapporteur groups in a framework that does not necessarily promote intersectionality. For example, the Group for Social and Health Questions (GR-SOC) prepares information concerning, among other things, the rights of people with disabilities and the rights of migrants.[244] Meanwhile, the Group for Human Rights (GR-H) focuses

[235] *See id.* ("These units co-operate in issue specific steering groups but tend to concentrate [*sic*] their 'own' basis of inequality and consult the civil society organizations that come within their remit. . . .").

[236] *See id.* at 46.

[237] NEWSLETTER SEPTEMBER 2019 (Comm. on Women's Rts. & Gender Equal., Eur. Parliament), Sept. 2019, at 1.

[238] Press Release, Eur. Parliament, Hearing of Commissioner-designate Helena Dalli (Oct. 2, 2019), https://www.europarl.europa.eu/news/en/press-room/20190926IPR62241/hearing-of-commissioner-designate-helena-dalli.

[239] *Id.*

[240] *See id.*

[241] *See id.*

[242] *See* Comm. of Ministers of the Council of Europe, Recommendation Rec (2002) 5. *See also* SOSA, *supra* note 200, at 131.

[243] *See* Comm. of Ministers of the Council of Europe, *supra* note 242, at pmbl.

[244] *See* Comm. of Ministers, *GR-SOC: Social and Health Questions*, COUNCIL OF EUR., https://www.coe.int/en/web/cm/gr-soc (last visited May 3, 2021).

on torture, minority rights, racism, and equality and diversity.[245] An intersectional approach, however, would likely require an approach that streamlined information about, for example, minority women with disabilities or the torture of migrant women.

The European system has increasingly incorporated intersectional analysis in soft law materials, although there is still room for improvement. Both the EU and Council of Europe systems have opportunities for increased communication across different entities that would encourage intersectional human rights analysis. Given the trend toward greater understanding of intersectional discrimination in the region, particularly in soft law, the European system will likely see intersectional principles expand from soft law into regional jurisprudence.

Intersectionality jurisprudence within the European system

The ECtHR has heard numerous cases concerning intersectional issues. The Court's responses to such cases often do not include robust intersectional analysis or the use of strong intersectional language. However, some of the rulings indicate that the Court is aware of the impact of intersecting forms of discrimination. There is great opportunity in the future for the ECtHR to embrace more intersectional analysis in their decisions.

In *Opuz v. Turkey*, the ECtHR considered a case concerning intimate partner violence in Turkey. The applicant alleged that Turkey's response to intimate partner violence was inadequate and discriminatory. According to the allegations, authorities routinely mistreated victims who reported abuse and failed to provide adequate protection to victims. The evidence submitted in support of the complaint included evidence suggesting that "women of Kurdish origin, illiterate or of a low level of education and without any independent source of income were particularly affected."[246] In a nod toward differentiated experiences of violence within the category of "women," the Court noted that "[w]omen from vulnerable groups, such as those from low-income families or who are fleeing conflict or natural disasters, are particularly at risk."[247] Despite this recognition, the Court neither engaged in a probing analysis nor mentioned intersectional discrimination or "multiple" discrimination in its decision. *Opuz v. Turkey*, however, is significant in the ECtHR's jurisprudence because it marks the first time the Court clearly articulated that gender-based violence was a form of discrimination against women.[248]

In July 2012, the ECtHR decided *B.S. v. Spain*.[249] The case involved a complaint from a Nigerian woman who was working as a sex worker in Spain. The complaint alleged that Spanish police officers had assaulted and racially abused the woman. The complainant, B.S., exhausted domestic remedies in Spain and then filed a complaint

245 *See id.*

246 SOSA, *supra* note 200, at 138.

247 Opuz v. Turkey, App. No. 33401/02, 48 I.L.M. 909, ¶ 99 (2009).

248 Keina Yoshida, *Towards Intersectionality in the European Court of Human Rights: The Case of* B.S. v. Spain, 21 FEMINIST LEGAL STUD. 195, 201 (2013).

249 B.S. v. Spain, App. No. 47159/08 (Oct. 24, 2012), https://hudoc.echr.coe.int/fre#{"itemid":["001-112459"]}.

with the ECtHR alleging several violations of the ECHR, including discrimination. B.S. asserted that she was a victim of intersectional discrimination and alleged that Spanish police discriminated against her based on her race, gender, and status as a sex worker. Although the ECtHR did not use intersectionality terminology in its decision, the Court determined that the Spanish Courts did not consider "B.S.'s special vulnerability inherent in her situation as an African woman working in prostitution."[250] The Court found that Spain violated B.S.'s rights to non-discrimination and to be free from torture, inhuman, or degrading treatment. The case is significant because it marks the first time that the Court expressed a willingness to consider intersecting forms of discrimination.[251]

In the 2016 decision for *Parris v. Trinity College Dublin (CJEU)*, the Court of Justice of the European Union (CJEU) rejected a claim of discrimination based on sexual orientation and age.[252] The university's pension scheme provides payment to a member's spouse after their death, but only if the couple is married before the age of sixty. In this case, the complainant lecturer turned sixty-four before the government recognized his longtime same-sex partnership. He entered into a civil partnership with his partner in 2009 when the United Kingdom legalized such partnerships. However, Ireland did not recognize same-sex civil partnerships until 2011.[253] Thus, the lecturer could not comply with the university's rules because he was not able to legally marry until after the age of sixty. The Court did not use intersectional analysis to assess the claim and concluded that there was neither age discrimination nor sexual orientation discrimination. According to the Court, because neither form of discrimination existed in isolation, then there could be no combined intersectional discriminatory effect. The Court's limited, sequential single-ground analysis failed to appreciate the ways in which discrimination based on sexual orientation and age intersected in the complainant's life and resulted in intersectional discrimination.[254]

In *Garib v. The Netherlands*, decided in 2017, the ECtHR heard a case concerning housing discrimination.[255] Ms. Garib alleged that the refusal by the city of Rotterdam to grant her a government-mandated housing permit for low-cost housing constituted income status discrimination.[256] Although a majority of the Court did not find a violation of Article 2 of Protocol No. 4 to the European Convention for the Protection of Human Rights and Fundamental Freedoms, one of the dissenting opinions focused on the intersectional nature of the multiple forms of discrimination experienced by Ms. Garib.[257] Judge Pinto de Albuquerque analyzed Ms. Garib's situation based on "being both a woman and impoverished" and how that status impacted "her vulnerability

[250] *See id.*

[251] *See* Yoshida, *supra* note 248, at 196 n.8 ("To my knowledge, the Court has not yet shown much awareness of intersectional discrimination in its case law. In this regard, *B.S.* represents an important development.") (citing Lourdes Peroni, STRASBOURG OBSERVERS (2012)).

[252] *See* Shreya Atrey, *Illuminating the CJEU's Blind Spot of Intersectional Discrimination in* Parris v Trinity College Dublin, 47 INDUS. L.J. 278, 278 (2018).

[253] *See id.* at 281.

[254] *See id.* at 295–96.

[255] Garib v. The Netherlands, App No. 43494/09 (Nov. 6, 2017), http://hudoc.echr.coe.int/eng?i=001-177406.

[256] *See id.* at 4.

[257] *See id.* at 70 (Pinto de Albuquerque, J., dissenting).

vis-à-vis the Dutch housing policy."[258] He further encouraged the Court to "reach a global and comprehensive understanding of the various discrimination situations" in order to "guarantee the effectiveness of the Convention rights."[259] However, Judge Pinto de Albuquerque's intersectional analysis failed to persuade a majority of the Court to adopt this approach to the case.

The example of Roma women's rights within the European system

The Roma population in Europe numbers six million individuals and has a history of discrimination by other Europeans.[260] A history of traditional gender structures and entrenched xenophobia makes Romani women highly likely to experience intersecting levels of discrimination.[261] Romani women have filed several cases before the ECtHR seeking redress for violations of their rights.

Originally filed in 2004, *I.G. and Others v. Slovakia* was the first case brought in front of, but the third case decided by, the ECtHR against Slovakia relating to the forced sterilization of Romani women. In its 2012 decision, the Court insisted that shortcomings in legislation and practice relating to sterilizations were liable to affect members of the Roma community in particular, so their discrimination in these cases would be only indirect and unintentional.[262] In other words, poor public policies that affected different demographics were responsible for the poor treatment of Romani woman rather than targeted, bad-faith discrimination.[263] The case involved three Romani women—I.G., M.K., and R.H.—who were sterilized in 2000, 1999, and 2002, respectively. While in the hospital, they were asked to sign a document that, they learned only a few years later, was a request form for sterilization. In addition to not providing informed consent, both I.G. and M.K. were minors at the time, and the doctors sterilized them without the consent of their legal guardians. R.H. died during course of the legal process, so her case was dismissed from the ECtHR. The Court provided redress for I.G. and M.K. for violation of their rights under Articles 3 and 8.67, but unfortunately, for the third time, refused to consider the discriminatory character of forced sterilizations of Romani women. The Court found that it could not be established that the doctors acted in bad faith, that the applicants' sterilizations were a part of an organized policy, or that the conduct of the hospital staff was intentionally racially motivated.[264]

258 *See id.* at 76 Pinto de Albuquerque, J., dissenting).
259 *See id.* at 72 Pinto de Albuquerque, J., dissenting).
260 Sandrine Charlotte Bartos, Romani Women: The European Union's Most Stigmatized Minority 4 (2017).
261 *See id.* at 5–7.
262 Eur. Roma Rts. Ctr., Coercive and Cruel: Sterilisation and Its Consequences for Romani Women in the Czech Republic (1966–2016) 20 (2018), http://www.errc.org/uploads/upload_en/file/coercive-and-cruel-28-november-2016.pdf (articulating the multiple forms of discrimination and their intersectional effects on Romani women and girls, then setting out recommendations for governments to follow in order to address their specific concerns).
263 *Id.*
264 *See id.*

The ECtHR decided *V.C. v. Slovakia* in 2011. The case involved a Roma woman in Slovakia who was sterilized in a public hospital without her free and full consent. The Court missed an opportunity to explore the intersection of discrimination based on ethnicity and gender. In fact, the Court declined to consider the allegation of discrimination at all. Instead, it found that Slovakia had violated V.C.'s right to respect for private and family life under Articles 3 and 8. The Court never reached the claim that Slovakian doctors discriminated against her based on her ethnicity and gender. In dissent, Judge Mijović disagreed with the majority's decision not to address the discrimination allegations. Noting that V.C. was targeted because of her ethnicity, the judge wrote, "that represents the strongest form of discrimination and should have led to a finding of a violation of Article 14 with the violations found of Articles 3 and 8 of the Convention."[265]

In 2012 in *N.B. v. Slovakia*, the Court once again declined to address discrimination under Article 14 in a case involving involuntary sterilization of a Roma woman. The victim claimed violations of her rights to private and family life (under Articles 3 and 8) and to non-discrimination based on ethnicity and gender under Article 14. The Court declined to depart from the majority's reasoning in *V.C. v. Slovakia* because there was no evidence of bad faith or a hospital policy favoring sterilization of Roma women. As human rights lawyer Keina Yoshida observes:

> Whilst the Strasbourg Court has recognised that the particularities and vulnerabilities of the situations of some Roma people, the Court has failed to recognise the discriminatory nature of the forced sterilisations on the ground of the Roma women's sex *and* ethnicity in these cases. An intersectional approach to Article 14 would have led the Court to look at the specific historical exclusion of Roma women and to conceive of the forced sterilisations as a form of gender violence in breach of the prohibition of non-discrimination. The failure to recognise the discrimination in the cases of Roma sterilization thus fails to address the root cause of the harm. By focusing on the harm suffered by the individual women, the structural discrimination affecting Roma women due to their gender and race was obfuscated by the Court.[266]

In addition to the troubled history of forced sterilizations, Romani women also experience discrimination in access to healthcare and education on the basis of their ethnicity.[267] The European Commission established the EU Framework for National Roma Integration Strategies to encourage Member States to establish policies that address the discrimination faced by the Roma population.[268] The 2019 report included intersectional language, discussing the multiple discrimination Romani women face because of their gender and ethnicity.[269] The report highlighted that few Member

[265] *See* V.C. v. Slovakia, App. No. 18968/07 (Aug. 2, 2012), http://hudoc.echr.coe.int/eng?i=001-107364 (Mijovic, J., dissenting).
[266] *See* Yoshida, *supra* note 248, at 202.
[267] *See* BARTOS, *supra* note 260, at 6–7.
[268] *See id.* at 7.
[269] *See generally* EUR. COMM'N, REPORT ON THE IMPLEMENTATION OF NATIONAL ROMA INTEGRATION STRATEGIES (2019), https://op.europa.eu/en/publication-detail/-/publication/3e0fe26c-3749-11ea-ba6e-01aa75ed71a1#.

States had implemented any policies to address the complex issues faced by Romani women.[270]

Trends in regional approaches to intersectionality

Like the UN treaty body system, the regional human rights systems have begun to embrace intersectionality. Each system is moving at its own pace and facing its own challenges in fully incorporating an intersectional framework into its work. In each of the regional systems, there is reason to be optimistic that intersectionality is taking hold and gaining ground. As we have seen, the African Court has demonstrated its willingness to expand its jurisdiction beyond the African Charter to consider other relevant human rights treaties, a jurisdictional move that may facilitate intersectional analysis of human rights claims. The European human rights system has witnessed an explosion of scholarly exploration of intersectionality in the context of rights, even as the CJEU has demonstrated its reluctance to adopt an intersectional lens. The Inter-American Court and Commission, respected for their treatment of gender-based violence as a human rights abuse, have increasingly shown a willingness to examine gender-based violence claims using an intersectional framework. Although the particular approaches and obstacles to intersectionality vary among the regional systems, several broad patterns emerge: additive approaches to intersectionality, a move from a focus on vulnerability to intersectionality, and a willingness to embrace intersectionality in soft law rather than jurisprudence.

Additive approaches to intersectionality

The three regional systems discussed in this chapter tend to view intersectional issues through an additive lens, meaning that the regional systems look at different grounds for discrimination as compounding each other.[271] Many of the regional bodies use the word *intersectionality* but then conduct an additive analysis of a person's experience with discrimination.[272] For example, in *I. V. v. Bolivia*, the IACHR looked at I.V.'s status as a woman and as an immigrant, rather than analyzing her case as an immigrant woman.[273] If the IACHR had analyzed I.V.'s case in a truly intersectional way, the Court would have realized that her statuses as an immigrant and as a woman are inseparable and cannot be divorced when understanding her experience in the hospital. An intersectional lens can shed light on the different forms of structural inequality that combine to produce the complex human rights violations faced by a complainant like I.V. An intersectional framework allows a human rights body to fully understand

270 *See id.*

271 GENDERACE: FINAL REPORT 72 (Isabelle Carles & Olga Jubany-Baucells eds., 2010), https://www.tu-berlin.de/fileadmin/f27/PDFs/Forschung/GENDERACE_FINAL_REPORT.pdf.

272 *See supra* note 121 and accompanying text.

273 *See generally* I.V. v. Bolivia, Preliminary Objections, Merits, Reparations and Costs, Judgment, Inter-Am. Ct. H.R. (ser. C) No. 329, ¶ 19 (Nov. 30, 2016).

and remediate the violations, including both individual remedies and remedies designed to dismantle structural subordination.

An additive discrimination analysis is certainly a step in the right direction for these regional systems. This type of analysis shows that the regional bodies understand that different grounds for discrimination interact and influence the situation that led to the complaint. However, a fully intersectional analysis, where the bodies appreciate that the discriminatory experience cannot be fully understood by solely examining one ground for discrimination,[274] would facilitate a richer body of human rights law and ideally lead to better outcomes for victims of human rights violations.

Moving from vulnerability to intersectionality

In both the jurisprudence of quasi-judicial bodies in the European system and in the soft law of European human rights institutions, intersectionality is often equated with additive notions such as "particular vulnerability." Treating intersectionality as a form of "added" vulnerability is problematic for three primary reasons. The first is that the EU often uses "particular vulnerability" to convey a physical vulnerability, such as pregnancy. The concept of vulnerability within the European system refers to corporeal or "embodied" vulnerability. Rather than an understanding of vulnerability grounded in the contextual analysis of structural inequality that renders one "vulnerable" to intersecting systems of power, the Council of Europe refers to physical vulnerability as "the vulnerability of a pregnant, defenceless, ill, physically or mentally handicapped or dependent victim."[275] The ECHR and the ECtHR use a particular form of vulnerability that focuses on individual corporeality rather than structural inequality and social systems. The preference for a biological or physiological vulnerability over true intersectional analysis surfaces in both "soft" law and "hard" law within the European system.

The second problem with an emphasis on "particular vulnerability" is that the concept leaves little conceptual space for agency and focuses on individual experiences rather than structural inequality. By focusing on particular vulnerability rather than intersectionality, the ECHR conveys that certain circumstances, like age or disability, may make some women particularly vulnerable to gender-based violence. The focus on vulnerability defines whole categories of women solely in terms of victimhood. Vulnerability downplays agency and leaves little room to recognize the many ways that women struggle against intersectional forms of oppression in their lives.[276] In addition, the focus on vulnerability tends to concentrate attention on the individual

[274] *See supra* note 76–78 and accompanying text.

[275] Comm. of Ministers of the Council of Europe, Recommendation Rec (2002) 5, app'x ¶ 35. As Lorena Sosa notes: "Similarly to the ECHR, however, these references do not necessarily suggest an 'intersectional approach' since vulnerability is not suggested as the result of structural and social constructions. Instead, they address 'embodied' vulnerability." SOSA, *supra* note 200, at 132.

[276] *See* Pok Yin S. Chow, *Has Intersectionality Reached Its Limits? Intersectionality in the UN Human Rights Treaty Body Practice and the Issue of Ambivalence*, 16 HUM. RTS. L. REV. 453, 481 (2016) ("[A]n individual's multiple identities may give rise to a form of uncertainty . . . raising complex questions of individual agency, self and identity.").

human rights victim rather than the systems of subordination that intersect to harm victims. Within UN discourse, the abbreviated concept of "particular vulnerability" takes the place of more searching inquiry concerning the ways in which power operates within intersecting systems of subordination.

The idea of "particular" vulnerability establishes as a baseline the experience of non-marginalized populations. In the case of women's rights, for example, the ECHR and the ECtHR have embraced a view that characterizes all women as vulnerable and some women as "particularly vulnerable" to gender-based violence. This is the third problem with vulnerability: it is cast as "extra"—meaning, for example, that wealthy white women are seen as the norm and that any additional sites of potential discrimination or oppression render one "extra," or particularly, vulnerable.[277] This type of analysis centers women who are privileged racially, economically, and geopolitically, among other things. Human rights bodies might consider, for example, women to be vulnerable to gender-based violence and Indigenous women to be "particularly vulnerable." This framework sets up non-native women as the baseline against which the "extra" or "added" vulnerability is measured.[278]

In this way, the focus on "particular vulnerability" parallels additive approaches. According to this understanding, intersectional identity is merely an added layer of vulnerability. The analysis fails to capture the truly intersectional, mutually constitutive nature of multiple, intersecting systems of oppression. This use of "particular vulnerability" as an anemic substitute for intersectional analysis stands in stark contrast to Crenshaw's invocation of vulnerability. Crenshaw notes that intersectional subordination "is frequently the consequence of the imposition of one burden that interacts with preexisting vulnerabilities to create yet another dimension of disempowerment."[279] Crenshaw's trenchant analysis of intersectionality encompasses the notion of people who are made vulnerable by the complex, mutually constitutive systems of subordination that intersect in their lives. We cannot expect the enervated concept of "particular vulnerability" frequently used by the UN and regional human rights systems to do the heaving lifting of Crenshaw's intersectional analysis.

A willingness to embrace intersectionality in soft law but not jurisprudence

Intersectionality is more prevalent in the soft law across all three regional systems than in their respective jurisprudence. One explanation for the more frequent appearance of intersectionality in soft law is that certain stakeholders representing marginalized groups have a larger voice in crafting soft law than they

[277] *See* Joanne Conaghan, *Intersectionality and UK Equality Initiatives*, 23 S. Afr. J. on Hum. Rts. 317, 320 (2007) ("As a consequence, feminism failed to get to grips with the complex ways in which racism and sexism worked through one another to produce forms of subordination with which feminism—and anti-racism—unwittingly conspired.").

[278] Carbado & Harris, *supra* note 120 at 2223 ("This baseline position of white women obscures their intersectional subjectivity.").

[279] Kimberlé Crenshaw, *Mapping the Margins: Intersectionality, Identity Politics, and Violence Against Women of Color*, 43 Stanford L. Rev. 1241, 1249 (1991).

do in formulating jurisprudence. For example, both the African system and the inter-American system consist of special rapporteurs that focus on a specific marginalized group. The creation of these positions demonstrates a recognition of the importance of devoting resources to addressing problems that implicate intersectional issues.

Jurisprudence depends on wronged parties bringing claims to the court to seek redress for the discrimination that the parties suffered. The decisions of the Inter-American Court are only binding on states that have expressly accepted the Court's jurisdiction. The decisions reached by the African Court and the ECtHR are binding on the member states, though member states may not always abide by the rulings of these courts. Regional system jurisprudence may be hesitant to embrace intersectionality without a true means of enforcing these new norms. Additionally, gender may play a role in the reticence to embrace intersectionality, as only 27 percent of judges worldwide are female.[280] Soft law, however, can still impact jurisprudence and encourage the hard law components of regional systems to embrace intersectionality through the changing social policy and norms.[281]

Future developments

Regional human rights systems offer victims of human rights violations a mechanism through which to seek redress that, in theory, reflects regional norms and is responsive to regional particularities in human rights interpretation. In broad strokes, regional systems offer many of the same human rights enforcement channels that the global UN system does, including state reporting on implementation and, in many cases, individual complaint mechanisms. Both these primary vehicles for human rights enforcement provide opportunities for state, NGOs, and regional human rights bodies to engage with and adopt an intersectional framework for human rights analysis.

As is the case at the global level, regional human rights systems are increasingly willing to adopt intersectional analysis in their human rights work. Not surprisingly, the soft law mechanisms are more susceptible to change and tend to reflect greater openness to adoption of an intersectional human rights framework. This openness to intersectionality in soft law will promote intersectionality in ways that will eventually be reflected in the enforceable treaty law or "hard law" in the region. Human rights jurisprudence at the regional level already indicates that regional bodies are grappling with individual complaints that are grounded in intersectional rights violations. The willingness of these bodies to consider intersectional dimensions of rights complaints varies, but the human rights bodies will likely become more consistently

[280] *See* Sital Kalantry, *Women in Robes*, Americas Q. (Jul. 24, 2012) https://www.americasquarterly.org/women-in-robes ("About 33 percent of state and federal court judges in the U.S. are women, slightly higher than the global average of 27 percent.").

[281] *See* Dinah L. Shelton, *Soft Law* in Routledge Handbook of International Law 68 (David Armstrong et al. eds., 2009).

supportive of intersectional approaches over time. The trends at the global and local levels point toward increased acceptance and adoption of intersectionality in our understanding of human rights. There is no indication that the regional systems will be any different, although each system will move at its own pace toward greater acceptance of intersectionality in its work.

5
Intersectionality in Treaty Body Decisions

In many cases, the treaty body system allows human rights victims to seek justice for rights violations by submitting a human rights complaint to one of the treaty bodies. The ability to bring a complaint to an international body offers victims a chance at compensation, remedies that may prevent future violations, and an acknowledgment that the state violated their rights. Although the complaint process cannot bring back a family member who was, for example, murdered by representatives of the state, holding the government accountable for its actions can be a powerful remedy for many victims.

Most of the major human rights treaties have an optional protocol that accompanies the primary treaty.[1] The optional protocol allows individuals in countries that have ratified the primary human rights treaty and separately ratified the optional protocol to bring individual complaints to the treaty body. Complainants cannot simultaneously pursue rights claims with the regional human rights bodies and the UN treaty bodies. They must first pursue their rights claim at the national level, and only if unsuccessful there, they must choose a regional or international venue. The decisions or communications in these cases form the jurisprudence of the treaty bodies. This jurisprudence provides another lens through which to explore the use of, or the failure to use, intersectionality theory in evaluating complex human rights violations.

This chapter's exploration of how intersectionality surfaces in the treaty body jurisprudence focuses primarily on the Committee on the Elimination of Discrimination Against Women (CEDAW), where consideration of intersectional human rights issues often come into play. Although the other UN treaty bodies have grappled with unstated intersectional issues, few cases from the other treaty bodies explicitly or implicitly identify intersectional rights violations. Legal and human rights scholar Shreya Atrey notes, "Intersectionality remains largely wanting in the Human Rights Committee's jurisprudence."[2] Writing about the treaty bodies more generally, human rights scholars Ivona Truscan and Joanne Bourke-Martignoni observe, "While the evolving and constantly growing list of grounds of discrimination prohibited by international human rights law would seemingly provide the basis for a systematic

[1] *See Human Rights Bodies—Complaint Procedures*, United Nations, https://www.ohchr.org/EN/HRBodies/TBPetitions/Pages/HRTBPetitions.aspx#individualcomm (last visited May 13, 2020) (listing the human rights bodies that may receive and consider individual complaints: CCPR, CERD, CAT, CEDAW, CRPD, the Committee on Enforced Disappearances (CED, CESCR, and the Committee on the Rights of the Child (CRC); and noting that the complaint mechanism for the Committee on Migrant Workers has not yet entered into force).

[2] Shreya Atrey, *Fifty Years On: The Curious Case of Intersectional Discrimination in the ICCPR*, 35 Nordic J. Hum. Rts. 220, 239 (2017).

Global Intersectionality and Contemporary Human Rights. Johanna Bond, Oxford University Press.
DOI: 10.1093/oso/9780198868835.003.0006

consideration of intersectional forms of discrimination, to date this has not been the case."[3] Nevertheless, several cases, three involving the Human Rights Committee and one involving the Committee on the Elimination of Racial Discrimination, offer insight into their respective treatment of intersectional complaints.

The chapter then looks at CEDAW jurisprudence specifically. I probe for evidence of intersectional analysis in the Committee's consideration of individual complaints, dividing the cases into four categories: (1) cases dealing with intersectional facts in which the Committee fails to address intersectionality; (2) cases in which CEDAW makes a passing reference to intersectionality but fails to explore intersectional issues comprehensively; (3) cases in which the Committee addresses intersectionality but does not include intersectional remedies; and (4) cases that include intersectional analysis and recommend intersectional remedies. In all, the Committee's jurisprudence reveals that it is moving cautiously toward an intersectional approach. Because intersectional rights violations are not unique to CEDAW, it is highly likely that the other treaty bodies will also move toward more systematic consideration of intersectional human rights issues that fall within the normative confines of their respective treaties.

Procedure and working methods for individual complaints

Each of the treaty bodies that allows individuals to submit human rights complaints follows a similar process for submission and consideration of an alleged human rights violation.[4] Complainants submit their complaint to the specific treaty body that correlates with the type of human rights violation that has been alleged. CEDAW is one of the eight human rights bodies that may evaluate individual complaints alleging a human rights violation. For example, in the case of CEDAW, individual communications must be directed against a State party that has ratified the Convention on the Elimination of All Forms of Discrimination Against Women and is a party to the Optional Protocol to the CEDAW Convention.[5] Any individual may file a complaint against such a State party alleging that their rights under the Convention were violated. The treaty body then evaluates the claims and issues its decision or view on the claim.[6]

[3] Ivona Truscan and Joanna Bourke-Martignoni, *International Human Rights Law and Intersectional Discrimination*, 16 Equal Rts. Rev. 103, 109 (2016).

[4] *See Human Rights Treaty Bodies—Individual Communications*, United Nations, https://www.ohchr.org/EN/HRBodies/TBPetitions/Pages/IndividualCommunications.aspx#proceduregenerale (last visited Sept. 30, 2020) (explaining the procedures open to individuals who claim that they are a victim of a violation of rights contained in international human rights treaties).

[5] A state's adoption of the Optional Protocol affirms the State party's recognition of the Committee's competence to evaluate claims that it has violated the Convention. G.A. Res. 54/4, Optional Protocol to the Convention on the Elimination of All Forms of Discrimination against Women (Oct. 15, 1999).

[6] *Human Rights Treaty Bodies—Individual Communications*, United Nations, https://www.ohchr.org/EN/HRBodies/TBPetitions/Pages/IndividualCommunications.aspx#overviewprocedure (last visited May 13, 2020) ("Final decisions adopted by the Committees are made public. Therefore, if complainants wish their identity not to be disclosed in the final decision, they are requested to so indicate.").

Although there is no required format for a complaint, CEDAW provides guidelines to help victims compose their communication.[7] The complaint must include the complainant's basic personal information, as well as specify the state against which the communication is directed.[8] In addition, the communication should provide a complete chronological statement of the facts on which the complaint is based, as well as the steps the complainant has taken to exhaust domestic remedies through the State party's judicial system.[9] The Committee recommends that victims also detail the specific rights under the treaty the complainant alleges were violated and the remedies sought. (Non-governmental organizations (NGOs) often assist complainants; the broader role of NGOs and other civil society groups is explored in chapter 7.)

Next, the Committee, through its Working Group on communications, evaluates the admissibility of the complaint. The Working Group will confirm that the following requirements are met: the complaint is brought by an individual, or on behalf of an individual (provided appropriate consent is given or other special circumstances are met); the victim was directly affected by the state action that the complainant alleges constitutes a violation; the complaint invokes a right protected by the treaty; the complaint alleges sufficient facts, arguments, or both to support a violation of the treaty; the treaty was in force at the time of the alleged violation;[10] the complaint has not been submitted to multiple international bodies for evaluation; all domestic remedies have been exhausted (i.e., the claim has proceeded through the national court system);[11] the complaint is not precluded by the State party's reservation to a particular provision of the treaty; and the complaint is not frivolous, harassing, vexatious, or otherwise unmeritorious.[12] If the communication meets all of these requirements, the Working Group will register the case for a decision and notify the parties.

After registration, the Working Group gives the State party an opportunity to respond to the complaint. Specifically, "the State party . . . has six months to respond on both its admissibility and merits (two months if the State party challenges admissibility only)."[13] Once the State party has completed its response, it is sent back to the complainant, who may comment on the state's response. The Committee may also ask the complainant or the State party for written responses to specific questions.[14] After

[7] Fact Sheet—How to Submit an Individual Complaint under the Optional Protocol to CEDAW, UNITED NATIONS, https://www.ohchr.org/EN/HRBodies/TBPetitions/Pages/IndividualCommunications.aspx#overviewprocedure (scroll to the section titled "What information do you need to provide in your complaint?"; click the second hyperlink within the paragraph).

[8] *Human Rights Treaty Bodies—Individual Communications*, UNITED NATIONS, https://www.ohchr.org/EN/HRBodies/TBPetitions/Pages/IndividualCommunications.aspx#overviewprocedure (last visited May 13, 2020).

[9] *See id.* (noting that complaints should be filed as soon as possible after the exhaustion of domestic remedial structures).

[10] *See id.* ("As a rule, a Committee does not examine complaints where the facts occurred prior to [the entry into force]. . . . There are, however, exceptions to this rule, for instance in cases where the effects of the event in question result in a continuous violation of the treaty.").

[11] *See id.* ("[T]he complainant must have exhausted all relevant remedies. . . . There are . . . exceptions to this rule, when proceedings at the national level have been unreasonably prolonged, or the remedies are unavailable or would plainly be ineffective.").

[12] *See id.* ("[F]or example if the same individual brings repeated claims to the Committee on the same issue when the previous identical ones have already been dismissed.").

[13] *See* Fact Sheet—How to Submit an Individual Complaint under the Optional Protocol to CEDAW, *supra* note 7, at 6.

[14] *See Human Rights Treaty Bodies—Individual Communications*, *supra* note 8.

the Committee receives all the required responses, the case is ready for a decision on the merits of the complaint.[15]

Cases are decided in closed session based on the facts presented in the written submissions. After reaching a decision, the Committee transmits its decision to both parties simultaneously and posts the decision on the Office of the High Commissioner for Human Rights (OHCHR) website, where it is available to the public. The decisions of the Committee are final and cannot be appealed.[16]

If the Committee decides that the complaint does not allege a violation of the treaty, the process ends there. However, if the Committee finds that the State party did violate the complainant's rights under the treaty, it will issue recommendations[17] to the State party to remedy the violation and invite the state to provide information, within a set time, that describes its efforts to effectuate those recommendations.[18] The treaty bodies' rules of procedure generally require that the treaty body only adjudicate claims that arise from the rights in the treaty that established the treaty body.[19] In other words, the Committee on the Elimination of Racial Discrimination (CERD) generally hears claims related to race or ethnicity and CEDAW generally hears claims related to gender. Nothing in this restriction, however, would prevent CERD, for example, from considering the *intersection* of rights related to race or ethnicity and gender. The presence of racial or ethnic discrimination brings the rights claim within the purview of the treaty, even if the claim focuses on a subset of individuals who are specifically affected by intersectional discrimination.

Although outside the parameters of this chapter, several human rights treaties also allow a State party to submit complaints about violations of the treaty allegedly committed by another State party. States parties rarely use the inter-state complaint procedure. Some treaties permit another procedure, the inquiry procedure, in which a State party may initiate an inquiry with the treaty body based on "reliable information containing well-founded indications of serious or systematic violations of the conventions."[20] Like the inter-state complaint procedure, States parties infrequently use the inquiry procedure.

CEDAW, for example, has used the inquiry procedure under its optional protocol six times as of 2020: Mexico (2005), Canada (2015), Philippines (2015), United Kingdom of Great Britain and Northern Ireland (2018), Kyrgyzstan (2018), and Mali (2019). The 2015 inquiry into Canada's treatment of missing and murdered Indigenous women is particularly noteworthy for our purposes.[21] None of the other

[15] *Id.*

[16] *Id.*

[17] *See id.* ("The kinds of recommendations that the Committee make[s] include: Measures to end ongoing violations against the victim; restitution, compensation and rehabilitation for the victim; law reform and changes in policies and practices that are in violation of the Convention; steps to prevent the repetition of the violation found.").

[18] *Id.*

[19] Committee on the Elimination of Discrimination Against Women, Rules of Procedure of the Committee on the Elimination of Discrimination Against Women, https://www2.ohchr.org/english/bodies/cedaw/docs/CEDAW_Rules_en.pdf (last visited Mar. 10, 2021); Committee on the Elimination of Racial Discrimination, Rule of Procedure of the Committee on the Elimination of Racial Discrimination, U.N. Doc. CERD/C/35/Rev.3 (1986).

[20] *See Human Rights Treaty Bodies—Individual Communications*, *supra* note 4.

[21] Comm. on the Elimination of Discrimination against Women, Rep. of the Inquiry Concerning Canada of the Comm. on the Elimination of Discrimination against Women under Article 8 of the Optional

inquiry reports addressed intersectionality, with the exception of a passing mention of multiple forms of discrimination in the report on the United Kingdom.[22] CEDAW's report on gender-based violence against Indigenous women in Canada, by contrast, is replete with references to intersectionality. Because the Canadian inquiry specifically focused on violence against Indigenous women, the Committee framed the investigation in explicitly intersectional terms.[23]

Intersectional jurisprudence of treaty bodies generally

Excluding CEDAW, few cases from the human rights treaty bodies have meaningfully grappled with intersectional human rights issues. This is not to say that intersectional issues are absent but rather that the treaty body jurisprudence beyond CEDAW rarely names or even implicitly gestures at intersectional violations, There are, however, some exceptions, as I describe below. As intersectionality gains traction within human rights discourse, I anticipate that all the treaty bodies will increasingly examine human rights violations through an intersectional lens.

HRC and *Lovelace v. Canada*

Factual background

In 1981, the Human Rights Committee, which oversees implementation of the International Covenant on Civil and Political Rights (ICCPR), considered an individual communication from a woman named Sandra Lovelace. Lovelace, an ethnic Maliseet Indigenous woman living in Canada, claimed that Canada's Indian Act[24] discriminated against her on the basis of sex, in violation of the ICCPR.[25] The Indian Act states that when an Indigenous woman marries a non-Indigenous man, the woman

Protocol to the Convention on the Elimination of All Forms of Discrimination against Women, U.N. Doc. CEDAW/C/OP.8/CAN/1 (Mar. 30, 2015).

[22] Comm. on the Elimination of Discrimination against Women, Inquiry Concerning the United Kingdom of Great Britain and Northern Ireland under Article 8 of the Optional Protocol to the Convention on the Elimination of All Forms of Discrimination against Women, ¶ 72(d), U.N. Doc. CEDAW/C/OP.8/GBR/1 (Mar. 6, 2018), ("The concentration of sexual and reproductive services in Belfast and the abdication of responsibility to ensure access to abortion in Northern Ireland by exporting the problem to England has serious impacts on disadvantaged groups unable to travel for socioeconomic reasons, exacerbating the multiple forms of discrimination already suffered by rural, migrant, asylum-seeking and refugee women and women in situations of poverty.").

[23] Report of the inquiry concerning Canada, *supra* note 21, ¶ 204 ("The Committee considers that, although the State party recognizes the general consequences of intersecting forms of discrimination based on gender and race, which lead to the increased vulnerability of aboriginal women, it has failed to take sufficient account of the particular problems of aboriginal women living on reserves, in breach of article 14(1) of the Convention.").

[24] When describing Lovelace, I use the term "Indigenous," but when referring to the Canadian statute, I use the term "Indian," as that is the language of the statute.

[25] Lovelace v. Canada, U.N. Doc. Supp. No. 40 (A/36/40) (July 30, 1981).

loses her ability to register, stripping her of her legal status as an Indigenous person.[26] However, an Indigenous man who marries a non-Indigenous woman does not lose his status.[27] In 1970, Lovelace had married a non-Indigenous man,[28] and in her complaint claimed that she was thereafter denied her right to live on a reserve.[29] This fact became particularly important when she and her husband later divorced and Lovelace sought housing for herself and her children.[30]

Canada asserted that Lovelace lived on the reserve at times during her marriage and after her divorce and that the reserve's Band Council did not prevent her from doing so.[31] However, Canada acknowledged that if she wished to live permanently on the reserve and obtain a new house, she would have to apply to the Band Council.[32] Creating an additional barrier, housing on reserves is provided with money set aside by Parliament for the benefit of Indigenous people who are *registered* as such.[33] Lovelace acknowledged that although she was living on a reserve, she had no right to remain there and was in violation of the law of the Band Council.[34] In addition to these residency issues, Lovelace also lost access to federal programs for Indigenous people[35] when she married a non-Indigenous person and lost her status.

HRC's analysis

Procedurally, the Human Rights Committee (HRC) can only consider alleged violations of human rights that occur after a state's accession to the ICCPR.[36] Because Lovelace's marriage occurred in 1970, six years before Canada acceded to the Covenant, the HRC could not consider the original cause of Lovelace's lost status.[37] However, the HRC did consider the continuing effects of the Indian Act's provisions.[38]

[26] *Id.* ¶ 1.

[27] *Id.*

[28] *Id.* ¶ 10.

[29] *Id.* ¶ 9.6. As Canada admits, "Section 14 of the Indian Act provides that '(an Indian) woman who is a member of a band ceases to be a member of that band if she marries a person who is not a member of that band' ... An Indian (including a woman) who ceases to be a member of a band ceases to be entitled to reside by right on a reserve [among other things]. None the less it is possible for an individual to reside on a reserve if his or her presence thereon is tolerated by a band or its members." *Id.* ¶ 9.3. However, the Band Council can pursue legal remedies for trespass if it chooses. *Id.*

[30] *See id.* ¶ 17 ("It is natural that in such a situation she wishes to return to the environment in which she was born, particularly as after the dissolution of her marriage her main cultural attachment again was to the Maliseet band.").

[31] *Id.* ¶ 9.6.

[32] *Id.*

[33] *Id.*

[34] *Id.* ¶ 9.3.

[35] For a more comprehensive list of the consequences of losing Indigenous status, *see id.* ¶ 9.9 (including loss of right to inherit possessory interest in land from parents or others; right to be buried on a reserve; access to loans from Consolidated Revenue fund; medical and health services; seed without charge; traditional hunting and fishing rights; the cultural benefits of living in an Indigenous community, emotional ties to home family friends, and loss of identity).

[36] *See id.* ¶ 10 ("[T]he Committee is not competent, as a rule, to examine allegations relating to events having taken place before the entry into force of the Covenant and the Optional Protocol.").

[37] *See id.* ("In the case of Sandra Lovelace it follows that the Committee is not competent to express any view on the original cause of her loss of Indian status, i.e. the Indian Act as applied to her at the time of her marriage in 1970.").

[38] *Id.* ¶ 11.

The HRC narrowed the issue and its analysis to whether Lovelace, having been denied a legal right to reside on a reserve, had been denied the rights guaranteed in article 27 of the Covenant, which states:

> In those States in which ethnic, religious or linguistic minorities exist, a person belonging to such minorities shall not be denied the right, in community with the other members of their group, to enjoy their own culture, to profess and practice their own religion, or to use their own language.[39]

The HRC concluded that the right to live on a reserve is not guaranteed by article 27[40] and that the Indian Act did not directly interfere with rights expressly mentioned in the article.[41] The HRC also found that not every interference can constitute a denial of rights within article 27, because Indigenous communities need to define the category of persons entitled to live on a reserve to protect resources and preserve the identity of its people.[42] The HRC observed, however, that in order to interfere with an individual's right to reside on a reserve, the state must have a reasonable and objective justification consistent with other provisions of the Covenant.[43]

The HRC found that in Lovelace's case, in light of her divorce, it was logical that she would want to return to the reserve.[44] The Committee also found it was her right to access her native culture and language and that the denial of her right to reside on the reserve was unreasonable and unnecessary to preserve the identity of the tribe.[45] The interference of this right was exacerbated because there was no place outside the reserve where the community existed in a similarly strong and vibrant way.[46]

The HRC determined that its finding allowed it to avoid examining whether Lovelace's specific situation violated the Covenant's general provisions against gender discrimination.[47] The HRC also found that other potential breaches of the Covenant (i.e., the right to choose one's residence and the rights concerning family life and children) were only indirectly related[48] and therefore unnecessary to examine.[49]

One member of the HRC appended a separate opinion onto the Committee's decision, agreeing that Canada violated Lovelace's rights under article 27 but indicating that the Committee should have found further rights violations. This member, Mr. Nejib Bouziri, stated:

[39] *Id.* ¶ 13.2.
[40] *Id.* ¶ 15.
[41] *See id.* ¶ 14 ("[T]he Indian Act deals primarily with a number of privileges which do not as such come within the scope of the Covenant.").
[42] *Id.* ¶ 15.
[43] *Id.* ¶ 16.
[44] *Id.* ¶ 17.
[45] *Id.* ¶ 18.
[46] *See id.* ¶ 15 ("[T]here is no place outside the Tobique Reserve where such a community exists.").
[47] *See id.* ¶ 18 ("In view of this finding, the Committee does not consider it necessary to examine whether the same facts also show separate breaches of other rights invoked.").
[48] *Id.*
[49] *Id.*

> In the Lovelace case, not only article 27 but also articles 2 (para. 1), 3, 23 (paras. 1 and 4) and 26 of the Covenant have been breached, for some of the provisions of the Indian Act are discriminatory, particularly as between men and women. The Act is still in force and, even though the Lovelace case arose before that date on which the Covenant became applicable in Canada, Mrs. Lovelace is still suffering from the adverse discriminatory effects of the Act in matters other than that covered by Article 27.[50]

The HRC stated that it could not consider the event that gave rise to the discrimination but could discuss the enduring effects.[51] Lovelace's inability to live lawfully on the reserve because of her sex was an enduring effect of discrimination under the Indian Act. Therefore, the HRC could have found that the law had an ongoing, persistent discriminatory impact. Further, the law *continued* to prohibit Lovelace from registering because of her sex and marriage every day after Canada ratified the Convention. Therefore, the HRC was able to rule on whether the law had a persistent discriminatory effect on the basis of sex (and ethnicity). The HRC simply did not take advantage of the opportunity to fully explore the ongoing violations.

A decision lacking intersectional analysis

The HRC failed to explore Lovelace's discrimination as intersectional. In some ways, this is unsurprising since the concept of intersectionality had not yet been formally articulated as such. Nevertheless, the case stands as an example of a human rights situation in which intersectional analysis would have improved the outcome and increased understanding of intersectional human rights generally.

As legal scholar Michael Addo states, "The *Lovelace* case is one such instance in which the gender inequality issue was overwhelmed by a focus on cultural rights."[52] Lovelace experienced unique (although not uncommon) discrimination in the sense that it was grounded in the intersection of her sex and ethnicity. As Rebecca Brown, Lilian Chenwi, and Michael Ashley Stein note, "Lovelace's identity as both indigenous and as a woman inextricably created the particular violation she experienced."[53] Lovelace's identity, writes professor Pok Yin S. Chow, "rendered it difficult for her to pursue discrimination on the basis of sex alone or on the basis of race alone."[54] While the HRC may have avoided incorporating an intersectional analysis to avoid admissibility issues, the Ontario Human Rights Commission states that

> [t]he failure to address multiple grounds discrimination at the international level has important consequences. If the European Court of Human Rights or the Human Rights Committee establishes a violation, the states concerned are to amend the law

[50] Lovelace v. Canada, at Appendix, U.N. Doc. Supp. No. 40 (A/36/40) (July 30, 1981).

[51] *Id.* ¶¶ 10–11.

[52] Michael K. Addo, *Practice of United Nations Human Rights Treaty Bodies in the Reconciliation of Cultural Diversity with Universal Respect for Human* Rights, 32 HUM. RTS. Q. 601, 639 (2010).

[53] THE OPTIONAL PROTOCOL TO THE INTERNATIONAL COVENANT ON ECONOMIC, SOCIAL AND CULTURAL RIGHTS: A COMMENTARY 289 (Malcolm Langford et al. eds., 2016).

[54] Pok Yin S. Chow, *Has Intersectionality Reached Its Limits: Intersectionality in the UN Human Rights Treaty Body Practice and the Issue of Ambivalence*, 16 HUM. RTS. L. REV. 453, 468–69 (2016).

> or practice accordingly. Thus, an incomplete analysis can affect the remedy or outcome. As well, the cases are used as examples and precedents by other states when enacting or amending laws, writing their reports under various international instruments and applying principles before their own national courts.[55]

Further, the HRC could have looked more carefully at how this discrimination was a result of the intersection of Lovelace's identities as both a member of the Maliseet community and a woman. The discrimination she experienced would not have occurred if she were not Indigenous or if she were not female. Although the HRC considered the other rights (to decide where to live and to make family life decisions) too attenuated,[56] the right to decide where one lives and the right to enjoy one's culture are at the heart of this case. Family life and one's culture are interrelated and difficult to tease apart. The HRC simply chose not to view the rights at stake as inextricable and the discrimination as intersectional. Based on the trends I identify in this volume, which demonstrate a gradually increasing willingness on the part of the treaty bodies to consider intersectional human rights, I suspect that if the HRC were to revisit the case today, it might be more willing to entertain claims of intersectional discrimination.

CERD and *A. Yilmaz-Dogan v. The Netherlands*

Factual background

In 1984, the Committee on the Elimination of Racial Discrimination considered an individual complaint from a Turkish national living in the Netherlands named A. Yilmaz Dogan. In 1982, when Ms. Yilmaz Dogan was pregnant, her employer sought permission from the Dutch Cantonal Court to terminate her employment. In its July 1982 termination request, Ms. Yilmaz Dogan's employer stated:

> When a Netherlands girl marries and has a baby, she stops working. Our foreign women workers, on the other hand, take the child to neighbors or family and at the slightest setback disappear on sick leave under the terms of the Sickness Act. They repeat that endlessly.[57]

In September 1982, the Cantonal Court gave the employer permission to terminate Ms. Yilmaz Dogan's employment, leaving her no opportunity to appeal the decision.[58] Ms. Yilmaz Dogan pursued numerous strategies to reverse the decision, including seeking annulment by the Supreme Court and seeking prosecution of her employer

[55] Ontario Human Rights Commission, Discussion Paper, *An Intersectional Approach to Discrimination: Addressing Multiple Grounds in Human Rights Claims*, 15 (Oct. 9, 2001), http://www3.ohrc.on.ca/sites/default/files/attachments/An_intersectional_approach_to_discrimination%3A_Addressing_multiple_grounds_in_human_rights_claims.pdf.

[56] *See* Lovelace, ¶ 19 (claiming that articles 17, 23, and 24 were only indirectly at stake).

[57] A. Yilmaz-Dogan v. Neth., ¶ 2.2, U.N. Doc. CERD/C/36/D/1/1984e (Aug. 10, 1988).

[58] *Id.*

on the basis of his discriminatory petition to the Cantonal Court.[59] The Netherlands Court of Appeal declined to prosecute the employer.[60]

CERD's analysis and decision

Ms. Yilmaz Dogan's complaint alleged that the Netherlands had violated the Convention on the Elimination of All Forms of Racial Discrimination by failing to guarantee equality as it related to the right to work and for failing to provide adequate legal remedies. With respect to the allegations of racial discrimination in the right to work context, the CERD stated: "After careful examination, the Committee considers that the petitioner's dismissal was the result of a failure to take into account all the circumstances of the case."[61] As a result, the Committee concluded that the Netherlands failed to protect Ms. Yilmaz Dogan's right to work under article 5(e)(i) of CERD.[62]

Ms. Yilmaz Dogan's complaint did not allege gender discrimination even though her dismissal was based, at least in part, on her pregnancy. The discrimination she faced, therefore, was intersectional in that it arose from the intersection of race and gender. The racial bias is evident in the racist communication from the employer to the Cantonal Court.[63] CERD recognized that the Netherlands had failed to protect Ms. Yilmaz Dogan from racial discrimination in her employment.[64] The fact that her pregnancy triggered the termination demonstrates the gender dimensions of the discrimination. However, Ms. Yilmaz Dogan did not allege intersectional discrimination, and CERD failed to acknowledge the operation of intersectional discrimination in her case. Even when the complainant does not explicitly frame her claim in intersectional terms, the treaty bodies can request further information from the parties to clarify intersectional issues, and they should do so more often.

CERD's failure to provide intersectional remedies

The CERD Committee missed an opportunity to provide remedies for the intersectional discrimination to which Ms. Yilmaz Dogan was subjected. Instead, CERD required the Netherlands to provide equitable relief to Ms. Yilmaz Dogan and to ensure that she was hired back or employed in an alternative job.[65] Had the Committee explored the full range of intersectional violations and remedies, it might have required the Netherlands to provide employers with anti-discrimination training that addresses the combined effects of both racial and gender-based stereotypes.

As with the *Lovelace* case, Ms. Yilmaz Dogan filed her complaint in the early to mid-1980s, at a time when the notion of intersectionality had not yet taken hold and was not widely understood. It is likely that the Committee would be more willing to address the intersectional issues if the case were filed today. In fact, in 2002, CERD issued General Recommendation No. 29, which emphasized that States parties

[59] *Id.* ¶ 2.3.
[60] *Id.*
[61] *Id.* ¶ 9.3.
[62] *Id.*
[63] *See id.* ¶ 8.1 ("[P]etitioner's counsel ... reiterates that the State party violated article 5 (e) (i) in that the cantonal judge failed to protect the petitioner against unemployment, although the request for her dismissal was, allegedly, based on racially discriminatory grounds.").
[64] *Id.* ¶ 9.3.
[65] *Id.* ¶ 10.

must ensure that descent-based groups enjoy the right to employment without discrimination, including intersectional discrimination faced by minority women in employment.[66]

As both the *Lovelace* and *Yilmaz Dogan* cases illustrate, intersectional rights violations may arise in the context of many of the human rights treaties. Many treaty body decisions, however, have historically missed the opportunity to incorporate intersectional analysis and remedies into the resolution of complaints, sometimes leaving complainants with incomplete remedies and an unsatisfactory process. As treaty body jurisprudence develops, it seems likely that treaty bodies will increasingly address intersectional issues such as those ignored in *Lovelace* and *Yilmaz-Dogan*.

HRC and *L.N.P. v. Argentina*

Factual Background

In 2003, three young men allegedly raped L.N.P., a fifteen-year-old Indigenous girl belonging to the Qom ethnic group, in a village in the north of the Chaco Province of Argentina.[67] Immediately after the assault, L.N.P. went to the village police station to report the crime. Even though she arrived bleeding and crying, the local police kept her waiting for several hours before attending to her and eventually sending her to the local medical center, where she was again kept waiting for several more hours. L.N.P. alleged that medical staff also subjected her to painful and unnecessary tests, including a virginity test.

Argentinian authorities eventually arrested and tried the three young men. According to her complaint, a court-appointed social worker investigated L.N.P.'s sexual history in an effort to impugn her character and undermine the prosecution rather than investigating the actions of the three men. L.N.P. alleged that the court failed to inform her of her right to appear in court and failed to provide an interpreter. The men were eventually acquitted of raping her. The authorities did not notify L.N.P. of the outcome, which she discovered two years later.

HRC's analysis and decision

Among other alleged violations of the ICCPR, L.N.P. alleged that she was a victim of discrimination based on gender and ethnicity in violation of Article 26. Although the HRC did not use the term intersectional or even multiple discrimination, it specifically noted that L.N.P.'s allegations of discrimination were based on both gender and ethnicity.[68] The HRC determined that the Argentine court engaged in harmful stereotyping designed to cast doubt on L.N.P.'s credibility, including multiple references to her sexual history and possible prostitution. Ultimately, the HRC determined that the

[66] Comm. on the Elimination of Racial Discrimination [CERD], General Recommendation No. 29 (2002), https://tbinternet.ohchr.org/_layouts/15/treatybodyexternal/TBSearch.aspx?Lang=en&TreatyID=6&DocTypeID=11 (select General recommendation No. 29 on article 1, paragraph 1, of the Convention; choose document in appropriate language).

[67] L.N.P. v. Argentina, U.N. Doc. CCPR/C/102/D/1610/2007 (Aug. 16, 2011).

[68] *Id.* ¶ 13.3.

facts before it revealed "the existence of discrimination based on the author's gender and ethnicity in violation of article 26 of the Covenant."[69]

In its decision, the HRC did not discuss intersectionality or acknowledge that discrimination based on both gender and ethnicity might intersect to produce intersectional, mutually constitutive forms of discrimination. The decision acknowledges that L.N.P. was the victim of both gender and ethnic discrimination but does not demonstrate an understanding of intersectional discrimination. Although the HRC concludes that L.N.P. was targeted both because she was a girl and because she was a member of the Indigenous Qom ethnic group, it takes an additive approach to the alleged discrimination and does not grapple with its intersectional aspects. The discrimination L.N.P. experienced was different in kind from gender-based violence targeting ethnic majority women and girls and violence directed at Qom men. The HRC's recognition that L.N.P. was a victim of both gender and ethnic discrimination is an important first step. In the years to come, however, the HRC should strive for a more nuanced understanding of intersectional discrimination that recognizes the complex lived experience of victims such as L.N.P.

HRC and *Yaker v. France* and *Hebbadj v. France*

Factual background

In 2011, French authorities in Nantes, France stopped two women, each of whom was wearing a niqab or full-face veil, for an identity check.[70] Both Sonia Yaker and Miriana Hebbadj are French nationals born in 1974 and both are Muslim women. The authorities convicted and fined the women for wearing a niqab in violation of a 2010 French law that criminalized concealing one's face in public.[71]

HRC's analysis and decision

The complaints in both cases allege that the French law banning facial coverings violated their rights to freedom of religion under Article 18 and the right to non-discrimination under Article 26 of the ICCPR. The Committee found that the ban restricted Yaker's and Hebbadj's rights to manifest their religion under Article 18 because it forced them to renounce their religious clothing or face penalties for wearing it.[72] Article 18(3) allows restrictions on the right to manifest one's religion only when the limitations are "prescribed by law and are necessary to protect public safety, order, health or morals, or the fundamental rights and freedoms of others."[73]

Addressing the violation of Article 18, the HRC determined that the wholesale prohibition on women wearing the niqab did not meet the requirements of the exceptions

[69] *Id.*

[70] Sonia Yaker v. France, U.N. Doc. CCPR/C/123/D/2747/2016 (July 17, 2018); Miriana Hebbadj v. France, U.N. Doc CCPR/C/123/D/2807/2016 (July 17, 2018).

[71] The French law, Act No. 2010-1192, states, "No one may, in a public space, wear any apparel intended to conceal the face [unless it is] authorized by law or justified for health or professional reasons, sports practices, festivities, or artistic or traditional manifestations." *Id.*, Yaker v. France, ¶ 2.2.

[72] *Id.*, Yaker v. France, ¶ 8.3.

[73] *Id.* ¶ 8.4.

listed in Article 18(3). In other words, a *blanket* ban on facial coverings was unnecessary and disproportionate to the state's need for identification and security. The Committee also noted that the public safety justification for the ban on facial coverings did not make sense in light of exceptions to the prohibition on facial coverings for non-religious reasons such as sporting events.[74] In response to France's argument that the ban was important to protect the "rights of others" and necessary to establish trust among people, the HRC concluded that there was an insufficient connection between the fundamental rights of others and the ability to see women's faces in public. The HRC decided that the prohibition was not necessary to serve a legitimate interest and therefore violated the religious freedom rights of Yaker and Hebbadj.[75]

Next, the HRC considered whether the ban violated Yaker's and Hebbadj's right to non-discrimination under Article 26 of the ICCPR and found that it did. The Committee noted that the prohibition on facial coverings had a disproportionate impact on Muslim women who chose to wear a niqab. The HRC noted that the legislation allowed face coverings for sporting and other events and was enforced primarily against women wearing a full-face veil. Differential treatment under Article 26 may be permissible if the Committee determines that the rule or measure is reasonable, objective, and furthers a legitimate state aim.[76] In this case, however, the Committee determined that France's ban on facial coverings in public failed to meet this test and was impermissible.

Most importantly for our purposes, the HRC specifically noted that Yaker and Hebbadj faced intersectional discrimination that was based on both gender and religion.[77] The HRC neither elaborated on its meaning of intersectionality nor provided specifically intersectional remedies. It is, nevertheless, significant that the Committee appreciated the intersectional nature of the discrimination faced by Yaker and Hebbadj.

Like *Yaker* and *Hebbadj*, two other 2018 cases from the Human Rights Committee expressly recognized intersectional discrimination but did so without developing the concept of intersectionality or exploring its meaning in the context of the cases. These cases also involved women who experienced intersectional discrimination on the basis of both gender and religion. In *Türkan v. Turkey.* the HRC determined that the refusal of university admission to a woman who chose to cover her hair constituted a violation of her non-discrimination rights. The HRC noted that "the restriction on covering the head in a university constituted a form of intersectional discrimination against the author as a Muslim woman who chose to cover her hair, and thus violated . . . the Covenant."[78] In the 2018 case *FA v. France*, the HRC explicitly recognized intersectional discrimination on the basis of gender and religion in a case involving a

[74] *Id.* ¶ 8.7.

[75] *Id.* ¶ 8.12.

[76] *Id.* ¶ 8.14 ("The Committee must therefore decide whether the differential treatment . . . meets the criteria of reasonableness, objectivity, and legitimacy of the aim.").

[77] *Id.* ¶ 8.17 ("The Committee hence concludes that this provision and its application to the author constitutes a form of intersectional discrimination based on gender and religion, in violation of article 26 of the Covenant.").

[78] Türkan v. Turkey, U.N. Doc. CCPR/C/123/D/2274/2013/Rev.1, July 17, 2018.

Muslim woman who refused to stop wearing her veil in France.[79] Although the HRC did not deeply engage with the concept of intersectionality in these decisions, it mentions the concept and recognizes its applicability to the complex human rights issues at stake in these cases.

In the French cases, the complainants experienced subordination based on the intersection of gender and religious discrimination, making them targets for French law enforcement. This intersectional discrimination was different in kind from the discrimination faced by Muslim men in France and by non-Muslim women in France. The HRC expressed willingness to consider the intersectional nature of the violations, which will help future complainants to frame similar claims in explicitly intersectional terms and underscore the responsibilities of states to protect against intersectional violations. In the future, the HRC should consider intersectional remedies that provide more comprehensive redress for victims of intersectional violations and incentivize States parties to protect intersectional rights within their borders.

Prior to the decisions in *Yaker* and *Habbadj*, CERD and CEDAW had considered the validity of France's prohibition on facial coverings for Muslim women and girls. In the context of France's reporting to CERD and CEDAW on its progress in implementing the treaties, both treaty bodies had a chance to consider the merits of a French ban on religious symbols and clothing in state schools. Neither CERD nor CEDAW specifically rejected the bans in their concluding observations to France's report in 2005 (CERD) and 2006 (CEDAW).[80] Instead, CERD urged France to continue to monitor the implementation of the ban to ensure that it did not have discriminatory effects on students' education.[81] Similarly, CEDAW recommended that France continue to monitor the implementation of the school ban to ensure that it had no negative effect on girls' education.[82] The failure of CERD and CEDAW to frame the rights in intersectional terms in their concluding observations to France makes the HRC's 2018 decisions in *Yaker* and *Habbadj* even more significant.

HRC and *Nyaya v. Nepal*

Factual Background

In April 2002, Fulmati Nyaya, a fourteen-year-old girl who is a member of the Indigenous Tharu community in Nepal, was abducted by the Royal Nepalese Army and a paramilitary group that had entered her village in western Nepal looking for

[79] FA v. France, U.N. Doc. CCPR/C/123/D/2662/2015, July 16, 2018 ("The Committee thus concludes that the author's dismissal, based on the internal regulations of the childcare centre imposing neutrality on employees and the Labour Code, was not based on reasonable and objective criteria and therefore constitutes intersectional discrimination based on gender and religion, in violation of article 26 of the Covenant.").

[80] Monika Zalnieriute & Catherine Weiss, *Reconceptualizing Intersectionality in Judicial Interpretation: Moving Beyond Formalistic Accounts of Discrimination on Islamic Covering Provisions*, 35 Berkeley J. Gender, Law & Just. (2020).

[81] Comm. on the Elimination of Racial Discrimination (CERD), Consideration of Reports Submitted by States Parties Under Article 9 of the Convention, ¶ 18, U.N. Doc. CERD/C/FRA/CO/16 (Apr. 18, 2005).

[82] Comm. on the Elimination of Discrimination against Women (CEDAW), Concluding Comments of the Committee on the Elimination of Discrimination against Women: France, ¶¶ 20–21, U.N. Doc. CEDAW/C/FRA/CO/6 (Apr. 8, 2008).

suspected members of the Maoist party.[83] Mistaking her for someone else, soldiers took Nyaya into custody and transported her to an army detention center by truck. While on the truck in transit to a detention center, soldiers sexually assaulted her for the first time.[84] During her detention, which lasted over two months, she was raped multiple times and suffered other forms of sexual violence, causing severe lasting physical and emotional harm. She also suffered violent beatings and was forced to perform arduous labor at the detention center.

Her father eventually secured her release, but the paramilitary police force that was responsible for her detention forced her to report back to them regularly on any suspected Maoist activities. Nyaya returned to her village only to face ostracism and ridicule from the community as a rape victim.[85] For many years, she suffered from the devastating physical and psychological consequences of the violence. She married but her husband quickly shunned her after learning of the rape and sexual assaults. Upon learning in 2011 that she could seek relief as a victim of the armed conflict in Nepal, Nyaya sought relief from the Nepalese courts. Authorities rejected her claim because they viewed it as time-barred under the thirty-five-day statute of limitations for reporting a rape.[86] After pursuing her claims at the national level, Nyaya submitted her complaint to the HRC alleging, among other things, that she was a victim of gender, ethnic, and age discrimination.[87]

HRC's analysis and decision

Despite the explicitly intersectional nature of her complaint, which included allegations of discrimination based on gender, Indigeneity, and age, the HRC considered only the gender dimensions of the complaint. The HRC acknowledges that Nyaya "claims she was a victim of triple discrimination: as a child, as a woman, and as an indigenous person."[88] The HRC, however, addressed only the gender discrimination she faced and largely ignored her claims of intersectional rights violations. Recognizing the severity of the harm she suffered, the HRC found multiple violations of the ICCPR, including non-discrimination.

The HRC's 2019 decision granted reparations to Nyaya in her individual capacity, including a thorough investigation, prosecution, and punishment for those responsible for the sexual violence and other harms, rehabilitation and treatment, compensation, and an official apology.[89] In terms of general remedies, the HRC decision requires Nepal to make changes to its criminal law, guarantee more effective investigation of sexual violence, and improve access to justice for victims. The HRC's discussion of general remedies highlighted the committee's missed opportunity to consider intersectionality in this case. Had the HRC embraced an intersectional analysis, its general remedies would have taken into account the particular challenges of Indigenous victims of gender-based violence. An intersectional framework would have prompted the HRC to consider, for example, whether

83 F. Nyaya v. Nepal, U.N. Doc. CCPR/C/125/D/2556/2015 (June 11, 2019).
84 *Id.* ¶ 2.2.
85 *Id.* ¶ 2.7.
86 *Id.* ¶ 2.12.
87 *Id.* ¶ 3.1.
88 *Id.* ¶ 3.3.
89 *Id.* ¶ 9.

additional measures were necessary to ensure access to the court system in Indigenous villages, whether there might be a need for greater representation of Indigenous people within the ranks of police, prosecutors, and court personnel, or whether specific, culturally sensitive campaigns were necessary to address the stigma of sexual assault. The HRC's singular focus on gender discrimination—even in the face of a complaint that was specifically framed in intersectional terms—demonstrates that intersectional analysis continues to be inconsistent.

Other relevant cases from the treaty bodies

In addition to the cases described in detail above, the complaints in a number of other cases before the treaty bodies have presented intersectional rights claims. In some cases like *Nyaya v. Nepal*, the complainants framed their arguments in intersectional terms and the treaty bodies failed to use intersectional analysis in evaluating the claims. In others, although the facts suggested intersectional violations, neither the complainant nor the treaty body recognized the intersectional nature of the claims. In some of these cases, the treaty bodies took an additive approach to the rights claims. In *X. v. Sri Lanka*, for example, the HRC considered the complainant's alleged gender and ethnic discrimination in isolation but failed to acknowledge the intersectional nature of the claims.[90] Similarly, in its 2016 decision in *Pjetri v. Switzerland*, CERD noted that the complainant raised a "double discrimination" argument, but the committee addressed each form of alleged discrimination separately.[91] The Committee Against Torture (CAT) issued a similar decision in *A. v. Bosnia and Herzegovina*, in which the committee observed that the claim of rape during the Bosnian War "represent[ed] a form of discrimination on the basis of [the complainant's] gender and ethnicity."[92] It did not explore intersectionality further in its decision.

The 2018 decision in *Trujillo Calero v. Ecuador* by the Committee on Economic, Social and Cultural Rights (CESCR) offers hope that the treaty bodies will more explicitly and systematically adopt an intersectional analytical framework. In that case, the CESCR noted that the "intersection of alleged gender and age discriminations makes [the complainant] particularly vulnerable."[93] Even with an explicit reference to intersectionality, however, the CESCR did not delve deeply into the intersectional nature of the rights claims.

A closer look: CEDAW jurisprudence

Like most of the other treaty bodies, and to varying degrees, CEDAW has begun to incorporate intersectional analysis into its consideration of human rights violations and their remedies. In recent years, for example, CEDAW's reports and other documents

[90] X. v. Sri Lanka, U.N. Doc. CCPR/C/120/D/2256/2013 (Aug. 22, 2017).
[91] Pjetri v. Switzerland, U.N. Doc. CERD/C/91/D/53/2013 (Jan. 23, 2017).
[92] A. v. Bosnia and Herzegovina, U.N. Doc. CAT/C/67/D/854/2017 (Sept. 11, 2019).
[93] Trujillo Calero v. Ecuador, U.N. Doc. E/C.12/63/D/10/2015 (Nov. 14, 2018).

have included references to "multiple" discrimination, discrimination affecting "particularly vulnerable" women, and in some cases "intersectional" forms of discrimination. On balance, however, the Committee has been slow to adopt an explicitly intersectional approach.

As discussed in chapter 3, CEDAW has embraced intersectionality, to some extent, in its General Recommendations, which describe the obligations of State parties under particular provisions of the treaty. The Committee has also addressed intersectionality, to varying degrees, in the cases that come before it pursuant to the Optional Protocol. It is useful to examine and tease out the distinctions in the cases that involve intersectional issues, as well the extent to which the Committee undertook an intersectional analysis in its decision-making. This section explores some of the decisions by the Committee in which intersectional human rights issues were prominent and were raised by the complainant, or could have been raised by the complainant or by the Committee in its decision. As I will explore in the following pages, in some of these cases, the Committee failed to address intersectionality despite the presentation of clearly intersectional human rights issues in the complaints. In some cases, the Committee mentioned multiple or intersectional discrimination in passing but failed to grapple with the intersectional human rights violations in a significant way. In a few cases, CEDAW used an intersectional analysis of the rights at stake and has required States parties to provide intersectional remedies. Finally, in at least one decision, CEDAW recommended intersectional remedies.

Decisions that failed to address intersectionality

In several cases, the authors of the complaints allege facts indicating that intersectional discrimination is at play. Despite the clearly identifiable intersectional issues, CEDAW, in some cases, failed to address intersectionality in its decisions. In these cases, the Committee missed important opportunities to address in full the discrimination faced by complainants. By failing to address the intersectional nature of the alleged violations, the Committee's analysis falls short in two primary ways. First, it fails to recognize a significant dimension of the harms suffered by the complainant. Failing to recognize the complexity of the harms signals that the intersectional dimensions of the discriminatory experience are unimportant. Second, by failing to recognize the intersectional nature of discrimination in its decisions, the Committee cannot fully redress the harms suffered by complainants.

A.S. v. Hungary

In the case of *A.S. v. Hungary*, the complaint, a Roma woman living in Hungary, alleged that she had been involuntarily sterilized by Hungarian doctors.[94] In 2001, A.S. suffered a miscarriage and required surgery shortly thereafter. A.S. alleged that moments after the hospital admitted her, and while she was still in a state of shock, she was asked to sign a form consenting to a cesarean section. She signed the form while

[94] A.S. v. Hung., U.N. Doc. CEDAW/C/36/D/4/2004 (Aug. 29, 2006).

on the operating table. The form also contained a handwritten, barely legible note at the bottom, which used the Latin word for sterilization. A.S. had no idea she was consenting to be sterilized and did not find out until after the surgery when she asked medical personnel when it would be safe to try to have another child.

A.S. alleged that doctors sterilized her without her full and informed consent in violation of CEDAW's right to health information (Article 10), right to non-discrimination in health (Article 12), and right to decide freely on the number and spacing of children (Article 16(1)(e)). In its 2006 decision, CEDAW found that Hungary had failed to protect A.S.'s reproductive rights. The decision is significant in that, as one NGO remarked, it "marks the first time that an international human rights tribunal has held a government accountable for failing to provide necessary information to a woman to enable her to give informed consent to a reproductive health-related medical procedure."[95]

Despite the significance of the case for women's reproductive rights more generally, the Committee failed to consider A.S.'s Roma identity as a salient part of her claim. The Roma population suffers systemic discrimination in Hungary and throughout the region. In addressing A.S.'s claims, CEDAW missed an opportunity to engage in intersectional analysis that would have reflected the crux of her complaint more comprehensively. A.S. complained that being subjected to forced sterilization violated rights related to her Roma identity—namely her Catholicism and Roma traditions and culture, which value having children. The Committee had an opportunity to engage in intersectional analysis in analyzing Article 12 claims—the right to non-discrimination in healthcare. The Committee failed to discuss how being both a member of the Roma community and a woman resulted in discriminatory treatment in accessing healthcare.

As discussed in chapters 2 and 4, discrimination against the Roma is well-documented. Sterilization campaigns that target women from oppressed communities are also well-documented. The case presented a perfect opportunity to address the complex discrimination that results from the intersection of gender and ethnic/religious discrimination. Instead, the Committee focused exclusively on gender as the relevant axis of oppression. This more superficial analysis had a direct impact on the remedies provided by the Committee. The Committee directed Hungary to provide accessible information about sexual and reproductive health to everyone. It missed an important opportunity, however, to urge the state to specifically target information campaigns within Roma communities, to require training of medical care providers about the sexual and reproductive health needs of Roma women—in particular—and to invest in medical infrastructure that is accessible to Roma women.

As a member of the Roma minority in Hungary, A.S. suffered a high degree of systemic discrimination. As a Roma *woman*, A.S. suffered a form of discrimination different from that suffered by Roma men and by non-Roma women. Nothing short of intersectional analysis captures the discrimination that exists for women living at the intersection of Roma identity, gender, and socioeconomic status. Instead of a nuanced

[95] CENTER FOR REPRODUCTIVE RIGHTS, A.S. V. HUNGARY: INFORMED CONSENT: A SIGNATURE IS NOT ENOUGH, CENTER FOR REPRODUCTIVE RIGHTS (2008).

and far-reaching analysis of intersectional discrimination in the enjoyment of the right to health, CEDAW focused narrowly on gender and health.

A.S.'s complaint specifically identifies her plight as "a woman who would lose her child and as a member of a marginalized group of society—the Roma."[96] In the early 2000s when CEDAW considered the case, the concept of intersectionality was broadly recognized among many international human rights activists. Indeed, even CEDAW's General Recommendation No. 24 on women and health, adopted in 1999, alludes to identity factors other than gender that may affect a woman's health status. General Recommendation No. 24 notes:

> [W]hile biological differences between women and men may lead to differences in health status, there are societal factors that are determinative of the health status of women and men and vary among women themselves. For that reason, special attention should be given to the health needs and rights of women belonging to vulnerable and disadvantaged groups.[97]

Despite the invitation in General Recommendation No. 24 to give special attention to vulnerable groups of women, and despite the available information on the plight of Roma women in particular, the Committee failed to acknowledge that A.S.'s claims were intersectional in nature. As such, the Committee failed to provide remedies that adequately addressed the harms that she suffered.

In many of these cases, the complainant may have experienced intersectional discrimination that goes unrecognized as intersectional by both the complainant and the treaty body. In these cases, the complainant does not specifically allege an intersectional violation and the treaty body does not raise intersectionality in its consideration of the complaint or in its decision. In cases in which the treaty body has not presented the facts in a way that surfaces intersectionality, it is difficult to identify specific intersectional issues. For example, without a sensitivity to possible intersectional violations, CEDAW might consider a complainant's ethnic identity irrelevant to her claim when, in fact, ethnic bias has intersected with gender bias to construct the complainant's experience of discrimination. In these situations, the Committee may present the facts without mentioning the possible intersectional dimensions of the claim.

Because individual complainants may or may not frame their rights claims as intersectional, the Committee should be attuned to intersectionality and willing to explore intersectional rights violations that are implicit in the complaint. As its commitment to providing redress for intersectional human rights violations evolves, the Committee will need to actively engage with complainants, at times, to explore potential intersectional dimensions of the human rights violations at issue. To the extent possible within the Committee's time and resource constraints, the Committee should probe for intersectional dimensions of complaints to ensure that recommended remedies address the underlying subordination as broadly and comprehensively as possible. Procedural rules generally allow the treaty body to request additional information from the

[96] A.S. v. Hung., at 12, U.N. Doc. CEDAW/C/36/D/4/2004 (Aug. 29, 2006).

[97] Comm. on the Elimination of Discrimination against Women [CEDAW], Rep. of the Comm. on the Elimination of Discrimination against Women, at 3, U.N. Doc. A/54/38/Rev.1 (1999).

complainant or the State party and to allow the other party time to comment on the additional submissions.[98] The treaty bodies could use this procedural mechanism to explore intersectional claims more assertively regardless of whether the complainant framed them as such in the original complaint.

Decisions that recognized intersectionality but offered little to no analysis

In a handful of cases decided between 2015 and 2017, the Committee superficially acknowledged the existence of intersectional rights violations but failed to meaningfully grapple with what that means for victims or for states attempting to fulfill their obligations under the treaty. In some cases, this passing recognition of intragroup difference takes the form of additive notions of discrimination. In those cases, remarks from the Committee suggest that complainants face an added disadvantage or "special vulnerability." In these "gender plus" references, the Committee suggests that complainants face a form of gender discrimination that is complicated by some additional disadvantage. The recognition is often brief and falls short of intersectional analysis. This section describes several such cases in which the Committee makes a passing reference to intragroup differences in the form of "multiple discrimination," "particular or special vulnerability," or intersectionality, but does not engage in meaningful intersectional analysis.

E.S. & S.C. v. Tanzania

The case of *E.S. & S.C. v. Tanzania*[99] involved two women who faced the intersection of gender and religious or ethnic discrimination. E.S. and S.C. were Tanzanian nationals. After their husbands died, they sought to inherit their husband's money and property. Tanzania has three different "inheritance schemes": Islamic law, customary law, and the Indian Succession Act. Customary inheritance law, which is the most common, states that widows shall have "no share of the inheritance if the deceased left relatives of his clan." The deceased man's other living female relatives, such as a daughter, mother, or sister, also have limited inheritance rights because the law ranks male relatives ahead of women.

E.S. and her husband shared a home together. Upon her husband's death, E.S.'s brother-in-law ordered her to vacate the home because "under Sukuma customary law she could not inherit her husband's estate."[100] S.C. has a similar story. E.S. and S.C. had no relief in the Tanzanian courts and brought their complaint to CEDAW.

CEDAW recognized that Tanzania's inheritance schemes violated several of the Convention's articles. Specifically, CEDAW declared that Tanzania "denied the authors

[98] *See, e.g.*, Comm. on the Elimination of Discrimination Against Women, Rules of Procedure of the Committee on the Elimination of Discrimination Against Women, https://www2.ohchr.org/english/bodies/cedaw/docs/CEDAW_Rules_en.pdf (last visited Mar. 10, 2021); Comm. on the Elimination of Racial Discrimination, Rule of Procedure of the Committee on the Elimination of Racial Discrimination, U.N. Doc. CERD/C/35/Rev.3 (1986).

[99] E.S. & S.C. v. United Republic of Tanz., U.N. Doc. CEDAW/C/60/D/48/2013 (Apr. 13, 2015).

[100] *Id.* ¶ 2.5.

equality in respect of inheritance and failed to provide them with any other means of economic security."[101]

Regarding intersectionality, CEDAW noted that "the authors have been subjected to Sukuma customary law on the basis of their ethnicity."[102] In footnote 32, CEDAW cites General Recommendations No. 29 and 28 "on intersectional discrimination."[103] In its recommendations, CEDAW advised Tanzania to provide women and girls with equal inheritance rights "irrespective of their ethnicity or religion."[104] It also recommended educational training to spread knowledge of women's rights "in particular in rural and remote areas."[105] The case presented an opportunity for the Committee to more thoroughly explore the intersection of gender, rurality, and ethnicity/religion in women's lives. Instead, the Committee focused only on the gender discrimination at play in the case and mentioned intersectionality only in a passing footnote.

L.R. v. Republic of Moldova

The Committee decided *L.R. v. Republic of Moldova*[106] in 2017. L.R. was a victim of domestic violence, whose husband abused her physically and psychologically. L.R. is "a person with an average degree of disability"[107] who suffered discrimination resulting from the intersection of gender and disability subordination. She received state assistance in the form of a disability pension and other government financial support totaling the equivalent of about US$2.50 monthly.[108] L.R. reported the abuse to authorities several times.[109] Her complaint to the CEDAW Committee alleged that the Moldovan government refused to enforce a protection order and failed to promptly investigate other reports. According to her complaint, prosecutors threatened her and attempted to submit L.R. to in-patient psychiatric examination rather than investigating her allegations against her husband.[110]

CEDAW found that Moldova failed to fulfill its obligations under the convention.[111] CEDAW specifically acknowledged the intersectional issues present in L.R.'s case. The Committee recommended that Moldova take steps to "ensure that all women and girls, including in particular older women, Roma women and girls and women with disabilities, are protected from violence and have access to immediate means of redress."[112] Still, although the Committee acknowledged that discrimination affects different groups of women differently, it missed an opportunity to delve more deeply into the intersection of gender and disability. The Committee

[101] *Id.* ¶ 7.9.
[102] *Id.* ¶ 7.6.
[103] *Id.* at 11 n.32.
[104] *Id.* ¶ 9(b)(ii).
[105] *Id.* ¶ 9(b)(vi).
[106] L.R. v. Republic of Moldova, U.N. Doc. CEDAW/C/66/D/58/2013 (Mar. 21, 2017).
[107] *Id.* ¶ 4.4.
[108] *Id.*
[109] *See id.* ¶ 2.2 ("The author's continuous complains were met with accusations by the police of improper conduct on her part, and she was even placed under police supervisions and labelled a 'family troublemaker' in respect of whom preventative measures needed to be taken.").
[110] *Id.* ¶ 11.2.
[111] *Id.* ¶ 14 (Acting under article 7(3) of the Optional Protocol to the Convention, the Committee is of the view that the State party has failed to fulfil its obligations and has thereby violated the rights of the author.").
[112] *Id.* ¶ 14(b)(xi)(a).

did not inquire about the nature of L.R.'s disability and how it might have affected her experiences of abuse or how it might have led authorities to undermine her credibility in reporting the abuse.

The intersection of gender and disability discrimination exposes women with disabilities to extraordinarily high rates of violence. (See chapter 2 for a more detailed discussion of the intersectional nature of intimate partner violence perpetrated against women with disabilities.) Aside from the passing reference mentioned above, the Committee failed to make recommendations to the government of Moldova that would have ensured better protection against violence for women with disabilities. Those recommendations could have included, for example, the passage of domestic laws or policies supporting women with disabilities who report intimate partner violence, recommending that the state hire women with disabilities to take reports of violence, creating a hotline to serve women with disabilities in reporting violence, and training law enforcement agents on the prevalence and seriousness of violence against women with disabilities.

Anna Belousova v. Kazakhstan

In the 2015 case *Anna Belousova v. Kazakhstan*,[113] CEDAW found that Kazakhstan had violated its obligations under articles 2(e) and 5(a) of the treaty.[114] Anna Belousova lived in a rural town and worked at a primary school. The director of the school "indicated that her continued employment would be dependent upon her engaging in a sexual relationship with him."[115] Upon her refusal, the director asked for payment to allow her to keep her job. Later, her contract was not renewed with the school.[116]

This case presented intersectional issues because Belousova alleged that by living in a rural area, "she and other women from that area belong to a specific group that is particularly subjected to discrimination."[117] CEDAW pointed out that Kazakhstan has "no legal provision prohibiting sexual harassment in the workplace,"[118] and the Committee had "already expressed its concern" about the state's lack of legal protections.[119] But the Committee failed to address intersectionality in its recommendations in any meaningful way. The Committee merely observed that the State party should "raise awareness of the public at large, including in rural areas, of sexual harassment in the workplace as a punishable offence."[120]

The brief recognition that women living in rural areas need to be included in remedial measures, such as awareness campaigns, does not amount to meaningful intersectional analysis. Had the Committee conducted probing intersectional analysis it would have been able to make more targeted recommendations to ensure that women

113 Belousova v. Kazakhstan, U.N. Doc. CEDAW/C/61/D/45/2012 (Aug. 25, 2015).

114 *Id.* ¶ 11.

115 *Id.* ¶ 2.2.

116 *See id.* ¶ 2.4 ("[T]he author made an oral complaint about her situation and the harassment by her employer. . . . [The inspection] concluded that the author's allegations were unfounded. The author was neither approached nor questioned.").

117 *Id.* ¶ 3.4.

118 *Id.* ¶ 9.4.

119 *Id.*

120 *Id.* ¶ 11(a)(iii).

living in rural areas enjoyed the same equality and employment rights as men living in rural areas and women living in urban areas. Specifically, the Committee neglected an opportunity to discuss what kinds of remedial measures are necessary to ensure the rights of women living at the intersection of gender subordination, rurality, and in some cases, low socioeconomic status.

Decisions that included intersectional analysis but failed to provide intersectional remedies

Jallow v. Bulgaria

A further set of cases involves those in which CEDAW engaged in intersectional analysis yet failed to provide remedies directed at those intersections. In *Jallow v. Bulgaria*,[121] CEDAW considered a complaint from Jallow, a Gambian citizen who migrated to Bulgaria in 2008 to be with her Bulgarian husband. The Committee describes Jallow as "an illiterate women with no education who can speak only her native language and English at an average level."[122] Jallow and her husband had a child together. Shortly after Jallow arrived in Bulgaria, she began experiencing physical and psychological abuse at the hands of her husband. Her husband began sexually abusing their young daughter as well as directing racist comments toward Jallow.[123]

Jallow's complaint alleged that Bulgaria failed to address her husband's domestic violence and that Bulgaria lacks legal provisions to prevent violence against women.[124] Jallow also alleged that she had limited access to the Bulgarian court system because she could not speak Bulgarian and could not understand the proceedings unless she paid for her own interpreter. Jallow asserted that "this disproportionately affects women, in particular those with low social status and income."[125]

CEDAW concluded that Bulgaria violated the Convention. The Committee recognized that Jallow and her daughter "were in a vulnerable position, in particular because the author is an illiterate migrant woman without a command of Bulgarian."[126] The Committee acknowledged that Jallow experienced discrimination on multiple axes, noting, "[T]he State party's authorities failed to act with due diligence, to provide her with effective protection and to take into account her vulnerable position, as an illiterate migrant woman with a small daughter without a command of Bulgarian or relatives in the State party."[127] Beyond these passing references to her vulnerability as an illiterate migrant woman, however, the Committee did not explore how intersectionality constructed her experiences of intimate partner violence and her subsequent interactions with Bulgarian authorities.

121 Jallow v. Bulg., U.N. Doc. CEDAW/C/52/D/32/2011 (Aug. 28, 2012).

122 *Id.* ¶ 2.1.

123 *Id.* ¶ 2.2.

124 *See id.* ¶ 2.1 ("The author claims that articles . . . of the Convention were violated by the State party as a result of the discriminatory treatment that she and her daughter, as women, received from its authorities, and its failure to protect them from domestic gender-based violence.").

125 *Id.* ¶ 3.4.

126 *Id.* ¶ 8.5.

127 *Id.* ¶ 8.2.

The Committee asserted that gender-based stereotypes influenced the Bulgarian authorities, noting that "the authorities based their activities on a stereotyped notion that the husband was superior and that his opinions should be taken seriously."[128] The Committee did not explore the extent to which racist stereotypes and attitudes may have also complicated Jallow's interactions with authorities. The Committee could have more accurately identified the intersection of racial and gender-based harms by analyzing the racist remarks made by her husband during the abuse. Also, by using data on Bulgarian attitudes toward migrants, and migrant women in particular, the Committee could have explored whether Jallow was likely to have faced intersectional discrimination based on gender and race from the Bulgarian police and other authorities.

CEDAW made several recommendations aimed at increasing access to justice in Bulgaria. It recommended that Bulgaria "take measures to ensure that women victims of domestic violence, in particular migrant women, have effective access to services related to protection against domestic violence and to justice."[129] The Committee observed that Bulgaria needs "interpretation or translation" services for women.[130] CEDAW also recommended that Bulgaria provide training for its judges, prosecutors, and other child protective agencies "in a gender-sensitive manner, having particular regard to multiple discrimination."[131] These recommendations acknowledge that Jallow's circumstances are different from that of a non-migrant woman or a migrant man. In this way, the recommendations represent progress toward a more rigorous intersectional analysis. The references to migrant status and vulnerability, however, appear as passing references in a decision otherwise focused on gender.

Alyne da Silva Pimentel Teixeira v. Brazil

In a landmark 2011 case, *Alyne da Silva Pimentel Teixeira v. Brazil*,[132] CEDAW engaged in a limited intersectional analysis to decide the case of a poor Afro-Brazilian woman who died because of inadequate emergency obstetric care. Legal scholar Rebecca Cook notes that *Alyne* marks "the first decision of an international treaty body holding a government accountable for a preventable maternal death."[133] The case also offers an example in which CEDAW engaged in an intersectional analysis that led to more comprehensive remedies than would result from traditional gender-based analysis alone.

Alyne da Silva Pimentel Teixeira died on November 16, 2002, in a Brazilian hospital following complications from childbirth.[134] She had visited a private hospital on November 11 because she was suffering from severe nausea and abdominal pain.[135] After this visit, which was in her sixth month of pregnancy, da Silva Pimentel

[128] *Id.* ¶ 8.6.
[129] *Id.* ¶ 8.8(2)(a).
[130] *Id.*
[131] *Id.* ¶ 8.8(2)(c).
[132] Alyne da Silva Pimentel Teixeira v. Braz., U.N. Doc. CEDAW/C/49/D/17/2008 (Sept. 27, 2011).
[133] Rebecca J. Cook, *Human Rights and Maternal Health: Exploring the Effectiveness of the* Alyne *Decision*, 41 J. L., Medicine & Ethics 103, 103 (2013).
[134] Alyne da Silva Pimentel Teixeira, ¶ 2.12 ("An autopsy found the official cause of death to be digestive haemorrhage. According to the doctors, this resulted from the delivery of the stillborn fetus.").
[135] *Id.* ¶ 4.9 (describing the health center as a private, for-profit hospital).

Teixeira was sent home. The private hospital scheduled blood and urine tests for November 13.[136]

When her condition worsened between November 11 and 13, she returned to the private hospital on November 13, and was admitted around 8:30 a.m. An ultrasound a few hours later found no fetal heartbeat. The doctors induced labor at 2 p.m., and da Silva Pimentel Teixeira delivered a stillborn fetus around 8 p.m.[137] Although it should have happened earlier, doctors waited fourteen hours before surgically removing the placenta.

At this point, da Silva Pimentel Teixeira began hemorrhaging severely and required a blood transfusion. The private hospital, hoping to transfer her, spent November 14 contacting other hospitals with better facilities. Da Silva Pimentel Teixeira was in critical condition for eight hours while she awaited an ambulance. On November 15, she arrived at a municipal hospital at 9:45 p.m., over two days after first being admitted to the clinic.[138] The medical transport did not bring any medical records with them when they transported her to the municipal hospital, so doctors relied on an oral account of her symptoms. Da Silva Pimentel Teixeira's mother tried to retrieve medical records, but she was questioned and had to wait.[139] On November 16, da Silva Pimentel Teixeira died.[140]

Da Silva Pimentel Teixeira's family filed suit in 2003 in the Brazilian courts on her behalf. Ten years later, the trial court in Rio de Janeiro awarded damages to her family but refused to hold the state directly responsible for the inadequate healthcare she received at the private hospital.[141] Her family also filed an international human rights claim before CEDAW in 2007.

The claim alleged that Brazil failed to ensure Da Silva Pimentel Teixeira's human rights in violation of Articles 1 (right to non-discrimination), 2 (access to justice), and 12 (right to health) of CEDAW. Specifically, the family claimed that Brazil violated Pimentel Teixeira's right to access to justice under Article 2 since it had not issued a decision in the domestic case. Article 2(c) ensures "legal protection of the rights of women ... through competent national tribunals."[142] Her mother, Maria de Lourdes da Silva Pimentel, argued that their family had not been provided redress for the hospital's actions. Specifically, the family claimed that the delay in domestic court proceedings demonstrated that "women's health, especially that of women from vulnerable groups ... are not given priority in the court system." Additionally, the family argued that Brazil failed to provide "a meaningful and timely response from the judiciary" based on the "extraordinary delay" in the trial court's decision.[143]

The claim argued further that Brazil failed to ensure access to quality medical treatment for pregnancy, thus violating Article 12 of CEDAW.[144] According to the

[136] *Id.* ¶ 2.2.

[137] *Id.* ¶ 2.5.

[138] *Id.* ¶ 2.9.

[139] *See id.* ¶ 2.10 ("The medical attendants did not bring her medical records to the hospital. Instead, they provided the treating physician with a brief oral account of her symptoms.").

[140] *Id.* ¶ 2.12.

[141] Ctr. Reprod. Rights, Alyne v. Brazil: Case of Alyne da Silva Pimentel Teixeira ("Alyne") v. Brazil 2 (2014).

[142] G.A. Res. 34/180, at 195 (Dec. 18, 1979).

[143] Alyne da Silva Pimentel Teixeira, ¶ 3.15.

[144] *Id.* ¶ 3.8.

complaint, Brazil violated Article 12 by failing to provide access to quality medical care during delivery. Specifically, the complainant claimed that there was no reasonable access to emergency services because her daughter had to travel two hours to receive care, only one hospital had enough space, and the doctors were negligent in providing care.[145] The family claimed, therefore, that Brazil failed to provide accessible care as required by its Article 12 obligations.

Brazil asserted that its Federal Constitution explains the obligations with respect to public health services. The state drew a distinction between the right to health and the right to health assistance under its constitution, "wherein the latter is restricted to medical actions performed to detect and treat illnesses."[146] Brazil explained that the private sector hospitals may only participate in health assistance. Broader health policies are in "the exclusive domain of the political sphere."[147] The acts of private sector hospitals, therefore, did not reflect Brazil's healthcare policies. Brazil argued that da Silva Pimentel Teixeira's death was the result of the private hospital's health assistance failure, and not a failure of the State to provide a right to health. Brazil blamed errors on the "mechanisms used to contract private health services ... not a lack of commitment on the part of the State to combat discrimination against women."[148] Brazil also denied that da Silva Pimentel Teixeira's death was linked with her pregnancy.[149] It pointed to a report by the State Committee on Maternal Mortality which concluded that the "probable cause of death was digestive haemorrhage."[150] Further, Brazil argued that there was no link between da Silva Pimentel Teixeira's death and gender discrimination.[151]

The family replied that Brazil's arguments did not address the unreasonable delay in judiciary action on this case[152] and that these judicial delays are even worse for Afro-descendant women and women of lower socioeconomic backgrounds who cannot get redress for acts of discrimination.[153] CEDAW concluded that da Silva Pimentel Teixeira's death was related to her pregnancy and that the failure of the health center to act appropriately caused her death.[154] It concluded that da Silva Pimentel Teixeira's death must be viewed as a maternal death because the lack of access to adequate healthcare was related to her pregnancy. The Committee found that the lack of appropriate maternal services discriminates against women's right to life and health.[155] The

[145] *See id.* ¶ 3.10–3.12 ("[N]umerous studies on material mortality in Brazil that identify poor quality of health care in treating obstetric emergencies as a major reason for Brazil's high maternal mortality rate.").

[146] *Id.* ¶ 4.1.

[147] *See id.* ¶ 4.4 ("The private sector is authorized to provide health assistance, which encompasses medical and pharmaceutical services, while municipalities retain sole responsibility over the health services intended for the general population.").

[148] *Id.* ¶ 4.7.

[149] *Id.* ¶ 4.8.

[150] *Id.*

[151] *Id.* ¶ 4.7 ("The state ... refers to the finding of the technical visit report ... which concluded that the failures in the medical assistance ... did not fall under discrimination against women, but rather deficient and low-quality service provision.").

[152] *Id.* ¶ 5.3.

[153] *Id.* ¶ 5.3.

[154] *See id.* ¶ 5.15 ("Despite the obvious need for immediate treatment and her continually worsening condition, she was not transferred .... This chain of events clearly demonstrates that [her] death resulted from the series of negligent medical interventions following intrauterine foetal death.").

[155] *Id.* ¶ 7.6.

Committee determined that States parties have an obligation to "meet the specific, distinctive health needs and interests of women."[156] Brazil's failure to provide adequate maternal health services, together with the delays in domestic court proceedings, therefore violated Articles 12, 2(c), and 2(e) of CEDAW.[157]

The Committee concluded that da Silva Pimentel Teixeira "was discriminated against, not only on the basis of her sex, but also on the basis of her status as a woman of African descent and her socio-economic background."[158] The Committee recognized that da Silva Pimentel Teixeira "suffered from multiple discrimination."[159] It further recognized intersectional discrimination by recalling its General Recommendation No. 28.[160] This recommendation acknowledges that State parties' obligations under Article 2 include addressing discrimination against women that is linked to "race, ethnicity, religion or belief, health, status, age, class, cast, and sexual orientation and gender identity."[161]

Still, while the Committee recognized intersectional discrimination in its considerations of the case, it did not explicitly address intersectional discrimination in its recommendations. The Committee recommended reparations, including financial compensation to Alyne da Silva Pimentel Teixeira's family.[162] In addition, the Committee's more general recommendations required Brazil to: ensure "women's right to safe motherhood and affordable access for all women"; "provide adequate professional training for health workers, especially on women's reproductive health rights"; "ensure access to effective remedies in cases where women's reproductive health rights have been violated"; "ensure that private health facilities comply with relevant national and international standards on reproductive health care"; "ensure that adequate sanctions are imposed on health professionals who violate women's reproductive health rights"; and reducing "preventable maternal deaths."[163]

Given the Committee's willingness to recognize the intersectional nature of the violations in its analysis of the merits, the failure to specifically address intersectional discrimination and corresponding intersectional remedies in this case is surprising. Describing the case, one scholar noted: "The circumstances leading to [da Silva Pimentel Teixeira's] death highlighted gross inadequacies and failures in the quality of maternity care and emergency obstetric care provided to poor, Afro-descendant women in Brazil."[164] Given the obvious intersectional nature of the rights violations and the Committee's acknowledgment of the intersection of race, gender, and socio-economic status in the case, it is curious that the Committee did not specifically target intersectional remedies in its recommendations. Instead, it relied on the more general notion that States parties must ensure healthcare access to *all* women.

156 *Id.*

157 *Id.* ¶ 8.

158 *Id.* ¶ 7.7.

159 *Id.*

160 *See generally* Comm. on the Elimination of All Forms of Discrimination Against Women [CEDAW], Gen. Recommendation 28, U.N. Doc. CEDAW/C/GC/28 (Dec. 16, 2010).

161 Alyne da Silva Pimentel Teixeira, ¶ 7.7.

162 *Id.* ¶ 8(1).

163 *Id.* ¶ 8(2)(a)–(f).

164 Kia Lilly Caldwell, Health Equity in Brazil: Intersections of Gender, Race, and Policy 1 (2017).

The failure to include intersectionality in its discussion of appropriate remedies represents a lost opportunity for CEDAW. In this case, the complainant explicitly asserted intersectional claims. To its credit, the Committee acknowledged and validated the intersectional nature of the claims, as shown above, but it would have been a straightforward matter to continue that intersectional analysis to the remedy stage. Instead, the Committee focused on general remedies stemming from the gender discrimination that Ms. da Silva Pimentel Teixeira experienced.

Had the Committee extended its intersectional analysis to its discussion of appropriate remedies in the case, it could have included numerous remedies that specifically address the discrimination in healthcare that arises from the intersection of gender, race, and socioeconomic biases in Brazil. In this vein, the Committee's analysis could have relied on existing data concerning disparities in Brazilian healthcare more extensively. As discussed in chapter 2, Afro-Brazilian women are disproportionately affected by numerous reproductive health issues, including fibroid tumors, maternal mortality, and clandestine abortions. "Maternal mortality is particularly problematic among low-income, Afro-Brazilian, and indigenous women, as well as women living in rural areas and in the Brazilian north and northeast," notes the NGO that assisted Ms. de Lourdes da Silva Pimentel with her petition.[165] Indeed, the Brazilian government acknowledges that "poverty is concentrated [among] black or Afro-descending women."[166] Poverty, racism, and sexism intersect to limit access to reproductive healthcare for Afro-descendant women in Brazil.

The *Alyne* case serves as an apt example of the discrimination that Black women in Brazil face with regard to reproductive healthcare. Many believe that Black women have been subjected to sterilization, including forced sterilization, at higher rates than white women.[167] As noted in chapter 2, race is a significant factor in the increasingly disproportionate health status of Black women as compared to white women in Brazil.[168] Many in the Black women's movement believe that Black and Brown women, both common descriptors of the Afro-descendant population in Brazil, commonly experience higher rates of pilgrimage, in which "women travel to more than one maternity hospital because they are unable to receive care at a hospital when they arrive."[169] Pilgrimage disproportionately affects Afro-Brazilian women and stems from the intersection of race, gender, and class-based discrimination.[170] By all accounts, Alyne da

[165] *See* CTR. REPROD. RIGHTS, *supra* note 141, at 1.

[166] *Id.* (*citing* Comm. on the Elimination of Discrimination Against Women [CEDAW], Brazil: Consideration of Reports Submitted by States Parties under Article 18 of the Convention on the Elimination of All Forms of Discrimination Against Women, at 60, U.N. Doc. CEDAW/C/BRA/1-5 (2002)).

[167] *See* Caldwell, *supra* note 164, at 51.

[168] *See id.* at 49 ("Black women health activists have also argued that race plays a major role in worsening the health status of black women when compared to white women.").

[169] *Id.* at 117.

[170] Kia Lilly Caldwell describes the race-based phenomenon of pilgrimage in Brazil:

> [Researchers] found that 31.8% of *negras* (black women), 28.8% of *pardas* (brown women), and 16.4% of *brancas* (white women) traveled to more than one maternity hospital in the municipality of Rio de Janeiro in order to give birth. Racial disparities in access to anesthesia during childbirth were also found .... [D]iscrimination by health professionals based on race and educational level had a noticeable impact on the prenatal and childbirth experiences of low-income black and brown women in Rio de Janeiro.

Id. at 117–18 (internal citations omitted).

Silva Pimentel Teixeira appears to have been a victim of the pilgrimage phenomenon in Brazil.

With respect to each of its recommendations, the Committee should have included remedies that specifically address the intersectional nature of the violations. Regarding safe motherhood and affordable access, the Committee notes its own General Recommendation No. 24, which concerns women and health:

> While biological differences between women and men may lead to differences in health status, there are societal factors that are determinative of the health status of women and men and can vary among women themselves. For that reason, special attention should be given to the health needs and rights of women belonging to vulnerable and disadvantaged groups, such as migrant women, refugee and internally displaced women, the girl child and older women, women in prostitution, indigenous women and women with physical or mental disabilities.[171]

Given the established phenomenon of pilgrimage, which disproportionately affects Black and low socioeconomic status women in Brazil and which appears to have prevented Alyne da Silva Pimentel Teixeira's access to quality care in this case, CEDAW missed an important opportunity to address intersectional discrimination. CEDAW cannot effectively address "access to safe motherhood" without specifically addressing the intersectional impediments to safe motherhood for Black women in Brazil. The Committee should have specifically recommended that Brazil work to eliminate pilgrimage by creating regulations and policies that punish, fine, or otherwise disincentivize hospitals and health clinics that engage in this discriminatory and life-threatening behavior.

The Committee recommended training for health workers "especially on women's reproductive health rights."[172] The Committee should have specifically recommended that the training include non-discrimination training that would educate medical professionals about the existence of racial and socioeconomic bias that intersects with gender bias in ways that substantially interfere with the enjoyment of women's reproductive health rights. Without such intersectional training, healthcare providers may improve treatment for racially and socioeconomically privileged women without improving the standard of care for poor and Afro-descendant women in Brazil.

In all, the Committee failed to provide comprehensive recommendations that adequately addressed the deeply intersectional nature of the violations at issue in this case. Instead, the Committee limited its recommendations to a narrow assessment of gender discrimination in healthcare. Despite having recognized the operation of intersectionality in Alyne da Silva Pimentel Teixeira's experience of the human rights violations in this case, the Committee failed to extend these intersectional insights to its recommendations, thereby limiting the effectiveness of the decision.

[171] *See* CEDAW, *supra* note 97, at 3.

[172] Alyne da Silva Pimentel Teixeira, ¶ 8(2)(b).

R.P.B. v. Philippines

A third case provides a window into CEDAW jurisprudence at the intersection of gender and disability. In its 2014 decision in *R.P.B. v. Philippines*,[173] the Committee considered the case of R.P.B. who is hearing impaired and unable to speak. R.P.B. was seventeen when she reported to police, using sign language and her sister as an interpreter, that her neighbor had raped her. In her case before the Committee, she alleged that the state had discriminated against her in the legal process under Articles 1 and 2 of CEDAW.[174] She also alleged a violation of the Convention on the Rights of Persons with Disabilities (CRPD), but she brought the complaint to CEDAW.[175]

This case was the first time CEDAW considered rights violations at the intersection of gender and disability in an individual complaint brought under the Optional Protocol. In its decision, the Committee acknowledged that the state failed to provide fair and impartial trial proceedings that were unaffected by stereotypes regarding the victim's gender, age, and disability.[176] Unfortunately, that is as far as the intersectional analysis went. The Committee gave primacy to the gender discrimination claims, citing the potential for "double discrimination," which suggests a kind of "gender plus" additive notion of increased vulnerability.[177]

R.P.B.'s complaint specifically asserted an intersectional claim of discrimination based on gender, age, and disability. Her complaint is replete with references to her identity as a young, disabled female victim of sexual violence. It was reasonable for CEDAW to conclude that it could not render a decision about any potential violation of the Convention on the Rights of Persons with Disabilities. Potential violations of another convention are clearly outside the purview of the Committee. CEDAW could, however, have carefully considered the intersectional dimensions of the discrimination that R.P.B. suffered and could have directed remedies at the intersection of gender, age, and disability.

The Committee's analysis falls short in several ways. First, with regard to stereotypes about the victim's behavior—R.P.B.'s complaint "argues that the [Philippine] court's decision is discriminatory, given that it requires that the victim display a 'reasonable standard of human conduct' in a rape case and that it discounts the wide range of behavioural responses exhibited by victims threatened with rape, in particular by a woman with [a] disability."[178] The Committee summarizes R.P.B.'s view, noting, "The author further contends that deaf women, especially girls, occupy a difficult position in Philippine society because they are disadvantaged both to men (men with or without disability, including deafness) and women (women without or with disability

[173] R.P.B. v. Phil., U.N. Doc. CEDAW/C/57/D/34/2011 (Mar. 12, 2014).

[174] *Id.* ¶ 1.

[175] *See id.* ¶ 3.8 ("The court ignored the reality . . . that 'women and girls with disabilities are often at greater risk, both within and outside the home, of violence, injury or abuse, neglect or negligent maltreatment.'").

[176] *Id.* ¶ 8.11 ("The Committee further recognizes that the author has suffered material and moral damage and prejudice . . . by the . . . use of the stereotypes and gender-based myths and disregard for her specific situation as a mute and deaf girl in the judgement.").

[177] *See* Truscan & Bourke-Martignoni, *supra* note 3, at 118 ("Although the Committee made progress in taking account of the complex circumstances that formed the background to R.P.B.'s situation, the decision also demonstrates the limits of its capacity to follow an intersectionality-based analysis through to its natural conclusion.").

[178] R.P.B. v. Phil., ¶ 3.4.

other than deafness)."[179] The complaint explicitly and compellingly opens the door for the Committee to explore how the stereotypes encountered by disabled women differ from those of disabled men and able-bodied women. Instead, the Committee focused largely on delegitimizing the gender-based stereotypes that have traditionally led courts to discount the credibility of female victims of sexual assault.

Second, CEDAW's discussion of remedies was insufficient. Given the sophisticated understanding of intersectionality articulated in R.P.B's complaint, it is unsurprising that the remedies she requests are comprehensive and reflect multiple aspects of her identity.[180] The Committee's list of mandated remedies is constrained and fails to comprehensively address the intersectional nature of R.P.B.'s complaint. Among other requested remedies, R.P.B. "asks the Committee to establish that she has been a victim of discrimination *as a deaf girl-child victim of rape*." In short, R.P.B. sought recognition from the Committee that she suffered discrimination at the intersection of gender, age, and disability. The Committee, however, emphasized the existence of gender discrimination, albeit gender discrimination that results in additional vulnerability for women with disabilities. The Committee's decision states: "In this context, the Committee emphasizes that it is crucial to ensure that women with disabilities enjoy effective protection *against sex and gender-based discrimination* by States parties and have access to effective remedies."[181] Although the Committee acknowledged that women and girls with disabilities face "double discrimination,"[182] its analytical focus remained on the additive formulation of "gender plus."

In other words, the Committee asserted that R.P.B.'s disability is relevant only to the extent that it renders her "extra" vulnerable to gender discrimination. True intersectional analysis would facilitate the Committee's understanding of R.P.B.'s discrimination as stemming from the intersection of disability, age, and gender and resulting in a qualitatively different experience of discrimination to that of men with disabilities and able-bodied women. The risks of sexual violence that R.P.B. faces are qualitatively different from those faced by majority-age, able-bodied women. For example, hearing-impaired women may be more isolated within families and communities and, as such, may lack access to information about sexual assault and about services for victims.

R.P.B.'s complaint specifically claims that the Philippine court relied on discriminatory gender-based stereotypes defining the degree of resistance expected from a rape victim.[183] It goes further, however, to argue that gender bias in the expectations of victim resistance should not be applied in a case involving a hearing-impaired victim. R.P.B notes that the Philippine court dismissively stated that "her being a deaf mute does not render her incapable of creating noise."[184] She argues that the court "not only rendered judgement against the author using gender stereotypes and myths, but also reasoned with manifest prejudice against her as a deaf minor."[185] The Committee

[179] *Id.* ¶ 3.8.
[180] *See id.* (requesting a remedy that focuses "on the intersectionality of gender, disability and age.").
[181] *Id.* ¶ 8.3 (emphasis added).
[182] *Id.*
[183] *Id.* ¶ 3.4.
[184] *See id.* ¶ 2.5 (listing the court's reasoning for finding that the author had failed to prove that the sexual intercourse was not consensual).
[185] *Id.* ¶ 3.8.

clearly condemns the use of gender-based stereotypes that require a victim to resist by "slapping, punching, kicking, or pushing the offender."[186] These assertions, however, also opened the door for the Committee to explore the court's dismissal of R.P.B.'s disability in its assessment of her reaction to the attack. Although the Committee notes that the Philippines must ensure that sexual assault proceedings are free from stereotypes about the victim's gender, age, and disability, it does so only in passing. Instead, the Committee chose to address only the gender-based stereotypes in a meaningful way. By leaving stereotypes about people who are deaf mute largely unchallenged, CEDAW itself reifies those disability-related stereotypes.

As with the previous cases, a robust intersectional analysis would have led the Committee to a more expansive view of appropriate remedies. R.P.B.'s complaint seeks a wide range of remedies, including compensation, free counseling for herself and her family including sign language interpreting, and barrier-free education and employment opportunities. After determining that the Philippines was responsible for violations of the treaty, the Committee recommended that the government provide R.P.B. with the compensation, counseling, and barrier-free education she sought in her complaint. The Committee also made the following broad recommendations: review of rape laws to focus on consent rather than force or violence; review of legislation and practice to guarantee access to sign language interpretation at all stages of judicial proceedings; ensure that all sexual assault proceedings are impartial, fair, and free from stereotypes based on gender, age, and disability; and provide adequate training for judges and lawyers on CEDAW's requirements to ensure that "stereotypes and gender bias do not affect court proceedings and decision-making."[187]

These are undoubtedly important remedies in this case. R.P.B., however, sought more. The additional remedies she sought reflected her self-understanding as a "deaf girl-child victim of rape."[188] She also wanted the Committee to address the structural dimensions of the discrimination she faced more comprehensively.[189] To that end, R.P.B's complaint cites statistics on the high rates of sexual violence within deaf communities in the Philippines. R.P.B.'s complaint asks the Committee to recommend that the Philippines take measures across all branches of government "and with particular focus on the intersectionality of gender, disability and age."[190] She also requests that "issues resulting from the intersectionality of gender, disability, and age be addressed in programmes and services of the relevant agencies of the State party."[191] She seeks a deaf sexual violence hotline, professional interpretation in legal and mental health counseling programs, inclusion of sexual violence awareness in university curricula, educational programming for deaf girls and women including sexuality and gender studies, and fully accessible guidance and counseling, among other things. The

[186] *Id.* ¶ 3.6.
[187] *Id.* ¶ 9(iv).
[188] *Id.* ¶ 3.16.
[189] *See id.* ¶ 3.17 (requesting "a law be enacted making mandatory the use of interpreting in all judicial, quasi-judicial and investigative proceedings . . . involving deaf individuals; [and] that issues resulting from the intersectionality of gender, disability and age be addressed in programmes and services of the relevant agencies of the State party.").
[190] *Id.*
[191] *Id.*

comprehensive remedies R.P.B. sought in her complaint reflect her focus on intersectional discrimination stemming from *both* gender and disability discrimination. With their focus on gender discrimination (and at times, "gender plus" discrimination), the more limited remedies from the committee do not fully embrace an intersectional view of R.P.B.'s experience.

Although the Committee could have discussed how R.P.B.'s disability may have affected her experience of the rape and the authorities' perception of her as a victim, it chose not to do so. Through a more expansive intersectional analysis, the Committee could have enumerated the requirements for States parties to eliminate barriers to the justice system for women and girls with disabilities. In the end, the Committee found a violation of R.P.B.'s right to be free from gender discrimination and a "disregard" for her disability and age. Although the implicit recognition of "double discrimination" represents progress for CEDAW, it is a shallow form of intersectionality. I have consistently argued that the treaty bodies, particularly CEDAW, can do better in their assessment of intersectional claims. The treaty bodies must do better, in fact, if they are to begin to fully comprehend the profound complexity of human rights violations. To do anything less is to provide partial remedies for partially legitimized claims.

A decision that recommended intersectional remedies

My analysis of CEDAW jurisprudence reveals one decision that both recognized intersectional harms and suggested intersectional remedies. The fact there is only one CEDAW decision that meaningfully grapples with the intersectional nature of the rights violations at issue is indicative of the treaty bodies' reluctance to engage fully with intersectionality. Because intersectionality is gaining traction within treaty body jurisprudence, I expect to see more decisions that incorporate intersectional remedies in the effort to compensate victims and combat structural inequality.

In its 2012 decision in *Kell v. Canada*,[192] CEDAW warmed to the notion of intersectionality. Decided eight years after *A.S. v. Hungary* and after considerable international attention to intersectionality as a valuable theoretical lens, the *Kell* case presented another opportunity for the Committee to recognize the intersectional nature of certain rights violations. In this case, the Committee succeeded in capturing the intersectional harms suffered by Cecilia Kell, an Aboriginal woman from the Rae-Edzo community in the Northwest Territories of Canada. In 1990, Kell's common-law partner, William Senych, applied for housing that the Canadian government reserved for members of the Rae-Edzo community. Because he was not a member of the community, Senych's application was denied. Advised to do so by the housing authority, Kell then applied for the housing and listed Senych as a spouse.[193] Senych and Kell then became co-owners of the property pursuant to an agreement with the Northwest Territory Housing Corporation.

Over the next three years, Senych subjected Kell to intimate partner violence. Without her knowledge, Senych requested that the Housing Corporation remove

[192] Kell v. Canada, U.N. Doc. CEDAW/C/51/D/19/2008 (Apr. 26, 2012).
[193] *Id.* ¶ 2.2.

Kell's name from the document certifying co-ownership of the property. The Housing Corporation, acting on information from the Rae-Edzo Housing Authority, of which Senych was a representative at the time, granted the request and removed Kell's name, making Senych the sole owner of the property in 1993.[194]

After two more years of abuse, Kell filed a complaint in the Northwest Territory Supreme Court seeking compensation for the abuse, including assault, battery, sexual assault, intimidation, trespass to chattels, loss of use of her home, and the resulting housing expenses she bore.[195] For his part, Senych denied her access to the property and sought an eviction.

Kell was represented by a series of legal aid lawyers, most of whom urged her to settle. Early in the legal battle, doctors diagnosed Senych with cancer, leading to a delay in the proceedings, and he later died. Kell's lawyers failed to represent her interests, and the Supreme Court eventually dismissed her case for "want of prosecution."[196] Subsequent appeals failed. When, in 2004, Kell filed another action to reclaim her property, the Court dismissed the claim because the property had already been sold.

Having exhausted domestic remedies, Kell submitted a communication to CEDAW in 2008. Her communication alleged violations of CEDAW's Articles 1, 2(d), 2(e), 14(2)(h), 15(1)—15(4), and 16(1)(h).[197] Kell alleged that the Canadian government and its housing authority agents discriminated against her based on sex, marital status, and cultural heritage with respect to her property rights.

Describing the ineffectiveness of her lawyers, Kell's communication to CEDAW stated: "As an aboriginal person, she experienced racism, and as a woman, she experienced sexism. Both of these aspects of discrimination contributed to a pattern of behavior that was at best bullying and at worst abusive."[198] In addition to Kell's own invocation of intersectionality in her complaint, CEDAW was able to draw on its own growing understanding of intersectionality as articulated in General Recommendation No. 28.[199] That General Recommendation asserts that intersectionality is part of the core non-discrimination obligation that states undertake when they ratify the CEDAW Convention.

Thanks to both General Recommendation No. 28 and a growing recognition among international scholars and activists of the value of intersectional analysis, CEDAW offered a commitment to and an emerging understanding of intersectionality. In its decision, the Committee observed, "[a]s the author is an aboriginal woman who is in a vulnerable position, the State party is obliged to ensure the effective elimination of intersectional discrimination."[200] In its most complete embrace of intersectionality in an individual case, the Committee further stated:

194 *Id.* ¶ 2.5.
195 *Id.* ¶ 2.7.
196 *Id.* ¶ 2.10.
197 *Id.* ¶ 1.
198 *Id.* ¶ 9.3 (internal citations omitted).
199 *See supra* note 160 and accompanying text.
200 Kell, ¶ 10.3. In its decision in the Kell case, the Committee also observed, "The discrimination of women based on sex and gender is inextricably linked with other factors that affect women, such as race ethnicity, religion or belief, health, status, age, class, caste, and sexual orientation and gender identity." Id. ¶ 10.2.

> States parties must legally recognize and prohibit such intersecting forms of discrimination and their compounded negative impact on the women concerned .... Accordingly, the Committee finds that an act of intersectional discrimination has taken place against the author.[201]

Unlike some of the cases discussed above, CEDAW extended its intersectional analysis to its discussion of appropriate remedies in the *Kell* case. The Committee recommended that Canada provide Kell with "housing commensurate in quality, location and size to the one that she was deprived of" and with monetary compensation for the violations of her rights.[202] More generally, the Committee took an intersectional approach in its recommendations to Canada, specifically recommending that the Canadian government "recruit and train more aboriginal women to provide legal aid to women from their communities, including on domestic violence and property rights."[203] The Committee also recommended that Canada "review its legal aid system to ensure that aboriginal women who are victims of domestic violence have effective access to justice."[204] These recommendations, unlike those in other cases, reflect the Committee's understanding of Kell's experience as intersectional. As such, the Committee's recommendations specifically refer to remedies that target Indigenous women.

Reflecting on CEDAW jurisprudence

CEDAW's treatment of intersectional issues, although evolving, continues to be sporadic and inconsistent. In the previous section I took a closer look at CEDAW jurisprudence and its use of intersectional analysis and remedies—or, as my analysis reveals, often a lack thereof. Grouping these cases by degree of intersectional analysis and remedies allows us to note patterns and areas of growth. In some cases, the Committee fails to recognize the human rights violations at issue as intersectional. In these cases, the Committee misses an opportunity to request further information about possible intersectional violations from the author of the complaint and the relevant State party.[205] In its decisions in this type of case, the Committee often presents the facts in a way that does not acknowledge the potential of an intersectional violation. In the future, greater sensitivity to and awareness of potential intersectional violations will help the Committee to identify areas in which it needs to probe for further information.

[201] *Id.* ¶ 10.2.
[202] *Id.* ¶ 11(a)(i).
[203] *Id.* ¶ 11(b)(i).
[204] *Id.* ¶ 11(b)(ii).
[205] As part of CEDAW's complaint process, "the Committee may request the State party or the author [of the complaint] to submit additional written explanations or statements relevant to the issues of admissibility or merits and, if it does so, will give the other party an opportunity to comment within a fixed time frame." Comm. on the Elimination of Discrimination Against Women, Rules of Procedure of the Committee on the Elimination of Discrimination against Women, https://www2.ohchr.org/english/bodies/cedaw/docs/CEDAW_Rules_en.pdf (last visited Mar. 10, 2021).

In the second subset of cases, CEDAW mentions intersectional violations in passing but failed to offer an intersectional analysis of the rights at stake. In these cases, the Committee sometimes treats the rights violations as additive rather than truly intersectional. In other words, the Committee may recognize that poverty or ethnic identity makes a complainant "particularly vulnerable" or adds to the complainant's vulnerability. In some cases, the Committee might even refer to intersectionality or intersectional violations. In many cases, however, the Committee treats these multiple aspects of identity as severable rather than mutually constitutive. This approach allows the Committee to focus solely on the gender discrimination at play. It fails to recognize that the experience of gender discrimination is socially constructed in combination with other aspects of identity and is, therefore, theoretically inseparable.

In the third group of cases, the Committee engages in intersectional analysis in describing the harms the complainant suffered. In the cases of *Alyne da Silva Pimentel Teixeira* and *R.P.B.*, for example, the Committee explored the human rights violations as intersectional and offered analysis that reflects a commitment to intersectional complexity. In *Alyne*, the Committee explored the ways in which the victim's identity as a poor, Afro-descendant woman Brazil intersected with gender discrimination, resulting in intersectional discrimination in healthcare access. Similarly, in *R.P.B.*, the Committee recognized how the victim's status as a person with a disability intersected with gender subordination, resulting in a particular experience of sexual violence. In both cases, however, the Committee failed to extend its intersectional analysis to the question of appropriate remedies.

In each of those cases, the Committee recommended compensation at the individual level but failed to capture intersectionality in its general recommendations for the State party. The general recommendations are an opportunity for the Committee to make recommendations that affect laws and social structures, and thereby combat structural discrimination. It is particularly important for these general recommendations to encapsulate and attempt to remedy intersectional discrimination. In *Alyne* and *R.P.B.*, intersectional remedies would have specifically targeted the social structures that create hierarchies based on poverty, race, and disability. In *Alyne da Silva Pimentel Teixeira*, for example, intersectional remedies would have included more extensive recommendations targeting programs to create access to maternal healthcare *specifically* within impoverished Afro-descendant communities. The Committee's recognition of the intersectional nature of the violations in these cases is a beginning, but the Committee must include intersectional remedies more systematically if it is to effect real change.

In the final category of cases, CEDAW did just that. In *Kell*, the Committee took an intersectional approach and extended intersectional analysis to the question of appropriate remedies. In *Kell*, the Committee recognized the ways in which the complainant's Indigenous identity intersected with her gender to construct an intersectional form of discrimination based on both gender and indigeneity. In its decision, the Committee makes specific recommendations to combat similar types of human rights violations, including a recommendation to increase the number of Indigenous women providing legal assistance to women in their communities. Because it includes intersectional analysis in its recommendations to the offending State party, *Kell* represents a more comprehensive intersectional approach. These recommendations aimed at systemic change along intersectional lines have the most potential to reverse intersectional discrimination. The treaty bodies must continue to engage in a broader and deeper intersectional analysis, including remedies, if they hope to provide true redress for victims of complex, intersectional human rights violations.

Past and future shifts

As understanding of intersectional violations evolves, the treaty bodies show a growing openness to consideration of intersectional violations. The growth in understanding of intersectional issues between *Lovelace* (1981) and *Kell* (2012) is remarkable and indicates that treaty bodies have the capacity to successfully incorporate intersectional analysis into their decisions. It is troubling, however, that *Kell* remains the only CEDAW case to date to incorporate a comprehensive intersectional approach. Just as treaty bodies need to improve their identification of intersectional issues, individual complainants should firmly and more consistently represent human rights violations through an intersectional lens.

Although CEDAW provides the most fertile ground for examining intersectional issues in treaty body jurisprudence, the benefits of intersectional analysis apply with equal force to the other treaty bodies. As the *Lovelace* and *Yilmaz-Dogan* cases illustrate, the HRC and the CERD Committee have also grappled with intersectional rights violations. With all the treaty bodies, it can be difficult to identify which cases involve claims of intersectional human rights violations, because the complainants themselves may not have included facts in the complaint that would indicate that intersectionality is at play. In addition, even when the complainant frames the complaint in intersectional terms, the treaty bodies sometimes do not take up intersectional issues in their analysis of the rights issues at stake, complicating the identification of intersectional rights claims. Most importantly when the treaty bodies fail to explore the intersectional dimensions of rights claims, they inevitably fail to provide comprehensive remedies to victims. Partial remedies, in turn, do little to break down the structural subordination that leads to further rights violations. Together, the treaty bodies have an opportunity to more systematically address and remedy intersectional rights claims.

6
Intersectionality in the State Reporting Process

When a state becomes a party to one of the primary UN human rights treaties, it assumes a number of obligations including, in many cases, to undertake the necessary legal and policy changes to achieve the treaty's goals. States parties also agree to certain reporting obligations pursuant to the human rights treaties, which generally require states to report periodically to the oversight committee on the state's efforts to fulfill the terms of the treaty. The reporting process "focuses governments' attention on the treaty obligations and requires them to evaluate progress, and it also provides an opportunity for civil society to engage with government during the preparation of the report and the Committee's review, as well as in following up on the Committee's concluding observations."[1]

The state reporting process has been a catalyst for change in some countries. In one example from 1995, Pramila Patten, who was then a women's rights leader in Mauritius and who now serves as UN Special Representative of the Secretary-General on Sexual Violence in Conflict, engaged the press in Mauritius to counter the government's description of its report to the CEDAW Committee. When the government of Mauritius presented its report to the Committee in 1995, the Committee was critical of its failure to pass non-discrimination legislation. Despite this criticism from the Committee, government representatives selectively presented positive excerpts of the Committee's concluding observations to the domestic press. Patten offered a more complete account of the Committee's dialogue with the state representatives, and the government publicly attacked her credibility. Ultimately, Patten was able to provide a complete set of the Committee's concluding observations to the press and was vindicated. The prime minister "was reprimanded for the misrepresentation";[2] shortly after that the government amended the Constitution to prohibit discrimination on the basis of sex.

In a number of similar stories,[3] the reporting process has led to scrutiny of domestic laws and prompted States parties to bring law and policy into compliance with the terms of the treaty. Non-governmental organizations (NGOs) have embraced the reporting process as a way to engage their governments in national conversations about the protection of human rights. These organizations have brought to those conversations important insights borne of working at the grassroots level with actual victims of human rights violations. NGOs have seen up close the ways in which victims of

[1] ANDREW BYRNES & MARSHA FREEMAN, WORLD BANK, THE IMPACT OF THE CEDAW CONVENTION: PATHS TO EQUALITY 13 (2011).

[2] UNIFEM, BRINGING EQUALITY HOME: IMPLEMENTING THE CONVENTION ON THE ELIMINATION OF ALL FORMS OF DISCRIMINATION AGAINST WOMEN 37 (Ilana Landsberg-Lewis ed., 1998), https://iknowpolitics.org/sites/default/files/bringingequalityhome_eng.pdf.

[3] *See* BYRNES & FREEMAN, *supra* note 1, at 17–50.

Global Intersectionality and Contemporary Human Rights. Johanna Bond, Oxford University Press. © Johanna Bond 2021.
DOI: 10.1093/oso/9780198868835.003.0007

rights violations achieve, or fail to achieve, justice. Part of this critical perspective is an appreciation for the ways in which human rights violations span multiple treaties and intersect across multiple identities, such as ethnicity and disability. It is not surprising, therefore, that NGOs are, in some cases, initiating important conversations about intersectionality in the context of the state reporting process. In the next chapter, I will look at NGOs' efforts to integrate intersectionality into their own human rights advocacy work and to encourage the UN human rights treaty bodies to do the same.

The human rights treaty bodies have increasingly engaged in intersectional analysis in the context of the reporting process. As noted above and described in more detail in chapter 3, states that have ratified the relevant treaty must report to the treaty body on their efforts to fulfill the treaty's obligations. In 2014, the UN General Assembly adopted a resolution encouraging the treaty bodies to streamline these reporting obligations by offering a simplified reporting procedure.[4] Prior to any discussions of a simplified procedure, each treaty body required States parties to submit an initial report within the first year after ratification and then subsequent reports periodically after that. The reporting intervals for periodic reports differed slightly depending on the treaty. Despite some changes to the reporting process, the treaty bodies continue to invite reporting states to send a representative to the UN meeting, during which the treaty body and the state representatives engage in a "constructive dialogue" about the state's efforts to implement the provisions of the treaty. After the dialogue, the treaty bodies typically adopt concluding observations that highlight how the State party is successfully implementing the treaty as well as the challenges that remain. The treaty bodies make recommendations to improve the State party's compliance with treaty provisions.

For States parties with minimal resources and a large number of ratifications, the reporting burden can be overwhelming. The reporting burden has led a number of states to be out of compliance with their obligations under the treaties. In addition to the burden on States parties, the treaty bodies themselves are behind in their examinations of the reports submitted by states, creating a backlog of years in many cases. Lack of adequate funding at the United Nations has also hampered the effectiveness of the treaty bodies over the years. The UN High Commissioner for Human Rights, Navanethem Pillay, has noted that states may be overwhelmed by receiving recommendations from multiple treaty bodies as part of the reporting process. In a period of four to five years, she noted, a State party may be asked to implement anywhere from 100 to 350 recommendations.[5]

The significant burden on states, the lack of funding, and the treaty bodies' backlog of reports have led to numerous proposals to reform the reporting process for the UN treaty body system. Although conversations about strengthening the treaty body system are ongoing, the treaty bodies have embraced several reform proposals beginning in 2014, when the General Assembly endorsed the idea of a simplified reporting

[4] *See* G.A. Res. 68/268, Strengthening and Enhancing the Effective Functioning of the Human Rights Treaty Body System, at 3 (Apr. 21, 2014) (encouraging treaty bodies to offer simplified reporting procedures to states).

[5] *See* UN HUMAN RIGHTS TREATY BODIES: LAW AND LEGITIMACY 18 (Helen Keller & Geir Ulfstein eds., 2012) (quoting a December 19, 2009 statement by Pillay).

procedure.[6] Instead of submitting periodic reports to a treaty body, states can submit answers to the treaty body's questions or list of issues, and those answers will constitute the periodic reports required under the terms of the treaty. According to the UN Sustainable Development Group, "[t]reaty bodies are progressively introducing this new reporting procedure."[7] The Committee on the Elimination of All Forms of Discrimination Against Women (CEDAW), for example, began offering the option of a simplified reporting procedure in 2014 and adopted new reporting guidelines in late 2019.[8] In chapter 8, I will discuss these and other reform proposals in greater depth. I applaud the UN's efforts to simplify reporting obligations not only because it eases the reporting burden on states but also because combined or integrated reports allow for greater exploration of intersectionality throughout the reporting process.

This chapter takes a deep dive into the reporting process, using CEDAW as a case study, to explore the extent to which intersectionality has surfaced in the Committee's responses to state reports. This offers a barometer for assessing the Committee's acceptance of intersectionality as an analytical framework more generally. The first half of the chapter discusses a trend analysis of information generated in the state reporting process. This analysis of terms and signifiers used in CEDAW's concluding observations (defined below) reveals that the Committee is trending toward more consistently using an intersectional lens.

As we will discuss, the patterns and variations in the analysis of the Committee's concluding observations illuminate inconsistencies and areas for growth. In particular, the Committee's use of vulnerability to describe intersectional rights violations remains problematic. The language of vulnerability, or in the Committee's words, those who are "particularly vulnerable," fails to capture the full insight of intersectionality and—worse—reduces those who have experienced intersectional violations to the embodiment of vulnerability. This elides the agentic lives of these individuals, casting those with multiple intersecting and subordinated identities solely in the reductionist terminology of victimization. By equating vulnerability with victimization and intersectionality, we send the message that intersectional identities are exclusively sites of subordination with layers of vulnerability stacked one on top of the other, rather than mutually constituted, intersecting aspects of identity that variously privilege, oppress, or both. As in earlier discussion, we will continue to explore what is problematic about an exclusive focus on vulnerability.

Building on the observation that CEDAW has increasingly named and explored intersectional human rights issues, the latter half of the chapter studies the circumstances in which CEDAW has undertaken intersectional analysis in the reporting process. Specifically, I look at the extent to which CEDAW embraces intersectionality

[6] *See* G.A. Res. 68/268, *supra* note 4, at 3 (encouraging treaty bodies to offer simplified reporting procedures to states).

[7] *UN Human Rights Treaty Bodies: What Do They Do? How Are They Relevant to My Work?*, United Nations Sustainable Dev. Grp., https://unsdg.un.org/2030-agenda/universal-values/strengthening-international-human-rights/un-treaty-bodies (last visited May 3, 2021).

[8] Comm. on the Elimination of All Forms of Discrimination Against Women, Guidance Note for States Parties for the Preparation of Reports Under Article 18 of the Convention on the Elimination of All Forms of Discrimination Against Women in the Context of the Sustainable Development Goals, U.N. Doc. CEDAW/C/74/3 (2019).

when NGOs have framed the relevant human rights as intersectional rights, when the Committee has taken intersectional issues up on its own initiative, and when the Committee has embraced intersectional analysis because of a reporting government framing the rights at stake as intersectional rights. Although it is impossible to draw definitive causal links between the discursive framing of intersectionality by various actors and the Committee's willingness to adopt an intersectional framework in any particular case, it is useful to think about how NGOs, reporting governments, and the Committee itself may push the UN's dialogue toward a more robust embrace of intersectionality in the decades to come.

Intersectionality in CEDAW's concluding observations: analyzing the trends

CEDAW working methods

After states submit their reports to CEDAW, a pre-sessional working group of the Committee, with the support of the secretariat, meets to draft a list of issues related to the report.[9] This list focuses on any concerns about the state's implementation of the Convention and is intended to help the state prepare for its constructive dialogue with the Committee. The pre-sessional working group comprises five members of the Committee, with the goal of achieving a balanced geographical distribution among committee members.[10]

In March 2018, CEDAW reinstated a simplified reporting procedure, or SRP, to which a state may opt in, provided that the state has "(1) previously submitted an initial report which was considered under the regular procedure; and (2) . . . submitted an updated common core document."[11] Under the SRP, states receive a list of issues prior to reporting, or LOIPR, which is intended to guide the state in drafting a report that is focused on the issues with which the Committee is concerned.[12] The state then has an opportunity to respond to the LOIPR. The Committee does not provide any further questions before evaluating the state's report, which gives states which report under this procedure priority in scheduling.

If a member of a committee is a national of the state at issue, or if there is a conflict of interest or appearance of a conflict, that member will abstain from considering reports and drafting concluding observations after the constructive dialogue.[13] After the constructive dialogue evaluating a state's report, the Committee holds a closed meeting to identify the main issues to be discussed in the concluding observations. The

[9] *See Committee on the Elimination of Discrimination Against Women: Working Methods*, OHCHR, https://www.ohchr.org/EN/HRBodies/CEDAW/Pages/WorkingMethods.aspx (last visited May 4, 2021).

[10] *Id.*

[11] *Committee on the Elimination of Discrimination Against Women: Simplified Reporting Procedure*, OHCHR, https://www.ohchr.org/EN/HRBodies/CEDAW/Pages/ReportingProcedures.aspx (last visited May 4, 2021).

[12] *See id.* (outlining the process of submission and recommended use of LOIPRs).

[13] *See Working Methods*, *supra* note 9 (noting that impartiality is required for compliance with "Addis Ababa guidelines on the independence and impartiality of treaty body experts").

Committee designates a member to serve as the country rapporteur for that country and to draft the concluding observations for consideration by the Committee.[14] After a full draft is completed, the Committee holds another closed meeting to adopt the Concluding Observations. The Committee has a procedure, revised in April 2020, for following up with reporting states on up to four of the recommendations it includes in its concluding observations.[15]

The CEDAW Committee divides concluding observations by subheadings. Typically, the document begins with an introduction, followed by a section commending the country for recent legislation and other steps it has taken to implement the treaty in the time since the last reporting cycle. Many concluding observations also contain a section defining discrimination and describing the country's constitutional framework. The remainder of the observations contain individual sections on issues such as health, education, public and political life, disadvantaged groups of women, and so on. Within each section, the Committee mentions positive steps the country has taken to address the particular issues in the section and then highlights the persistent obstacles to full implementation of the relevant treaty provisions. The Committee then offers the State party recommendations to advance its implementation of the treaty.

It is noteworthy that many of CEDAW's concluding observations include separate sections discussing specific "groups" of women—for example, rural women, migrant women, women with disabilities. Sometimes these group-specific sections stand alone. In other instances, these discussions exist as subsections within a section titled "Disadvantaged groups of women."

The reporting process provides CEDAW with an opportunity to assess the status of women in all participating countries. When the Committee incorporates tenets of intersectionality theory, it conducts a more comprehensive assessment and provides reporting countries with more meaningful recommendations, leading to a more complete and nuanced understanding of the human rights issues at stake in many cases. The concluding observations of CEDAW and the other human rights treaty bodies should reflect this insight if the committees hope to use their concluding observations to maximize the enjoyment of human rights in reporting states.

Trends as reflected in terminology

To track CEDAW's engagement with intersectional concepts in the context of state reporting, I examined CEDAW's concluding observations from 2013 to 2019 to identify references to intersectionality or intersectional concepts. For the concluding observations I examined, I tracked the use of multiple words and phrases: vulnerable, multiple discrimination, intersectional/intersectionality, disadvantage, lesbian, intersex,

[14] *See id.* (explaining the duties of a state's rapporteur).

[15] *See* Information on the Follow-Up Procedure: CEDAW, OHCHR, https://www.ohchr.org/en/hrbodies/cedaw/pages/cedawindex.aspx (last visited May 4, 2021) (follow the "Follow-up to concluding observations procedure" hyperlink on the left-hand side; then follow the "View document" hyperlink next to "INFORMATION ON THE FOLLOW-UP PROCEDURE"; then click the document icon next to the desired language).

homophobia, transgender, transsexual, and disabilities. Although this was in no way a quantitative analysis, I hoped to identify broad patterns in the use or disuse of terms related to intersectional analysis. I reviewed the CEDAW Committee's concluding observations from 2013 to 2019. I searched each concluding observation for the words and partial versions of the words listed above and examined the sentences that contained the search terms. If the sentence simply referred to areas in which women are "disadvantaged" vis-à-vis men, I did not consider this an effort to include intersectional analysis.

The trend analysis revealed broad patterns of references to intersectional concepts, the parameters of which point to increasing attention to intersectionality within the CEDAW Committee's state reporting process. I base these observations on an assumption that the Committee's terminology and nomenclature reflect the theoretical framework it uses to identify and address human rights violations. On the path toward a more robust embrace of intersectionality, the Committee uses a range of signifiers to indicate its openness to intersectionality. At times, it uses terms such as "particularly vulnerable" to describe groups of women who experience intersectional discrimination. In other instances, the Committee notes that some women experience "multiple discrimination." Yet in other circumstances, the Committee uses the language of intersectionality to describe the complex human rights violations that people face at the intersection of subordination based on race, ethnicity, gender, religion, socioeconomic status, disability, and sexual orientation and gender identity.

The data drawn from seven years of CEDAW concluding observations suggest that the Committee is gradually moving away from descriptions of intersectional human rights abuses as affecting "particularly vulnerable" women or "disadvantaged" groups of women. The examination of concluding observations suggests a shift in the Committee's approach, moving toward more explicit references to "intersectional" rights. From 2013 to 2019, the Committee refers to the specific challenges faced by women with disabilities with increasing frequency. Expressed as a percentage of the concluding observations in a given year, the references to the rights violations for women with disabilities increased from 77 percent in 2013 to 100 percent in 2019. In other words, in 2013, roughly three-quarters of CEDAW's concluding observations mentioned women with disabilities compared with all of the concluding observations in 2019. In both years, some of the references in the concluding observations are mere mentions of the need for disaggregated data on women with disabilities. Others involve deeper analysis of the intersectional issues confronting women with disabilities. Considering both its superficial and probing references, the Committee has demonstrated that it is increasingly cognizant of the unique human rights violations that women with disabilities face across the globe.

Similarly, the Committee has increasingly recognized in its concluding observations the intersectional human rights violations facing LBT women.[16] Expressed as a percentage of the concluding observations each year, the references to the rights violations for LBT women increased from 9 percent in 2013 to a high of 67 percent in

[16] The designation "LBT" is used here because the CEDAW Committee specifically limits its analysis to the rights of individuals who identify as women, including lesbians, bisexual women, and transgender women.

2018.[17] Trend lines indicate that the Committee is taking intersectional rights violations for LBT women more seriously than it did nearly a decade ago. By including references to LBT rights in its concluding observations, the Committee reminds states that they have an obligation to protect, respect, and fulfill intersectional rights related to sexual orientation and gender identity.

Revisiting the problems with additive approaches and the language of vulnerability

Since the early days of state reporting, the CEDAW Committee has used concluding observations to draw attention to the plight of particular groups of women. As noted, over the years, the Committee has used a variety of terms to describe subsets of women who face specific, particular challenges within a reporting state. For many years, and to some extent still today, the Committee took an additive approach. This approach amounted to a conclusion that "if it's bad for women generally, it's particularly or especially bad for [some subset of women]." This approach communicated that most women experienced a particular type of discrimination or violation, but "X" subset had it worse. In other words, the subset experienced discrimination "plus," or some other kind of discrimination added to an already existing form of gender discrimination.

As discussed in earlier chapters, this additive model fails to capture the full complexity of intersectional discrimination, which involves forms of subordination that are mutually constitutive. For example, additive models might capture how a woman experiences discrimination based on her gender and her disability separately. CEDAW might observe that women with disabilities face challenges such as a lack of access to technical training programs (a challenge that may be faced by all people with disabilities in the country). The Committee might also observe that educational inequalities based on gender compound the challenges faced by women with disabilities, leaving them particularly vulnerable. This analysis omits the intersecting dimensions of the subordination faced by women with disabilities, including those aspects that affect neither men with disabilities nor non-disabled women. Intersectional discrimination such as coerced sterilization may affect women with disabilities in a particular country in ways that leave men with disabilities and non-disabled women largely unaffected. The intersection of disability-based subordination and gender-based subordination may significantly alter the experience of subordination for women with disabilities. The Committee oversimplifies this complex intersectional subordination when it uses additive terminology to describe the phenomenon.

Perhaps more importantly, the Committee's use of the concept of vulnerability to describe the experience of intersectional subordination stigmatizes victims, as I discussed in chapter 4. It defines "vulnerability" solely in terms of the experience of victimization in the human rights context. Those who experience subordination based

[17] The percentage of concluding observations referencing LBT-related rights violations for women for the 2013–2019 period were as follows: 9 percent in 2013; 35 percent in 2014; 26 percent in 2015; 56 percent in 2016; 57 percent in 2017; 67 percent in 2018; and 59 percent in 2019.

on multiple intersecting forms of identity, such as race, socioeconomic status, and gender, are described as "particularly vulnerable." As Martha Fineman notes, "labeling some individuals and herding them into 'populations' defined as differently or particularly vulnerable (and therefore somehow inadequate) stigmatises those individuals."[18] Fineman constructs a theory of vulnerability that is based on universal applicability to all humans. As Frank Rudy Cooper points out, however, Fineman's theory of vulnerability relies on a notion of universality that ignores the reality of hierarchical identity construction. In the context of racial identity, for example, Cooper notes that Fineman's vulnerability theory uses whiteness as the norm by which we measure the vulnerability of racial "others."[19]

Although Fineman proposes a theory of vulnerability that is universally applicable to the human condition, her modified and more progressive attempt to reclaim the concept of vulnerability is outside the scope of this book. For our purposes, the notion of vulnerability is a pre-Fineman idea that relies on the traditional concept of vulnerability. The CEDAW Committee invokes the term in the vein that Fineman criticizes, to denote a subset of people who are differently or "particularly" vulnerable. In addition to Cooper's critique that vulnerability discourse both normalizes and obscures privilege, layered vulnerability does not contemplate how systems of subordination intersect, define, and mutually reinforce each other.[20] If the treaty bodies invoked vulnerability in the spirit of robust intersectional analysis, the concept could highlight the ways in which systems of subordination intersect to subordinate certain groups in distinct and mutually reinforcing ways. In its most common use by the treaty bodies, however, "particularly vulnerable" is meant to substitute for meaningful engagement with intersectional analysis. Crenshaw notes, "'[O]ther' women are silenced as much by being relegated to the margin of experience as by total exclusion. Tokenistic, objectifying, voyeuristic inclusion is at least as disempowering as complete exclusion."[21] Feeble attempts to draw attention to vulnerability or marginalization rarely accomplish the important analytical work that intersectionality sets out to do.

This notion of vulnerability relies on an underlying assumption of victimization. The label of "particularly vulnerable" will not resonate, for example, with every woman who identifies as an ethnic minority lesbian. Vulnerability, or the accentuated "particular vulnerability," focuses too much on victimization or, in Fineman's words, inadequacy.[22] It neglects the potential axes along which an ethnic minority lesbian might

[18] Martha Albertson Fineman, *Vulnerability and Inevitable Inequality*, 4 Oslo L. Rev. 133, 147 (2017).

[19] *See* Frank Rudy Cooper, *Always Already Suspect: Revising Vulnerability Theory*, 93 N.C. L. Rev. 1339, 1365–66 (2015) ("For example, in the West, the 'universal' perspective has been based on the experiences and viewpoints most common to straight, white, able-bodied Christian men who are economically advantaged.... [W]e end up installing a particular group's experiences and worldview as an objective vantage point. That is a crucial reason that we cannot replace identities theory with an assumption of a universal vulnerability.").

[20] In this way, characterizing someone as "particularly vulnerable" evokes the additive formulation of multiple forms of subordination that I describe above and in chapter 1. The layers of vulnerability that make one "particularly vulnerable" are simply added together, resulting in an additive analysis that is devoid of the rich insights of intersectionality.

[21] Kimberlé Crenshaw, *Mapping the Margins: Intersectionality, Identity Politics, and Violence Against Women of Color*, 43 Stanford L. Rev. 1241, 1261 (1991).

[22] Fineman's revision of this concept imagines a post-identity world in which vulnerability is a universal part of being human. Frank Rudy Cooper offers a helpful modification of vulnerability theory in which he argues for the recognition of privilege within the theoretical model. He notes, "Identities ... are a principal

enjoy privilege, such as socioeconomic status, majority religion, status as able-bodied, and others.[23] The label reduces her experience to one of vulnerability and is therefore viewed exclusively as a negative, while the very qualities that are typically defined as vulnerable can be significant sources of identity, strength, and community. We must modify the discourse of vulnerability to focus on systemic, structural changes rather than individual characteristics.

"Particular vulnerability" conveys an added or heightened susceptibility to abuse. The treaty bodies often invoke the term in a passing reference that generically acknowledges that the experience of subordination is different for different groups. It connotes a sense of intersectional identities as additive, increasing the risk of victimization, without examining the ways in which multiple identities are mutually constitutive. It also focuses examination inward, to the individual traits that may subject one to abuse. Instead, the focus should be external, addressing the intersecting systems of power that cause, allow, and maintain subordination. Intersectionality maintains a focus on the types of structural discrimination that intersect to mutually reinforce systems of subordination.

Language matters. Political scientists Cosette Creamer and Beth Simmons observe, "[A]s socialization research makes clear, the nature of the dialogue with treaty bodies is central to successful internalization of rights norms."[24] The choices that treaty body members make in describing rights violations in their constructive dialogue with the States parties may shape the willingness of a state to engage in the dialogue that is at the heart of the reporting process.[25] Similarly, the ways in which treaty body members describe and address rights violations affect the process of norm socialization. The use of intersectional language in treaty body dialogue with States parties is a telling metric for assessing the extent to which they have internalized norms around intersectionality.

CEDAW, as well as other human rights treaty bodies, has struggled to capture the insights of intersectionality in full. Only in the last decade has the Committee shifted away from additive descriptors such as "particular vulnerability" and multiple discrimination and begun to more consistently use the language of intersectionality to describe these particularized, multifaceted human rights violations. The treaty bodies have variously described intersectional rights in terms of "particular vulnerability," multiple discrimination, and in the last decade, intersectionality. The trends mentioned above suggest that the CEDAW Committee is moving toward greater use of intersectional terminology to describe complex, intersectional human rights violations.

CEDAW's working methods, as described above, shed some light on the variability of descriptors. The Committee is made up of twenty-three independent experts with varying degrees of understanding of and commitment to intersectionality as a

means by which privilege is maintained in this society. If it is to create a better society for all, vulnerability theory will have to acknowledge that identity groups are differentially privileged." Cooper, *supra* note 19, at 1375.

[23] *See id.* at 1374.

[24] Cosette D. Creamer & Beth A. Simmons, *The Proof is in the Process: Self-Reporting Under International Human Rights Treaties*, 114 Amer. J. Int'l L. 1, 46 (2020).

[25] *See id.* at 13.

framework for analysis. Not surprisingly, some concluding observations highlight intersectionality more than others, depending in part on who was involved in drafting the concluding observations. The Office of the High Commissioner for Human Rights (OHCHR) supports the work of committee members, including when they are assigned to draft concluding observations. Accordingly, the OHCHR could be pivotal in regulating the approach to intersectionality across concluding observations. By providing technical expertise and encouraging intersectional analysis, the OHCHR could standardize approaches, not only within the CEDAW Committee but across the treaty bodies, facilitating intersectional analysis in the work of each body.

The hopeful and positive trend toward the language of intersectionality will likely continue as the Committee and other treaty bodies become more habituated to using an intersectional lens for analysis and more comfortable with the terminology. The increased use of explicitly intersectional language within the treaty bodies in their concluding observations for States parties will affect national and sub-national discourses on human rights. The "constructive dialogue" between states and the treaty bodies will reinforce the need for national human rights institutions to explore human rights from an intersectional perspective. States that are already engaged in intersectional human rights conversations at the national and sub-national level will continue to push the treaty bodies to consider intersectionality in their analyses. The ongoing dialogues between national human rights institutions and the treaty bodies will play a mutually reinforcing role as intersectional analysis continues to take hold at both the national and international levels.

CEDAW's initiative (or lack thereof) in taking up intersectionality

During the State party reporting process, there are several junctures at which intersectional analysis may enter the conversation. First, the State party may raise intersectional issues in its report to the Committee. Second, the Committee may raise questions about intersectional rights violations in the list of issues it submits to the reporting State party. In many cases, NGOs that submit shadow reports, also called alternative reports, raise the issue of intersectionality in their descriptions of human rights abuses that they are working to combat in their country. Ideally, the Committee uses both the state report and the civil society shadow reports to inform the list of issues it drafts and submits to the State party. Third, there are instances in which the Committee raises intersectional issues on its own accord without specifically referencing the issues in shadow reports or the state's report itself.

When the Committee does acknowledge intersectional issues in its concluding observations, it is impossible to know with certainty whether that recognition originated with the state report, the shadow reports, or the Committee members themselves. Nevertheless, the following analysis tentatively links intersectional analysis to possible sources of information in the reporting process. This section offers examples of how the Committee addresses, or fails to address, intersectionality in the context of the state reporting procedure. In selecting these examples, I looked for state reports within the last ten years that illustrated varying degrees of commitment within CEDAW to embracing intersectional analysis. To that end, I have organized the examples according to whether an intersectional framework was proposed by NGOs, the Committee itself, or the reporting state government. In some cases, the Committee actively embraced intersectionality, while in others it missed the import of intersectionality in its analysis.

An example of mixed success with intersectionality in the reporting process: Vietnam

The reporting process surrounding Vietnam's submission of its seventh and eighth periodic reports reveals the Committee's embrace of intersectionality in some areas but not in others. To its credit, CEDAW's concluding observations for Vietnam include two recommendations that the state collect information disaggregated by sex, age, disability, ethnicity, location, and socioeconomic rights.[26] The Committee also notes with concern "that girls belonging to ethnic minorities have limited access to all levels of education" and recommends that the government increase educational access to ethnic minority girls.[27] The Committee recognizes the intersection of gender and ethnic bias as a contributor to the structural discrimination that minority ethnic girls face within Vietnam's education system. Although it does not use the language of intersectionality or even multiple discrimination, the Committee signals its appreciation of the potential educational risks for ethnic minority girls. In the context of health, the Committee also notes its concerns about high rates of maternal mortality among ethnic minority women in some regions.[28] With respect to structural discrimination arising from the intersection of gender and ethnicity, the Committee does an admirable job identifying specific risks in the areas of education and health.

This intersectional focus on gender and ethnicity does not stem from Vietnam's periodic report on its compliance with the terms of the treaty. Consistent with the process in place at the time,[29] Vietnam filed its periodic report in January 2013. The report focuses largely on the different treatment of women and men, with only a few passing references to the intersectional impact of ethnicity.[30] The Committee developed a list of issues for Vietnam, which contained several requests for information that pertain to intersectional issues, including a request for "updated information on

[26] *See* Comm. on the Elimination of All Forms of Discrimination Against Women, Concluding Observations on the Combined Seventh and Eighth Periodic Reports of Viet Nam, ¶¶ 19(g), 43, U.N. Doc. CEDAW/C/VNM/CO/7-8 (2015).

[27] *See id.* ¶¶ 26(d), 27(d) [hereinafter Concluding Observations on Viet Nam].

[28] *See id.* ¶ 32(b). The Committee's recommendations on health also include protections "regardless of . . . marital status, disability, ethnicity or geographical location" and "without distinction of any kind, including sex, disability, health, economic or social status and ethnicity." *Id.* at ¶ 33(b)–(c).

[29] A new simplified reporting procedure involves the treaty body developing a list of issues, submitting that to the reporting country, and treating the country's response to the list of issues as the periodic report itself.

[30] *See* Comm. on the Elimination of All Forms of Discrimination Against Women, Consideration of Reports Submitted by States Parties under Article 18 of the Convention, Seventh and Eighth Periodic Reports of States Parties Due in 2011: Viet Nam, ¶ 144, U.N. Doc. CEDAW/C/VNM/7-8 (2014). For example, the report states, "Classes are organized in remote areas to provide opportunities for ethnic minority boys and girls to attend school." *Id.*

the reported law on ethnic minorities and indicate whether it will deal with the situation of minority women and the multiple forms of discrimination to which they are subjected."[31] The list of issues also notes that "the Committee has also been informed that significant disparities persist in educational opportunities and outcomes, with girls belonging to minorities at a particular disadvantage."[32] Through the development of its list of issues, the Committee focused the government of Vietnam on some of the intersectional human rights issues it deemed to be particularly important.

Vietnam then had an opportunity to respond to the list of issues. In most instances, the government of Vietnam failed to respond meaningfully to the Committee's attempt to solicit information about intersectional rights. In response to the Committee's request for information related to multiple discrimination under the "Non-discrimination" subheading, for example, Vietnam simply did not address intersectional concerns at all.[33] In the context of temporary special measures, the government response merely observed the existence of a 2013 Employment Law that emphasizes equal employment opportunities for people with disabilities and "female workers from ethnic minority groups."[34] It does not elaborate further. In the education context, the government offered two statistics indicating that literacy programs have included women from ethnic minority groups.[35]

The question of LGBTQI rights in Vietnam is particularly noteworthy. Here, it appears that the Committee did have information at its disposal that could have informed its concluding observations. In the concluding observations, however, the Committee does not express any concerns or issue any recommendations involving LGBTQI rights. In its List of Issues, the Committee requests clarification concerning whether the Marriage and Family Law recognizes same-sex relationships. The government responded by noting that the constitution (amended in 2013) states that "[m]en and women have the right to marry."[36] Vietnam's response also observed, however, that the 2014 Marriage and Family Law removed the prohibition on same-sex marriage.[37] This conflict requires clarification, and it would seem to warrant mention in the concluding observations. In its "Marriage and Family Relations" subsection, however, the Committee focuses only on issues related to age of marriage and women in de facto unions, and makes no mention of same-sex marriages or same-sex de facto unions.

During the drafting of its concluding observations, the Committee had received a detailed shadow report entitled *The Rights of Lesbian, Bisexual, Transgender and*

[31] Comm. on the Elimination of All Forms of Discrimination Against Women, List of Issues and Questions in Relation to the Combined Seventh and Eighth Periodic Reports of Viet Nam, ¶ 3, U.N. Doc. CEDAW/C/VNM/Q/7-8 (2014). Other references include a request for detailed information on temporary special measures designed to promote women's equality and "to ensure the rights of women belonging to minorities, elderly women and women with disabilities." *Id.* ¶ 6.

[32] *Id.* ¶ 13.

[33] Comm. on the Elimination of All Forms of Discrimination Against Women, List of Issues and Questions in Relation to the Combined Seventh and Eighth Periodic Reports of Viet Nam: Replies of Viet Nam, ¶¶ 15–21, U.N. Doc. CEDAW/C/VNM/Q/7-8/Add.1 (2015).

[34] *Id.* ¶ 41.

[35] *Id.* ¶ 92.

[36] *Id.* ¶ 130.

[37] *Id.*

Intersex (LBTI) Women in Viet Nam,[38] which repeatedly urged the Committee to include in its concluding observations several recommendations promoting the rights of LBTI individuals (it uses the narrower acronym LBTI), including non-discrimination protection and marriage rights for LBTI individuals in Vietnam. Although it is impossible to include all relevant human rights issues in the concluding observations, the decision to exclude LGBTQI rights from the concluding observations in the face of the Committee's own unanswered queries about LGBTQI rights and the reliable information from shadow reports on file with the OHCHR is disappointing. As it relates to LGBTQI rights, the Committee missed an opportunity to address important intersectional rights in its concluding observations. Had the concluding observations included such a discussion, it could have enhanced the government's understanding of intersectional rights violations generally and of LGBTQI rights more specifically.

Examples of intersectional analysis originating within the Committee

The Committee's concluding observations for Cameroon in 2014 suggest that the Committee included some intersectional issues without being prompted to do so by either Cameroon's state report or the shadow reports submitted by civil society organizations. NGO shadow reports addressed intersectional issues related to Indigenous women[39] and LBT women,[40] and the state report briefly addressed women with disabilities[41] and refugee women.[42] The Committee's concluding observations included these issues but also included references to women with albinism and older women.[43] Although it is impossible to make conclusions with certainty, it appears that the Committee included these intersectional issues in the concluding observations on its own accord. These instances in which the Committee included intersectional issues without prompting from states or civil society organizations helps us gauge the extent to which the Committee has internalized intersectional analysis in its routine state reporting process.

[38] *See* KALEIDOSCOPE FOUND. ET AL., THE RIGHTS OF LESBIAN, BISEXUAL, TRANSGENDER AND INTERSEX (LBTI) WOMEN IN VIET NAM: SHADOW REPORT FOR THE 61ST SESSION OF THE COMMITTEE ON THE ELIMINATION OF DISCRIMINATION AGAINST WOMEN (2015), https://tbinternet.ohchr.org/Treaties/CEDAW/Shared%20Documents/VNM/INT_CEDAW_NGO_VNM_20790_E.pdf. The organization uses the narrower acronym (LBTI) in this report to CEDAW.

[39] *See* Letter from Okani et al., to CEDAW Secretariat & Palais Wilson, OHCHR (June 19, 2013), https://www.ecoi.net/en/file/local/1111202/1930_1373985231_jointngosubmission-pswg-cameroon-cedaw57-e.pdf ("Request that the Situation of Indigenous Women of Cameroon be Included in the list of Questions Arising from the Cameroon Government's Periodic Report . . . .").

[40] *See* CAMEROONIAN FOUND. FOR AIDS ET AL., HUMAN RIGHTS VIOLATIONS AGAINST LESBIANS, BISEXUAL WOMEN AND TRANSGENDER PEOPLE IN CAMEROON (2014), https://tbinternet.ohchr.org/Treaties/CEDAW/Shared%20Documents/CMR/INT_CEDAW_CSS_CMR_16117_E.pdf.

[41] *See* Comm. on the Elimination of Discrimination Against Women, Consideration of Reports Submitted by States Parties Under Article 18 of the Convention, Combined Fourth and Fifth Periodic Report of States Parties Due in 2011: Cameroon, ¶¶ 14, 15, 116, U.N. Doc. CEDAW/C/CMR/4-5 (2012).

[42] *See id.* ¶ 227.

[43] *See* Comm. on the Elimination of Discrimination Against Women, Concluding Observations on the Combined Fourth and Fifth Periodic Reports of Cameroon, ¶¶ 36–37, U.N. Doc. CEDAW/C/CMR/CO/4-5 (2014).

In the CEDAW Committee's 2019 concluding observations in response to Ethiopia's eighth periodic report, the Committee noted several intersectional rights violations that NGOs included in shadow reports submitted as part of the country review process. One shadow report, for example, offers a detailed discussion of the challenges that girls and women with disabilities face in education, employment, and healthcare.[44] The concluding observations, in turn, mention that women with disabilities in Ethiopia have difficulty accessing healthcare.[45]

In addition to the intersectional issues raised by civil society organizations, the Committee also included intersectional issues that it raised on its own, or with little prompting, in its concluding observations. The Committee, for example, included an extensive discussion of women and girls affected by leprosy.[46] The issue of leprosy was not raised in any of the shadow reports submitted to and filed within the UN Treaty Body Database in conjunction with Ethiopia's 2019 reporting cycle. Although the state report made a passing reference to the issue, the Committee's concern appears to be traceable to the deliberations of the Committee itself rather than an external source. Similarly, the concluding observations also mention discrimination faced by Rastafarian women in Ethiopia, who "have limited access to basic social services and are exposed to discrimination and gender-based violence."[47] The civil society organizations that filed shadow reports with the OHCHR did not raise the issue of intersectional rights violations of Rastafarian women in Ethiopia. The Committee raised this intersectional rights issue without being prompted either by the state report or by shadow reports.

In its 2019 concluding observations on Guyana, the Committee incorporated an intersectional approach by citing issues and offering recommendations related to Indigenous women; women with disabilities; and lesbian, bisexual, and transgender women and intersex persons.[48] The Committee's inclusion of the latter two groups—women with disabilities and lesbian, bisexual, and transgender women and intersex persons—appears to be an example of the Committee making its own observations about intersectional issues.[49] Although one 2019 shadow report mentioned these categories, it did so briefly and only in the context of climate change.[50] With respect to

[44] *See* Setaweet Movement & Dev. Alts. for a New Era, *Gender at the Juncture of Political Reform: Shadow Report to the CEDAW Committee, Review of the 8th Periodic Report on Ethiopia* (Feb. 2019), https://tbinternet.ohchr.org/_layouts/15/treatybodyexternal/Download.aspx?symbolno=INT%2fCEDAW%2fCSS%2fETH%2f33740&Lang=en. *See also* Unrepresented Nations & People's Org., Alternative Report to the Committee of the United Nations Convention on the Elimination of All Forms of Discrimination Against Women 8 (2018), https://tbinternet.ohchr.org/Treaties/CEDAW/Shared%20Documents/ETH/INT_CEDAW_ICO_ETH_31503_E.pdf.

[45] Comm. on the Elimination of All Forms of Discrimination Against Women, Concluding Observations on the Eighth Periodic Report of Ethiopia, ¶ 37(c), U.N. Doc. CEDAW/C/ETH/CO/8 (2019).

[46] *See id.* ¶¶ 39–40.

[47] *Id.* at ¶¶ 47–48.

[48] Comm. on the Elimination of All Forms of Discrimination Against Women, Concluding Observations on the Ninth Periodic Report of Guyana, ¶¶ 15, 22, 28, 32, 37–38, 40, 43–48, U.N. Doc. CEDAW/C/GUY/CO/9 (2019) [hereinafter Concluding Observations on Guyana].

[49] Guyana's state report includes a fleeting reference to "transgendered persons" but it is unlikely that this brief reference is the source of the Committee's more extensive comments on the discrimination that LBT women face.

[50] *See* Ctr. for Int'l Env't L. et al., *Joint Parallel Report*, at 3 (July 12, 2019), https://tbinternet.ohchr.org/_layouts/15/treatybodyexternal/Download.aspx?symbolno=INT%2fCEDAW%2fCSS%2fGUY%2f35463&Lang=en. With respect to women with disabilities, an NGO had filed a shadow report on this topic for a

disabilities, the Committee may have referred back to a shadow report on the topic filed in an earlier reporting cycle in 2012.[51] The Committee also included in the concluding observations a separate section titled "Lesbian, bisexual, transgender women and intersex persons."[52] Referring back to previous concluding observations on the topic of LBTI rights, the Committee expressed its concern that "lesbian, bisexual, transgender women and intersex persons face discrimination in law and in practice in the State party, as well as physical and sexual violence, including at the hands of law enforcement officers."[53] All in all, the Committee devotes considerable space to discussing intersectional issues, including those facing Indigenous women, women and girls with disabilities, and LBT women and intersex persons.

In some cases, the Committee first raises the issue of intersectional rights violations in its list of issues for the State party. In developing the list of issues, the Committee can shape the parameters of the "constructive dialogue" with the reporting state. For example, in its list of issues for Armenia in 2016, the Committee requested "information on measures taken to counter stereotypical attitudes towards women and girls, who experience multiple forms of discrimination on account of their ethnicity, age or disability, for being lesbian, bisexual, transgender or intersex women and girls, or for any other characteristic."[54] The list of issues provides an effective way for the Committee to focus reporting states on intersectional rights and serves to raise awareness of states' obligations to protect intersectional rights.

Examples of apparent reliance on shadow reports to surface intersectionality

NGOs that submit shadow reports to the Committee offer critical insights about the reality of rights on the ground. As noted above, shadow reports have become an indispensable tool for NGOs to communicate with the treaty bodies about ways in which the government has or has not effectively implemented the rights guaranteed in the treaties. Before NGOs began submitting shadow reports on a large scale, the treaty bodies were forced to rely primarily on the state report and the government

prior reporting cycle in 2012, so the Committee presumably had access to this information in preparing for its review.

[51] *See* INT'L DISABILITY ALLIANCE, SUGGESTIONS FOR DISABILITY-RELEVANT QUESTIONS TO BE INCLUDED IN THE LIST OF ISSUES: PRE-SESSION WORKING GROUP OF THE CEDAW COMMITTEE FOR THE 52ND SESSION, https://tbinternet.ohchr.org/Treaties/CEDAW/Shared%20Documents/GUY/INT_CEDAW_NGO_GUY_52_8982_E.pdf (last visited May 4, 2021); Concluding Observations on Guyana, *supra* note 48. For reference, the Committee cited issues faced by women with disabilities and offered recommendations in multiple sections in the document: "National machinery for the advancement of women" (Observations ¶¶ 17–18); "Temporary special measures" (Observations ¶¶ 21–22); "Trafficking and exploitation of prostitution" (Observations ¶¶ 27–28); "Employment" (Observations ¶¶ 37–38); "Health" (Observations ¶¶ 39–40); and a separate section on women with disabilities (Observations ¶¶ 45–46).

[52] *See* Concluding Observations on Guyana, *supra* note 48, at 14.

[53] *Id.* ¶¶ 47–48.

[54] Comm. on the Elimination of All Forms of Discrimination Against Women, List of Issues and Questions in Relation to the Combined Fifth and Sixth Periodic Reports of Armenia, ¶ 6, U.N. Doc. CEDAW/C/ARM/Q/5-6 (2016).

representative's description of treaty implementation. The governmental descriptions of treaty implementation often painted a particularly rosy picture of the state's success in implementing the treaty. NGO shadow reports often confirm the progress that a particular state has made in implementation but also point to areas in which the state has fallen short of its commitments.

It is common for the treaty bodies to rely on shadow reports in addition to the state's report. In one example, the Committee appears to have relied on at least three shadow reports in drafting its 2018 concluding observations on Australia. First, Intersex Human Rights Australia submitted a shadow report in which they noted the "pattern of human rights abuses on infants, children and adolescents born with intersex traits occurs in Australia, without effective, independent oversight, often based on gender stereotypes, and lacking a scientific basis."[55] Presumably drawing on information in the shadow report, the Committee mentioned intersex issues in several different sections within its concluding observations for Australia: stereotypes,[56] education,[57] and health.[58] Second, the National Aboriginal and Torres Strait Islanders Women's Alliance submitted a shadow report highlighting the issues that Aboriginal and Torres Strait Islander women face in Australia. The Committee not only mentioned Indigenous women in multiple sections[59] but also dedicated a section of the concluding observations specifically to Aboriginal and Torres Strait Islander women.[60] Finally, the National Council of Jewish Women of Australia submitted a report focused on marriage, family violence, and divorce rights (*Gett*; spelled *get* in the concluding observations). The Committee specifically referred to Jewish *Gett/get* within the marriage and family relations section, observing that "[r]eligious practices, such as the Jewish *get*, prevent women from exercising their right to remarry freely after divorce, leaving them in situations of forced continuation of religious marriage, also referred to as 'marital captivity.'"[61]

Similarly, the Committee is likely to have relied on a shadow report in drafting its concluding observations for the Bahamas in 2018. Equality Bahamas submitted a report advocating for the needs of women and LGBTQI people in the Bahamas.[62] In addition to highlighting the issues that LBGTQI people encounter, Equality Bahamas detailed the plight of rural women and women married to non-Bahamian men.[63] The

[55] Intersex Hum. Rts. Austral., Shadow Report Submission: Australia 1 (2018), https://tbinternet.ohchr.org/Treaties/CEDAW/Shared%20Documents/AUS/INT_CEDAW_NGO_AUS_31448_E.pdf.

[56] *See* Comm. on the Elimination of All Forms of Discrimination Against Women, Concluding Observations on the Eighth Periodic Report of Australia, ¶¶ 23–24, U.N. Doc. CEDAW/C/AUS/CO/8 (2018) [hereinafter Concluding Observations on Australia].

[57] *See id.* ¶¶ 41–42.

[58] *See id.* ¶¶ 49–50.

[59] *See id.* ¶¶ 23–24 (Stereotypes); *id.* ¶¶ 41–42 (Education); *id.* ¶¶ 49–50 (Health); *id.* ¶¶ 55–56 (Women in Detention).

[60] *See id.* ¶¶ 51–52.

[61] *See id.* ¶¶ 57–58.

[62] *See* Equal. Bah., CEDAW Shadow Report on the Bahamas for the 71st Session ¶ 1 (2018), https://tbinternet.ohchr.org/Treaties/CEDAW/Shared%20Documents/BHS/INT_CEDAW_CSS_BHS_32599_E.pdf.

[63] *See id.* at art. 9 ("As it stands, women married to non-Bahamian men cannot pass on citizenship to their children born outside of The Bahamas, women married to Bahamian men cannot pass on citizenship to them, and men cannot pass on citizenship to their children born to non-Bahamian women when the parents are not married to each other.").

Committee, in its 2018 concluding observations on the Bahamas, addressed these very topics. For example, the Committee specifically noted "[t]he failure to eliminate discrimination, notably intersecting forms of discrimination, in particular against women of Haitian descent, migrant women, women with disabilities, lesbian, bisexual and transgender women, intersex persons and women living in the Family Islands."[64] It is impossible to know with certainty whether the Committee would have raised the issue of LGBTQI rights in the absence of a shadow report on the subject. Neither the state report from the government of the Bahamas nor the Committee's list of issues, however, addressed LGBTQI rights violations, increasing the likelihood that the shadow report informed the Committee's subsequent drafting of the concluding observations.

These two examples demonstrate that NGO shadow reports are significant in the promotion of intersectional analysis in the state reporting process. Shadow reports that explore intersectional rights can push the treaty bodies to consider the many ways in which rights violations and systems of subordination intersect in peoples' lives. The treaty bodies have framed the state reporting process as a dialogue between states and the treaty bodies. Since the early 1990s, NGOs have increasingly become an essential voice in the conversation around state reporting on treaty implementation. International Women's Rights Action Watch (IWRAW), one of the earliest NGOs to use shadow reports to inform the treaty bodies, has published guides for producing shadow reports for submission to the UN.[65] These guides for the production and submission of shadow reports also provide a mechanism for encouraging other NGOs and the treaty bodies themselves to engage in intersectional analysis.

Examples of failing to recognize intersectional analysis

It is impossible, of course, for any one treaty body to address all relevant human rights violations occurring in a particular country at a particular time. Each treaty body must routinely prioritize some human rights issues over others. We expect this kind of triage in the reporting process. Often this prioritization of issues occurs when the treaty body drafts the list of issues that the State party must address. This section offers examples of instances in which the CEDAW Committee did not raise significant intersectional issues despite having relevant information from NGO shadow reports filed with the Committee. The list is not exhaustive but is intended to provide examples in which the Committee declined to pursue certain intersectional issues despite being briefed on those issues by civil society organizations.

[64] Comm. on the Elimination of All Forms of Discrimination Against Women, Concluding Observations on the Sixth Periodic Report of the Bahamas, ¶ 11, U.N. Doc. CEDAW/C/BHS/CO/6 (2018).

[65] Int'l Women's Rts. Action Watch [IWRAW], *Producing Shadow Reports to the CEDAW Committee: A Procedural Guide*, UNIV. MINN. HUM. RTS. LIBR., http://hrlibrary.umn.edu/iwraw/proceduralguide-08.html(last visited May 4, 2021). *See also* INT'L WOMEN'S RTS. ACTION WATCH [IWRAW], ASSESSING THE STATUS OF WOMEN IN THE 21ST CENTURY: A GUIDE TO REPORTING UNDER THE CONVENTION ON THE ELIMINATION OF ALL FORMS OF DISCRIMINATION AGAINST WOMEN (2000), http://hrlibrary.umn.edu/iwraw/Publications.html.

In one example, the Committee included some intersectional analysis in its concluding observations for Austria in 2013. It highlighted the need to protect migrant women, women living in rural areas, and women with disabilities.[66] One shadow report submitted by Frauen: Rechte jetzt NGO Forum included discussions of these topics and may have informed the Committee's draft of the concluding observations. One issue that the group included in its shadow report, however, did not surface in the Committee's concluding observations: the issue of LBT rights, a topic discussed in detail in the shadow report.[67]

Although the Committee incorporated somewhat of an intersectional approach in its 2015 concluding observations on Portugal,[68] it failed to address two intersectional issues raised by civil society organizations through the shadow-reporting process: the discrimination faced by women with disabilities and LBT women in Portugal. The Disability and Human Rights Observatory of the School for Social and Political Sciences at the University of Lisbon partnered with other disability rights organizations to submit a shadow report entitled *The Situation of Women and Girls with Disabilities in Portugal*.[69] The report highlighted Portugal's lack of recognition "of the risk for multiple discrimination facing women and girls with disabilities," and noted that women with disabilities are particularly susceptible to gender-based violence."[70] The organizations also detailed the "[p]oor visibility of issues linked to the sexual and reproductive rights of women with disabilities in the national normative framework."[71] Nevertheless, the Committee did not reference women with disabilities in any section within its concluding observations for Portugal.[72] Additionally, the Committee failed to include any information or recommendations related to the discrimination LGBTQI women face, despite the fact that the International Lesbian Gay, Bisexual Trans and Intersex Association of Portugal submitted a report on the matter.[73]

[66] *See* Comm. on the Elimination of All Forms of Discrimination Against Women, Concluding Observations on the Seventh and Eighth Periodic Report of Austria, Adopted by the Committee at its Fifty-Fourth Session (11 February–1 March, 2013), ¶¶ 27, 40–41, 42–47, 48–49, U.N. Doc. CEDAW/C/AUT/CO/7-8 (2013).

[67] *See* Frauen: Rechte Jetzt, NGO Shadow Report Complementing the Seventh and Eighth Country Report of the Austrian Government 52–55 (2012), https://tbinternet.ohchr.org/Treaties/CEDAW/Shared%20Documents/AUT/INT_CEDAW_NGO_AUT_13221_E.pdf.

[68] Comm. on the Elimination of All Forms of Discrimination Against Women, Concluding Observations on the Combined Eighth and Ninth Periodic Reports of Portugal, U.N. Doc. CEDAW/C/PRT/CO/8-9 (2015) [hereinafter Concluding Observations on Portugal]. The Committee recognized that Roma women, migrant women, and older women have trouble within Portugal's labor market. *Id.* ¶¶ 34–35. The Committee also dedicated a separate section to issues and recommendations related to Roma women living in Portugal. *Id.* ¶¶ 42–43.

[69] Disability & Hum. Rts. Observatory et al., The Situation of Women and Girls with Disabilities in Portugal (2015), https://tbinternet.ohchr.org/Treaties/CEDAW/Shared%20Documents/PRT/INT_CEDAW_NGO_PRT_22005_E.pdf.

[70] *Id.* at 1–2.

[71] *Id.*

[72] With the exception of noting that Portugal adopted the Convention on the Rights of Persons with Disabilities in 2009. *See* Concluding Observations on Portugal, *supra* note 68, ¶ 6.

[73] ILGA Portugal, ILGA Portugal Shadow-Report: Complementing the Eighth and Ninth Periodic Country Reports of the Portuguese Government to the CEDAW Committee for its 62nd Session, https://tbinternet.ohchr.org/Treaties/CEDAW/Shared%20Documents/PRT/INT_CEDAW_NGO_PRT_21872_E.pdf (last visited May 4, 2021).

The Committee's 2018 concluding observations in response to the report by Australia included several examples of intersectional analysis in relation to intersex individuals, Indigenous women, and Jewish women.[74] The concluding observations reflect important insights concerning the discrimination that Indigenous and migrant women face in the healthcare sector. The Committee separately notes that lesbian, bisexual, and transgender women may also face discrimination in healthcare. The Committee failed to explore how these forms of discrimination may further intersect, despite the submission of a shadow report from the Queer Sisterhood Project that explores the discrimination faced by LGBTQI migrant and refugee women in Australia.[75]

Lastly, the Committee's 2019 concluding observations on Ethiopia included some important intersectional analysis, as described above. The report, however, failed to address certain intersectional human rights issues raised by civil society organizations in shadow reports filed with the OHCHR and available to the Committee. For example, the organizations and report cited above also briefly discussed discrimination against ethnic and religious minorities, lesbian and bisexual women, and women who identify as intersex.[76] The organizations noted that these women "are completely ignored even within the Ethiopian human rights discourse that does not include sexuality, or the rights of sexual minorities, as an issue at all."[77] The concluding observations neglect to address these topics. Additionally, the Unrepresented Nations and Peoples Organization submitted a report on "the double discrimination Somali, Oromo and other minority women face in a context of internal conflicts and social exclusion of their communities."[78] These issues are not mentioned in the concluding observations.

Despite these instances, as well as others in which the Committee did not discuss intersectional human rights violations that were raised by civil society organizations, the Committee is trending toward increased analysis of intersectional issues in its state reporting process. As noted, it is impossible for the Committee to address every pertinent human rights issue in its concluding observations. Nevertheless, there is value in exploring when and with respect to which issues the Committee undertook an intersectional analysis or failed to do so.

The centrality of data: encouraging states to keep disaggregated statistics

As we have seen throughout this chapter, CEDAW's acceptance of intersectionality in human rights reporting has grown considerably since the early 2000s. The early, almost exclusive focus on sex discrimination has evolved into a more sophisticated

[74] *See* Concluding Observations on Australia, *supra* note 56, ¶¶ 24, 12(b), 57(b).

[75] Queer Sisterhood Project, Human Rights Violations of Lesbian, Gay, Bisexual, Transgender and Intersex Asylum-Seeking and Refugee Women in Australia: A Shadow Report for Australia 4–5 (2018), https://tbinternet.ohchr.org/Treaties/CEDAW/Shared%20Documents/AUS/INT_CEDAW_NGO_AUS_31444_E.pdf.

[76] *See* Setaweet Movement, *supra* note 44 and accompanying text.

[77] *Id.* at 15.

[78] unrepresented nations & people's org., *supra* note 44, at 8.

Table 6.1 Requests for disaggregated data, 2004 versus 2019

Year	Number of concluding observations	Number containing requests for data disaggregated by multiple factors	Percentage
2004	16	2	12.5%
2019	22	20	90.9%

understanding that gender subordination intersects with other mutually reinforcing forms of structural discrimination, leading to different experiences of subordination for different groups of women. This intersectional insight is evident in the Committee's requests for disaggregated data and how those requests have changed over time.

In 2004, for example, the CEDAW Committee reviewed the reports of sixteen States parties in its thirtieth and thirty-first sessions. Within the concluding observations to those sixteen reports, the Committee regularly requested that states provide data disaggregated by sex, gender, or both. In fact, across the sixteen sets of concluding observations, requests for data disaggregated by sex occur thirty times. In fourteen of the sixteen concluding observations, the Committee exclusively requested data disaggregated by sex and no other factors. The two exceptions were the concluding observations for Ethiopia, in which the Committee requested data disaggregated by gender, age, and disability, and for Latvia, in which the Committee requested data disaggregated by sex and nationality.[79] With the exception of Latvia and Ethiopia, however, the Committee's focus on sex and gender is clearly demonstrated by its desire for data disaggregated only by sex, gender, or both.

Fifteen years later, in 2019, the CEDAW Committee's approach to disaggregated data is different. The Committee routinely requested that States parties collect data "disaggregated by sex, age, disability, ethnicity, location, and socio-economic status."[80] Although the descriptors differ depending on the country situation and the inclinations of those drafting the concluding observations, most of the Committee's requests for disaggregated data in 2019 included, at a minimum, sex or gender (or both), age, disability, and ethnicity.

In striking contrast to 2004, the 2019 concluding observations demonstrate the Committee's burgeoning commitment to intersectional analysis. In twenty of the twenty-two concluding observations in 2019, the Committee requested data disaggregated by multiple factors, reflecting a significantly deeper commitment to intersectional analysis than existed in 2004 (see Table 6.1). The precise parameters of the requests for disaggregated data in the concluding observations differ to some extent, but 90 percent of the 2019 concluding observations expressed a commitment to data

[79] *See* Comm. on the Elimination of All Forms of Discrimination Against Women, Rep. of the Comm. on the Elimination of Discrimination Against Women, Thirtieth Session and Thirty-first Session, at 48 & 110, U.N. Doc. A/59/38 (2004). The Committee requested only sex-disaggregated data in the following fourteen countries: Nepal, Nigeria, Belarus, Bhutan, Germany, Kuwait, Kyrgyzstan, Malta, Angola, Equatorial Guinea, Bangladesh, Dominican Republic, Spain, and Argentina, *id.*

[80] *See e.g.*, Concluding Observations on Viet Nam, *supra* note 26, ¶ 43.

disaggregated by intersectional identity factors such as gender, race, ethnicity, religion, migration status, age, disability, geographic location, socioeconomic status, and sexual orientation and gender identity.

Unlike twenty of the twenty-two concluding observations for 2019, the Committee's 2019 concluding observations for Congo and Myanmar did not include a request for data disaggregated by multiple factors. A few others included requests for disaggregated data based on limited intersectional factors, such as the Committee's concluding observations for Serbia, which requested data disaggregated by "age, gender, and geographical location."[81] In the case of Seychelles, the Committee choose not to list all intersectional factors but instead used the catch-all phrase "other relevant factors" to request data on women disaggregated by "age and other relevant factors."[82] Meanwhile, in the concluding observations for the United Kingdom of Great Britain and Northern Ireland, the Committee specifically invoked the language of intersectionality in its request for disaggregated data. The Committee expressed "further concern regarding the lack of systematic collection of data, disaggregated by sex, gender, ethnicity, disability and age, in particular with regard to intersecting forms of discrimination."[83]

The Committee's focus on intersectional data serves several important purposes.[84] First, it helps raise awareness of intersectionality in human rights discourse. By systematically signaling to States parties that the Committee is concerned with the intersection of gender subordination and other forms of subordination, the Committee communicates that States parties should themselves be concerned about intersectional human rights violations. Second, it does so in the relatively non-threatening context of data. The Committee's request for data disaggregated along intersectional lines is a modest request that does not, at first blush, require States parties to make radical changes to their approaches to treaty implementation. A truly intersectional approach to the protection of human rights will require significant shifts in thinking about human rights enforcement, but the requirement of intersectional data is a measured step toward wholesale adoption of an intersectional approach. The third role of data is a practical one. If States parties provide intersectional data, this will provide the Committee with the information it needs to conduct more probing, far-reaching intersectional analysis in its constructive dialogues with states in the future.

[81] Comm. on the Elimination of All Forms of Discrimination Against Women, Concluding Observations on the Fourth Periodic Report of Serbia, ¶ 30(c), U.N. Doc. CEDAW/C/SRB/CO/4, (2019).

[82] *See* Comm. on the Elimination of All Forms of Discrimination Against Women, Concluding Observations on the Sixth Periodic Report of Seychelles, ¶ 34(c), U.N. Doc. CEDAW/C/SYC/CO/6, (2019) ("Provide, in its next periodic report, data, disaggregated by age and other relevant factors, on school dropout rates among adolescent girls . . . .").

[83] Comm. on the Elimination of All Forms of Discrimination Against Women, Concluding Observations on the Eighth Periodic Report of the United Kingdom of Great Britain and Northern Ireland, ¶ 25, U.N. Doc. CEDAW/C/GBR/CO/8, (2019).

[84] *See Counted and Visible: Global Conference on the Measurement of Gender and Intersecting Inequalities*, UN WOMEN (Feb. 26, 2020), https://data.unwomen.org/news/counted-and-visible-global-conference-measurement-gender-and-intersecting-inequalities (demonstrating the commitment of other divisions of the United Nations to intersectional data).

Promoting intersectionality

The state reporting process has been and will continue to be a useful way to promote intersectional analysis within UN treaty bodies. Recent studies "help establish a causal connection between the fact of iterated [human rights] reporting and improved rights practices and gesture toward mechanisms of public attention and political mobilization as potential explanations for this connection."[85] NGOs from all regions of the world have engaged with the reporting process by producing shadow reports that provide credible information about the real human rights situation on the ground. Many of those NGOs have explicitly or implicitly adopted an intersectional approach to rights violations, such as organizations devoted to women with disabilities or ethnic minority women. In many cases, these shadow reports push the treaty bodies to consider intersectional rights violations that they might not otherwise consider. In other cases, the treaty bodies themselves draw attention to intersectional rights issues and often push States parties to consider intersectionality in drafting their state report or response to the treaty body's list of issues for consideration. The list of issues, in fact, offers treaty bodies a vehicle for focusing the state's attention on intersectional rights violations. Whether intersectional analysis enters the conversation because of an NGO shadow report, the state report submitted by the government, or the treaty body itself, intersectionality will continue to transform our understanding of complex human rights violations and the remedies necessary to make victims whole again.

Reporting to the treaty bodies on compliance with the human rights treaties generates attention and dialogue about rights at the international, national, and subnational levels. The increased awareness that stems from such dialogues contributes to enhanced rights protection at the national level, benefiting people by preventing abuses and providing more fulsome remedies when abuses are committed. Focusing the reporting dialogue on intersectionality, as is increasingly happening, will go a long way toward internalizing norms around intersectionality at the state level.

[85] *See* Creamer & Simmons, *supra* note 24, at 2. The most rigorous evidence to date establishes a plausible connection between the cumulative effects of participating in the reporting process and improved human rights outcomes. Recent research shows that the more frequently states participate in the reporting process, the better they perform on relevant indicators of rights outcomes. In particular, repeated and cumulative dialogues with treaty bodies have contributed to lower levels of discrimination against women and physical integrity rights violations.

7

Putting Intersectionality to Work: Non-governmental Organizations

Just as the UN treaty bodies have been increasingly willing to consider intersectionality in the international human rights context, many non-governmental organizations (NGOs) have also incorporated an intersectional approach into their human rights advocacy. NGOs enjoy a symbiotic relationship with the treaty bodies, holding the treaty bodies accountable for their human rights work while also accepting guidance from the treaty bodies as to how best to engage with the UN system. This reciprocal dynamic makes NGOs a fruitful source for exploring their potential to advocate for intersectional approaches within the United Nations and for examining ways in which the treaty bodies might also encourage NGOs to use intersectional frameworks in their own advocacy work. The growing acceptance of intersectionality within the United Nations and within the civil society sector is mutually reinforcing and holds the promise of more comprehensive remedies for human rights victims.

When NGOs use an intersectional approach in their own work, they can better address the complexity of human rights violations and improve their capacity for coalitional work. As intersectionality is increasingly recognized as a salient and effective approach to human rights work, the civil society sector will continue to push the United Nations to embrace intersectionality in its work. Likewise, the United Nations plays a role in fostering a commitment to intersectionality within the human rights work of NGOs. Through this mutual engagement of intersectionality, human rights work will continue to become more responsive to the complex realities of modern human rights violations. This chapter considers the work of human rights NGOs and their relationship to UN treaty body work and advocacy. The interplay between UN entities and NGOs, as well as national human rights institutions (independent but state-founded entities that also conduct human rights work), provides a range of ways to inform, encourage, and equip groups with the growing ability to engage intersectional analysis in the redress of human rights abuses.

Mobilizing intersectionality and coalition-building

Jill Irvine, Sabine Long, and Celeste Montoya acknowledge that intersectionality requires a shift in thinking. They observe, "Intersectionality asks scholars (and activists) to complicate their understanding of the world, moving from an oversimplified single-axis analysis of oppression to a more complete and nuanced examination of multiple, interacting, and dynamic dimensions."[1] In this context, they discuss how

[1] Gendered Mobilizations and Intersectional Challenges: Contemporary Social Movements in Europe and North America 3 (Jill Irvine et al. eds., 2019).

Global Intersectionality and Contemporary Human Rights. Johanna Bond, Oxford University Press. © Johanna Bond 2021.
DOI: 10.1093/oso/9780198868835.003.0008

intersectionality affects the ability of activists to create unifying momentum within a social movement while also acknowledging the different positionalities of social movement participants.[2] Political theorist Anna Carastathis argues that Kimberlé Crenshaw originally conceptualized intersectionality itself as a form of coalition in action. Carastathis notes,

> For women of color, queer people of color, and other multiply oppressed groups, conceptualizing identity groups as "in fact" coalitions shifts our attention to the "intersectionalities within"—the multiplicity and contradictions of our identities politicized by social movements that have failed to grasp the social totality and lived experiences of multiple oppressions in a nonfragmented way.[3]

Carastathis observes that identity groups are "always already multiple," making them fertile ground for exploring intersectionality and coalescing around goals that reflect the heterogeneity of group members' experiences.[4] Similarly, Edwina Barvosa-Carter suggests that identities are, by definition, intersectional and are therefore primed to "connect people to a number of social groups and communities that can, in turn, potentially become politicized and mobilized in order to achieve particular social justice goals."[5]

Coalitional work is not easy. It is often fraught with power dynamics that reflect institutionalized white supremacy, colonialism, and other forms of oppression that privilege certain voices over others. Crenshaw, nevertheless, remains hopeful in her characterization of identities *as* coalitions: "[A]ny attempt to mobilize identity is a negotiation, a discussion among those in identity groups to put forth an agenda that fully recognizes the various political interests, conflicting though they may be, that exist within an identity category."[6] Other critical race theorists, such as Richard Delgado, are more pessimistic about the potential of coalition-building. Delgado believes that coalitions detract from the goals of oppressed groups and distract members by requiring that they familiarize themselves with each other.[7] Conceptualizing identity as intersectional, however, requires coalition members to interrogate their own positions within the coalition and to dismantle hierarchies within the coalition itself. Carastathis hopefully notes, "Perhaps we can be most fully ourselves in relation to others in movements that advance coalitional conceptions of identity and that articulate the connections between what have been theorized as discrete systems of oppression."[8]

[2] *Id.* at 9.

[3] ANNA CARASTATHIS, INTERSECTIONALITY: ORIGINS, CONTESTATIONS, HORIZONS 188 (2016); *see also* Kimberlé Crenshaw, *Mapping the Margins: Intersectionality, Identity Politics, and Violence against Women of Color*, 43 STAN. L. REV. 1241, 1299 (1991) ("A beginning response to these questions requires that we first recognize that the organized identity groups in which we find ourselves in are in fact coalitions, or at least potential coalitions waiting to be formed.").

[4] CARASTATHIS, *supra* note 3, at 190.

[5] Edwina Barvosa-Carter, *Multiple Identity and Coalition Building: How Identity Differences Within Us Enable Radical Alliances Among Us*, 2 CONTEMP. JUST. REV. 111, 123 (1999).

[6] CARASTATHIS, *supra* note 3, at 190 (*quoting* Kimberlé Williams Crenshaw, *The Identity Factor in Multiculturalism*, 81 LIBERAL EDUCATION 6, 12 (1995)).

[7] *Id.* at 191 (quoting Delgado, who suggests that "little is gained from coalition; working in concert may even diminish efficiency because it takes time to . . . become familiar with each other").

[8] *Id.* at 194–95.

Exploring intersectionality within coalition work demands that individuals recognize when they experience both subordination and privilege and when they act in ways that perpetuate inequality. These conversations around identity are fraught, complex, and fluid. At times, a coalition may highlight one aspect of identity as a strategic matter. As noted in chapter 1, strategic essentialism "is best thought of as a political practice whereby an individual or group foregrounds one or more aspects of identity as significant in a given situation."[9] Strategic essentialism recognizes that identity is not static and fixed but rather fluid and changeable. It reflects an understanding that individuals or groups might prioritize some aspect of identity to organize and galvanize support for political action.[10] Patricia Hill Collins and Sirma Bilge offer an example, explaining: "Black women in Brazil were able to incorporate so many different groups into their movement because they had shifting alliances with many groups. One sees in their work the use of strategic essentialism as an important legitimate political tactic in a struggle for social justice."[11] Viewed in this way, strategic essentialism is consistent with intersectionality, and both lay the foundation for coalition-building.

To craft an intersectional social movement successfully, human rights NGOs must take the charge of intersectionality within their organizational work seriously. This requires "the fostering of intersectional consciousness, an awareness of the identities and needs of the most marginalized members of the movement as well as a sense of the particular, and multiple challenges they face."[12] Many human rights NGOs are already doing this, and the commitment to intersectionality is gaining traction. Irvine, Long, and Montoya observe that this intersectional social movement work occurs within four different focus areas: creating intersectional capacity, finding voice, forming alliances, and acting politically.[13] Intersectional capacity requires a recognition of inequalities *within* the group and a commitment to adopt decision-making practices that bring the most marginalized group members to the table.[14] Finding voice within an intersectional social movement often means finding "common identities while acknowledging difference," explicitly recognizing "power differentials based on group identities," identifying collective action built on shared goals rather than shared identities, or a combination thereof.[15] "Forming alliances," write the editors, "gets at the heart of intersectional activism, which points to the necessity of building alliances across both 'intracategorical difference' within groups as well as across 'intercategorical difference' among different social movements."[16] Finally, the focus on political action reveals that particular strategic choices in advocacy campaigns can be helpful or unhelpful in achieving intersectional goals. Those goals require that activists be intentionally focused on intersectionality in setting priorities and strategizing collective action.[17]

[9] Patricia Hill Collins & Sirma Bilge, Intersectionality 133 (2016).
[10] *Id.*
[11] *Id.*
[12] Gendered Mobilizations and Intersectional Challenges, *supra* note 1, at 10.
[13] *Id.* at 10–15.
[14] *Id.* at 10.
[15] *Id.* at 12–13.
[16] *Id.* at 13.
[17] *Id.* at 15–16.

NGOs that are already using or seeking to embrace an intersectional approach will likely need to train their staff to understand intersectionality theory and recognize its importance in human rights work. In some cases, the shift in approach may stem from an organizational assessment. For example, two NGOs working in Lebanon, the International Foundation for Electoral Systems (IFES) and the Lebanese Union for People with Physical Disabilities (LUPD), worked in partnership to eliminate barriers to participation in political life. As a first step, the NGOs conducted an assessment using IFES's Intersectionality Assessment Framework, which resulted in findings such as "[d]isabled people's and LGBTQ [lesbian, gay, bisexual, trans, and queer and/or questioning] organizations are not currently working together, but there is an interest and an acknowledgement of the benefits of intersectional coalition-building."[18] The assessment identified intersectional barriers to political participation among a number of groups, and this knowledge informed the NGOs' efforts to build coalitions among advocacy groups.[19] The project has focused on building intersectional coalitions among diverse organizations and uniting them in "Power to Persuade" policy platform workshops. In so doing, the coalition has "engage[d] in dialogue around shared values, experiences and opportunities to pursue common goals to defend their rights and reduce violence and discrimination impacting political participation."[20] The strategy of beginning with an intersectionality assessment and then using that information to build coalitions should be explored in other countries and regions.

The role of NGOs in treaty body work generally

The evolution of NGO interventions in treaty body work

NGOs play a significant role in the UN human rights system. From its inception, the United Nations has envisioned a role for NGOs, and that role has grown and shifted over time. Article 71 of the UN Charter first opened the door, inviting the Economic and Social Council (ECOSOC) to "make suitable arrangements for consultation" with NGOs.[21] Initially, NGO representatives served in a consulting role to country delegations during UN conferences and drafting sessions.[22] NGOs had a more limited function during the Cold War era for several reasons, including states' concern about the dominance of Western-influenced NGOs and criticism of some governments by human rights NGOs.[23] NGOs, however, still found areas in which to assert their

[18] *Building Intersectional Coalitions to Address Discrimination and Violence in Lebanon*, Int'l Found. for Electoral Sys. (IFES) (Apr. 11, 2019), https://www.ifes.org/news/building-intersectional-coalitions-address-discrimination-and-violence-lebanon.

[19] IFES reports that after the intersectionality assessment, "[t]he next step for the project is coalition-building between Lebanese CSOs so they can recruit and engage allies, policymakers, political parties, human rights advocates and other strategic partners for reform." *Id.*

[20] *Id.*

[21] Barbara K. Woodward, *The Role of International NGOs: An Introduction*, 19 Willamette J. Int'l L. & Disp. Resol. 203, 206 (2011).

[22] Steve Charnovitz, *Two Centuries of Participation: NGOs and International Governance*, 18 Mich. J. Int'l L. 183, 250–51 (1997).

[23] Dianne Otto, *Nongovernmental Organizations in the United Nations System: The Emerging Role of International Civil Society*, 18 Hum. Rts. Q. 107, 113–14 (1996).

influence, specifically the areas of human rights and nuclear disarmament[24] as well as environmental policies.[25]

Since the Cold War era concluded and a new time of globalization began, "NGOs' activities and roles have increased dramatically, challenging the role of the State and States' traditional dominance of international law."[26] Scholars point to several factors that facilitated the growing role of NGOs in international policy, including the integration of the global economy, movement away from state polarization in global politics, a worldwide media platform for publicization of NGOs' views, and the spread of democratic norms.[27] NGOs play an important function in planning international conferences, contributing to international agreements, and monitoring state regimes and participation in multilateral treaties.[28] Environmental NGOs, for example, expanded on the activities of the International Whaling Commission and recruited the state members necessary to impose a moratorium on commercial whaling.[29]

States still occasionally oppose UN accreditation of NGOs that may be critical of state practices, especially in the realm of human rights.[30] For example, conservative factions in the United States opposed the UN accreditation of the International Lesbian, Gay, Bisexual, Trans and Intersex Association (ILGA) as a recognized NGO.[31] Additionally, some Asian and African countries strongly opposed the UN accreditation of Human Rights Watch in 1993.[32] The vetting process for NGOs is important and despite occasional challenges with the process, modern NGOs are increasingly active in international policy-making.[33]

NGOs with intersectional missions

NGOs have come a long way since the early days of single-issue organizing. It is far more common today to see NGOs engaged in intersectional work, both in terms of the process and methods of the organization's work and in terms of setting agendas for the substantive work itself. NGOs that have incorporated intersectionality into their mission statements may find it easier to incorporate intersectional goals systematically into all their projects and work. In turn, work that centers intersectional analysis will come closer to providing protection against and remedies for intersectional human rights violations. NGOs using intersectional methods tend to focus on specific

[24] Karsten Nowrot, *Legal Consequences of Globalization: The Status of Non-Governmental Organizations Under International Law*, 6 IND. J. GLOB. LEGAL STUD. 579, 585 (1999).

[25] Charnovitz, *supra* note 22, at 260.

[26] Woodward, *supra* note 21, at 204.

[27] Charnovitz, *supra* note 22, at 265–66.

[28] Nowrot, *supra* note 24, at 585–86.

[29] Charnovitz, *supra* note 22, at 263.

[30] Otto, *supra* note 23, at 116. NGOs may apply for consultative status with the UN's Economic and Social Council (ECOSOC). As of April 2020, 5451 NGOs from around the world have consultative status, which allows them to participate in a variety of UN meetings, conferences, and processes. *Basic Facts about ECOSOC Status*, NGO BRANCH: DEPT. OF ECON. & SOC. AFFS., http://csonet.org/index.php?menu=17 (last visited Dec. 12, 2020).

[31] *Id.* at 116–17.

[32] *Id.* at 116.

[33] Charnovitz, *supra* note 22, at 265.

geographic regions and attempt to influence their regional treaty bodies. Below, I review a cross-section of intersectionality-focused NGOs in different geographic regions. The examples help elucidate the ways that some NGOs have explicitly or implicitly incorporated intersectionality into their human rights work.

The Americas

The Office for the Defense of Rights and Intersectionality (ODRI) explicitly incorporates intersectionality into its organizational mission. Founded in 2017 in Lima, ODRI uses an intersectional approach in "the protection of human rights and the promotion of inclusive sustainable development."[34] ODRI regularly submits shadow reports that focus on intersectional human rights violations to the UN human rights treaty bodies (a later section discusses several of their reports).[35] ODRI takes an expansive view of intersectional human rights violations in its work, although it focuses geographically on Latin America.[36]

Similarly, the DisAbled Women's Network Canada (DAWN Canada) recognizes intersectionality in its mission statement, emphasizing the experiences of disabled women from different ethnicities, sexual orientations, marital statuses, and ages.[37] In May 2020, DAWN Canada completed an intersectional analysis of disabled young women and girls in Canada.[38] DAWN Canada frequently collaborates with similarly focused NGOs around the world.[39] It also helps monitor Canada's implementation of the United Nations Convention on the Rights of People with Disabilities (CRPD).[40] Through its robust commitment to intersectionality, DAWN Canada encourages regional and international recognition of intersectional issues.

Asia

A range of smaller human rights NGOs in Asia also incorporate intersectionality into their work. For example, the Indigenous Women's Network of Thailand (IWNT) combines a focus on gender and indigeneity to advocate for the specific and intersectional needs of indigenous women in the country.[41] Their 2017 shadow report to the CEDAW Committee covers indigenous women's access to services in Thailand, human trafficking, land rights, and gender-based violence.[42] The IWNT notes that the

[34] *El Corazón y los Lineamientos de ODRI*, Off. for the Def. of Rts. & Intersectionality, https://odriintersectionalrights.org/lineamientos/ (last visited Nov. 6, 2020).

[35] *Acerca de ODRI*, Off. for the Def. of Rts. & Intersectionality, https://odriintersectionalrights.org/acerca-de-odri/ (last visited Nov. 6, 2020).

[36] *Id.*

[37] *Our Mission and Vision*, DAWN Can., https://dawncanada.net/about/our-mission-and-vision/ (last visited Nov. 6, 2020).

[38] DAWN Can., Girls Without Barriers: An Intersectional Feminist Analysis of Girls and Young Women with Disabilities in Canada 10–12 (2020).

[39] *In Focus From the United Nations*, DAWN Can., https://www.dawncanada.net/news/in-focus-from-the-united-nations/ (last visited May 25, 2020).

[40] *More Than a Footnote: A Research Report on Women and Girls with Disabilities in Canada*, DAWN Can., https://www.dawncanada.net/projects/beyond%20uncrpd/?wbdisable=true (last visited Nov. 6, 2020).

[41] Indigenous Women's Network of Thai. & Asia Indigenous Peoples Pact, NGO CEDAW Shadow Report on Behalf of Indigenous Women in Thailand 4 (2017).

[42] *Id.* at 4–5.

Thai government's policies fail "to acknowledge [indigenous women's] indigeneity/ ethnicity and the intersectional discrimination that they experience."[43]

Similarly, the China LBT Rights Initiative is a coalition of Chinese LBT Women's NGOs that submitted a shadow report to the CEDAW Committee in 2014.[44] The coalition's shadow report frames its arguments in terms of the CEDAW Committee's General Recommendation No. 28, which notes the inextricable links between gender and "other factors that affect women, such as race, ethnicity, religion or belief, health, status, age, class, caste, and sexual orientation and gender identity."[45]

Europe

In 2009, the European Roma Rights Centre (ERRC) released a report entitled *Multiple Discrimination* that addressed the importance of intersectionality in its work within European Roma communities.[46] The report observes, "Roma may find themselves discriminated against not only because of their racial or ethnic origin, but also because they are female, disabled, homosexual or elderly (or any combination of these). It will often be impossible to separate these different aspects of their identity."[47]

The ERRC report discusses intersectionality in the context of a range of human rights issues facing Roma populations in Europe. In one example, Spain denied a Roma woman widow's benefits because the Spanish government did not recognize the validity of her Romani customary marriage.[48] The report also discusses the intersection of age discrimination and discrimination on the basis of Roma ethnicity, suggesting that restricted public assistance to the Roma in Bulgaria would disproportionately affect elderly members of Roma communities.[49] The report also offers a first-hand look at life in Serbia for a gay Romani man. The author observes that "among his gay acquaintances, membership in one discriminated group did not necessarily sensitise members of that group to the discrimination faced by other groups: gay men were sometimes as intolerant to him as a Roma as non-gay men were."[50] This anecdote illustrates the intersectional principle that one may simultaneously face discrimination along one axis of identity and subject others to discrimination along another axis. One may be both oppressed and oppressor at the same time.

ERRC, at times, characterizes multiple identities in an additive way. The organization asserts, for example, that "Muslim Roma will face discrimination when dealing with islamophobic [*sic*] people but also the regular anti-Roma discrimination. Now

[43] *Id.* at 4.

[44] China LBT Rts. Initiative, Information Submitted by the China LBT Rights Initiative (a Coalition of Chinese LBT Women NGOs) to the Committee on the Elimination of Discrimination Against Women (2014).

[45] *Id.* (quoting Comm. on the Elimination of Discrimination Against Women, Gen. Recommendation No. 28 on the Core Obligations of States Parties Under Article 2 of the Convention on the Elimination of All Forms of Discrimination Against Women, ¶ 18, UN Doc. CEDAW/C/GC/28 (Dec. 16, 2010)).

[46] Rob Kushen, *The Challenge of Multiple Discrimination*, 2 Roma Rts.: J. Eur. Roma Rts. Ctr. 3, 3 (2009).

[47] Gay Moon, *Multiple Discrimination: Justice for the Whole Person*, 2 Roma Rts.: J. Eur. Roma Rts. Ctr. 5, 5 (2009).

[48] Kushen, *supra* note 46, at 3.

[49] *Id.*

[50] *Id.*

those are just examples of double discriminations."[51] In this case, ERRC expresses support for intersectionality even as its own understanding of the concept is evolving.

Africa

Some civil society organizations have explicitly embraced intersectionality as a way of securing basic human rights for lesbian, gay, bisexual, trans, queer and/or questioning, and intersex (LGBTQI) communities. One such organization, first mentioned in chapter 4, is the Coalition of African Lesbians, or CAL, an NGO headquartered in Johannesburg, South Africa. CAL's website notes, "We believe that our multiple sets of realities and contexts intersect and are linked. Our race, class, gender, sexual orientation, [dis]ability, geographic location amongst others are connected in a web of oppression."[52] CAL's story, however, cautions against relying too heavily on regional human rights bodies to advocate for intersectional approaches.

CAL has faced an uphill battle in the sub-Saharan African region, and its advocacy campaigns suggest that NGOs are vital to moving international and regional human rights bodies to embrace intersectionality more comprehensively. As described earlier, in 2008, CAL applied for observer status at the African Commission, which is similar to consultative status with ECOSOC and would allow CAL to regularly appear before the Commission, participate in select proceedings, and enjoy the credibility that comes from official recognition by the Commission.[53] Before submitting its application, CAL met all the Commission's requirements for observer status, including submitting required documentation and satisfying other administrative criteria.[54] The African Commission delayed a decision on CAL's observer status three times before rejecting its application in 2010.[55] The African Commission noted, "[T]he activities of the said organisation (CAL) do not promote and protect any of the rights enshrined in the African Charter."[56] The Commission failed to recognize that many people who identify as LGBTQI are frequently targeted for violence and denied rights enshrined in the Charter on the basis of LGBTQI individuals' real or perceived sexual orientation or gender identity. This targeted discrimination and violence makes them victims of gender discrimination as it is commonly defined in contemporary human rights discourse.

In 2014, CAL again applied for observer status.[57] In the same year, the African Commission adopted a resolution entitled Protection against Violence and other Human Rights Violations against Persons on the basis of their real or imputed Sexual

[51] Benjamin Ignac, *Dipping our Toes in the Waters of Intersectionality*, Eur. Roma Rts. Ctr. (Feb. 20, 2017), http://www.errc.org/news/dipping-our-toes-in-the-waters-of-intersectionality.

[52] *Why We Exist*, coal. afr. lesbians, https://www.cal.org.za/about-us/why-we-exist/ (last visited Nov. 7, 2020).

[53] Ctr. for Hum. Rts., Univ. of Pretoria & Afr. Comm'n for Hum. & Peoples' Rts., Celebrating the African Charter at 30: A Guide to the African Human Rights System 39–40 (2011).

[54] *Id.* at 40.

[55] *Id.*

[56] *Id.*

[57] Coal. of Afr. Lesbians, *Coalition of African Lesbians Granted Observer Status by the African Commission on Human and Peoples' Rights*, Ass'n for Progressive Commc'ns (Apr. 27, 2015), https://www.apc.org/en/blog/coalition-african-lesbians-granted-observer-status-african-commission-human-and-peoples-rights (last updated Aug. 6, 2020).

Orientation or Gender Identity (hereinafter Resolution 275).[58] In the resolution, the African Commission expressed alarm at the increasing rate of violence against LGBTQI communities in the region and violence directed at the human rights defenders and civil society organizations working to protect those communities.[59] Resolution 275 condemned such violence and urged states to take action to combat violence against people "on the basis of their imputed or real sexual orientation or gender identities."[60] The next year, the African Commission granted CAL observer status at the Commission's 56th Ordinary Session.[61]

Despite these steps, the African Union has not consistently articulated a commitment to LGBTQI rights. The Executive Council of the African Union (AU), for example, has been reluctant to recognize LGBTQI rights. The Executive Council supports the AU Assembly, reports to the AU Assembly of Heads of State and Government, and supports work on issues of common concern to member states.[62] Notably, the Executive Council interfered with the Commission's work on LGBTQI rights, and pressured the Commission to review its 2015 decision to grant CAL observer status.[63] The Executive Council called on the African Commission to consider "African values" when reviewing applications for observer status.[64] In 2018, after initially resisting pressure from the Executive Council, the African Commission revoked CAL's observer status.[65] Human rights organizations have expressed concern that the African Commission is not operating as an independent human rights body.[66] The 2018 decision calls into question the African Commission's commitment to LGBTQI rights and illustrates the importance of treaty bodies working in tandem with NGOs and using an intersectional lens to analyze human rights work.

Many NGOs, such as CAL, frequently interact with UN human rights treaty bodies and regional human rights treaty bodies in the context of individual communications (as described in chapter 5) and human rights reporting (as described in chapter 6). Through these processes, NGOs discursively engage with human rights bodies as to the content and meaning of rights. When an organization like CAL takes an explicitly intersectional approach in its human rights work, it influences the ongoing human rights dialogue and encourages intersectional approaches. Through this dialogic process, NGOs may push the treaty bodies to incorporate intersectional approaches in their work. The treaty bodies will, in turn, influence other NGOs and encourage them to adopt intersectional analysis through a variety of mechanisms, including guidance documents on engaging with the state reporting process, guidance on submitting

[58] Afr. Comm'n on Hum. & Peoples' Rts. Res. 55/275 (2014).

[59] *Id.*

[60] *Id.* ¶ 4.

[61] AFR. COMM'N ON HUM. & PEOPLES' RTS., FINAL COMMUNIQUÉ OF THE 56TH ORDINARY SESSION OF THE AFRICAN COMMISSION ON HUMAN AND PEOPLES' RIGHTS 7 (2015).

[62] *The Executive Council*, AFR. UNION ADVISORY BD. ON CORRUPTION, http://www.auanticorruption.org/organs/the-executive-council (last visited Nov. 7, 2020).

[63] *ACHPR: Withdrawing Coalition of African Lesbians' Observer Status Threatens Civil Society Participation*, ARTICLE 19 (Oct. 18, 2018), https://www.article19.org/resources/achpr-concern-with-decision-to-withdraw-coalition-of-african-lesbians-observer-status/.

[64] *Id.*

[65] *Id.*

[66] *See id.* ("The decision raises questions about the ACHPR's independence and impartiality, and has triggered concerns of a further assault by the AU's Executive Council on the ACHPR's human rights work.").

individual complaints, the work of special rapporteurs, and many other actors in the UN and regional human rights systems.

Asserting intersectional rights in litigation

In addition to advocating for intersectional rights in reports to treaty bodies, NGOs may also emphasize the importance of intersectional analysis in litigation. This emphasis is crucial because many human rights treaties do not explicitly reflect an intersectional approach in the treaty text. As I described in chapter 3, the treaties often list competing and discrete grounds for discrimination, and treaty bodies tend to focus on one type of discrimination at a time in assessing individual complaints.[67]

In 2012, the European Court of Human Rights (ECtHR) heard the case of *B.S. v. Spain*, which involved a Nigerian woman who alleged that Spanish police assaulted and racially abused her.[68] B.S. alleged that the police discriminated against her on an intersectional basis because of her race, gender, and status as a sex worker, and thus violated the European Convention on Human Rights.[69] Women's Link Worldwide (WLWW), which represented B.S. in this litigation,[70] intentionally brings "a gender perspective and an intersectional analysis to the legal framework of human rights [law]."[71] It operates a network of NGOs and other organizations to identify intersectional issues and facilitate "access to justice for victims of discrimination."[72]

WLWW illustrates the significance of different NGOs reinforcing each other to provide a broad network of support for all aspects of a marginalized person's identity. In its briefs before the court, WLWW continually emphasized and explained the nature of intersectional discrimination and encouraged its NGO partners to submit third-party briefs supporting this notion.[73] WLWW's commitment to intersectional analysis influenced the ECtHR finding that the police officers violated B.S.'s rights and that she had a "special vulnerability inherent in her situation as an African woman working as a prostitute."[74] Although the court did not use the specific phrase "intersectional discrimination" in its decision, *B.S. v. Spain* still marks an important step in human rights jurisprudence toward intersectionality.[75]

WLWW also played a role in *Atala Riffo and Daughters v. Chile*, a 2012 case before the Inter-American Court of Human Rights (IACHR).[76] The case, which I also

[67] MariaCaterina La Barbera & Marta Cruells López, *Toward the Implementation of Intersectionality in the European Multilevel Legal Praxis*: B. S. v. Spain, 53 L. & Soc'y Rev. 1167, 1169 (2019).

[68] B.S. v. Spain, App. No. 47159/08, ¶¶ 7–10, 21–22 (July 24, 2012), https://hudoc.echr.coe.int/eng#("itemid":["001-112459"]).

[69] *Id.* at ¶ 29.

[70] La Barbera & López, *supra* note 67, at 1177.

[71] *About Women's Link*, Women's Link Worldwide, https://www.womenslinkworldwide.org/en/womens-link/about-us (last visited Nov. 7, 2020).

[72] La Barbera & López, *supra* note 67, at 1180.

[73] *Id.* at 1185–86.

[74] Eur. Ct. of Hum. Rts., Information Note on the Court's Case-Law: No. 154, 24 (2012).

[75] La Barbera & López, *supra* note 67, at 1191–92 (2019).

[76] *Atala Riffo and Daughters v. Chile*, Women's Link Worldwide, https://www.womenslinkworldwide.org/en/gender-justice-observatory/court-rulings-database/atala-riffo-and-daughters-v-chile (last visited Nov. 7, 2020).

describe in chapter 4, involved a Chilean court that denied Ms. Riffo custody of her three daughters because of her sexual orientation as a lesbian.[77] WLWW filed an amicus brief supporting Ms. Riffo and emphasizing that the state discriminated against her both as a woman and on the basis of her sexual orientation.[78] Both WLWW and Ms. Riffo's lead attorney argued that Chile's actions violated Ms. Riffo's rights as stated in the American Convention on Human Rights (ACHR), specifically her rights to equality, honor, private and family life, and freedom from discrimination.[79] While it did not use specifically intersectional language, the IACHR adopted a broad reading of Section 1.1 of the ACHR to include discrimination on the basis of sexual orientation.[80] Some scholars have found the IACHR's "open interpretation to the prohibition of discrimination" encouraging to recognition of intersectionality, as it lays the foundation for the court's understanding of multiple, intersectional forms of discrimination.[81]

The European Roma Rights Center (ERRC) has also incorporated an intersectional approach into its litigation before the UN human rights treaty bodies. ERRC represented six Romani women after doctors in the Czech Republic sterilized them without their consent.[82] ERCC submitted an individual communication to the CEDAW Committee under the Optional Protocol. The complaint asserted egregious violations of the CEDAW Convention and alleged that the six women were targeted for coercive sterilization because of gender and racial stereotypes affecting women in the Czech Republic.[83] Although CEDAW's outcome found that the complainants needed to exhaust domestic remedies before turning to the treaty body, ERRC's articulation of the importance of considering such complaints through an intersectional lens was a valuable contribution to the record.[84]

The examples given here demonstrate the significance and necessity of NGOs raising intersectional issues and including intersectional analysis in their approach to litigation before human rights bodies. In doing so, NGOs push human rights bodies to consider the harms caused by complex, intersectional rights violations. Correspondingly, the more that human rights treaties recognize intersectional violations, the more that NGOs will highlight intersecting violations in their complaints.

[77] Atala Riffo and Daughters v. Chile, Merits, Reparations and Costs, Judgment, Inter-Am. Ct. H.R. (ser. C) No. 239, ¶ 3 (Feb. 24, 2012).

[78] Brief for Women's Link Worldwide as Amici Curiae Supporting Petitioners, Atala Riffo and Daughters v. Chile, Inter-Am. Ct. H.R. (ser. C) No. 239 (Feb. 24, 2012).

[79] *Atala Riffo and Daughters v. Chile*, *supra* note 76.

[80] Atala Riffo and Daughters v. Chile, Merits, Reparations and Costs, Judgment, Inter-Am. Ct. H.R. (ser. C) No. 239, ¶ 91 (Feb. 24, 2012); Rosa M. Celorio, *The Case of Karen Atala and Daughters: Toward a Better Understanding of Discrimination, Equality, and the Rights of Women*, 15 CUNY L. Rev. 335, 356 (2012).

[81] *Id.* at 361–62.

[82] Comm. on the Elimination of Discrimination against Women, Decision Adopted by the Committee Under Article 4(2)(c) of the Optional Protocol, Concerning Communication No. 102/2016, U.N. Doc. CEDAW/C/73/D/102/2016 (Sept. 10, 2019).

[83] *Id.* ¶ 3.1.

[84] *Id.* ¶ 8.2–8.3.

Integrating intersectionality into shadow reports

Opportunities for intervention in treaty body reviews of state reports

NGOs have several opportunities to provide information to treaty bodies in advance of the latter's review of a State party's report. CEDAW specifically invites NGOs to submit shadow reports at several different stages of its review process. CEDAW guidelines for NGO submissions invite international and national NGOs to submit shadow reports at the pre-sessional working group, which is when the working group determines the list of issues that the Committee will focus during its review of the state's report.[85] NGO submissions to the pre-session working group can be done orally or in writing.[86] CEDAW also welcomes shadow report submissions for treaty body sessions and encourages coordination among NGOs in the writing of shadow reports.[87] During CEDAW sessions, NGOs are permitted to organize side events for the members of CEDAW.[88]

The UN Office of the High Commissioner for Human Rights also invites NGOs to submit written reports in advance of the pre-session working group and the CEDAW session itself. It also encourages NGOs to attend and present information orally at both the committee session and the pre-session working group.[89] NGOs may also provide country-specific information through private briefings to CEDAW members during CEDAW sessions.[90]

NGOs themselves also sometimes draft guidelines for the submission of alternative or shadow reports to the treaty bodies. International Women's Rights Action Watch (IWRAW) provides guidance to other NGOs seeking to submit shadow reports or participate in other aspects of monitoring state compliance with CEDAW.[91] IWRAW provides specific manuals and guides for NGOs participating in monitoring and evaluation efforts and also facilitates a network of NGOs for coordination purposes.[92]

International Women's Rights Action Watch–Asia Pacific, originally a sister program to IWRAW and now a separate entity, serves as a liaison between other NGOs and the CEDAW Committee for purposes of submitting shadow reports.[93] IWRAW–Asia

[85] COMM. ON THE ELIMINATION OF DISCRIMINATION AGAINST WOMEN, INFORMATION NOTE PREPARED BY OHCHR FOR NGO PARTICIPATION 1, https://www2.ohchr.org/english/bodies/cedaw/docs/NGO_Participation.final.pdf (last visited Mar. 10, 2021).

[86] *Id.*

[87] *Id.*

[88] *Id.* at 3.

[89] *Id.* at 1–2.

[90] *Participation by Non-Governmental Organizations (NGOs)*, COMM. ON THE ELIMINATION OF DISCRIMINATION AGAINST WOMEN, at 4 (2019), https://tbinternet.ohchr.org/_layouts/15/treatybodyexternal/SessionDetails1.aspx?SessionID=1190&Lang=en (scroll to "Participation by Non-Governmental Organizations (NGOs)"; click "View document"; click the desired language).

[91] *Our History*, INT'L WOMEN'S RTS. ACTION WATCH, http://hrlibrary.umn.edu/iwraw/ (last visited Nov. 9, 2020).

[92] *Id.*

[93] *What We Do*, INT'L WOMEN'S RTS. ACTION WATCH ASIA PACIFIC, https://www.iwraw-ap.org/ourwork/what-we-do/ (last visited Nov. 9, 2020).

Pacific created guidelines that offer comprehensive guidance for NGOs seeking to research, prepare, and submit shadow reports to the CEDAW Committee.[94] The guidelines encourage NGOs to include information relevant to the rights included not only in the CEDAW Convention but also in other human rights treaties.[95] To that end, the report states:

> While collecting data and preparing your report, try to consider how issues and rights under CEDAW intersect with those under other treaties, and include relevant information about those issues and rights. For example, make sure you have information about how girl children are affected under the CEDAW articles, since that information can easily be sent to the Committee on the Rights of the Child.[96]

These guidelines can be helpful to NGOs in terms of preparation of reports and overall participation in CEDAW activities. The guides also present an opportunity for NGOs such as IWRAW–Asia Pacific to promote intersectionality by encouraging other NGOs to adopt an intersectional framework in their human rights work and thereby raising intersectionality awareness within NGO communities.

Examples of intersectional frameworks in shadow reports

Examples abound of NGOs using intersectional analysis and language in their shadow reports. As part of its human rights advocacy work, the Office for the Defense of Rights and Intersectionality regularly submits shadow reports to the human rights treaty bodies. In 2018, ODRI submitted a report to the Committee on the Elimination of Racial Discrimination (CERD) in connection with the Committee's review of Peru's compliance with the treaty.[97] In its shadow report, ODRI highlighted the discrimination faced by indigenous Peruvian women, taking an explicitly intersectional approach to human rights in Peru and noting that despite modest gains, "indigenous women still experience intersecting forms of discrimination."[98] In particular, the report described accusations of witchcraft leveled against indigenous Peruvian women and the violence and discrimination they face as a result.[99] As in many of its reports, ODRI recommended, among other things, that the government of Peru collect and keep data disaggregated by "sex, color and descent, nationality or ethnic origin, indigenous origin, sexual orientation and gender identity."[100] Such disaggregated data

[94] INT'L WOMEN'S RTS. ACTION WATCH ASIA PACIFIC, PARTICIPATION IN THE CEDAW REPORTING PROCESS: PROCESS AND GUIDELINES FOR WRITING A SHADOW/ALTERNATIVE REPORT 1 (2010).
[95] *Id.* at 3.
[96] *Id.*
[97] OFF. FOR THE DEF. OF RTS. & INTERSECTIONALITY, WRITTEN SUBMISSION ON PERU 95TH SESSION (2018).
[98] *Id.* at 1.
[99] *Id.* at 1–3.
[100] *Id.* at 4.

would allow for intersectional analysis and targeted, intersectional human rights recommendations.

In a similar 2019 submission to the Committee on the Protection of the Rights of All Migrant Workers and Members of their Families (CMW), ODRI examined the plight of migrant workers in Belize, with a focus on people for whom migrant status intersects with other facets of identity such as gender, gender identity and sexual orientation, socioeconomic status, Indigeneity, and age.[101] The report made several recommendations, including that the Committee discuss with the government representatives from Belize their plans for implementing legislation "with clear time frames, indicators, monitoring and evaluation benchmarks to guarantee the access to HIV/AIDS treatment and sexual and reproductive health services by indigenous and Afro descendants' [*sic*] migrant workers."[102]

Additionally, ODRI requested that the CEDAW Committee address the health of intersex women and girls in Pakistan.[103] ODRI is highly attuned to intersectionality in its advocacy on behalf of intersex women and girls in the country, noting the need for heightened awareness of harmful practices, including coerced medical treatment.

Amnesty International also submitted a shadow report to the CEDAW Committee in 2019 concerning the Committee's examination of Canada's progress in implementing the women's rights convention.[104] The report urged the Canadian government "immediately [to] address violence against indigenous women and girls" and highlighted the ways in which the government has failed to adequately protect the safety and security of those populations.[105] Although the Amnesty report applauded the creation of the National Inquiry into Missing and Murdered Indigenous Women and Girls, it found fault with Canada's efforts to implement "previously identified solutions."[106] Canadian Prime Minister Justin Trudeau issued a response to the Inquiry's report, noting that "reducing the rate of violence against Indigenous women and girls, and Indigenous LGBTQ and two-spirit people, is a priority for the Government of Canada."[107] Other NGOs such as WLWW continue to assist in monitoring the status of indigenous women and girls in Canada.

In 2018, Equality Bahamas submitted a shadow report to the CEDAW Committee in advance of its 71st Session.[108] The report indicated that the effort to amend the

[101] Off. for the Def. of Rts. & Intersectionality, *Contribution to the Committee on the Protection of the Rights of All Migrant Workers and Members of their Families in Relation to the Adoption of the List of Issues to the Periodic Report of Belize (September 2019)* (Aug. 12, 2019), https://tbinternet.ohchr.org/_layouts/15/treatybodyexternal/Download.aspx?symbolno=INT%2FCMW%2FICS%2FBLZ%2F35799&Lang=en.

[102] *Id.*

[103] Off. for the Def. of Rts. & Intersectionality, *Contribution to the Committee on the Elimination of All Forms of Discrimination Against Women (CEDAW) in Relation to the Adoption of the List of Issues to the Periodic Report of the Islamic Republic of Pakistan (75th Pre-Sessional Working Group (22 July 2019–26 July 2019))*, at 3 (June 9, 2019), https://www.ecoi.net/en/document/2012188.html.

[104] Amnesty Int'l, Canada: Submission to the United Nations Committee on the Elimination of Discrimination of Women Follow-Up, June 2019, 4 (2019).

[105] *Id.* at 9–10.

[106] *Id.* at 9.

[107] *Id.* "Two-spirit people" is a pan-Indian term encompassing sexual, gender, and/or spiritual identity. *Two-Spirit Community*, Univ. of Toronto & Ctr. for Addiction & Mental Health, https://lgbtqhealth.ca/community/two-spirit.php (last visited Nov. 9, 2020).

[108] Equal. Bah., CEDAW Shadow Report: Submitted by Equality Bahamas for the 71st Session (2018).

Bahamian Constitution to prohibit discrimination on the basis of sex was defeated in 2016 largely because of concerns that the ban on sex discrimination would allow for same-sex marriage.[109] The defeat of the constitutional amendment suggests a high degree of homophobia and continued discrimination against LGBTQI communities in the Bahamas. Although Equality Bahamas was formed in 2014 as a women's rights organization,[110] the NGO approaches its mission expansively and reflects an intersectional understanding of the links between gender and sexual orientation and gender identity.

Similarly, the Central Asian Gender and Sexuality Advocacy Network (CAGSAN) submitted a shadow report to the CEDAW Committee that focused on the intersection of gender discrimination and discrimination on the basis of sexual orientation and gender identity in Tajikistan, particularly for lesbian and bisexual women and transgender people.[111] The report examined police violence, including both physical and sexual violence, targeting the LBT population in Tajikistan.[112] It also sought to alert the CEDAW Committee to the police practice of blackmailing LBT individuals as well as the targeting of civil society groups working on behalf of LBT communities.[113]

In its 2014 shadow report to the CEDAW Committee, the Association Concerning Sexual Violence Against Women (ACSVAW) in Hong Kong specifically addressed the plight of female migrant domestic workers and ethnic minorities who suffered from what it referred to as "double jeopardy in the crime of sexual violence."[114] Although this analysis reflects a limited, additive understanding of complex identity that does not rise to the level of intersectional analysis, it represents a step toward acknowledging intersectionality in the human rights context. A similar submission to the CEDAW Committee from Americans for Democracy and Human Rights in Bahrain in 2018 highlights the intersection of gender and ethnicity discrimination in the treatment of women migrants in that country.[115] The report described the intersection of discrimination because of gender and migrant status and the resulting harms for female domestic workers in Bahrain, such as withholding of wages, confiscation of passports, and sexual abuse.[116]

The Unrepresented Nations and Peoples Organization (UNPO) in the Lao People's Democratic Republic submitted a shadow report to the CEDAW Committee in October 2018.[117] The report focused on the plight of indigenous Hmong women in

[109] *Id.* at 3–4.

[110] *Id.* at 20.

[111] Cent. Asian Gender & Sexuality Advoc. Network, Shadow Report: Discriminatory Policies and Practices, Hate Speech and Hate Crimes against LBT Communities of Tajikistan 1 (2018).

[112] *Id.*

[113] *Id.*

[114] Ass'n Concerning Sexual Violence Against Women, Shadow Report to the CEDAW Committee On Sexual Violence in Hong Kong SAR, China 2 (2014).

[115] Ams. for Democracy & Hum. Rts. in Bahr., Submission for Bahrain's List of Issues Prior to Reporting (LOIPR) Under the Convention on the Elimination of Discrimination Against Women (CEDAW) 4 (2018).

[116] *Id.*

[117] Unrepresented Nations & Peoples Org., Alternative Report Submitted to the UN Committee on the Elimination of Discrimination against Women Lao People's Democratic Republic 1 (2018).

Laos.[118] Noting the intersection of gender and ethnicity, UNPO remarked, "[W]omen in different ethnic groups have distinct experiences and are affected in different ways by government neglect, marginalisation and disregard, while, at the same time, profiting on different levels and to a different extent from efforts made and developments related to gender equality."[119] As such, the report acknowledged a fundamental tenet of intersectionality theory—that women enjoy different levels of privilege and subordination depending on the intersection of gender with other aspects of identity such as ethnicity or Indigeneity. The report used an intersectional lens to discuss the particular challenges that Hmong women face with respect to education, participation in decision-making processes at the local and national level, language discrimination, maternal mortality, and human trafficking.[120]

As these examples demonstrate, a number of NGOs have begun to embrace intersectionality in their shadow reports to international and regional human rights bodies. This effort pushes treaty bodies to consider complex, intersectional rights violations and often gives them the analytical tools to do so. NGO shadow reports that use an intersectional analysis are critical for raising awareness of intersectionality among the members of the treaty bodies. NGOs that offer guidance to other NGOs on using an intersectional approach to human rights further amplify intersectionality as an analytical tool.

Interactions with special rapporteurs and other advocacy opportunities

In addition to interacting with treaty bodies through litigation and shadow reporting, NGOs also communicate with UN Special Rapporteurs and other UN entities, including to advocate on behalf of marginalized populations. In one 2018 example, the International Women's Development Agency (IWDA) submitted a report to the UN Special Rapporteur on Human Rights Defenders concerning the health and security of those working on behalf of women's rights.[121] The report documents four types of activism that increase the risk to women's human rights defenders: environmental/land rights activism and activism spearheaded by women in remote or rural areas, LGBTQI individuals, and those advocating for sexual rights.[122] Among other things, the IWDA report advocates for support services that are gender-sensitive and "accessible for women in all of their diversity—linguistic, location, religious, ethnicity/race and age."[123] It also urges support for "[n]etworks that link disadvantaged groups."[124] Although the report does not explicitly address intersectionality, it reflects a commitment to serving women in some of the most marginalized populations and reflects

[118] *Id.* at 2.
[119] *Id.*
[120] *Id.* at 6–11.
[121] Int'l Women's Dev. Agency, *Survey Response to the UN Special Rapporteur on Human Rights Defenders on the Status of Women Human Rights Defenders*, at 1–2 (Sept. 26, 2018).
[122] *Id.* at 2.
[123] *Id.* at 4.
[124] *Id.*

the core understanding that multiple, intersecting marginalized identities may subject some women to greater risk than others.

At the regional level, in 2017, the International Institute on Race, Equality and Human Rights (hereinafter Race and Equality) published a report assessing the accomplishments of the Inter-American Commission's Rapporteurship on the Rights of Persons of African Descent and Against Racial Discrimination.[125] Race and Equality applauded the Commission for creating the Rapporteurship and emphasized the need for a focus on structural racism against Afro-descendant people in the Inter-American region,[126] but it criticized the Rapporteurship for its limited human rights record over the last decade, suggesting that the Rapporteurship has accomplished very little in the region.[127] Without using the language of intersectionality, Race and Equality recommended that the Rapporteurship undertake a substantial study that includes consideration of

> women of African descent and trans women, with emphasis on the differentiated impact of the racial factor on violence based on gender and/or sexual orientation; Afro-descendent children, with emphasis on situations of violence and limitations on access to education; ... economic, social, and cultural rights ... poverty and racism: the differentiated impact of the racial factor on access to public services and discrimination in educational, work and health areas.[128]

The work that Race and Equality envisions for the Rapporteurship has a decidedly intersectional gloss. The NGO recommends that the Rapporteur focus on women and children of African descent, laying the foundation for human rights analysis at the intersection of race, gender, and age. The recommendations also include a focus on poverty and race, implicitly adopting an intersectional approach to race and socioeconomic status.

In a final example, the Asian-Pacific Resource and Research Centre for Women (ARROW) submitted a statement to the 55th Session of the Commission for Social Development in 2017 which focused on poverty eradication and sustainable development.[129] ARROW takes an intersectional approach in its submission, linking poverty to a range of human rights: "[e]radicating poverty requires addressing social exclusion and inequalities of opportunity—whether based on gender, age, ethnicity, caste, socioeconomic status, disability, sexual orientation and gender expression, health status, marital status, occupation, or citizenship status—as these lead to powerlessness, poor social status, and lack of agency thus leading to poverty."[130] The statement discusses the particular challenges of older women, LGBTQI individuals, and women

[125] Int'l Inst. on Race, Equal. & Hum. Rts., First Decade of the Rapporteurship on the Rights of Persons of African Descent and Against Racial Discrimination, Inter-American Commission on Human Rights: Challenges and Opportunities 2 (2017).

[126] *Id.* at 8.

[127] *Id.* at 8–9.

[128] *Id.* at 12.

[129] *ARROW Submission to the 55th Session Commission for Social Development*, Asian-Pacific Res. & Rsch. Ctr. for Women (Jan. 17, 2017), https://arrow.org.my/arrow-csd55/.

[130] *Id.*

with disabilities living in poverty, while recognizing that these issues cannot be fully addressed in isolation.[131]

Collaboration with national human rights institutions

Another branch in the network of human rights advocacy work is that of national human rights institutions, or NHRIs, which occupy a space between governments and NGOs.[132] NHRIs differ from NGOs in that NHRIs are created and funded by the government of a state.[133] Examples include human rights commissions and ombuds agencies. NHRIs promote and protect human rights in various ways, through monitoring the status of human rights within a state, educating the public and the government on human rights best practices, handling complaints, and reporting to treaty bodies.[134] The UN Office of the High Commissioner for Human Rights works with NHRIs to promote human rights and provides support and communication across NHRIs.[135] In 1993, the UN adopted the Paris Principles, which "are international standards and serve as minimum conditions that an NHRI must meet to be considered credible by its peers and within the United Nations system."[136] NHRIs must balance independence from both governments and NGOs with fostering a productive working relationship with both types of entities.[137]

The relationship between NGOs and NHRIs may take many different forms. The human rights commission of Togo, for example, provided protection for human rights NGOs as they established themselves in the state, with some NGO members serving as part of the commission.[138] In other countries, such as Uganda and Ghana, NHRI cooperation with existing, well-respected NGOs lent credibility to the mission of a state-sanctioned NHRI.[139] Additionally, NGOs can use their influence to

[131] *Id.*

[132] *See* Anne Smith, *The Unique Position of National Human Rights Institutions: A Mixed Blessing?*, 28 Hum. Rts. Q. 904, 905 (2006) ("It is this conceptual space [between government and NGOs] which gives NHRIs a potentially distinctive role in society.... However, ... NHRIs have to grapple with the uncomfortable dilemma of how to be independent from both government and NGOs, while at the same time establishing working relationships with both actors.").

[133] *Id.* at 906. In the 1990s, the United Nations High Commissioner for Human Rights and donors around the world encouraged the creation of NHRIs. When funding became available NHRIs proliferated, although sometimes without the long-term funding commitments to make the institutions viable over long term. Int'l Council on Hum. Rts. Pol'y, Performance and Legitimacy: National Human Rights Institutions 10 (2000).

[134] Smith, *supra* note 132, at 905.

[135] *UN Human Rights and NHRIs*, Off. of the High Comm'r of Hum. Rts., https://www.ohchr.org/EN/Countries/NHRI/Pages/NHRIMain.aspx (last visited Nov. 10, 2020).

[136] Off. of the High Comm'r of Hum. Rts., National Human Rights Institutions: History, Principles, Roles and Responsibilities 30 (2010).

[137] Smith, *supra* note 132, at 931.

[138] Livingstone Sewanyana, *Building Strategic Partnerships Between NGOs and National Human Rights Institutions (NHRIs): Human Rights in Conflict and Counter-Terrorism Situations*, 3 E. Afr. J. Hum. Rts. & Democracy 53, 54 (2005); Smith, *supra* note 132, at 931.

[139] Smith, *supra* note 132, at 931.

apply pressure on states to establish NHRIs.[140] One study found that the robust presence of human rights NGOs had a significant effect on a country establishing one or more NHRIs.[141]

Since NHRIs are state-sanctioned organizations tasked with promoting and protecting human rights, they present a unique opportunity to promote intersectionality. The Carter Center is an international NGO that publishes implementation guides for NHRIs on topics such as gender discrimination and election security.[142] The Carter Center argues that because many NHRIs make "vulnerable groups an NHRI priority" they "are uniquely placed to effectively tackle situations of intersectional violations of rights."[143] The Center encourages NHRIs to use their resources to collect data on marginalized groups that can help highlight instances of intersectional discrimination.[144] It also suggests NHRIs collaboration with NGOs that have more subject-matter expertise and connections within marginalized communities.[145] This type of NGO-NHRI collaboration could produce widespread intersectional analysis within NHRIs.

Similarly, the NHRI Toolkit published by the UN Development Programme in collaboration with OHCHR refers to the opportunity for intersectional collaboration between NGOs and NHRIs. Specifically, the UN promulgated the Paris Principles to guide NHRI activity and to call for collaboration with NGOs in the field of human rights.[146] While NGOs can provide much-needed expertise on marginalized groups, NHRIs ideally have the backing of the state to protect individuals from intersectional discrimination.[147] Successful coalition-building among NGOs and between NGOs and NHRIs reflects a commitment to intersectional analysis and has the potential to redress complex human rights violations more fully. Greater exploration of intersectionality by both NGOs and NHRIs will be mutually reinforcing and will lead to more widespread adoption of intersectional analysis.

[140] Catherine Shanahan Renshaw, *National Human Rights Institutions and Civil Society Organizations: New Dynamics of Engagement at Domestic, Regional, and International Levels*, 18 Glob. Governance 299, 303 (2012).

[141] *See* Dongwook Kim, *International Governmental Organizations and the Global Diffusion of National Human Rights Institutions*, 67 Int'l Org. 505, 506 (2013) (explaining that the study analyzed "149 developing UN member states and eighty-five NHRI founding acts for the period from 1979 to 2004").

[142] *Human Rights Program*, The Carter Ctr., https://www.cartercenter.org/peace/human_rights/index.html (last visited Nov. 10, 2020); *Democracy Program*, the carter ctr., https://www.cartercenter.org/peace/democracy/index.html (last visited Mar. 10, 2021).

[143] The Carter Ctr., Election Obligations and Standards: An Implementation Guide for National Human Rights Institutions 22–23 (2017). The Carter Center has explored the role of NHRIs in ensuring participatory rights and the intersection of socio-economic exclusion and political rights. In the context of political rights, the Carter Center notes, "Neglect of minority areas by state authorities and service providers, lack of information and materials in local languages, or lack of adapted access to state services to people with disabilities impact vulnerable groups rights concurrently." *Id.* at 22–23.

[144] *Id.* at 23.

[145] *Id.* at 21.

[146] *See* united nations dev. programme & united nations off. of the high comm'r for hum. rts., UNDP-ohchr toolkit for collaboration with national human rights institutions 36 (2010) ("The Principles require NHRIs to maintain ties with other bodies active in the human rights area, particularly with NGOs that work in the promotion and protection of human rights.").

[147] *Id.* at 2–3, 60.

Reviewing the relationship between NGOs and the United Nations

NGOs are critical drivers of human rights discourse. They often work in coalition to expand their reach, increase their political power, and achieve their advocacy goals. Coalitions are diverse by definition. Because they are "always already multiple,"[148] coalitions are fertile ground for intersectional work. Indeed, the characteristics of coalitional work led Crenshaw and others to link the concepts of coalition and intersectionality. Coalitions open the door for NGOs to internalize the practice of examining the multiple ways members both enjoy and lack privilege. When these points of intersectional awareness inform advocacy campaigns, NGOs become more habitually and intentionally intersectional over time.

NGOs, UN treaty bodies, UN Special Rapporteurs, NHRIs, and other intergovernmental entities all have a role to play in encouraging intersectional human rights work. NGOs must continue to raise intersectional claims in shadow reports and individual complaints where applicable, and they must also continue to raise awareness of intersectionality within human rights discourse more generally. NGOs have always guided and pushed the treaty bodies to be more effective in preventing abuses and promoting human rights; emphasizing intersectional analysis is a natural continuation of this work.

The UN treaty bodies, in turn, play a critical role fostering an environment where an intersectional lens is understood as necessary and valuable in the effort to provide redress for human rights violations. The treaty bodies have an opportunity to create guidelines for NGOs that integrate intersectionality into their recommendations for shadow report submissions. Guidelines that explicitly encourage NGOs to explore intersectional human rights violations and offer guidance on intersectional analysis would improve the quality of NGO reporting from an intersectional perspective. Furthermore, the UN Office of the High Commissioner for Human Rights and individual national governments should incentivize NHRIs to incorporate intersectional analysis in the critical national-level human rights work of NHRIs. Because they often work with NGOs, NHRIs are also well-positioned to influence human rights discourse and actively incorporate intersectional analysis into the work they do in furtherance of human rights.

NGOs can have maximum impact in promoting intersectionality by intentionally engaging a variety of actors, including UN treaty bodies, regional bodies, UN Special Rapporteurs and other special mechanisms, and NHRIs in the discourse of intersectional human rights. They often push the UN and other human rights bodies to embrace a more capacious vision of human rights. Within this dialectic, human rights bodies also conversely influence the work of NGOs, particularly when they offer guidelines about how NGOs should interpret certain rights. Intersectionality will offer maximum benefit to victims of human rights violations when all the actors in the human rights ecosystem embrace intersectionality and center the concept in all of the work that they do.

[148] CARASTATHIS, *supra* note 3, at 188, 190.

8

Strategies for Reform: Facilitating Intersectionality in Human Rights Advocacy

An intersectional human rights framework offers victims of human rights violations the best chance to recover remedies that fully address the complex and structural dimensions of the violations. To be effective within any national, regional, or international human rights system, however, intersectionality must be part of the institutional culture. Members of the human rights bodies must be conversant with the theory and comfortable applying it in a variety of human rights scenarios. Chapter 7 explored the ways in which NGOs can facilitate intersectional analysis by engaging human rights bodies in the discourse of intersectionality. This chapter examines structural reforms within the UN human rights system that will foster intersectional analysis. Breaking down the silos in the treaty body system and creating opportunities for collaboration will help to facilitate system-wide intersectional analysis, all of which will benefit victims of human rights violations around the world.

Since the late 1990s, there has been widespread acknowledgment that the UN human rights treaty body system does not operate at peak effectiveness. Many States parties to the treaties have failed to submit reports on time, with some states failing to submit multiple reports over several years. As of 2016, only 13 percent of States parties had submitted all of their obligatory reports to the treaty bodies.[1] The current system, however, *depends* on the delinquency of states in their reporting obligations. In fact, in 2008, the International Commission of Jurists concluded that "[i]f all overdue reports were submitted at once it would take the treaty bodies more than eight years at the current pace to get through the backlog."[2] In other words, the backlog of reports is such that if States parties were to submit their past-due reports, the treaty bodies simply would not have the time and resources to review them.

Moreover, the treaty bodies are woefully behind in their reviews of the reports that have been submitted. In 2012 some committees reported taking up to four years to review a state report.[3] A 2014 General Assembly resolution specifically allocated

[1] *See* Geneva Acad. of Int'l Humanitarian L. & Hum. Rts., Optimizing the UN Treaty Body System: Academic Platform Report on the 2020 Review 11 (2018), https://www.geneva-academy.ch/joomlatools-files/docman-files/Optimizing%20UN%20Treaty%20Bodies.pdf (citing U.N. Secretary-General, *Status of the Human Rights Treaty Body System*, ¶ 5, UN Doc. A/71/118 (July 18, 2016)).

[2] Int'l Comm'n of Jurists, Study on the Reform of the United Nations Human Rights Treaty Body System 19 (2008), https://www.icj.org/wp-content/uploads/2012/04/ICJ-Report-on-the-Reform-of-the-United-Nations-Human-Rights-Treaty-Body-System-Themetic-reports-2008.pdf.

[3] *See* Jan Lhotský, Human Rights Treaty Body Review 2020: Towards an Integrated Treaty Body System 25 (2017) (Master's thesis, Global Campus Europe) (on file with EMA).

Global Intersectionality and Contemporary Human Rights. Johanna Bond, Oxford University Press. © Johanna Bond 2021.
DOI: 10.1093/oso/9780198868835.003.0009

treaty body meeting time to discuss the prevention of backlogs.[4] Nevertheless, a 2016 General Assembly report found that "the overall backlog of the treaty body system has increased rather than decreased, in spite of the increased output and productivity of the treaty bodies."[5]

One reason for the increased backlog is the UN's adoption, since the early 2000s, of four new human rights treaties, bringing the number of primary human rights treaties to ten.[6] This expansion has resulted in additional reporting obligations for states. The UN's adoption of Universal Periodic Review (described below) in 2006 also increased the number of State party ratifications of the human rights treaties, compounding the reporting burden for both states and treaty bodies.[7] In 2012, for example, the average delay between the time that a State party submitted its report to the Committee on the Rights of Persons with Disabilities (CRPD) and the Committee's consideration of the report was six to seven years.[8] Human rights scholar Suzanne Egan has noted that the General Assembly's refusal to adequately fund the treaty body system also contributes to the challenges of timely review.[9] Overall, the combination of all of these factors has led to an inefficient system in need of reform.

Reform efforts have almost exclusively focused on improving efficiency and reducing costs. Although these are critical goals, they should not be the only goals of reform. Reform conversations must also include potential normative benefits, such as a shared understanding of and commitment to intersectionality, collaboration between treaty bodies, educating members on intersectional issues, and framing reporting questions to encourage reporting on specific issues. Specifically, proponents of reform must consider the ramifications for intersectional analysis and work to ensure that reform encourage rather than discourage an intersectional approach to human rights. Widespread adoption of an intersectional framework within the United Nations will lead to better outcomes for victims of human rights violations and more complete remedies for the harms they have suffered. Any reforms that facilitate intersectional analysis must be accompanied by training and education for treaty body experts, representatives of reporting states, and other individuals working within the UN human rights system.

This chapter examines past and ongoing reform efforts, including the efforts since the early 2000s to strengthen the treaty bodies. Building on these reform efforts, I argue that any future reform agenda should focus on facilitating intersectional analysis in addition to improving the efficiency and decreasing the cost of the current system. In particular, I name and discuss how and where the United Nations—as well

[4] *See* G.A. Res. 68/268, ¶ 26, Strengthening and Enhancing the Effective Functioning of the Human Rights Treaty Body System (Apr. 21, 2014).

[5] U.N. Secretary-General, *Status of the Human Rights Treaty Body System*, ¶ 31, U.N. Doc. A/71/118 (July 18, 2016).

[6] *See* GENEVA ACAD. OF INT'L HUMANITARIAN L. & HUM. RTS., *supra* note 1, at 11.

[7] *See* Suzanne Egan, *Strengthening the United Nations Treaty Body System*, 13 HUM. RTS. L. REV. 209, 211 (2013).

[8] *See id.* at 212.

[9] *See id.* ("The expansion of the system, together with the persistent refusal of the General Assembly to fund it with commensurate resources, has led to a perfect storm whereby the challenges facing the system threaten to overwhelm it and leave it vulnerable to charges of incoherence, ineffectiveness, and increasing marginalisation.").

as other human rights entities—can incorporate an intersectional framework into its own work.

Reform efforts in the treaty body system

Early conversations: 1989–2003

Much of the conversation about the effectiveness of the treaty body system has focused on procedural and funding issues. As noted, efforts to reform and fortify the treaty body system stem from concerns about resources, efficiency, and reporting backlog. This is understandable given the urgency of funding needs and the range of benefits that may come from careful and strategic changes in the working methods of the treaty bodies.

Philip Alston, an Independent Expert at the UN from 1989 to 1996, was an early proponent of reform who recommended improving the quality of the treaty bodies' concluding observations and harmonizing reporting guidelines.[10] Alston also envisioned that the treaty bodies might require significant structural reform to increase their effectiveness. Anne Bayefsky, a human rights scholar, published a report in 2001 calling for structural reforms to the treaty body system.[11] Acknowledging the need for lasting structural reform at the international level, Bayefsky's report also suggested smaller-scale reforms, such as consolidated reporting organized by theme.[12]

In 2002, then UN Secretary-General Kofi Annan called for more collaboration between treaty bodies and more uniform reporting requirements.[13] Secretary-General Annan also advocated for allowing states to submit a single comprehensive report.[14] In response to this call for collaboration, the governments of Australia and New Zealand met to determine how the reporting process could be streamlined from the countries' perspective.[15] They echoed the recommendation of numerous scholars: the submission of a single comprehensive report as a way to promote coordination among the treaty bodies and to streamline State reporting efforts.[16] At a 2005 meeting, the General Assembly resolved to promote more timely reporting and provide technical assistance to States to improve their internal reporting capabilities.[17] The resolution

[10] *See* U.N. Secretary-General, *Effective Implementation of International Instruments on Human Rights, Including Reporting Obligations Under International Instruments on Human Rights*, ¶ 175, U.N. Doc. A/44/668 (Nov. 8, 1989).

[11] *See* ANNE F. BAYEFSKY, THE UN HUMAN RIGHTS TREATY SYSTEM: UNIVERSALITY AT THE CROSSROADS 8 (2001).

[12] *See id.* at 21.

[13] *See* U.N. Secretary-General, *Strengthening the United Nations: An Agenda for Further Change*, ¶¶ 53–54, U.N. Doc. A/57/387 (Sept. 9, 2002).

[14] *See id.* ¶ 54.

[15] *See* U.N. Secretariat, Methods of Work Relating to the State Reporting Process, ¶ 26, U.N. Doc. HRI/ICM/2003/3 (Apr. 11, 2003).

[16] *See* U.N. Secretary-General, *supra* note 13, ¶ 54; Methods of Work Relating to the State Reporting Process, *supra* note 15, ¶ 27.

[17] *See* G.A. Res. 60/1, 2005 World Summit Outcome, ¶ 125 (Sept. 16, 2005).

did not elaborate on specific steps the United Nations would take to reach these goals.[18]

Like Alston, I was an early proponent of reform efforts. Since 2003, I have focused on the substantive benefits of procedural reform. With normative goals in mind, I have urged a more comprehensive examination of the benefits of both modest and far-reaching structural reform within the UN treaty bodies.[19] My argument, then and now, is that the procedural and structural reforms under consideration will have equally important benefits in terms of substantive rights. The changes focused on increasing communication and collaboration between treaty bodies will benefit rights holders by facilitating intersectional human rights analysis. Many of the reform proposals aimed at increasing the efficiency of the treaty bodies will have ancillary benefits in terms of opening channels for intersectional analysis.

As I suggested in 2003, the United Nations could undertake a range of modest structural reforms that would significantly increase the likelihood of the treaty bodies engaging in meaningful intersectional analysis.[20] The United Nations has, in fact, adopted some of those changes. One of my recommendations was for treaty bodies to issue more joint general recommendations and general comments.[21] Because general recommendations and comments provide guidance to States parties on the implementation of treaty provisions, they are a critical source of compliance information for states. Collaborating on the drafting and issuance of general recommendations and general comments offer treaty bodies the opportunity to align their interpretations of rights guarantees. This normative collaboration also invites the treaty bodies to consider intersectional violations that may straddle the bounds of the treaties, such as those involving discrimination based on the intersection of race, gender, ethnicity, religion, socioeconomic status, sexual orientation and gender identity, and disability.

I also recommended that the Office of the High Commissioner for Human Rights create an office or designated staff specifically charged with acting as a liaison between treaty bodies.[22] This Office of the Liaison would facilitate information-sharing between committees and encourage collaboration between them when possible and appropriate. The liaison would be well-positioned to stimulate intersectional analysis in its conversations with committees and in its efforts to encourage collaboration and information-sharing. If a country reports to the Committee on the Elimination of Racial Discrimination (CERD) and the CRPD within the same one- or two-year period, for example, the liaison could ensure that both committees receive information about rights violations targeting those at the intersection of non-majority racial or ethnic identity and disabilities in the reporting state. Conversations leading up to a review that the General Assembly was scheduled to undertake in 2020 suggest that some constituencies were recommending "focal points" that would perform much the same function as the liaisons that I recommended in the past.[23]

[18] *See* Methods of Work Relating to the State Reporting Process, *supra* note 15, ¶ 27; G.A. Res. 60/1, *supra* note 17, ¶ 125.

[19] *See* Johanna E. Bond, *International Intersectionality: A Theoretical and Pragmatic Exploration of Women's International Human Rights Violations*, 52 EMORY L.J. 71, 166, 179 (2003).

[20] *See id.* at 179.

[21] *See id.* at 163–64.

[22] *See id.* at 164–65.

[23] *See* GENEVA ACAD. OF INT'L HUMANITARIAN L. & HUM. RTS., *supra* note 1, at 31.

Although I realized that it was unlikely, I also suggested that the United Nations consider more radical structural reform. I proposed a dual committee structure with two consolidated committees: one with primary jurisdiction over individual communications and one with primary jurisdiction over State party reports.[24] This structure would differ significantly from the current structure, which involves nine core human rights bodies each monitoring the state reports and individual communications submitted pursuant to its mandate. The proposed consolidated committees would consist of expert representatives from the current committees, and I argued that the new structure would not require significantly more resources. Structural reforms of this magnitude would require amendment of the treaties, making this an unlikely outcome.

Over time, consolidated committee work would help reduce the backlog of State party reports. I recommended that the UN allow states to submit an omnibus state report to the consolidated committee handling state reports, instead of submitting individual reports to each body.[25] This would allow states to think more expansively about intersectional rights violations that may span the substantive rights of more than one treaty. It would, of course, also help the treaty bodies manage the backlog of state reports that plague the treaty body system by decreasing the total number of reports submitted. Requiring states to submit only one consolidated report reduces the reporting burden on states and makes the review process more streamlined for the treaty body. Equally important, however, are the benefits in terms of substantive rights. In a comprehensive review, the State party and the treaty body can explore rights violations that span multiple treaties. In other words, they can readily raise and consider intersectional human rights violations. For example, a state that has ratified the CEDAW, the CERD, the International Covenant on Economic, Social and Cultural Rights (ICESCR), and the International Covenant on Civil and Political Rights (ICCPR) might report that local authorities have been accused of requiring sexual favors in exchange for food in a food distribution program targeting an ethnic minority population in a poor, rural area of the country. To address the rights violation in full, a consolidated treaty body must explore intersectional rights affecting poor, ethnic minority women in the country and may refer to rights in multiple treaties.

Unlike most commentators, my rationale for significant structural reform was based primarily on opening channels for intersectionality in the work of the treaty bodies and secondarily on increasing the efficiency of the treaty bodies. By consolidating work in this way, I argued that the treaty bodies would be able to break down subject-specific silos and use an intersectional lens for analyzing human rights violations. The proposal was complicated and would have required amendment of the treaties, making the likelihood of its implementation low. My purpose, however, was to challenge the treaty bodies and civil society organizations to consider structural solutions that would facilitate intersectional analysis, including both solutions that require more dramatic reforms and solutions that require more modest structural or methodological changes.

[24] *See* Bond, *supra* note 19, at 169–75.

[25] *See id.* at 171–75.

Reform efforts 2005–2007: the Arbour proposal

In March 2005, the UN Secretary-General issued a further call for reform when he sought changes to promote the functioning of the treaty bodies as a "unified system."[26] In May 2005, in response to the Secretary-General's report, the Office of the High Commissioner for Human Rights (OHCHR) released a plan of action calling for relationship-building across and among treaty bodies and civil society to better support State actors.[27] The OHCHR emphasized the importance of cultivating current relationships as well as establishing new relationships both within and outside the existing treaty body system.[28] Then High Commissioner for Human Rights Louise Arbour submitted the OHCHR's plan of action as an addendum to the Secretary-General's remarks.[29] Under her leadership, the OHCHR developed a concept paper in 2006, building on the 2005 plan of action, that proposed a unified standing treaty body as a way to decrease costs and improve efficiency.[30] Arbour's proposal emphasized the need for greater interaction between her office and reporting states, increased financing, and harmonized reporting guidelines. It also proposed a unified standing treaty body. Several commentators criticized the concept paper because it failed to address concerns about privileging some rights and marginalizing others and did not provide alternatives to full-scale structural reform.[31] I will explore these critiques below.

The concept paper focused on the advantages a unified standing treaty body would bring to State parties and to victims of human rights. The concept paper states

> The treaty body system has developed ad hoc and it does not function as an integrated and indivisible framework for human rights protection.... The proposal of a unified standing treaty body is based on the premise that, unless the international human rights treaty system functions and is perceived as a unified, single entity responsible for monitoring the implementation of all international human rights obligations, with a single, accessible entry point for rights-holders, the lack of visibility, authority, and access which affects the current system will persist. The proposal is also based on the recognition that, as currently constituted, the system is approaching the limits of its performance, and that, while steps can be taken to improves its functioning in the short and medium term, more fundamental, structural change will be required in order to guarantee its effectiveness in the long term.[32]

[26] *See* U.N. Secretary-General, *In Larger Freedom: Towards Development, Security and Human Rights for All*, ¶ 147, U.N. Doc. A/59/2005 (Mar. 21, 2005). *See also* United Nations High Comm'r for Hum. Rts., The OHCHR Plan of Action: Protection and Empowerment ¶¶ 43–44 (2005), https://www2.ohchr.org/english/planaction.pdf.

[27] *See* united nations high comm'r for hum. rts., *supra* note 26, ¶¶ 43–44.

[28] *See id.*

[29] *See* U.N. Secretary-General, Letter dated May 26, 2005 from the Secretary-General to the President of the General Assembly, ¶ 147, U.N. Doc. A/59/2005/Add.3 (May 26, 2005).

[30] *See* U.N. Secretariat, Concept Paper on the High Commissioner's Proposal for a Unified Standing Treaty Body, ¶¶ 46, 50, U.N. Doc. HRI/MC/2006/2 (Mar. 22, 2006).

[31] *See* Suzanne Egan, The UN Human Rights Treaty System: Law and Procedure 462–63 (2011).

[32] U.N. Secretariat, *supra* note 30, ¶¶ 23, 27.

Arbour's proposal identified several possible structures for the unified standing treaty body. The options included a single chamber body, which would ensure consistency in the interpretation and meaning of rights. It is unlikely that such a structure would alleviate the backlog of reports, however, and if the body had a large number of members, it might make it more difficult to reach consensus. Another possibility was a single body with sub-units, or parallel chambers, with each of the chambers examining state reports and hearing individual complaints. This would allow the body to distribute the workload across the parallel chambers. Another option was to create the same structure of parallel chambers but allocate different responsibilities to each chamber, including examination of State parties' reports, individual complaints, follow-up and implementation, and country visits. A fourth possibility involved the creation of a single body with parallel chambers divided by treaty, although this would likely replicate some of the problems with the current system. A fifth option consisted of a single body with parallel chambers operating along thematic lines or "clusters of rights." Finally, the sixth option described a single body with parallel chambers focusing on different regions of the world.[33]

In addition to these major structural changes, the concept paper recommended streamlined reporting, such as an expanded core document supplemented by treaty-specific reports. In the alternative process, a State party's response to the list of issues could constitute its periodic report. The paper also identified other benefits to the unified standing treaty body, including improved follow-up procedures and early-warning and fact-finding responsibilities.[34]

Although Arbour's focus was on maximizing available resources and increasing the efficiency of the treaty body system, the concept paper also referenced a "holistic" approach to human rights. The concept paper noted that a unified standing body would offer a "framework for a comprehensive, cross-cutting and holistic approach to implementation of the treaties."[35] It did not elaborate on the advantages of a holistic approach to human rights or even explain the meaning of the term in the context of human rights. The references to a holistic approach, however, hint at an intersectional understanding of human rights. A later report concerning intersectionality within the work of the Special Rapporteur on violence against women, which was written by a team of experts in 2011, uses the term "holistic" to describe an intersectional approach that considers human rights violations that occur along multiple axes of identity, such as race and disability.[36]

The concept paper provoked a somewhat positive, albeit lukewarm, response among academics.[37] Other constituencies responded to the proposal with skepticism.

[33] *See id.* ¶¶ 40–45.

[34] *See id.* ¶¶ 52–54.

[35] *Id.* ¶ 28.

[36] *See* Lisa Crooms et al., *Intersectional and Multiple Forms of Discrimination in the Context of Violence Against Women: Background Paper Prepared for the Special Rapporteur on Violence Against Women, Its Causes and Consequences, Rashida Manjoo* ¶ 147 (Feb. 6, 2011).

[37] *See* EGAN, *supra* note 31, at 462 (citing Rachael Johnstone, *Cynical Savings or Reasonable Reform? Reflections on a Single Unified UN Human Rights Treaty Body*, 7 HUM. RTS. L. REV. 173 (2007); Michael O'Flaherty & Claire O'Brien, *Reform of UN Human Rights Treaty Monitoring Bodies: A Critique of the Concept Paper on the High Commissioner's Proposal for a Unified Standing Treaty Body*, 7 HUM. RTS. L. REV. 141 (2007)).

Liechtenstein hosted an informal meeting in July 2006 (commonly referred to as the Malbun II meeting) to brainstorm about and consider proposals to improve the efficacy of the treaty body system, including the OHCHR concept paper. Although some participants expressed support for the idea of a unified standing treaty body, many others expressed a desire for more information and more time to consider the proposal.[38]

According to the official record of the Liechtenstein meeting, the proposal "found little support."[39] The concerns articulated included the

> fear that the focus on specific issues which exists in the current system would be lost in a unified treaty body; that the creation of such a body would raise complex legal and political problems, not easily solved in the short or medium term; and that, fundamentally, there would be no guarantee that such a body would necessarily provide a solution to the current challenges facing the treaty system.[40]

Participants favored the more moderate approach, which is currently in use, of a core document that could be used by all committees along with subject-specific, supplementary reports for each of the relevant treaty bodies.

It is unsurprising that the expert members of the treaty bodies would be wary of a unified standing treaty body. The treaty body experts undoubtedly had concerns that a unified standing body would lead to a reduction in the number of treaty body experts, leaving some or many without an official role.[41] After this skepticism about the proposal, the subsequent High Commissioner for Human Rights, Navanthem Pillay, was more cautious in framing conversations about treaty body reform.[42] Arbour's proposal, nevertheless, stimulated important conversations about potential reform.

Another critique of consolidating into a unified standing treaty body or some less drastic form of consolidation is the legitimate concern that some rights will be systematically privileged over others. Not surprisingly, members of the CEDAW Committee have articulated this concern. They quite rightly express concern that women's rights could become lost or deprioritized in any consolidation of the treaty bodies. Advocates for women's rights fought for decades, and are still fighting, to ensure that gender equality rights do not receive less attention than other rights. The question then becomes whether it is possible to safeguard the specificity *and* breadth of human rights concerns within a more generalized system involving either one or two consolidated treaty bodies or a consolidated workload spread among multiple treaty bodies.

[38] *See* HUM. RTS. L. CTR., UNIV. OF NOTTINGHAM, THE DUBLIN STATEMENT ON THE PROCESS OF STRENGTHENING OF THE UNITED NATIONS HUMAN RIGHTS TREATY BODY SYSTEM: INFORMAL BACKGROUND PAPER 10 (2009), https://www2.ohchr.org/english/bodies/HRTD/docs/Informal_background_paper_Dublin_meeting.pdf.

[39] *See* EGAN, *supra* note 31, at 463 (citing Norbert Frick (Permanent Representative), Letter dated 18 September 2006 from the Permanent Mission of Liechtenstein to the United Nations Office at Geneva addressed to the High Commissioner for Human Rights, ¶ 12, U.N. Doc. A/HRC/2/G/5 (Sept. 25, 2006)).

[40] EGAN, *supra* note 31, at 464 (internal citations omitted).

[41] *Id.* at 463. Egan alludes to these "vested interests" in her observation that "[i]nterestingly, and perhaps predictably given some of the vested interests at stake, the reaction to the OHCHR's proposal on the part of the treaty bodies has been mostly negative." *Id.*

[42] *See id.* at 464.

To use CEDAW as an example, there have been sustained and effective efforts to mainstream gender equality across the United Nations and in regional and national human rights institutions. The success of those efforts has varied, but gender mainstreaming has generally become an expectation within human rights bodies. Building on the success of gender mainstreaming efforts, it is possible to establish structures and procedures that help keep gender equality prominent in discussions of human rights, even in the context of a consolidated, more generalized entity. Given the tendency to sideline gender, however, these efforts would require vigilance and some degree of oversight by the OHCHR, which would need staff dedicated for this purpose.

Such structures and strategies might include mandated coverage in the list of issues for each country. Gender equality concerns exist in every nation, and it would be reasonable to require coverage of gender or intersectional issues that include gender in every state report to a consolidated body or in a consolidated report. The US State Department Human Rights Report is an example of a country-specific report with mandated coverage of gender issues, which offers a structural solution that ensures coverage of gender equality. The OHCHR could require that the list of issues contain a minimum and maximum number of issues drawn from each of the relevant treaty bodies. To encourage thoughtful intersectional inquiry and discussion, the OHCHR would need to provide extensive training on intersectional human rights to treaty body members, staff at the OHCHR, and representatives of national human rights institutions.

In addition to the Arbour proposal and subsequent discussion, other conversations about human rights reform have also occurred outside of the context of the treaty body system. In 2006, the UN Human Rights Council created the Universal Periodic Review (UPR) mechanism, a process through which all 192 (now 193) UN member states are subject to a review concerning the status of human rights in the country. Unlike the UN treaty-based system, UPR is a peer review process in which other states form the reviewing body. NGOs participate in the process and may submit "credible and reliable" information to the OHCHR. Many of the treaty body reform conversations that have transpired since this process was established also discuss ways to ensure compatibility and reduce redundancy between the UPR process and the treaty body reporting process.

Reform efforts 2009–2012: the Dublin and "intergovernmental" processes

Conversations about potential reform or "strengthening" of the UN treaty body system have continued in the wake of Arbour's controversial concept paper. In 2014, human rights lawyer Michael O'Flaherty observed that for decades, different stakeholders had attempted to address UN treaty bodies issues, culminating in a 2009 initiative by Navi Pillay, the then-UN High Commissioner for Human Rights.[43] The 2009

[43] *See* Michael O'Flaherty, *The Strengthening Process of the Human Rights Treaty Bodies*, 108 Am. Soc'y of Int'l L. Proc. 285, 286 (2014).

reform process, known as the Dublin Process, included consultations with and recommendations by numerous stakeholders and led to two years of debate about the best ways to strengthen the treaty body system.[44] The reform process culminated in the UN High Commissioner's 2012 report, *Strengthening the United Nations Human Rights Treaty Body System.*[45]

The report offers a range of recommendations to ease the burden on reporting states, increase efficiency and visibility of the treaty bodies' work, and provide greater transparency in the election of independent experts who serve on the treaty bodies. Specifically, the report recommends changes to the schedule by which State parties report to the treaty bodies on their progress in implementing the terms of the treaties. High Commissioner Pillay's 2012 report recommends the establishment of a comprehensive reporting calendar for all of the treaty bodies, ensuring (at least theoretically) equal treatment of all State parties and greater compliance with reporting deadlines.[46] The report also recommends, "increasing coordination among the treaty bodies on their work on individual communications and their adoption of common guidelines on procedural questions" and "alignment of other working methods to the maximum extent without contradicting the normative specificities of the treaties."[47] These latter two recommendations involve the kind of collaboration that could, to a limited extent, create small openings for intersectional analysis within the work of the treaty bodies.

The Dublin Process was not entirely smooth. In 2012, a group of states organized a rival reform process called the "intergovernmental process" which threatened to restrict the access and participation of human rights defenders in treaty body processes.[48] The need for additional resources to support the treaty bodies and NGO participation in treaty body processes became flashpoints in the intergovernmental process. The intergovernmental process continued with state and NGO consultations in 2013. However, the higher-profile Dublin Process largely overshadowed the intergovernmental process.

Reform efforts 2014–2020

Efforts to fortify and reform the treaty body system continue to this day. In 2014, the UN General Assembly adopted Resolution 68/268, entitled "Strengthening and Enhancing the Effective Functioning of the Human Rights Treaty Body System," in which it committed to considering potential reforms to the system by April 2020.[49] In the lead-up to the General Assembly's 2020 efforts to strengthen the treaty body system, constituencies provided proposals and recommendations to the Assembly

[44] *See id.*

[45] *See* Navanethem Pillay (United Nations High Commissioner for Human Rights), *Strengthening the United Nations Human Rights Treaty Body System*, at 10, 37 (June 2012), https://www2.ohchr.org/english/bodies/HRTD/docs/HCReportTBStrengthening.pdf.

[46] *See id.* at 10.

[47] *Id.* at 10–11.

[48] *See* Int'l Serv. for Hum. Rts., *Update on Treaty Body Reform: Discussion Moves to the General Assembly*, 4 Hum. Rts. Monitor Q. 22, 22 (2012). The states who pushed for the creation of the intergovernmental process include China and Russia and are described as "less progressive." *Id.* at 23.

[49] *See* G.A. Res. 68/268, *supra* note 4, ¶ 41.

in three primary ways: (1) the Chairpersons of the treaty bodies issued a 2019 position paper articulating the reform priorities from the perspective of the treaty bodies themselves;[50] (2) forty-three states endorsed a proposal submitted by Costa Rica, which made recommendations for strengthening the system;[51] and (3) civil society organizations (CSOs) coalesced around a joint proposal, signed by thirty organizations, recommending changes to the working methods of the treaty bodies to improve the functioning of the system.[52] Outside groups and human rights organizations also engaged in reform discussion and proposal development, including expert group meetings and a far-reaching report from the Geneva Academy. The following pages explore these various proposals in response to Resolution 68/268.

Chairpersons' June 2019 position paper

The Chairpersons' June 2019 position paper suggests potential improvements to aid the functioning of the system. The paper focuses on aligning the working methods of the treaty bodies and addresses primarily procedural and methodological issues, such as simplified reporting procedures and expectations for the review of States parties' reports.[53]

The paper does not address aligning the treaty bodies' interpretations of substantive rights. Although the paper focuses on procedural concerns, the Chairpersons missed an opportunity to discuss the treaty bodies' approach to overlapping rights such as non-discrimination and to discuss strategies for addressing intersectional rights. The position paper does attempt to reduce "unnecessary overlap," stating, "All treaty bodies will coordinate their list of issues prior to reporting to ensure that their dialogues with State parties are comprehensive and do not raise substantively similar questions in the same time period."[54] This suggests a willingness to coordinate and collaborate on the content of the substantive dialog with states. Thus, if the treaty bodies committed to an intersectional normative framework, they would have opportunities to coordinate such an approach in their reviews of State parties' reports.

The Chairpersons could take a similar approach in coordinating the list of issues among the treaty bodies to address intersectional issues. This substantive coordination concerning the treaty bodies' agendas with reporting states offers an opportunity

[50] *See* U.N. Secretary-General, *Implementation of Human Rights Instruments: Position Paper of the Chairs of the Human Rights Treaty Bodies on the Future of the Treaty Body System*, at 19–21, U.N. Doc. A/74/256, annex III (July 30, 2019).

[51] *See* Permanent Mission of Costa Rica, Towards the 2020 Treaty Bodies Review, in letter dated June 20, 2019 from the Permanent Mission of Costa Rica to the United Nations addressed to the Human Rights Treaty Branch of the Office of the High Commissioner for Human Rights, at 2, REF. MPCR-ONUG/2019-231 (June 20, 2019), https://tbinternet.ohchr.org/Treaties/CHAIRPERSONS/Shared%20Documents/1_Global/INT_CHAIRPERSONS_CHR_31_28571_E.pdf?Mobile=1&Source=%2FTreaties%2FCHAIRPERSONS%2F%5Flayouts%2F15%2Fmobile%2Fviewa%2Easpx%3FList%3Da3af4f41%2D6269%2D4984%2D88f9%2D775592b28f41%26View%3D407df2ac%2Dbff1%2D4603%2D87e8%2D8e1d3c44912a%26RootFolder%3D%252FTreaties%252FCHAIRPERSONS%252FShared%2BDocuments%252F1%5FGlobal%26PageFirstRow%3D41%26wdFCCState%3D1.

[52] *See* Ctr. for Civ. & Pol. Rts. et al., Towards a Strengthened UN Treaty Body System: Civil Society Proposals 3–4 (Sept. 23, 2019), https://www.ishr.ch/sites/default/files/documents/joint_ngo_proposal_on_untb_reviews.pdf.

[53] *See* U.N. Secretary-General, *supra* note 50, at 19–20.

[54] *Id.* at 19.

to carefully include intersectional issues in the list of issues for the relevant treaty bodies and the relevant States. The position paper also commits treaty bodies to an aligned methodology with respect to concluding observations. The Chairpersons aim to create concluding observations that are "short, focussed [sic], concrete and prioritized, balancing immediate with longer term priorities and objectives."[55] Here, too, the process of aligning concluding observations could facilitate intersectional analysis if the treaty bodies pursued these conversations with purpose and intentionality. The treaty bodies, however, must first incorporate this normative objective into their conversations about strengthening the treaty body system.

Costa Rican proposal

The Costa Rican proposal presented the State parties' viewpoint on strengthening the treaty body system. Supported by forty-three State parties, the Costa Rican proposal highlighted several for improvement and named different factors that the General Assembly should keep in mind when implementing changes. For example, the proposal echoed similar suggestions for improvement by calling for the harmonization of treaty bodies' efforts to "avoid the overlapping of questions, topics and recommendations."[56]

One way to achieve harmonization is through a simplified reporting structure and coordination of deadlines to avoid overwhelming State parties with reporting requests.[57] Like the Chairpersons' policy paper and the CSO proposal, discussed below, the Costa Rican proposal mainly focused on procedural improvements rather than on the effect of any changes on substantive rights. Thus, the proposal missed the opportunity to promote an intersectional framework of analysis within the treaty body system.

Expert group meetings

The 2014 General Assembly resolution led human rights experts to hold several group meetings to discuss ways to improve the treaty body system. These expert group meetings often resulted in reports that summarized the meetings' conclusions and provided recommendations to the UN on strengthening the treaty body system.

Columbia University embarked on a research project entitled "Human Rights Treaty Body Reform Process: Towards a Stronger Human Rights Protection Regime."[58] The project consisted of three expert group meetings in 2016 and 2017. Topics included treaty body collaboration with outside organizations such as national human rights institutions (NHRIs) and CSOs and encouraging treaty bodies to follow up with State parties.[59] While the reports addressed the procedural hurdles faced by the treaty body system and ways to make the system more efficient, however, the meetings did not include a discussion of facilitating intersectional analysis.

[55] *Id.* at 20.

[56] *See* Permanent Mission of Costa Rica, *supra* note 51, at 3.

[57] *See id.*

[58] *See Human Rights Treaty Body Reform*, Colum. Univ. Inst. for the Study of Hum. Rts., http://www.humanrightscolumbia.org/research/treaty-body-reform(last visited May 4, 2021).

[59] *See* Colum. Univ. & Geneva Acad., Regional Consultation for Northern America 10 (2017), http://humanrightscolumbia.org/sites/default/files/pdf/treaty_reform_new_york_consultation_2017.pdf.

A similar meeting took place in 2015 at Wilton Park between UN stakeholders.[60] Participants noted the importance of focusing on long-term sustainability and improvements to the treaty body system.[61] Again, the bulk of the meeting focused on improving the processes and efficiency of the treaty body system, particularly for communications with State parties.[62]

Civil society organizations' proposal

The expert group meetings also provided a foundation for civil society organizations that initiated proposals for strengthening treaty bodies in light of the 2014 General Assembly resolution. A 2019 joint proposal from thirty CSOs[63] recommended improvements to the working methods of the treaty bodies but, like the 2019 Chairpersons' position paper, did not meaningfully address the interpretation of substantive rights.[64] The proposal largely failed to consider how procedural changes might influence consideration of substantive rights. As such, CSOs missed an opportunity to consider and recommend changes that might enhance the treaty bodies' ability to address intersectional human rights violations.

The CSO proposal did make one procedural recommendation that, if adopted, could positively influence the treaty bodies' ability to consider intersectionality in the state reporting process. The proposal recommended the creation of focal points in every treaty body "to liaise with each other on different matters, and systematically [hold] inter-Committee meetings ... to help coordination."[65] This recommendation is similar to my 2003 recommendation that the UN create liaisons between the treaty bodies to facilitate coordination and intersectional analysis. The CSO proposal does not, however, specifically articulate any benefits related to intersectional analysis in the recommendation to create focal points.

Geneva Academy report

The aforementioned proposals support modest methodological changes. Many explicitly articulate a commitment to incremental change, and all express a desire to avoid altering the legal framework of the treaties. Many forms of dramatic structural change would require amendment of the treaties, and some worry that this could undermine the effort to protect human rights around the world.

A few reports and proposals have considered the effects of more dramatic structural change, although almost all stop short of changes that would require legal amendment. An example comes from the Geneva Academy of International Humanitarian Law and Human Rights.[66] In anticipation of the General Assembly's 2020 treaty body

[60] *See* Wilton Park, Strengthening the UN Human Rights Treaty Monitoring System: What Are the Next Steps? (2015), https://www.wiltonpark.org.uk/wp-content/uploads/WP1375-Report.pdf.

[61] *See id.* at 3.

[62] *See id.* at 4–5.

[63] *See* towards a strengthened un treaty body system: civil society proposals, *supra* note 52, at 5–6. As of October 22, 2019, the number of signatory organizations was thirty.

[64] *See id.* at 2 ("The UNTBs should strengthen the coordination of their substantive work, in particular in relation to General Comments and Concluding Observations/Recommendations, in order to avoid inconsistencies and ensure complementarity in protection standards and mutual reinforcement.").

[65] *Id.* at 3.

[66] The Geneva Academy, which is part of the University of Geneva, offers postgraduate education and acts as a research center focusing on human rights, humanitarian law, and transitional justice.

review, the Geneva Academy solicited written submissions from stakeholders and organized regional and thematic consultations on the treaty body reform process. The Geneva Academy's resulting report, published in May 2018, reflects the recommendations and proposals of a large group of stakeholders, including academics, representatives of NGOs, members of NHRIs, treaty body members, and staff of the Office of the High Commissioner for Human Rights.[67]

The Geneva Academy report expresses a commitment to structural change that does not immediately require treaty amendment. The report, however, exhibits a higher tolerance for considering more dramatic, longer-term structural change that may be necessary to sustain the work of the treaty bodies over the long haul. As far as State reporting procedures go, the report recommends two possibilities for reform, both involving a consolidation of State reports. The first option is a single review of a consolidated State report.[68] In this case, a reporting State would submit one consolidated report to all treaty bodies, and all of the treaty bodies would examine the State during a one-week session that would include each of the treaty bodies. The single state report (SSR) would include a general section followed by treaty-specific sections. Before submitting its SSR, the reporting State would receive a consolidated list of issues from the treaty bodies. The treaty bodies would treat the State's response to the list of issues as its periodic report.[69] This cycle of reporting would require all the treaty bodies to sit in session during the same week every four to five years, or could accommodate a reporting cycle of every eight years.

The report's second option also consolidates state reporting but to a lesser extent. In this version, states would submit a report to a cluster of treaty bodies every four years.[70] The OHCHR might divide treaty bodies into two clusters, with the more general Covenant treaty bodies (the Human Rights Committee and the Committee on Economic, Social, and Cultural Rights) in one cluster and the subject-specific treaty bodies in another.[71] States would then alternate between reporting to the clusters, with states submitting one report every four years.

In either case, the treaty bodies would collaborate on a consolidated list of issues for each reporting State. If the treaty bodies adopted this approach, collaboration on the list of issues would open the door for the treaty bodies to systematically consider intersectional human rights issues that straddle the substantive rights in multiple treaties. To some extent, this is already happening in the context of individual treaty bodies' lists of issues. For example, in its prepared list of issues for Senegal in 2020, the CEDAW Committee specified:

> Please provide up-to-date data, disaggregated by relevant factors, on the enjoyment by disadvantaged groups of women, including women and girls with disabilities, lesbian, bisexual and transgender women, intersex persons and older women, of their rights and of access to basic services and accessible infrastructure, for example

[67] *See* GENEVA ACAD. OF INT'L HUMANITARIAN L. & HUM. RTS., *supra* note 1, at 3.
[68] *See id.* at 7.
[69] *See id.*
[70] *See id.*
[71] *See id.*

schools, workplaces and public spaces, and on measures to tackle the intersecting forms of discrimination and violence that such persons face.[72]

Although each treaty body would have opportunity to craft concluding observations for the reporting state, the secretariat would consolidate the concluding observations to reduce redundancy and contradictory recommendations from the various treaty bodies.[73] The secretariat could also use this opportunity to help identify intersectional issues and seek input from the treaty bodies on concluding observations that are ripe for intersectional analysis.

The Geneva Academy report also notes that the treaty bodies "could decide to establish an inter-committee working group to follow up their recommendations and views. This would help to reduce or avoid any protection gaps in relation to specific rights."[74] Any inter-committee working group would facilitate collaboration between the committees and lead to greater coordination of working methods. More importantly for purposes of extending the reach of intersectional analysis within the UN, inter-committee working groups would also help align committee interpretations of overlapping substantive rights. By extension, it could also encourage inter-committee conversations about intersectional rights. Some proposals reviewed by the Geneva Academy favored a joint working group on individual communications, which would better align the treaty bodies' approach to remedies for violations of individual rights.[75] The report observes, "The Committees could improve communication with each other, and harmonize their working methods, by sharing information and, more directly, holding joint meetings."[76] These efforts at harmonization and the establishment of joint meetings would undoubtedly create more opportunities for the treaty bodies to consider those intersectional rights that span multiple treaties.

In response to the Geneva Academy report, twenty-five human rights experts met in Oslo in 2018.[77] Their purpose was to discuss the report's proposals within the context of the experiences of human rights stakeholders and to discern whether stakeholders believed the proposals to be feasible and necessary.[78] Stakeholders voiced concern over the proposed eight-year reporting cycle, believing that it would create "too long a gap for effective human rights monitoring."[79] Participants also discussed ways to improve the State reporting process by introducing the use of standardized key words and shortening the time between State report submission and treaty body review.[80] Overall, this meeting focused on improving the treaty body reporting process rather than addressing gaps in substantive human rights analysis.

[72] Comm. on the Elimination of All Forms of Discrimination against Women, List of Issues and Questions in Relation to the Eighth Periodic Report of Senegal, ¶ 19, U.N. Doc. CEDAW/C/SEN/Q/8 (Mar. 11, 2020).

[73] *See* GENEVA ACAD. OF INT'L HUMANITARIAN L. & HUM. RTS., *supra* note 1, at 22.

[74] *Id.*

[75] *See id.* at 25.

[76] *Id.* at 27.

[77] *See* NORWEGIAN CTR. FOR HUM. RTS., THE UN HUMAN RIGHTS TREATY BODY REVIEW AGENDA 2020: SCOPE FOR LOCAL AND NATIONAL ENGAGEMENT 1 (2018), https://www.geneva-academy.ch/joomlatools-files/docman-files/Oslo%20Consultation%20-%20Final.pdf.

[78] *See id.*

[79] *Id.* at 2.

[80] *See id.* at 3.

It is important to note that the 2019 joint CSO proposal mentioned in the previous section was written after the Geneva Academy report and incorporated some of its suggestions.[81] The CSO proposal does not contemplate longer-term, dramatic changes in the same way that the Geneva Academy report does; instead, it focuses on short-term coordination and a strengthening of the role that CSOs play in the reporting process.[82] Additionally, the CSO proposal advocates for a four-year reporting cycle with comprehensive and focused reviews.

The Geneva Academy report notes that some constituencies proposed a standing, unified treaty body similar to that proposed by Louise Arbour in 2006 and by me in 2003.[83] The report comments that such a system would create the "strongest synergy between [treaty bodies]."[84] This standing, unified treaty body would require the reopening of the treaties, which would have its own costs.[85] There are, however, more moderate approaches that would increase opportunities for intersectional analysis, such as more efficient cooperation among the treaties and greater harmonization of their "working methods and jurisprudence."[86] Structural change that falls short of a unified standing treaty body could still facilitate intersectional analysis and improve the efficiency and effectiveness of the treaty bodies.

Building on past reform efforts to facilitate intersectional analysis within the treaty body system

So far I have considered the primary proposals to date for reforming the structure of the treaty body system. At their most extreme, these proposals, including my 2003 proposal, involve consolidation of the treaty bodies into one or two committees. This streamlined structure would likely allow the consolidated committee to better manage the influx of State parties' reports, reduce the reporting burden on States, and potentially reduce the financial pressure on the treaty body system. In addition to these practical benefits, consolidation has the potential to facilitate more thorough and more consistent intersectional human rights analysis. Breaking down the silos within which the treaty bodies conduct much of their work allows for an intersectional framework that cuts across multiple treaties.

A consolidated approach has drawbacks, including the risk that a consolidated committee would privilege certain rights over others and the risk that opening the treaties up for legal amendment could lead to backsliding. Although it may be possible to prevent or minimize the negative effects of consolidation, the OHCHR needs to study the benefits and drawbacks more extensively. To date, almost all reform discussions

[81] *See NGOs Meet in Geneva to Discuss Strengthening of UN Treaty Bodies*, CTR. FOR CIV. & POL. RTS. (July 8, 2019), http://ccprcentre.org/ccprpages/ngos-meet-at-geneva-to-discuss-strengthening-of-un-treaty-bodies.

[82] *See* TOWARDS A STRENGTHENED UN TREATY BODY SYSTEM: CIVIL SOCIETY PROPOSALS, *supra* note 52, at 4–5.

[83] *See* GENEVA ACAD. OF INT'L HUMANITARIAN L. & HUM. RTS., *supra* note 1, at 29.

[84] *Id.*

[85] *See id.*

[86] *Id.*

have focused exclusively on the practical benefits of reform, such as reducing the reporting burden on states, creating a manageable workload for treaty body representatives, and offering a predictable schedule for reporting states. Should the OHCHR assess the consolidation option, there must be a corresponding focus on the benefits and drawbacks in terms of substantive rights, including the possibility of enhanced intersectional analysis.

Some of the treaty bodies have already implemented a streamlined reporting procedure. Consistent with recommendations for reform,[87] the CEDAW Committee, for example, adopted a process in 2014 for developing its lists of issues for states, and those responses constitute the state's subsequent periodic report to the Committee.[88] For those committees adopting a similar approach,[89] the preparation of the list of issues allows treaty bodies to focus on the most pressing human rights concerns within the reporting state. It also provides an opportunity to focus states' reporting on relevant intersectional issues. By 2015, eight treaty bodies had agreed to offer states a simplified reporting procedure.[90]

[87] *See* G.A. Res. 68/268, *supra* note 4, ¶¶ 1–2.

[88] *See* Comm. on the Elimination of All Forms of Discrimination against Women, Guidance Note for States Parties for the Preparation of Reps. under Article 18 of the Convention on the Elimination of All Forms of Discrimination against Women in the Context of the Sustainable Development Goals, ¶ 7, U.N. Doc. CEDAW/C/74/3 (Dec. 18, 2019). This simplified reporting procedure was suspended in November 2016, but the Committee reinstated it in March 2018. *See Committee on the Elimination of Discrimination against Women: Simplified Reporting Procedure*, OFF. OF THE HIGH COMM'R OF HUM. RTS., https://www.ohchr.org/EN/HRBodies/CEDAW/Pages/ReportingProcedures.aspx (last visited May 4, 2021).

[89] Six committees have adopted a simplified procedure. *See Human Rights Committee: Simplified Reporting Procedure*, OFF. OF THE HIGH COMM'R OF HUM. RTS., https://www.ohchr.org/EN/HRBodies/CCPR/Pages/SimplifiedReportingProcedure.aspx (last visited May 4, 2021) (HRC Committee); *Committee on the Elimination of Discrimination against Women: Simplified Reporting Procedure*, OFF. OF THE HIGH COMM'R OF HUM. RTS., https://www.ohchr.org/EN/HRBodies/CEDAW/Pages/ReportingProcedures.aspx (last visited May 4, 2021) (CEDAW Committee); *Committee Against Torture: Optional Reporting Procedure*, OFF. OF THE HIGH COMM'R OF HUM. RTS., https://www.ohchr.org/EN/HRBodies/CAT/Pages/ReportingProcedures.aspx (last visited May 4, 2021) (Committee Against Torture); *Committee on the Rights of the Child: Simplified Reporting Procedure*, OFF. OF THE HIGH COMM'R OF HUM. RTS., https://www.ohchr.org/EN/HRBodies/CRC/Pages/ReportingProcedure.aspx (last visited May 4, 2021) (CRC); *Committee on Migrant Workers: Monitoring the Protection of the Rights of All Migrant Workers and Members of Their Families*, OFF. OF THE HIGH COMM'R OF HUM. RTS., https://www.ohchr.org/EN/HRBodies/CMW/Pages/CMWIndex.aspx (last visited Mar. 10, 2021) (CMW); *Committee on the Rights of Persons with Disabilities: Simplified Reporting Procedure*, OFF. OF THE HIGH COMM'R OF HUM. RTS., https://www.ohchr.org/EN/HRBodies/CRPD/Pages/Simplifiedreportingprocedure.aspx (last visited May 4, 2021) (CRPD). If the other committees—the Committee on Enforced Disappearances, the Committee on the Elimination of Racial Discrimination, and the Committee on Economic, Social and Cultural Rights—currently use a simplified procedure, it is not indicated on the face of the individual treaty pages on the OHCHR website.

[90] The report of the Meeting of the Treaty Body Chairpersons summarized those commitments to a simplified reporting procedure as follows:

> Eight treaty bodies agreed in principle to offer to States parties the simplified reporting procedure. Four treaty bodies, namely, the Committee against Torture (CAT), the Human Rights Committee (HR Committee), the Committee on the Protection of the Rights of All Migrant Workers and Members of Their Families (CMW) and the Committee on the Rights of Persons with Disabilities (CRPD), were already offering or had already decided to offer the simplified reporting procedure prior to the adoption of General Assembly resolution 68/268. Since the adoption of that resolution and the recommendation issued by the chairpersons on the subject at their twenty-sixth meeting, another four treaty bodies have decided to make available the simplified reporting procedure, namely, the Committee on the Rights of the Child (CRC), the Committee on Economic, Social and Cultural Rights (CESCR), the Committee on the Elimination of Discrimination against Women (CEDAW) and the Committee on the Elimination of Racial

The following pages highlight areas within past and current reform efforts that open the door for intersectional analysis. Any treaty body reform needs to include an intersectional framework and provide stakeholders, particularly State parties, with the tools to discuss and analyze intersectional issues. This section will examine ways in which the system currently allows for intersectional analysis as well as places where the opportunity for intersectional frameworks can be created.

General Recommendations and General Comments within and between treaty bodies

The treaty bodies should consider either individually or jointly adopting a general comment or general recommendation that comprehensively addresses intersectionality in human rights analysis.[91] General recommendations (or, depending on the committee, general comments) serve a dual purpose: (1) they seek to guide State parties in the implementation of treaty provisions, and (2) they serve to clarify state obligations for NGOs and the general public. These documents could serve as cogent mechanisms for promoting intersectionality within the human rights system.

The CEDAW Committee has addressed intersectionality in past general recommendations, specifically in General Recommendation No. 28. Adopted in 2010, it addresses states' core obligations pursuant to Article 2 of the treaty. As noted earlier, General Recommendation No. 28 mentions intersectionality in one paragraph[92] and includes several other brief references to intersecting rights or particularly vulnerable women, thereby articulating a commitment to intersectionality. It does not, however, offer an exhaustive or even thorough discussion of the concept and its centrality to the contemporary human rights framework. The issue of intersectionality, like the issue of gender-based violence, needs to be more fully addressed in a more comprehensive and

> Discrimination (CERD). Some are doing so on a pilot or trial basis (CESCR and CEDAW), some with certain modalities (CRC after it reduces the backlog, CEDAW on the condition that States parties submit an updated common core document in the preceding five years, or less in case of significant political or socioeconomic changes) and some for a limited number of periodic reports (CERD for reports more than five years overdue, CESCR as of the third periodic report). One committee (CEDAW) decided to limit strictly the number of questions asked in the questionnaire for the simplified reporting procedure, referred to as the list of issues prior to reporting, to 25.

U.N. Secretariat, Implementation by Treaty Bodies of the Conclusions and Recommendations of the Treaty Body Chairpersons at Their Twenty-sixth Meeting in the Framework of General Assembly Resolution 68/268, ¶ 6, UN Doc. HRI/MC/2015/2 (April 13, 2015).

[91] Some treaty bodies refer to these as general recommendations while others call them general comments.

[92] *See* Comm. on the Elimination of Discrimination against Women, Gen. Recommendation No. 28 on the Core Obligations of States Parties under Article 2 of the Convention on the Elimination of All Forms of Discrimination against Women, ¶ 18, U.N. Doc. CEDAW/C/GC/28 (Dec. 16, 2010).

> Intersectionality is a basic concept for understanding the scope of the general obligations of States parties contained in article 2. The discrimination of women based on sex and gender is inextricably linked with other factors that affect women, such as race, ethnicity, religion or belief, health, status, age, class, caste, and sexual orientation and gender identity. Discrimination on the basis of sex or gender may affect women belonging to such groups to a different degree or in different ways to men. States parties must legally recognize such intersecting forms of discrimination and their compounded negative impact on the women concerned and prohibit them.

far-reaching general recommendation that offers clear guidance to State parties concerning the adoption of an intersectional approach.

The CEDAW Committee's work since 2018 reflects a stronger commitment to an intersectional framework than has existed in the past. In 2019, for example, the Committee produced a draft General Recommendation on Trafficking in Women and Girls in the context of Global Migration. The draft specifically "identifies the higher risk faced by women and girls subjected to multiple and intersecting forms of discrimination, particularly women and girls in poverty, living in remote areas, forcibly displaced women and girls and women and girl migrants."[93] Indeed, the draft includes a subheading addressing "multiple forms and compounded discrimination." That subsection elaborates as follows:

> Discrimination on the basis of sex or gender may affect women belonging to groups in situations of vulnerability in different ways. Women are not a homogenous group and their experiences as trafficking victims are diverse. States parties are required to proactively identify as rights-bearers women and girls within the jurisdiction of the State party who are marginalized, being subjected to multiple forms of discrimination, including non-citizen, migrant, refugee, asylum-seeking and stateless women and girls, and women and girls with an irregular migration status.[94]

In another example from 2018, the CEDAW Committee adopted a general recommendation entitled "Gender-Related Dimensions of Disaster Risk Reduction in the context of Climate Change." It refers to intersectionality several times, reflecting the slowly emerging trend toward intersectionality in the Committee's work. Among other things, the general recommendation frames the discussion with the following observation:

> Situations of crisis exacerbate pre-existing gender inequalities and compound the intersecting forms of discrimination against, among others, women living in poverty, indigenous women, women belonging to ethnic, racial, religious and sexual minority groups, women with disabilities, refugee and asylum-seeking women, internally displaced, stateless and migrant women, rural women, unmarried women, adolescents and older women, who are often disproportionately affected compared with men or other women.[95]

General Recommendation No. 37 includes language that specifically rejects the reductionist practice of defining women and girls solely in terms of vulnerability. It states, "The categorization of women and girls as passive 'vulnerable groups' in need of protection from the impacts of disasters is a negative gender stereotype that fails to recognize the important contributions of women in the areas of disaster risk reduction,

[93] Comm. on the Elimination of Discrimination against Women, Draft Gen. Recommendation on Trafficking in Women and Girls in the Context of Global Migration, ¶ 12 (2019).

[94] *Id.* ¶ 18.

[95] Comm. on the Elimination of Discrimination against Women, Gen. Recommendation No. 37 (2018) on the Gender-Related Dimensions of Disaster Risk Reduction in the Context of Climate Change, CEDAW/C/GC/37, ¶ 2 (Mar. 13, 2018).

post-disaster management and climate change mitigation and adaptation strategies."[96] This critique of the notion of vulnerability represents progress in the committee's articulation of women's experiences of discrimination and subordination. As described in earlier chapters, the treaty bodies have often substituted reductionist notions of vulnerability for well-developed notions of intersectionality. In this poor approximation of intersectionality, the treaty bodies describe minority ethnic women and disabled women as "particularly vulnerable." This description elides agency and fails to recognize these women as potential agents of social change. As demonstrated by General Recommendation No. 37, the CEDAW Committee appears poised to recalibrate its own understanding of vulnerability and more comprehensively recognize women's experiences, which are multifaceted, intersecting, and agentic.

Although the integration of intersectional analysis into general recommendations and comments is beginning to happen in a piecemeal way, the CEDAW Committee and other treaty bodies should seek to do so more consistently. By providing this kind of authoritative substantive guidance on the meaning of treaty obligations, the treaty bodies can and should encourage States parties to systematically report on intersectional human rights violations.

In addition to publishing a general recommendation or comment that specifically and thoroughly addresses intersectionality, the treaty bodies should more frequently collaborate on their composition. Many human rights issues involve substantive rights from more than one human rights treaty. Joint general recommendations can help align the treaty bodies' approaches to normative human rights law. Joint recommendations or comments also offer the treaty bodies an opportunity to explore intersectional rights that straddle two or more treaties.

There are successful examples of this type of collaboration. In 2014, the CEDAW Committee and the Committee on the Rights of the Child (CRC) became the first treaty bodies to jointly issue a general recommendation/comment. It addressed harmful traditional practices that adversely affect women and girls.[97] It defines harmful practices in intersectional terms by emphasizing "discrimination on the basis of, among other things, sex, gender, and age in addition to multiple and/or intersecting forms of discrimination that often involve violence and cause physical and/or psychological harm or suffering."[98] The fact that the CEDAW Committee and the CRC jointly drafted the general recommendation/comment ensured that, at a minimum, the committees would address the intersection of gender and age. Other treaty bodies should explore the drafting and adoption of joint general recommendations/comments to more fully address intersectional rights.

Reporting guidelines to States parties

In addition to general recommendations and comments, many of the treaty bodies issue additional guidelines to states and NGOs about what should be included in the

[96] *Id.* ¶ 7.

[97] *See* Joint Statement, Comm. on the Elimination of Discrimination against Women & Comm. on the Rights of the Child, Joint Gen. Recommendation No. 31 of the Comm. on the Elimination of Discrimination Against Women/Gen. Comment No. 18 of the Comm. on the Rights of the Child on Harmful Practices, ¶ 17, U.N. Doc. CEDAW/C/GC/31-CRC/C/GC/18 (Nov. 14, 2014).

[98] *Id.* ¶ 15.

State parties' reports. These guidelines provide another critical opportunity for the treaty bodies to shape the type and content of reports they receive from States parties pursuant to the reporting requirements of the individual treaties.

For example, in late 2019, the CEDAW Committee issued a new guidance document for State parties that reinforces the simplified reporting procedure and offers guidance as to the substantive content of State parties' reports.[99] As of early 2020, this document represents the most robust embrace of intersectionality from the CEDAW Committee. The guidance document frames the reporting obligation in terms of a core commitment to discrimination against women, including "intersecting, multiple, vertical and horizontal forms of discrimination."[100] For each article of the convention, the document addresses three components of compliance: the legal framework, enforcement and monitoring measures, and data analysis. In the legal framework section for each article, the Committee identifies questions about the legal protection offered by the state. In some cases, the legal framework subsection specifically refers to intersectional rights, such as the discussion of Article 4 on temporary special measures, which requires reporting on "[w]hether there are specific measures (mandatory or voluntary) for women who may experience intersecting discrimination, such as migrant or indigenous women."[101]

The guidance document includes the most references to intersectionality in its data analysis section. As of early 2020, the Committee appeared to be most willing to hold states accountable for intersectionality in the collection and reporting of data. In its discussion of Article 11, for example, the Committee requires that State parties report on "[t]he social protection and retirement schemes (type, average amount, sex, urban and rural area, age, disability status and ethnicity)."[102] In fact, of the sixteen data points that the Committee seeks in relation to Article 11, thirteen of them require data disaggregated by some combination of intersectional identities such as age, disability, sex, and urban or rural area.[103] Read as a whole, the document represents a significant step forward in the recognition and embrace of intersectionality in the Committee's work.

The guidance document, nevertheless, omits important points regarding intersectional human rights analysis. In its discussion of the legal framework of Article 12 on the right to health, for example, the Committee fails to mention intersectionality, despite seeking information related to prohibitions on forced sterilization and coercive abortion. Given the considerable research that demonstrates that forced sterilization is often targeted at racial or ethnic minority women,[104] it is surprising that the guidance document omits any reference to intersectionality here. Although the document requires extensive health-related data disaggregated along intersectional lines,[105] the intersectional focus is limited to data collection in the context of health. Even here, the

[99] *See* Comm. on the Elimination of All Forms of Discrimination against Women, *supra* note 88, ¶¶ 7–13.
[100] *Id.* ¶ 16(b).
[101] *Id.* ¶ 22(b).
[102] *Id.* ¶ 42(m).
[103] *See id.* ¶¶ 42(a)–(p).
[104] *See supra* notes 65–67, 74–77 and accompanying text (chapter 2).
[105] *See* Comm. on the Elimination of All Forms of Discrimination against Women, *supra* note 88, ¶¶ 45 (a)–(j).

document seeks data on forced sterilization without any reference to data disaggregated by race, ethnicity, or any other facet of identity.[106]

Despite these shortcomings, the guidance document reflects a strong and growing commitment to intersectional human rights analysis within the CEDAW Committee's work. The document is designed to guide State parties in the preparation of their human rights reports and, as such, offers a vehicle fostering intersectional analysis at the national level. The guidance document serves an educative role at the national level and brings the Committee closer to a paradigmatic embrace of intersectionality. By adopting interpretive guidelines that express a similar commitment to intersectionality, each of the other treaty bodies could similarly foster intersectional analysis at the domestic level.

Joint statements: another opportunity for treaty body collaboration

Joint statements present another opportunity to explore intersectional human rights violations that span multiple human rights treaties. The Committee on the Rights of Persons with Disabilities (CRPD) and the CEDAW Committee, for example, issued a joint statement in 2019 entitled "Guaranteeing sexual and reproductive health and rights for all women, in particular women with disabilities."[107] The statement explicitly adopts an intersectional approach, noting that women with disabilities "continue to experience intersecting forms of discrimination."[108]

In another example, five treaty bodies issued a joint statement in 2019 addressing the harmful effects of climate change. CEDAW, the Committee on Economic, Social, and Cultural Rights (CESCR), the Committee on the Protection of All Migrant Workers and Members of their Families (CPMW), the CRC, and the CRPD expressed concern that victims of intersectional discrimination will disproportionately experience the harmful effects of climate change.[109] Significantly, the joint statement also notes that "[w]omen, children and other persons such as persons with disabilities, should not be seen only as victims or in terms of vulnerability."[110] Like the reference in the CEDAW Committee's General Recommendation No. 37, discussed above, this explicit reference to agency represents a departure from and progress over the treaty

[106] *See id.* ¶ 45(t).

[107] Joint Statement, Comm. on the Rights of Persons with Disabilities & Comm. on the Elimination of Discrimination against Women, Guaranteeing Sexual and Reproductive Health and Rights for All Women, in Particular Women with Disabilities (Aug. 29, 2018), https://www.ohchr.org/EN/HRBodies/CRPD/Pages/CRPDStatements.aspx.

[108] *Id.* at 1. The Committees issued another joint statement, along with UN Women, entitled "Ending Sexual Harassment against Women and Girls with Disabilities" in October 2020. *See* Joint Statement, UN Women, Comm. on the Rights of Persons with Disabilities & Comm. on the Elimination of Discrimination Against Women, Ending Sexual Harassment against Women and Girls with Disabilities (Oct. 22, 2020), https://www.unwomen.org/en/news/stories/2020/10/statement-joint-un-women-cedaw-and-crpd.

[109] *See Five UN Human Rights Treaty Bodies Issue a Joint Statement on Human Rights and Climate Change*, Off. of the High Comm'r for Hum. Rts. (Sept. 16, 2019), https://www.ohchr.org/en/NewsEvents/Pages/DisplayNews.aspx?NewsID=24998&LangID=E ("The risk of harm is particularly high for those segments of the population already marginalised or in vulnerable situations or that, due to discrimination and pre-existing inequalities, have limited access to decision-making or resources, such as women, children, persons with disabilities, indigenous peoples and persons living in rural areas.").

[110] *Id.*

bodies' prior practice of equating intersectional identities with "particularly vulnerable" populations.

Regular use of inter-committee meetings of treaty bodies

The many and ongoing conversations about strengthening the treaty bodies have often included discussion of the expanded use of inter-committee meetings, or ICMs.[111] ICMs allow representatives of the treaty bodies to convene and discuss possible methods of collaboration and harmonization. Early ICM discussions involved a range of issues, including the development of the list of issues for reporting states, follow-up to both state reporting and individual communications, cross-referencing the work of other treaty bodies, harmonizing terminology across treaty bodies, and drafting joint general comments.[112] Many of these strategies for harmonization, if implemented, would facilitate intersectional analysis.

Conversations across the treaty bodies would create an implicitly intersectional process, which would likely produce intersectional content and analysis. Conversations and collaborations between CERD and CRPD, for example, would naturally focus on the rights violations facing those who inhabit the intersections of race and disability subordination. If the treaty bodies were to systematically collaborate on the development of the list of issues for reporting states, discussions about which issues to highlight would likely involve discussion of intersectional human rights. Essentially, conversation across treaty bodies has intersectionality "baked in." This implicitly intersectional *process* would necessarily produce intersectional content and analysis. Once treaty bodies begin to consistently and deeply explore human rights issues that cut across multiple treaties, they open the door for consideration of rights violations that reflect intersectional identities. Depending on the pressing issues in the reporting country, for example, the list of issues might include a focus on women with disabilities or the intersection of migrant status and LGBTQI rights.

As I have noted in previous scholarship, the meeting of treaty body chairpersons could provide similar opportunities for collaboration on intersectional human rights issues.[113] In practice, however, treaty body chairperson meetings have proven less fruitful than other collaboration between the treaty bodies. The treaty body chairpersons have not always enjoyed the full support of their respective treaty bodies in decision-making on behalf of the treaty body.[114] As a result, these joint meetings may prove less useful than ICMs in generating support for an intersectional framework in the work of the treaty bodies. However, if the treaty body chairpersons articulated a collective commitment to intersectionality, it would signal an important leadership consensus on the issue.

[111] *See, e.g.*, HUM. RTS. L. CTR., *supra* note 38, at 13.

[112] *See id.* at 14.

[113] *See* Bond, *supra* note 19, at 164.

[114] *See* Hanna Beate Schöpp-Schilling, *Treaty Body Reform: The Case of the Committee on the Elimination of Discrimination Against Women*, 7 HUM. RTS. L. REV. 201, 204 (2007) (stating that annual meetings of chairpersons "suffer from a lack of immediate decision-making power" because the meetings can only make recommendations to the treaty bodies).

Professional development for treaty body experts and OHCHR staff

A final element necessary for substantive reform within the treaty body system is professional development specific to intersectionality theory. Although many members of the treaty bodies have already demonstrated an understanding of and commitment to principles of intersectionality, others may need additional exposure to the theory and its application to international human rights. OHCHR staff, although experts in human rights, may need the time and space to think more deeply about the application of intersectionality to international human rights. Treaty body leadership should work with OHCHR to provide professional development opportunities to treaty body members and those in OHCHR who support them.

The OHCHR has begun educating stakeholders about the value of intersectionality in human rights analysis. In response to a request from the Human Rights Council, the OHCHR produced a 2017 report on intersectional discrimination faced by women and girls around the globe.[115] As described in chapter 3, the report explores a range of intersectional rights violations that affect women and girls.[116] Although the report represents significant progress in the UN's willingness to explicitly embrace intersectionality in human rights analysis, it does so only in the context of gender. The next step for the OHCHR and the UN as a whole will be to expand this burgeoning interest in intersectionality beyond gender.

Special rapporteurs and other OHCHR special procedures mandate holders

Examples of intersectional analysis within special rapporteur work

The Human Rights Council's Special Procedure System, which is made up of Special Rapporteurs, independent experts, and working groups of experts,[117] is another system in which stakeholders should increase their understanding and application of intersectionality theory. Special Rapporteurs in particular are vital to promoting the application of intersectional analysis to international human rights because of their role in reporting and advising on human rights issues. Special Rapporteurs conduct country visits, issue communications to individual states, promote public awareness on issues, produce reports and studies, contribute to standard-setting, and organize and attend expert workshops and meetings,[118] signaling that they are indeed "a central element of the United Nations human rights machinery."[119] Although Special

[115] *See* U.N. High Comm'r for Hum. Rts., *Impact of Multiple and Intersecting Forms of Discrimination and Violence in the Context of Racism, Racial Discrimination, Xenophobia and Related Intolerance on the Full Enjoyment of All Human Rights by Women and Girls*, ¶ 1, U.N. Doc. A/HRC/35/10 (Apr. 21, 2017).

[116] *See supra* chapter 3, notes 131–136 and accompanying text.

[117] *See Special Procedures of the Human Rights Council*, OFF. OF THE HIGH COMM'R FOR HUM. RTS., https://www.ohchr.org/EN/HRBodies/SP/Pages/Introduction.aspx (last visited May 4, 2021).

[118] *See* U.N. High Comm'r for Hum. Rts., *Rep. on the Twenty-Fifth Annual Meeting of Special Rapporteurs/Representatives, Independent Experts and Chairs of Working Grps. of the Special Procedures of the Human Rights Council (Geneva, 4 to 8 June 2018), Including Updated Information on Special Procedures*, ¶¶ 5–30, U.N. Doc. A/HRC/40/38 (Sept. 18, 2019) (explaining the activities and duties of special rapporteurs). As of 2018, there were forty-four thematic mandates and twelve country-specific mandates. *Id.* ¶ 2.

[119] *Special Procedures of the Human Rights Council*, *supra* note 117.

Rapporteurs are required to work within their mandates, each post is filled by an individual who brings particular expertise and priorities to the assignment. Naturally, some mandate holders consistently prioritize intersectionality in their approaches and others do not.

Notably, some of the earliest references to intersectional rights in UN human rights work appeared in the reports of the UN Special Rapporteur on violence against women, its causes and consequences, Radhika Coomaraswamy, who served in that role from 1994 to 2003. In a 1999 country mission report on the United States, for example, Coomaraswamy demonstrated that the intersection of race and gender led to the imprisonment and custodial abuse of disproportionate numbers of African American and Latina women.[120] She also highlighted gender-based violence at the hands of non-state actors, including those who targeted "women who live their lives outside of heterosexuality."[121] Rashida Manjoo, the Special Rapporteur from 2009 through 2015,[122] also issued reports that explicitly highlight intersectionality as a research theme.[123]

Yakin Ertürk, Special Rapporteur from 2003 to 2009, also highlighted intersectionality in much of her work. Ertürk summarizes one late 2003 report as follows: "emphasis is placed on the *universality* of violence against women, the *multiplicity* of its forms and the *intersectionality* of diverse kinds of discrimination against women and its linkage to a system of domination that is based on subordination and inequality."[124] Ertürk also notes, "In view of the intersectionality of systems of domination, integrating an intersectional approach to gender analysis will contribute to identifying the multiple forms of discrimination and identifying State accountability for human rights."[125]

Recent reports indicate that Special Rapporteurs have continued to incorporate intersectionality. In the 2019 *Report of the Special Rapporteur on Violence Against Women, Its Causes and Consequences*, Dubravka Šimonovic, who began serving in that role in 2015, states that other special rapporteurs, including the Special Rapporteur on the rights of persons with disabilities, have started to include a gender perspective when examining the rights of disabled women and, in the case of another special

[120] *See* Radhika Coomaraswamy (Special Rapporteur), *Rep. of the Mission to the United States of America on the Issue of Violence Against Women in State and Federal Prisons*, ¶¶ 25–27, U.N. Doc. E/CN.4/1999/68/Add.2 (Jan. 4, 1999).

[121] Kim Vance et al., *The Rise of SOGI: Human Rights for LGBT People at the United Nations*, *in* ENVISIONING GLOBAL LGBT HUMAN RIGHTS 223, 229 (Nancy Nicol et al. eds., 2018).

[122] *See Special Rapporteur on Violence Against Women, Its Causes and Consequences*, OFF. OF THE HIGH COMM'R FOR HUM. RTS., https://www.ohchr.org/EN/Issues/Women/SRWomen/Pages/SRWomenIndex.aspx (last visited May 4, 2021) (noting that Dubravka Šimonovic was appointed as Special Rapporteur in 2015).

[123] *See* Rashida Manjoo (Special Rapporteur), *Rep. of the Special Rapporteur on Violence against Women, its Causes and Consequences*, ¶ 56, U.N. Doc. A/HRC/26/38 (May 28, 2014) (noting that Manjoo continued to build on the theme of intersectionality through her investigations on violence against women); Rashida Manjoo (Special Rapporteur), *Rep. of the Special Rapporteur on Violence against Women, its Causes and Consequences*, ¶¶ 26, 62, U.N. Doc. A/HRC/20/16 (May 23, 2012).

[124] Yakin Ertürk (Special Rapporteur), *Integration of the Human Rights of Women and the Gender Perspective: Violence Against Women, Rep. of the Special Rapporteur on Violence Against Women, Its Causes and Consequences*, summ., U.N. Doc. E/CN.4/2004/66 (Dec. 26, 2003).

[125] *Id.* ¶ 53.

rapporteur, the right to physical and mental health.[126] Since the appointment of the first Special Rapporteur on violence against women in 1994, each expert who has served in that role has, at various points in her tenure, highlighted the significance of intersectionality as an analytical tool.

Other Special Procedures documents explicitly reference intersectionality. In 2017, for example, the Special Rapporteur on the rights of persons with disabilities explored and reported on the intersectional rights violations faced by women and girls with disabilities in terms of their sexual and reproductive health[127] and in 2019 on the intersection between aging and disability.[128] In the 2019 *Report of the Special Rapporteur on the situation of human rights defenders*, Michel Forst described the experiences of human rights defenders as "diverse":

> They promote and protect human rights in very different circumstances. In doing so, they generally face greater risks and challenges than men do—risks that are gendered and intersectional. Aside from gender, aspects of their identities, such as age, religion, ethnicity, class, immigration or legal status, disability, sexual orientation, gender identity, gender expression, and the way those aspects intersect shape the way women human rights defenders are perceived and treated.[129]

One of Forst's recommendations also calls on stakeholders to view protection practices through the lens of intersectionality.[130]

In the 2019 *Report of the Independent Expert on protection against violence and discrimination based on sexual orientation and gender identity*, the Independent Expert highlights that intersectionality is one of the mandate holder's guiding principles.[131] The report lists specific examples of identities relevant to this guiding principle: (1) women who are lesbian, bisexual, trans and gender diverse; (2) young

[126] *See* Dubravka Simonovic (Special Rapporteur), *Rep. of the Special Rapporteur on Violence Against Women, Its Causes and Consequences*, ¶ 44, U.N. Doc. A/HRC/41/42 (June 20, 2019).

[127] *See* U.N. Secretary-General, *Sexual and Reproductive Health and Rts. of Girls and Young Women with Disabilities*, ¶ 21, U.N. Doc. A/72/133 (July 14, 2017).

[128] *See* Catalina Devandas-Aguilar (Special Rapporteur), *Rep. of the Special Rapporteur on the Rights of Persons with Disabilities*, ¶ 8, U.N. Doc. A/74/186 (July 17, 2019).

[129] Michael Forest (Special Rapporteur), *Situation of Women Human Rights Defenders, Rep. of the Special Rapporteur on the Situation of Human Rights Defenders*, ¶ 35, U.N. Doc. A/HRC/40/60 (Jan. 10, 2019). *See also id.* ¶ 3.

> Women of diverse backgrounds promote and protect rights in very different contexts. There are, for instance, women calling for gender equality, indigenous women fighting for land and environmental rights, women in rural areas pressing for socioeconomic rights, girls campaigning on social issues, trans women speaking up against discrimination, lesbians calling for equality, migrant and refugee women advocating for their rights and security, homeless women demanding the right to housing and shelter, women fighting for justice for the disappeared, gender non-conforming persons resisting gender-based violence, women promoting choice and bodily autonomy, women expanding digital rights, women with disabilities fighting for independent living, and women involved in peace processes.

[130] *See id.* ¶ 110(d).

[131] *See* Victor Madrigal-Borloz (Independent Expert), Rep. of the Independent Expert on Protection against Violence and Discrimination Based on Sexual Orientation and Gender Identity, ¶ 4, U.N. Doc. A/74/181 (July 17, 2019).

persons; (3) older persons; (4) persons living with disabilities; (5) asylum seekers, refugees, migrants and internally displaced persons; and (6) victims of humanitarian and natural disasters.[132]

Two 2019 reports from Tendayi Achiume, the Special Rapporteur on contemporary forms of racism, racial discrimination, xenophobia and related intolerance, mention intersectionality. The report to the Human Rights Council on the topics of global extractivism and racial equality highlights that "discrimination and inequality within the extractivism economy is intersectional" and notes the "gendered nature of racial inequality."[133] Achiume's report to the General Assembly indicates that she participated in an event titled "Intersectionality as politics and practice" in July 2019.[134] One of the recommendations within the report also displays Achiume's recognition of intersectional discrimination, calling on states to adopt a "comprehensive approach to reparations" which "entails an intersectional approach to understanding and fighting racial discrimination by accounting for gender, class, disability status and other social categories."[135]

Overall, reports from Special Rapporteurs in recent years indicate that those within the United Nation's Special Procedures system have begun to recognize intersectionality as an important aspect of their work. The Special Rapporteurs on violence against women, its causes and consequences have embraced intersectionality in a fairly consistent and robust way. Other Special Rapporteurs have also emphasized intersectionality in their analyses of human rights issues. The enthusiastic embrace of intersectionality within the Special Procedures will likely raise awareness of intersectionality among other UN mandate holders.

Opportunities for greater collaboration

In 2003, I recommended greater collaboration among Special Rapporteurs through joint fact-finding and report writing. There has been some progress on this front. For example, a 2009 review report on the Special Rapporteur on violence against women notes

> Intersectionality is also demonstrated by work methods in terms of the joint communications, country visits and reports undertaken by the SRVAW with other special procedures. Only a small fraction of the total number of communications issued by the SRVAW annually are sent singly; the bulk of the communications are sent jointly with other special mechanisms.[136]

[132] *See id.* ¶¶ 36–60.

[133] Tendayi Achiume (Special Rapporteur), *Rep. of the Special Rapporteur on Contemporary Forms of Racism, Racial Discrimination, Xenophobia and Related Intolerance*, ¶¶ 18–19, U.N. Doc. A/HRC/41/54 (May 14, 2019).

[134] *See* Tendayi Achiume (Special Rapporteur), *Contemporary Forms of Racism, Racial Discrimination, Xenophobia and Racial Intolerance*, ¶ 4, U.N. Doc. A/74/321 (Aug. 21, 2019).

[135] *Id.* ¶ 57.

[136] *See* UN SPECIAL RAPPORTEUR ON VIOLENCE AGAINST WOMEN, ITS CAUSES AND CONSEQUENCES, 15 YEARS OF THE UNITED NATIONS SPECIAL RAPPORTEUR ON VIOLENCE AGAINST WOMEN, ITS CAUSES AND CONSEQUENCES (1994–2009) 42 (2009), https://www.ohchr.org/Documents/Issues/Women/15YearReviewofVAWMandate.pdf [hereinafter 15 Year Review Report].

When Special Procedures mechanisms focus on different types of rights, as in, for example, a joint report between the Special Rapporteur on violence against women, its causes and consequences and the Special Rapporteur on the rights of persons with disabilities, there is significant potential for intersectional analysis.

In 2019, the Special Rapporteur on violence against women called for increased collaboration among the global and regional independent monitoring mechanisms and recognized that "[t]he current approach to addressing violence against women within the United Nations system is fragmented, with the different agencies often working in silos and with limited collaboration with the Special Rapporteur."[137] The author of the 2010 article "Women with Disabilities: The Forgotten Peace Builders" also calls for increased collaboration among Special Rapporteurs.[138] The author specifically recommends the creation of a mechanism that would allow the Special Rapporteur on violence against women and the Special Rapporteur on disability (now called the Special Rapporteur on the rights of persons with disabilities) to collaborate "with respect to violence against women with disabilities generally and conflict situations in particular."[139]

The frequency with which Special Rapporteurs engage in collaborative work is increasing. The Special Rapporteur on the rights of persons with disabilities, for example, collaborated with the Independent Expert on the enjoyment of all human rights by older persons in organizing an expert consultation on challenges faced by older persons with disabilities.[140] There is also evidence of increased collaboration between Special Rapporteurs and regional human rights bodies as well as the treaty bodies.[141]

There are, however, many missed opportunities for collaboration between Special Rapporteurs themselves and between Special Rapporteurs and other UN mandate holders. For example, a joint report from the Special Rapporteur on violence against women and the Special Rapporteur on contemporary forms of racism would be an important contribution. It would shed light on the many ways that structural discrimination based on race and ethnicity intersects with gender discrimination, resulting in different rates and effects of gender-based violence among women of color. An increase in collaboration among treaty bodies, Special Procedures mechanisms, and other UN entities would increase opportunities for meaningful intersectional analysis.

So far we have considered how ongoing reform efforts within the treaty body system and OHCHR special procedures might effectively incorporate intersectionality. There is evidence that the treaty body system and other entities within the UN are moving toward a gradual embrace of intersectionality. Given that other reform advocates and

[137] Simonovic, *supra* note 126, ¶¶ 79–85.

[138] *See* Stephanie Ortoleva, *Women with Disabilities: The Forgotten Peace Builders*, 33 Loy. L.A. Int'l & Comp. L. Rev. 83, 135–36 (2010).

[139] *Id.* at 135.

[140] *See* Off. of the High Comm'r for Hum. Rts., Concept Note, Virtual Side Event During the 13th Session of the Conference of States Parties to the CRPD (2020), https://www.ohchr.org/Documents/Issues/OlderPersons/Concept_Note.pdf.

[141] *See, e.g.*, Comm. on the Elimination of Discrimination against Women & Special Rapporteur of Violence Against Women, Framework of Cooperation Between the CEDAW Committee and the Special Rapporteur of Violence Against Women (SRVAW) (Nov. 8, 2018), https://tbinternet.ohchr.org/Treaties/CEDAW/Shared%20Documents/1_Global/INT_CEDAW_SUS_8787_E.pdf.

I called for these theoretical and practical shifts almost twenty years ago, however, the pace of change has been slow. The treaty bodies and other constituencies have made clear their distaste for sweeping structural change, such as the creation of one or two consolidated treaty bodies. The movement to adopt an intersectional framework to date has been piecemeal and relied largely on individuals in the system who appreciated the analytical benefits of intersectionality in the human rights regime. Human rights advocates, both within and outside of the UN, will need to find ways to foster a deep and structural commitment to intersectionality across the UN system.

Beyond the treaty bodies: the need for collaboration across UN agencies

The furtherance of intersectionality theory in the international human rights system requires more than just the efforts from the treaty bodies and OHCHR Special Procedures mandate holders; it requires commitment from other UN agencies as well. UN Women, the UN organization dedicated to women's rights around the world, has the potential to garner widespread global support for an intersectional human rights framework through its Gender Focal Points in UN offices and through its regional offices. The Gender Focal Points form a network throughout the UN called the Inter-Agency Network on Women and Gender Equality (IANWGE). At its 2019 annual meeting, the IANWGE expressed a commitment to intersectionality in its inter-agency work. For example, in its planning for the Beijing +25 meeting, which marked twenty-five years since the UN World Conference for Women in Beijing in 1995, the Network "emphasized its commitment to ensure that its engagement in Beijing +25 takes an intersectional approach, and that women's experiences are not homogenized but must be considered in all their diversity."[142] The network's 2019 report also recognizes that the planning process for the Beijing +25 meeting needed to include "the perspectives of groups that are likely to be left behind, including persons with disabilities, rural women, indigenous women, migrant women, and women with disabilities."[143]

The Inter-Agency Standing Committee (IASC), which brings together heads of UN agencies and non-UN leaders in furtherance of improved humanitarian responses, has taken on the issue of sexual exploitation, abuse, and harassment. In its report of the 2018 meeting on the topic, the group briefly mentions women in "vulnerable" situations but fails to mention intersectionality. Because this group brings together high-level leaders of numerous UN agencies, it has the potential to collaborate on intersectional issues and to inculcate a commitment to intersectional analysis in each of the represented agencies.

In 2018, the executive boards of UNICEF, UN Women, World Food Program (WFP), and UNDP/UNFPA/UNOPS held a joint meeting to discuss implementation of the

[142] U.N. Inter-Agency Network on Women and Gender Equality, *Report of the Eighteenth Annual Session of the Inter-Agency Network on Women and Gender Equality*, at 15, U.N. Doc. IANWGE/2019/Report (Mar. 14, 2019).

[143] *Id.* at 17.

2030 Agenda for Sustainable Development.[144] The 2030 Agenda was developed by the United Nations General Assembly to eradicate poverty; combat inequality; promote peace, inclusivity, and gender equality; and protect human rights as well as natural resources.[145] In her opening remarks of the joint meeting, the Deputy Secretary-General emphasized the need for UN agencies to join forces and collaborate in their efforts to achieve the 2030 goals.[146] The meeting stressed possibilities for collaboration to promote women's rights within the UN system. If achieved, this kind of inter-agency collaboration opens the door for greater consideration of intersectionality.

UN Women also plays a significant role in raising awareness of women's human rights by sponsoring topical programs. Together with other UN agencies, UN Women hosted a conference in early 2020 entitled "Counted and Visible: Global Conference on the measurement of gender equality, leave no one behind and intersecting inequalities." The concept note for the conference asked whether current data collection mechanisms are sufficient to capture the experiences of those who suffer intersectional forms of inequality. UN Women is well-positioned to expand and deepen conversations about intersectionality in human rights beyond the focus on intersectional data collection. UN Women liaison offices can also foster dialog about intersectionality in different regions of the globe.

Parallel human rights and humanitarian processes

Beyond the UN treaty bodies, OHCHR special procedures, and UN agencies, parallel processes offer opportunities to adopt an intersectional human rights framework. The Universal Periodic Review process, regional human rights mechanisms, and international courts and tribunals have the potential to increase intersectional human rights analysis. As described earlier in the chapter, the UPR process relies on peer review to hold states accountable for human rights violations. The process can foster interstate conversations about intersectionality. It may be difficult, however, to get widespread buy-in from states about the centrality of intersectionality in the human rights framework. Without entities such as the treaty bodies injecting intersectionality into the conversation through lists of issues and other agenda-setting means, it may be difficult to encourage states to hold each other accountable for intersectional violations. Those engaged with the UPR process, however, should explore ways to generate a commitment to intersectionality among countries reporting under this process.

As I described in chapter 4, regional human rights mechanisms offer complementary human rights systems for victims to seek redress for human rights violations. Those systems have developed their own jurisprudence and have grappled with intersectional human rights violations with varying degrees of success.[147] Several

[144] *See* United Nations Development Program et al., Report of the Joint Meeting of the Executive Boards of UNDP/UNFPA/UNOPS, UNICEF, UN-WOMEN, and WFP Held on 1 June 2018 ¶¶ 1–27 (2018), https://www.unfpa.org/sites/default/files/board-documents/main-document/Report_on_the_JMB_1_June.pdf.

[145] *See* G.A. Res. 70/1, ¶ 3, Transforming Our World: the 2030 Agenda for Sustainable Development (Oct. 21, 2015).

[146] *See* united nations development program et al., *supra* note 144, ¶ 2.

[147] *See supra* notes 270–280 and accompanying text (chapter 4).

steps would encourage the furtherance of intersectional frameworks. The UN treaty body system and the regional human rights bodies should create mechanisms for information-sharing concerning intersectionality. Events and trainings designed to promote awareness within the treaty body system should also include representatives from the relevant regional systems. In addition, UN Women should use its liaison offices to increase collaboration with the regional bodies in fostering a commitment to adopt an intersectional framework for human rights analysis.

Although detailed discussion is beyond the scope of this volume, international tribunals, such as the International Criminal Court (ICC), also confront intersectional violations of international humanitarian law, including genocide, crimes against humanity, and war crimes. Intersectionality is deeply relevant when an armed group targets women of a particular racial or ethnic group for mass rape or forced pregnancy. Atrocities committed in the former Yugoslavia, Rwanda, and Darfur, Sudan, offer devastating examples of intersectional rights abuses for which the law must provide a remedy.[148] International and regional human rights bodies and international criminal tribunals should collaborate in training and other awareness-raising activities to promote an appreciation of intersectional human rights harms within the international criminal context.

National strategies for incorporating intersectionality

As discussed in the previous chapter, non-governmental organizations and national human rights institutions have a symbiotic and mutually reinforcing relationship with the UN and other human rights entities. The embrace of intersectionality by NGOs and NHRIs would greatly facilitate the understanding of intersectional issues at both the state and UN level.

NGOs around the world have engaged with intersectionality theory, and some have incorporated the theory as a guiding principle in their organizational missions. Other NGOs may not view intersectionality as relevant to their work or may not have encountered an intersectional human rights framework. NGOs that have adopted an intersectional approach in their work are likely to continue to push the treaty bodies toward a more consistent and systematic embrace of intersectionality. Those groups are critical drivers of intersectionality within the treaty body system. At the same time, the treaty bodies play a role in engaging NGOs that have not yet considered intersectionality or recognized its importance in human rights analysis.

The treaty bodies and the regional human rights mechanisms have multiple tools at their disposal to raise awareness of intersectionality among the many NGOs that partner with them on initiatives or that advocate for human rights victims through the state reporting processes or individual complaint procedures. NGO communities must also collaborate to raise awareness of intersectionality within their own ranks.

NHRIs have proliferated around the world. These bodies perform a variety of functions depending on their individual mandates. Among other responsibilities, most

[148] *See, e.g.*, Aisha Nicole Davis, *Intersectionality and International Law: Recognizing Complex Identities on the Global Stage*, 28 HARV. HUM. RTS. J. 205, 222 (2015).

of them are charged with ensuring that the state fulfills its duties under the human rights treaties to which the state has agreed to be bound. As stated in chapter 7, NHRIs are well positioned to encourage intersectional frameworks at the national and local levels. They often look to the treaty bodies for guidance on the implementation of the rights contained in the treaties. Such guidance, like the 2019 CEDAW Committee guidance, should explicitly adopt an intersectional framework and should seek to inculcate a commitment to intersectionality at the national level. NHRIs naturally have greater insight into the domestic human rights landscape, and they also play an educative role for the treaty bodies. Once they have incorporated and internalized a commitment to intersectionality in their work, they can keep the treaty bodies and regional human rights mechanisms focused on intersectional violations and appropriate intersectional remedies.

The need for a paradigm shift: the example of gender-based violence

There is no question that a meaningful increase in collaboration in furtherance of intersectionality within the United Nations will require a system-wide commitment to this theoretical and pragmatic shift. Although it sounds daunting, the UN system and activists who engage with the system accomplished one such rapid and dramatic shift in the 1990s with respect to gender-based violence. The process, which I first described in chapter 2, led to widespread recognition that systemic gender-based violence committed by non-state actors constitutes a human rights abuse. That history offers insight into steps that the treaty bodies might take to more firmly entrench intersectionality in human rights analysis. The 1990s saw a dramatic, rapid, and comprehensive shift in human rights law and advocacy to bring gender-based violence firmly within the purview of human rights discourse. I have advocated for, and we are beginning to see, a similar paradigm shift toward systematically embracing an intersectional framework for human rights analysis.

In the context of violence against women, the CEDAW Committee proved to be nimble and enterprising. CEDAW's treatment of gender-based violence illustrates how the Committee responded to a human rights issue that was, for many years, considered to be outside of the scope of the treaty's obligations. Although the CEDAW Convention's text failed to mention gender-based violence as a human rights violation, when public discussion of the issue expanded in a meaningful way in the late 1980s, the Committee recognized that it needed to adapt to the growing recognition of the breadth and depth of the problem. As a result, the Committee adopted General Recommendation No. 19 in 1992.[149] The recommendation brought gender-based violence within the purview of the convention by recognizing it as a form of discrimination against women.

As noted in chapter 2, before the late 1980s, human rights violations were limited to the actions of government officials or private citizens whose actions were ordered

[149] *See* Comm. on the Elimination of Discrimination against Women, Gen. Recommendation No. 19 Violence Against Women, ¶¶ 1–6, U.N. Doc. CEDAW/C/GC/19 (1992).

or explicitly supported by the state. But women often suffered rights violations at the hands of family members or other non-state actors. Under the traditional rule, women were unable to claim a rights violation.

In 1988, however, the Inter-American Court of Human Rights decided the case of *Velásquez Rodríguez v. Honduras*.[150] The case involved the disappearance of Angel Manfredo Velásquez Rodríguez, one of a number of people whose disappearance was attributed to a quasi-governmental group in Honduras. Under the American Convention on Human Rights, states are obligated to "ensure" the full exercise of the rights contained in the convention.[151] The Court decided that Honduras had violated Velásquez Rodríguez's right to life by failing to prevent, investigate, and punish the disappearance. Even if it could not be proven that those responsible "acted under of cover of public authority," the Court declared, "the failure of the State apparatus to act, which is clearly proven, is a failure on the part of Honduras to fulfill" its duties.[152] In its decision, the Court required Honduras to "take reasonable steps to prevent human rights violations and use the means at its disposal to carry out a serious investigation of violations committed within its jurisdiction, to identify those responsible, to impose the appropriate punishment and to ensure the victim adequate compensation."[153] It also mandated that states act with "due diligence" to prevent, investigate, and punish human rights violations committed by private citizens.[154]

For women's rights activists, the *Velásquez Rodríguez* decision was monumental. It paved a way to hold a state accountable for neglecting to act with due diligence to protect women from "private" abuses long considered to be beyond state concern. The CEDAW Committee took note of the case's precedent-setting insights about due diligence. General Recommendation No. 19, adopted four years after the *Velásquez Rodríguez* decision, specifically mentions due diligence as a metric to determine whether states have fulfilled their obligations to combat violence against women.[155] Shortly thereafter, in 1993, the General Assembly of the United Nations issued the Declaration on the Elimination of Violence Against Women (DEVAW),[156] which reinforced the due diligence standard for measuring whether a state had met its obligation to eliminate violence against women.[157] The UN declaration is not binding but it represents the consensus of member states that all states have a responsibility to eradicate violence against women, regardless of whether the perpetrators are public or private actors.

The 1993 UN Human Rights Conference in Vienna also highlighted gender-based violence worldwide.[158] The subject was also a significant theme at the UN Fourth

150 Velásquez Rodríguez v. Honduras, Merits, Judgment, Inter-Am. Ct. H.R. (ser. C) No. 4 (July 29, 1988).

151 *See* Organization of American States, American Convention on Human Rights art. 1, Nov. 22, 1969, O.A.S.T.S. No. 36, 1144 U.N.T.S. 123.

152 *Velásquez Rodríguez*, Inter-Am. Ct. H.R. (ser.C) No. 4, ¶ 182.

153 *Id.* ¶ 174.

154 *See id.* ¶ 172.

155 *See* Comm. on the Elimination of Discrimination against Women, *supra* note 149, ¶ 9.

156 *See* G.A. Res. 48/104, Declaration on the Elimination of Violence Against Women (Feb. 23, 1994).

157 *See id.* art. 4.

158 *See World Conference on Human Rights, Vienna, 1993*, OFF. OF THE HIGH COMM'R FOR HUM. RTS., https://www.ohchr.org/en/aboutus/pages/viennawc.aspx (last visited May 4, 2021).

World Conference on Women in Beijing in 1995.[159] Various regional efforts paralleled these developments at the United Nations. These included the adoption of the Inter-American Convention on the Prevention, Punishment and Eradication of Violence Against Women (Convention of Belém Do Pará) by the General Assembly of the Organization for American States in 1994.[160] As described in chapter 3, the Committee adopted a follow-up recommendation in 2017 about gender-based violence, General Recommendation No. 35, which reflects a commitment to examining gender-based violence through an intersectional lens.[161]

There are several lessons to be learned from the successful effort to define gender-based violence quickly and comprehensively as a human rights issue. With the right internal and external pressure, the United Nations can, and does, adapt to changing norms. If ever there was a moment for the United Nations to embrace intersectionality unequivocally, that moment is now. As this volume has shown, there is already considerable movement in that direction within the UN treaty bodies, regional human rights systems, NHRIs, and NGOs. The effort to incorporate intersectionality in all aspects of human rights work is gaining momentum.

The dramatic expansion of our collective understanding of gender-based violence as a human rights issue offers lessons for intersectionality discourse. Numerous NGOs championed the cause of gender-based violence. They mobilized to create a highly visible force for change. One high-profile example of NGO mobilization took place at the 1993 UN Human Rights Conference in Vienna. NGOs organized extensive testimonials from victims of gender-based violence from around the globe. The testimonials underscored the scope and severity of the problem, and decision-makers both within and outside the United Nations took notice. There were, of course, countless other events designed to raise public awareness, lobby policymakers, change laws, create support programs for victims, and convince the treaty bodies to take seriously the issue of gender-based violence.

These important developments helped broaden the scope of cognizable human rights claims. The collective understanding of state action under international human rights law shifted dramatically to expand common approaches to women's human rights. These changes removed the divide between "public" and "private" rights. Previously, only violations of rights in the public realm were recognized for state attention and redress, but expanding notions of state responsibility forced states to reckon meaningfully with rampant abuses against women occurring in the private sphere.

The changes, which largely occurred during the 1990s, were fast and effective. Although gender-based violence remains a significant problem around the globe, the right to be free from such violence is now widely accepted as a human right. In many cases, victims can complain to human rights institutions and seek redress. In the case of CEDAW, the Committee dramatically expanded coverage for gender-based

[159] *See Fourth World Conference on Women*, UN WOMEN, https://www.un.org/womenwatch/daw/beijing/platform/ (last visited May 4, 2021).

[160] *See* Organization of American States, Inter-American Convention on the Prevention, Punishment, and Eradication of Violence against Women, June 9, 1994, 27 U.S.T. 3301, 1438 U.N.T.S. 63.

[161] *See supra* notes 126–127 and accompanying text (chapter 3).

violence by equating it with gender discrimination and using a general recommendation to bring it within the purview of the convention.

This type of widespread, committed, and coordinated activism is necessary—and achievable—in the context of intersectionality. CEDAW's General Recommendation No. 28 on the core obligations of State parties to the convention underscores the dynamic nature of the treaty, acknowledging that it may expand to include rights not specifically mentioned but consistent with the spirit of the convention.[162] General Recommendation No. 28's language invites a dramatic shift toward intersectionality.

The next step for CEDAW is a general recommendation that goes beyond the vague commitments of General Recommendation No. 28. Each of the treaty bodies, including CEDAW, should issue a detailed and far-reaching general comment or general recommendation that not only demonstrates its firm commitment to intersectionality but also provides States parties with a detailed road map for using an intersectional framework in the context of human rights. The OHCHR has a critical role to play in fostering these conversations at the treaty body level and for supporting the treaty bodies as they engage in this work.

Reviewing reforms

As illustrated in this chapter, the United Nations and related organizations can and must take steps to fully embrace and implement intersectionality theory. Although dramatic changes in the structure and operation of the treaty body system would encourage intersectional analysis and potentially increase efficiency, such significant reforms would need to overcome considerable resistance and are unlikely to be implemented. Increased collaboration among treaty bodies and partner organizations, as well as reporting requirements focusing on intersectionality, however, can facilitate intersectional human rights analysis. The treaty body system and other UN entities must lead by example by consistently incorporating such analysis in their work. Several treaty bodies and other UN offices have already increased communication and collaboration with each other, providing opportunities to foster intersectional human rights analysis.

The example of the UN system's rapid and resourceful embrace of gender-based violence as a human rights violation indicates that change is possible through enterprising interpretation of existing norms and procedural and structural changes within the system. This necessary accommodation by human rights law of gender-based

[162] *See* Comm. on the Elimination of Discrimination against Women, General Recommendation No. 28 on the Core Obligations of States Parties under Article 2 of the Convention on the Elimination of All Forms of Discrimination against Women, ¶ 7, U.N. Doc. CEDAW/C/GC/28.

> Article 2 of the Convention should be read in conjunction with articles 3, 4, 5 and 24 and in the light of the definition of discrimination contained in article 1. In addition, the scope of the general obligations contained in article 2 should also be construed in the light of the general recommendations, concluding observations, views, and other statements issued by the Committee, including the reports on the inquiry procedures and the decisions of individual cases. The spirit of the Convention covers other rights that are not explicitly mentioned in the Convention, but that have an impact on the achievement of equality of women with men, which impact represents a form of discrimination against women.

violence offers an example of norms that expanded to reflect contemporary rights violations. Similarly, human rights norms must expand to accommodate the critical insights of intersectionality theory. Comprehensive acceptance of intersectionality within the UN system would result in a more efficient and more effective understanding and resolution of human rights issues, all of which will greatly benefit victims seeking comprehensive remedies for rights violations.

Conclusion: An Intersectional Future for Human Rights

Adopting an intersectional framework is like putting on a pair of corrective glasses for the first time. The blur of human identity takes shape, and the intersectional lenses offer clarity in the exploration of the interconnected systems of privilege and oppression that shape our lives. The concept of intersectionality is regularly invoked in scholarly and colloquial discourse such that most students entering college now have some familiarity with the concept. It has become a theoretical staple of undergraduate women's, gender, and sexuality studies and inter-disciplinary programs. The ubiquity of the concept is evidence of its intellectual appeal and transformative potential.

The widespread embrace of intersectionality has also prompted a call from Black feminist theorists to maintain the integrity of the theory by continuing to honor its origins as grounded in Black feminist theorizing. I have argued in this volume that it is appropriate to locate the origins of intersectionality theory in the critical work of Black feminists in the United States even as we seek to explore new applications and new terrain for the theory. To artificially cabin its application runs counter to the aspirations of Kimberlé Crenshaw and other critical race feminists. As I outlined in chapter 1, Crenshaw imagined a range of applications and encouraged the use of the theory beyond the race and gender context within which she formally framed it. In applying intersectionality theory to a range of human rights issues, I have tried to remain true to its central tenets, including the importance of the theory in recognizing and breaking down structural oppression. In doing so, I have sought to be, in Ange-Marie Hancock's words, a good "steward" of the theory, cognizant of its wide-ranging potential and vigilant in ethically connecting the theory to its origins in Black feminist thought.[1]

In the context of human rights, intersectionality allows us to see how different forms of structural oppression intersect, construct, and mutually reinforce each other. Race, poverty, and gender, for example, intersect to limit the options of a Black woman who has experienced intimate partner violence, whether in the United States, South Africa, or Brazil. Similarly, age and disability may intersect to limit access to humanitarian aid in the aftermath of a natural disaster. Only by carefully considering the intersections of structural inequality in the lives of human rights victims can we hope to provide comprehensive human rights remedies.

[1] *See* Ange-Marie Hancock, Intersectionality: An Intellectual History 23 (2016). If we think of a steward as someone entrusted with caring for valuables that she does not herself own, then my role is to not only disavow ownership of intersectionality but to remember that while I am permitted to use it, I must do so ethically, which entails producing projects that hopefully leave intersectionality scholars better equipped to engage in knowledge production projects in intersectionality studies.

Global Intersectionality and Contemporary Human Rights. Johanna Bond, Oxford University Press. © Johanna Bond 2021.
DOI: 10.1093/oso/9780198868835.003.0010

As discussed in chapter 5, for example, CEDAW's decision in the *Kell v. Canada* case illustrates the potential of intersectional remedies.[2] In *Kell*, CEDAW recommended individual remedies for the complainant, an Indigenous woman who suffered discrimination based on Indigeneity and gender, including adequate housing and monetary compensation. In addition to these individual remedies, the Committee recommended that the Canadian government take steps to address the structural and intersectional discrimination faced by Indigenous women in Canada. Specifically, the Committee recognized the need for more Indigenous women among the ranks of legal aid providers working within Indigenous communities. The Committee recommended that the government take steps to eliminate the structural barriers that interfere with the recruitment and training of Indigenous women in the provision on legal aid. The Committee also recommended that the government work to ensure that Indigenous victims of intimate partner violence have access to legal remedies. The recommendations reflect an intersectional understanding that specific strategies to combat gender-based violence within Indigenous communities may significantly differ from strategies targeting non-Indigenous communities. This recognition allows CEDAW to recommend specifically tailored, intersectional, and more effective remedies.

Intersectionality's reach and potential impact in the context of international human rights is deep and broad. International human rights norms have evolved since the early 2000s in ways that reflect a burgeoning intersectional orientation. In the first decade of the new millennium, the United Nations was slow to embrace intersectionality in its human rights work. This had less to do with the transformative potential of the theory and more to do with the structure of the UN treaty bodies, the entities charged with implementing the primary global human rights treaties. The UN treaty bodies are siloed: the Committee on the Elimination of Racial Discrimination, for example, works almost exclusively on race-based violations, and the Committee on the Rights of Persons with Disabilities works almost exclusively on disability rights. The United Nations is slowly beginning to change this siloed approach as it recognizes the value of an intersectional framework for human rights. The treaty bodies are warming to the concept of intersectionality, and many are now actively embracing it as a conceptual lens.

This embrace of intersectionality in human rights is found at the regional and domestic levels as well. As I also explored in this volume, in the last two decades, the primary regional human rights systems (the European system, the inter-American system, and the African system) have begun to use intersectional analysis in their human rights work.

Although intersectionality is gaining traction at all levels—within the global UN human rights system, the regional human rights systems, the national human rights institutions, and the non-governmental organizations (NGOs) that work alongside these bodies—intersectional analysis in these contexts continues to be spotty, inconsistent, and underdeveloped. NGOs are a critical driver of change and will push global and regional human rights bodies to embrace intersectional analysis more actively.

[2] Kell v. Canada, U.N. Doc. CEDAW/C/51/D/19/2008 (Apr. 26, 2012).

In the symbiotic interplay between human rights entities, human rights bodies at all levels also have a role to play in encouraging NGOs to adopt an intersectional approach. There are many ways to do so. Many human rights bodies, for example, issue NGO guidelines for submitting human rights information and data to the human rights bodies. These guidance mechanisms shape and influence the work of collaborating NGOs and provide a powerful vehicle for promoting intersectional human rights analysis.

The methods by which NGOs engage the human rights bodies varies, but broad patterns exist. Many NGOs assist individual victims of rights violations to submit formal complaints to international and regional bodies. Those bodies, in turn, consider the individual complaints and issue decisions and, if appropriate, recommendations to the government that is the subject of the complaint. The complaint process, as discussed in greater detail using the example of the Committee on the Elimination of Discrimination against Women (CEDAW) in chapter 5, offers an opportunity for human rights bodies to adopt an intersectional approach in their analysis of the human rights issues at stake in individual communications. Of course, some violations are not intersectional in nature, but others present violations that occur at the juncture of various forms of structural discrimination, such as race and sexual orientation. The human rights bodies must more consistently recognize intersectional violations and provide remedies that address the complex, intersectional needs of victims. NGOs can facilitate this process by working to frame intersectional rights violations in explicitly intersectional terms.

The reporting process, which requires States parties to report periodically on their progress in implementing the human rights treaties, is a dialogic process. As such, it offers another way to encourage more consistent consideration of intersectional rights violations. Human rights reporting is a primary means through which the oversight bodies ensure that governments that have agreed to be bound by the human rights treaties are, in fact, implementing those treaties in their own territories. As outlined in chapter 6, the reporting process offers multiple opportunities for NGOs, reporting governments, or the treaty bodies themselves to adopt an intersectional framework for human rights analysis. The reporting process is a discursive process among NGOs, governments, and the treaty bodies. To the extent that NGOs adopt an intersectional lens in dialogue with their governments or with the treaty bodies, intersectionality as a discursive method will spread and gain momentum among NGOs, governments, and treaty bodies. Similarly, when the treaty bodies adopt guidelines for NGOs that emphasize intersectional analysis, more NGOs will embrace intersectional analysis in their own human rights work.

The beneficiaries of an analytical shift toward intersectionality are those harmed by human rights violations. As human rights bodies embrace intersectional analysis, their efforts to provide redress to human rights victims will increasingly reflect this more comprehensive and nuanced approach to human rights. Human rights bodies will be more attentive to the needs of, for example, migrant transgender women living in refugee camps and suffering disproportionate rates of violence. Recognizing that migrant trans women experience structural discrimination at the intersection of subordination based on gender, gender identity, ethnic identity, and socioeconomic status, human rights bodies can provide more complete remedies that address the challenges of occupying that particular intersectional space.

This volume is replete with examples of intersectional subordination. Intersectionality has proven itself to be a theory that travels well. It applies across disciplines and it evolves over time, with scholars and activists regularly invoking the theory in connection with new applications. As we consider global human rights in the twenty-first century, intersectionality offers enduring insight into appropriate remedies for a host of new and expansive rights violations.

Human rights advocates and policy-makers must adopt an intersectional lens to fully address contemporary issues such as data privacy, climate change, and global epidemiology. As social media, smartphones, and data-sharing become increasingly ubiquitous, concerns about privacy grow. Private data analytics firms, companies, and state actors capitalize on this newly available trove of data to "address previously intractable problems across wide-ranging fields including health care, education, retail, and banking."[3] Although the data have been put to good use in some instances, in many others the increasing access to data has compromised individual privacy.[4] Both private and government invasions of privacy in the form of government surveillance and private collection and sale of data on individuals are not equally experienced across populations.[5] The sociotechnical infrastructure that defines our relationship with technology reflects implicit bias and subtle but pernicious forms of racism and discrimination.[6] Women, particularly those facing intersecting forms of discrimination, experience threats to their privacy acutely, including disproportionate government surveillance.[7]

As with data privacy, the causes and impacts of climate change are not evenly distributed across the world's population.[8] While affluent countries and, to varying degrees, their citizens have typically been the largest polluters, marginalized communities and those living in poverty in developing countries often disproportionately suffer the consequences of climate change.[9] Geography and income, however, are not the only factors driving the unequal effects of climate change—the vast climate inequities we face also stem from inequalities in geopolitical power.[10] Intersectionality is a valuable tool for exploring how those unequal power structures are inextricably linked with and mutually defined by other systems of subordination.[11]

[3] Payal Arora, *Decolonizing Privacy Studies*, 20 Television & New Media 366, 366–67 (2018).

[4] *Id.* at 367.

[5] Jane Bailey, *Gendering Big Brother: What Should a Feminist Do?*, 12 J.L. & Equal. 157, 176 (2016).

[6] Ruha Benjamin, Race After Technology 34 (2019).

[7] *Id.* at 162; Violette Khammad et al., *Human Rights in the Digital Age: Inclusive Policies on Data Privacy*, *in* Strengthening the Rules-Based International Order: 2020 Global Trends Report 5 (2020).

[8] Anna Kaijser & Annica Kronsell, *Climate Change Through the Lens of Intersectionality*, 23 Env't Pol. 417, 418 (2014).

[9] *Id.*

[10] *Id.*

[11] Kaijser & Kronsell, *supra* note 8, at 421. Kaijser and Kronsell have compiled a list of questions for researchers to apply when examining issues of intersectionality and climate change, including "[w]hich social categories, if any, are represented in the empirical material? Which social categories are absent? ... What identities are promoted and considered to serve as grounds for political action? Are any other aspects of identity neglected or deemed insignificant?" and "How are relations between humans and between humans and the environment portrayed? How is nature represented? What type of environmental knowledge is recognised and privileged?" *Id.* at 229–30.

One consequence of climate change is an increase in the number and severity of natural disasters around the world, which often cause severe damage to marginalized communities that are unable to withstand and recover from the disasters. Natural disasters can be devastating for communities living in poverty, particularly for women and people with disabilities in those communities. Climate-related natural disasters disrupt mobility and communication devices on which some individuals with disabilities rely.[12] As Aleksandra George and Erin Flannery Keith note, "[f]or any community in the Caribbean and the global south, intersectional considerations complicate climate change preparedness and resilience."[13] Any climate resiliency and disaster response plans should therefore consider intersectionality and the implications for communities with multiple marginalized identities.[14] Intentional intersectionality can ensure that targeted outreach, emergency drills, and disaster planning address the needs those living at the intersection of multiple systems of subordination and save lives.[15]

As I described in the introduction to this volume, the COVID-19 pandemic has highlighted a range of inequities related to healthcare access and the human right to good health. Applying an intersectional framework to disparities in healthcare outcomes encourages medical professionals to challenge the status quo and to question "victim blaming" tactics that over-simplify disparate outcomes by attributing them solely to genetics or social behaviors.[16] Discrimination in healthcare may include the assumption that certain languages, such as English or other dominant-culture languages, are the primary spoken language for patients and their families, creating impediments to effective diagnosis and treatment.[17] LGBTQI communities may also face barriers to treatment based on a provider's assumption that patients are in heterosexual, gender-conforming relationships, which may lead a provider to fail to provide or inquire about vital information.[18]

Using an intersectional approach in analyzing questions related to health equity deepens our understanding of the systems of subordination that intersect and impede access to healthcare and lead to negative health outcomes for marginalized communities.[19] Applying this lens requires the researcher to reflect on how race, gender, sexual identity, class, disability, and other axes of inequality intersect to form vastly different lived experiences.[20]

These intersecting structural inequalities affected the lives of women, minorities, and other marginalized individuals during the COVID-19 pandemic. An

[12] Aleksandra George & Erin Flannery Keith, *Disability Rights and Dignity in Disasters*, 34 Nat. Res. & Env't 53, 54 (2019).

[13] *See id.* at 55 ("Without measures that center intersectional realities, individuals of color with disabilities are left alone to address the unique climate challenges that disproportionately impact the poorest and darkest communities.").

[14] *Id.*

[15] *Id.*

[16] Nancy López & Vivian L. Gadsden, *Health Inequalities, Social Determinants, and Intersectionality*, Nat'l Acad. Med., Dec. 5, 2016, at 2.

[17] *Id.* at 5.

[18] *Id.*

[19] *See id.* at 3 (citing Patricia Hill Collins & Sirma Bilge, Intersectionality 2 (2016)).

[20] *Id.* at 4–5.

intersectional approach to the coronavirus pandemic response and other public health emergencies that may arise in the future is vital to addressing the disparate outcomes in access to healthcare and treatment.[21] Approaches that fail to address the complex intersecting identities and power structures that affect people's lived experiences will fall short of addressing the pandemic's impact on work, caregiving, and health outcomes. Intersectionality is therefore an important tool to generate a robust response to this and other global public health emergencies, humanitarian crises, and large and small-scale human rights violations.

Intersectionality has changed the way we think about human rights. It offers a complex, comprehensive, and nuanced approach that redounds to the benefit of victims seeking redress. It allows victims to articulate the multiple and intersecting forms of subordination that have negatively affected their lives. Intersectionality rejects the anemic and siloed approach to human rights that invariably fails to capture and remedy the complex, intersectional violations that characterize the lived experience of subordination for many people. Intersectionality has positively influenced human rights discourse ranging from the UN human rights treaty bodies to local human rights organizations that have incorporated the theory into their organizational missions. The theory is gaining ground in international human rights discourse, and it will continue to transform and expand our vision of appropriate remedies for human rights violations. Only by more accurately conceiving of intersectional human rights violations can we hope to provide meaningful and comprehensive remedies to those who have experienced violations of their rights.

[21] *Id.*

Index

For the benefit of digital users, indexed terms that span two pages (e.g., 52–53) may, on occasion, appear on only one of those pages.

Tables are indicated by *t* following the page number